MANAGING INTELLECTUAL PROPERTY RIGHTS

LEWIS C. LEE

J. SCOTT DAVIDSON

Wiley Law Publications
JOHN WILEY & SONS, INC.
New York • Chichester • Brisbane • Toronto • Singapore

This text is printed on acid-free paper.

Copyright © 1993 by John Wiley & Sons, Inc.

All rights reserved. Published simultaneously in Canada.

Reproduction or translation of any part of this work beyond that permitted by Section 107 or 108 of the 1976 United States Copyright Act without the permission of the copyright owner is unlawful. Requests for permission or further information should be addressed to the Permissions Department, John Wiley & Sons, Inc., 605 Third Avenue, New York, NY 10158-0012.

This publication is designed to provide accurate and authoritative information in regard to the subject matter covered. It is sold with the understanding that the publisher is not engaged in rendering legal, accounting, or other professional services. If legal advice or other expert assistance is required, the services of a competent professional person should be sought. *From a Declaration of Principles jointly adopted by a Committee of the American Bar Association and a Committee of Publishers.*

Library of Congress Cataloging-in-Publication Data

Lee, Lewis E.
    Managing intellectual property rights / Lewis E. Lee, J. Scott Davidson.
    p.   cm. — (Business practice library)
    Includes index.
    ISBN 0-471-59728-7 (paper)
      1. Intellectual property—United States.   I. Davidson, Scott, 1954– . II. Title. III. Series.
KF2979.L44   1993
346.7304'8—dc20
[347.30648]   93-9881
                                             CIP

ISBN 0-471-59728-7

Printed in the United States of America

10 9 8 7 6 5 4 3

To my wife, Sarah,
and my children, Jordan and Brendan
L.C.L

To my wife, Julie, and my son, Samuel
J.S.D.

FOREWORD

Despite the obvious importance of intellectual property—patents, trademarks, copyrights, and trade secrets—to substantially all product-oriented businesses, these vitally significant business tools are not understood by a great many people who participate in these businesses. Similarly, many attorneys who counsel these businesses often do not understand the processes that produce the products and thus how best to advise implementation of intellectual property protection.

The scholastic curricula that prepare individuals for participation in such businesses totally fail to deal with intellectual property matters. For example, on his first day of employment by a product-oriented company, the average engineering school graduate will be presented with a paper dealing with patents and trade secrets and, more particularly, his relationship in these matters with his employer. That new engineer usually hasn't the foggiest notion of the implication of such a document. Furthermore, as his employment with the company continues, there is often no mechanism by which he can be trained to understand intellectual property despite its importance to the profits of the company and, in some cases indeed, to its survival.

Large companies with in-house patent departments tend to be better protected against errors concerning these matters; however, companies without such internal assistance frequently fail to obtain the maximum benefits available from intellectual property and often inadvertently place themselves at risk with respect to such property rights owned by others.

The growing importance of intellectual property in the business world has exacerbated this situation. In a company without an internal intellectual property department, business managers must have accessible, authoritative advice to help them attain intellectual property protection for their products. The authors of this book have provided precisely such a convenient, reliable, and profit-maximizing book. It is not intended to supplant the experienced lawyer; instead, the book will act as a guide as to when such a lawyer is necessary.

This book can help business managers, engineers, and attorneys better understand and protect valuable intellectual property. It provides basic information which is essential to profitability, and sometimes even existence, in today's highly competitive world. Managers of businesses in other countries frequently illustrate their familiarity with intellectual property matters and thereby maximize the potential of their businesses. The authors of this book have provided a much needed tool for business managers in this country to take the fullest advantage of the opportunities that intellectual properties present. There now is no excuse for any business to overlook the potentials, as well as the perils, that are inherent in intellectual property matters.

Washington, D.C.
February 1993

DONALD W. BANNER
Former United States Commissioner of Patents and Trademarks

PREFACE

Not too long ago, there was very little talk about patents, copyrights, or trademarks. While some companies maintained portfolios of these so-called "intellectual properties", there was never much importance placed on them. Today, the markets are more competitive, both domestically and globally. Intellectual property has evolved as a key ingredient for preserving a competitive posture. You cannot pick up a newspaper without reading headline stories of the impact of intellectual property in today's business world: "Judge Orders Kodak to Pay Over $900 Million," "Microsoft to Pay a Patent Fee In IBM Accord," "Wang's Patent Complaint Citing Japanese Firms Wins U.S. Inquiry," and "Hughes Case Could Send Patent Claims Into Orbit."

If your company or your client's company is like many U.S. companies, it tends to place too little emphasis on the value of intellectual property. It shouldn't. This book is intended to give you a plain look at intellectual property and how your company can profit by recognizing and exploiting its intellectual property opportunities. We think that you will find this book to be easy reading and written in a language we can all understand. You will also find practical cost-conscious methods that you can use to improve your recognition of intellectual property opportunities.

Even for those U.S. companies that are increasing their emphasis on intellectual property, we have found that many employees do not have a basic understanding of intellectual property. Our experience suggests that the typical company employee has heard of patents, copyrights, and trademarks, but is not familiar with what rights are granted by each of these, what legal requirements must be satisfied to obtain the properties, and what acts will cause forfeiture of the rights. Unfortunately, the typical employee lacks even a general understanding of what type of protection is the most effective for a particular idea or concept. This lack of a basic knowledge is damaging to a company, no matter how sophisticated its intellectual property legal department. Without managers' and engineers' input with respect to intellectual property opportunities in their respective departments, even the most qualified in-house counsel might not realize that protection is available or needed.

A dilemma thus arises. Those in the in-house intellectual property department are quite knowledgeable on the subject of intellectual property rights but are not in a position to initially identify protection opportunities and problems. On the other hand, those who are in a position to initially recognize intellectual property opportunities and problems (engineers, managers, and marketers) are not sufficiently knowledgeable concerning the procedures necessary to obtain, preserve, and exploit intellectual properties.

Recognizing this dilemma, we have prepared this book. It has grown out of our experience in working with small, medium, and large companies. It is written for company employees—such as managers, engineers, and marketing personnel—who are often faced with intellectual property opportunities, problems, and decisions *without even knowing it*. It is also written for attorneys who counsel businesses and are likely to confront such issues. With the knowledge gained from this book, employees and attorneys can work together to better inform and advise each other.

This book is designed to teach corporate employees a practical systematic approach to handling intellectual property situations. It is written for those in the best positions to recognize protection opportunities, specifically managers, engineers and marketers and others who handle the day-to-day operations of delivering products/services to the marketplace. These are the employees who often have the clearest perspective of intellectual property opportunities and yet these are the same employees who, through a lack of understanding, are most prone to unwittingly harm their company's chances to obtain or exploit intellectual property rights.

The solution, we believe, is to give engineers, business managers, and marketers the tools they need to make preliminary judgments about protection opportunities facing their company. The result is an informed and conscientious staff that is better able to recognize profitable intellectual property opportunities.

This book also is well suited for in-house attorneys and general practice attorneys. It will give them a clearer understanding of a company's day-to-day operations in order to better advise that company on appropriate legal procedures to follow. In addition, the legal requirements for each of the intellectual properties are defined in a brief, easy-to-reference manner and the primary issues arising from most intellectual property situations are discussed using real-life examples. We primarily focus on the general rules associated with intellectual property to provide a fundamental education in this legal area. While we recognize that each general proposition might have many corollaries or exceptions, we feel that discussion of tangential issues are inappropriate for the scope of this book.

The book presents a new approach to analyzing patents, copyrights, trademarks, and trade secrets as a coherent body of rights, rather than as disjointed individual properties, which proves useful to gaining a general understanding of intellectual property law. Topics and checklists are provided in this book to assist general attorneys, who are not familiar with the specialized legal area of intellectual property, when counseling their business clients on how to protect technology and goodwill.

PREFACE

The examples and cases employed in the book exemplify the general rules of intellectual property law and if more detail or legal support is required for any given topic, you should consult an intellectual property attorney. Similarly, each company or client may have special needs or circumstances. Because the suggestions offered in this book are general in nature, the wise manager or attorney may need to seek additional legal, accounting, or other advice to solve a unique or specialized situation.

The book is presented in three parts.

Part I is entitled "Understanding Intellectual Property." It contains **Chapters 1–4** and demonstrates the importance of intellectual property. It also provides an overview of the different types of intellectual property and the highlights of each.

Part II is entitled "Selecting Most Appropriate Intellectual Property Protection" and contains the primary thesis of this book. It involves an analytical model which provides a systematic managerial approach to evaluating intellectual property situations. The model synthesizes the different types of protection into a single, coherent flow diagram. The chapters of this Part also address the many factors weighing in any decision to select one type of protection over another. The model is discussed in detail throughout **Chapters 5–11.**

Part III is entitled "Intellectual Property Management Strategies." It contains a discussion of corporate policies and procedures designed to maximize a company's intellectual property opportunities and prevent premature loss of its rights. It also contains a discussion of why, from a legal perspective, such policies and procedures are necessary. Part III contains **Chapters 12–14.**

February 1993

LEWIS C. LEE
Spokane, Washington

J. SCOTT DAVIDSON
Washington, D.C.

ACKNOWLEDGMENTS

We would like to thank Richard St. John, Nancy Linck, Don Banner, Tom Morgan, and Jerry McBride for offering time from their busy schedules to review initial drafts of our book. Their comments, criticisms, and insights were invaluable.

ABOUT THE AUTHORS

Lewis C. Lee is a patent attorney with Wells, St. John, Roberts, Gregory & Matkin, a Northwest intellectual property law firm located in Spokane, Washington. He received his J.D. from George Washington University in Washington, D.C., and earned bachelors degrees in both Electrical Engineering and Business Administration from Washington State University. Mr. Lee is admitted to practice in Washington and is registered to practice before the U.S. Patent and Trademark Office.

J. Scott Davidson is a patent attorney at the intellectual property law firm of Cushman, Darby & Cushman in Washington, D.C. He received his J.D. from the University of Florida and a bachelors degree in Electrical Engineering from the University of South Florida. Mr. Davidson is admitted to practice in Florida and the District of Columbia, and is registered to practice before the U.S. Patent and Trademark Office.

SUMMARY CONTENTS

PART I	UNDERSTANDING INTELLECTUAL PROPERTY	
Chapter 1	Importance of Intellectual Property	3
Chapter 2	Legal Framework and Requirements	9
Chapter 3	Dangers of Failing To Consider Intellectual Property Issues	55
Chapter 4	Value and Benefits of Intellectual Property	71
PART II	SELECTING MOST APPROPRIATE INTELLECTUAL PROPERTY PROTECTION	
Chapter 5	Introduction to Protection Analysis Model	95
Chapter 6	Deciding Whether Protection Is Warranted	107
Chapter 7	Trade Secret Protection: A Threshold Level of Protection	123
Chapter 8	Is Patent Protection Appropriate?	127
Chapter 9	Choosing Between Trade Secret and Patent Protection	149
Chapter 10	Is Copyright Protection Appropriate?	163
Chapter 11	Is Trademark Protection Appropriate?	169
PART III	INTELLECTUAL PROPERTY MANAGEMENT STRATEGIES	
Chapter 12	Why Company Intellectual Property Policies and Procedures Are Necessary	183
Chapter 13	Company Policies and Procedures That Maximize Preservation of Intellectual Property Rights	205
Chapter 14	Managing the Intellectual Property Portfolio	237
Appendixes		247
Table of Cases		269
Index		275

DETAILED CONTENTS

PART I	UNDERSTANDING INTELLECTUAL PROPERTY
Chapter 1	**Importance of Intellectual Property**
§ 1.1	What Is Intellectual Property?
§ 1.2	Why Is Intellectual Property Important?
§ 1.3	—Litigation
§ 1.4	—Foreign Competition
§ 1.5	—Valuable Asset
§ 1.6	How to Use This Book
Chapter 2	**Legal Framework and Requirements**
PATENTS	
§ 2.1	Patent Definition
§ 2.2	—How to Read Patent Claim
§ 2.3	—Patent Claims Define Patented Subject Matter
§ 2.4	Legal Framework and Requirements of Patent
§ 2.5	—Subject Matter
§ 2.6	—Novelty
§ 2.7	—Nonobviousness
§ 2.8	—Utility
§ 2.9	—Enablement and Best Mode
§ 2.10	Right to Exclude
§ 2.11	Protection Extends to Equivalent Products
§ 2.12	Duration of Patent Protection
§ 2.13	Enforcement Against Patent Infringers
§ 2.14	How Company Secures Patent Protection
DESIGN PATENTS	
§ 2.15	Design Patent Definition
§ 2.16	Legal Framework and Requirements of Design Patent
§ 2.17	—Subject Matter
§ 2.18	—Ornamental
§ 2.19	—Originality
§ 2.20	—Novelty and Nonobviousness
§ 2.21	Scope of Design Patent Protection

§ 2.22   How Company Secures Design Patent Protection

COPYRIGHTS

§ 2.23   Copyright Definition
§ 2.24   Legal Framework and Requirements of Copyright
§ 2.25   —Subject Matter
§ 2.26   —Original Authorship
§ 2.27   —Fixation
§ 2.28   Actions Not Necessary but Recommended
§ 2.29   Exclusive Right to Copy and Distribute Work
§ 2.30   Duration of Copyright Protection
§ 2.31   Copyright Protection Very Narrow
§ 2.32   Enforcement Against Copyright Infringers
§ 2.33   How Company Secures Copyright Protection

TRADEMARKS

§ 2.34   Trademark Definition
§ 2.35   Legal Framework and Requirements of Trademark
§ 2.36   —Subject Matter
§ 2.37   —Affixation
§ 2.38   —Use or Intent to Use
§ 2.39   —Distinctiveness
§ 2.40   —Absence of Confusion with Similar Marks
§ 2.41   —Nonfunctionality
§ 2.42   Exclusive Use of Mark
§ 2.43   Duration of Trademark Protection
§ 2.44   Enforcement Against Trademark Infringers
§ 2.45   How Company Secures Federal Trademark Protection

TRADE SECRETS

§ 2.46   Trade Secret Definition
§ 2.47   Legal Framework and Requirements of Trade Secret
§ 2.48   —Subject Matter
§ 2.49   —Secrecy
§ 2.50   —Value
§ 2.51   —Novelty
§ 2.52   —Affirmative Steps
§ 2.53   Rights May Not Be Exclusive
§ 2.54   Trade Secrets Only Protected Against Improper Taking
§ 2.55   Duration of Trade Secret Protection
§ 2.56   Legal Recourse for Theft of Trade Secret
§ 2.57   Others May Patent Technological Trade Secrets
§ 2.58   How Company Secures Trade Secret Protection

KNOW-HOW

§ 2.59 Know-How Definition
§ 2.60 Intellectual Property Rights Checklist

Chapter 3 Dangers of Failing to Consider Intellectual Property Issues

§ 3.1 Lessons from Real-Life Cases
§ 3.2 Case 1: Loss of Patent Rights as a Result of Patent Holder's Marketing Activity
§ 3.3 Case 2: Loss of Patent Rights Caused by Business Partner's Sales Activities
§ 3.4 Case 3: Loss of Patent Rights as a Result of Prior Public Use
§ 3.5 Case 4: Loss of Trade Secret Rights as a Result of Inadvertent Disclosure
§ 3.6 Case 5: Loss of Trade Secret Rights as a Result of Failing to Adequately Identify Confidential Information
§ 3.7 Case 6: Loss of Trade Secret Rights as a Result of Failing to Take Affirmative Steps to Maintain Secrecy
§ 3.8 Case 7: Monetary Loss for Patent Infringement
§ 3.9 Case 8: Monetary Loss for Patent Infringement
§ 3.10 Case 9: Monetary Loss for Willful Patent Infringement
§ 3.11 Case 10: Monetary Loss for Trademark Infringement

Chapter 4 Value and Benefits of Intellectual Property

§ 4.1 Introduction
§ 4.2 Exclusive Rights
§ 4.3 Remedies for Infringement of Intellectual Property
§ 4.4 —Patent Remedies
§ 4.5 —Copyright Remedies
§ 4.6 —Trademark Remedies
§ 4.7 —Trade Secret Remedies
§ 4.8 Ability to Assign Rights
§ 4.9 Ability to License Rights
§ 4.10 —Royalty Revenue
§ 4.11 —Technology Exchanges
§ 4.12 —Grantbacks
§ 4.13 —Second Sources
§ 4.14 —Exploiting in Closed Markets
§ 4.15 —Prevent or Settle Lawsuit
§ 4.16 —Testing of Technology
§ 4.17 —Establishing Industry Standard
§ 4.18 Recoupment of Research and Development Expenditures

DETAILED CONTENTS

§ 4.19 Control Market Share
§ 4.20 Enter New Markets
§ 4.21 Secure Interest in Foreign Market
§ 4.22 Extend Product Life Cycle
§ 4.23 Valuable Intangibles
§ 4.24 Asset Value
§ 4.25 Increasing Strength of Patents
§ 4.26 —Creation of Federal Circuit
§ 4.27 —International Trade Commission

PART II   **SELECTING MOST APPROPRIATE INTELLECTUAL PROPERTY PROTECTION**

Chapter 5   **Introduction to Protection Analysis Model**

§ 5.1 What Is Best Protection?
§ 5.2 Common Scenario
§ 5.3 Protection Analysis Model
§ 5.4 —Know-How and Trade Secret Phases
§ 5.5 —Patent Phase
§ 5.6 —Copyright Phase
§ 5.7 —Trademark Phase
§ 5.8 —More Than One Type of Protection May Be Available

Chapter 6   **Deciding Whether Protection Is Warranted**

§ 6.1 Everything Begins as Know-How
§ 6.2 Weighing the Factors
§ 6.3 —Is Subject Matter Already Known?
§ 6.4 —Exclusive Ownership of Subject Matter
§ 6.5 —Preventing Competitors from Owning Subject Matter
§ 6.6 —Does Subject Matter Make Company's Products More Competitive?
§ 6.7 —Is Subject Matter Economically Practical?
§ 6.8 —Does Subject Matter Help Reduce Company's Costs?
§ 6.9 —Does Subject Matter Help Satisfy Customer Preference?
§ 6.10 —Company Goals
§ 6.11 —Company Market Position and Strategy
§ 6.12 —Is Market Mature and Ready to Accept Technology?
§ 6.13 —Company Profile
§ 6.14 —Does Subject Matter Have Licensing Potential?
§ 6.15 —Does Subject Matter Improve Corporate Bargaining Posture?

DETAILED CONTENTS

§ 6.16	—Is Subject Matter Sufficiently Valuable to Warrant Expenditure of Limited Resources?
§ 6.17	—Is Asset Value Important?
§ 6.18	Protection Factors Checklist
§ 6.19	All Things Being Equal, Favor Protection
§ 6.20	Protection Alternatives

Chapter 7   **Trade Secret Protection: A Threshold Level of Protection**

§ 7.1	Legal Requirements for Trade Secret Protection
§ 7.2	Attributes of Trade Secrets
§ 7.3	Maintaining Trade Secret Rights

Chapter 8   **Is Patent Protection Appropriate?**

§ 8.1	Patent Phase of Protection Analysis Model
§ 8.2	Does Subject Matter Satisfy Legal Requirements for Patent Protection?
§ 8.3	Is Patent Protection Economically Desirable?
§ 8.4	—Patent Value Formula
§ 8.5	—Factors Affecting Value Variable V
§ 8.6	—Factors Affecting Value Probability Variable P_v
§ 8.7	—Factors Affecting Cost Variable C
§ 8.8	—Checklist of Factors for Patent Value Formula
§ 8.9	Is Design Patent Protection Appropriate?
§ 8.10	—Does Subject Matter Satisfy Design Patent Requirements?
§ 8.11	—Is Design Patent Protection Desirable from Business Perspective?
§ 8.12	Trade Secret or Patent Protection?
§ 8.13	Conduct Patent Search and Reevaluate Patentability
§ 8.14	File for Patent Protection
§ 8.15	Duty to Disclose Information Known to Be "Material to Patentability"
§ 8.16	Label Products with *Patent Pending*
§ 8.17	Foreign Patent Applications
§ 8.18	Is a Patent Granted?
§ 8.19	Maintain and Commercialize Patent Rights

Chapter 9   **Choosing Between Trade Secret and Patent Protection**

§ 9.1	Introductory Story
§ 9.2	Weighing the Factors
§ 9.3	—Is Patent Protection Available?
§ 9.4	—Nature of Subject Matter: Can It Be Kept Secret?

§ 9.5	—Life Expectancy of Technology
§ 9.6	—Patent Protection Has Stricter Legal Requirements
§ 9.7	—Scope of Intellectual Property Rights
§ 9.8	—Subsequent and Independent Discovery by Another
§ 9.9	—Duration of Protection
§ 9.10	—Cost of Obtaining and Maintaining Protection
§ 9.11	—Preservation of Intellectual Property Rights
§ 9.12	—Breadth of Intellectual Property
§ 9.13	—Policing
§ 9.14	—Risk of Losing Intellectual Property Rights
§ 9.15	—Enforcement and Burden in Court
§ 9.16	—Cost of Enforcing
§ 9.17	—Remedies
§ 9.18	—Is Technology Pioneering?
§ 9.19	—Is Market Ready?
§ 9.20	—Licensing
§ 9.21	Checklist of Trade Secret versus Patent Protection Factors

Chapter 10 Is Copyright Protection Appropriate?

§ 10.1	Copyright Phase of Protection Analysis Model
§ 10.2	Does Subject Matter Satisfy Legal Requirements for Copyright Protection?
§ 10.3	Place Copyright Notice on the Work
§ 10.4	Is Work to Be Published?
§ 10.5	Advantages of Registration
§ 10.6	Commercialize Rights Afforded by Copyright

Chapter 11 Is Trademark Protection Appropriate?

§ 11.1	Trademark Phase of Protection Analysis Model
§ 11.2	Does Subject Matter Satisfy Legal Requirements for Trademark Protection?
§ 11.3	Conduct Trademark Search
§ 11.4	Is Trademark Registration Desirable?
§ 11.5	Checklist of Registration Factors
§ 11.6	Registering Trademark
§ 11.7	—Intent to Use Application
§ 11.8	—Regular Application for Mark in Use
§ 11.9	When Trademark Registration Is Not Allowed
§ 11.10	—Select New Mark
§ 11.11	—Keep Mark and Generate Secondary Meaning
§ 11.12	Trademark Registration Is Allowed

DETAILED CONTENTS

§ 11.13	—Intent to Use
§ 11.14	—Mark Is in Use
§ 11.15	Maintain, Properly Use, and Commercialize Trademark

PART III   **INTELLECTUAL PROPERTY MANAGEMENT STRATEGIES**

Chapter 12   **Why Company Intellectual Property Policies and Procedures Are Necessary**

§ 12.1	Introduction
§ 12.2	Trade Secret Laws
§ 12.3	Satisfying Secrecy and Affirmative Steps Requirements
§ 12.4	Preventing Unnecessary Loss of Trade Secrets
§ 12.5	—Inadvertent Disclosure
§ 12.6	—Former Employee and Innocent New Employer
§ 12.7	—Trade Secret Matters in Business Relationships
§ 12.8	Patent Laws
§ 12.9	Failing to Satisfy Novelty Requirement: Self-inflicted Bars to Patentability
§ 12.10	—Printed Publication Bar
§ 12.11	—Public Use Bar
§ 12.12	—On-Sale Bar
§ 12.13	—Experimentation Incident to Public Use or Sale Activity
§ 12.14	—Loss of Foreign Patent Rights
§ 12.15	First Inventorship
§ 12.16	Checklist

Chapter 13   **Company Policies and Procedures That Maximize Preservation of Intellectual Property Rights**

§ 13.1	Need for Policies and Procedures
§ 13.2	Employer/Employee Relationships
§ 13.3	—Preemployment Disclosure
§ 13.4	—Hiring New Employees from Competitor
§ 13.5	—Orientation for New Employees
§ 13.6	—Employee Agreement
§ 13.7	—Employment Manuals
§ 13.8	—Periodic Reminders of Intellectual Property Obligations
§ 13.9	—Seminars to Educate Employees
§ 13.10	—Procedures for Departing Employees
§ 13.11	Laboratory Procedures
§ 13.12	—Record Daily Activities of Engineers

DETAILED CONTENTS

§ 13.13 —Corroboration by Disinterested Employee
§ 13.14 —Maintain Progress Records
§ 13.15 —Catalog Engineering and Progress Notebooks
§ 13.16 —Maintain Records Pertaining to Daily Time Sheets of Personnel
§ 13.17 Security Procedures
§ 13.18 —Facility Restrictions
§ 13.19 —Handling Confidential Material
§ 13.20 Release Review Procedures
§ 13.21 —Distribution of Advertisements and Brochures
§ 13.22 —Publications in Trade and Professional Journals
§ 13.23 —Demonstrations of New Technology
§ 13.24 —Test Marketing New Products
§ 13.25 Patent Marking
§ 13.26 Copyright Marking
§ 13.27 Trademark Marking
§ 13.28 Technological Relationships with Other Companies
§ 13.29 —Initially Disclose Only General Information
§ 13.30 —Confidentiality Agreements
§ 13.31 —Stamp *CONFIDENTIAL* on All Documents Transferred to Business Partner
§ 13.32 —Record Transfer of Proprietary Information
§ 13.33 —Research and Development Relationships with Other Companies
§ 13.34 Channel New Ideas to Intellectual Property Counsel
§ 13.35 —Keep Decisions at Grass-roots Level
§ 13.36 —Educate Employees
§ 13.37 —Provide Incentive to Innovate
§ 13.38 Handling Unsolicited Ideas
§ 13.39 —Designate One Employee to Field All Unsolicited Ideas
§ 13.40 —Nonconfidential Disclosure Agreement
§ 13.41 —Reviewing Unsolicited Idea
§ 13.42 —Procedures for Designated Employee
§ 13.43 Intellectual Property Audit

Chapter 14 **Managing the Intellectual Property Portfolio**

§ 14.1 Monitoring the Industry
§ 14.2 —Monitoring Activities of Other Companies
§ 14.3 —Product Clearance
§ 14.4 —Policing for Infringers of Company's Rights
§ 14.5 —Checklist

§ 14.6	Intellectual Property Program Review	
§ 14.7	—Roundtable Meetings to Plan Protection Strategies	
§ 14.8	—Product Team Meetings on Intellectual Property Issues	

Appendixes

A	Example of a Patent
B	Example of a Design Patent
C	Sample Trademark Registration
D	Form for Registration of a Copyrighted Work

Table of Cases

Index

PART I
UNDERSTANDING INTELLECTUAL PROPERTY

CHAPTER 1

IMPORTANCE OF INTELLECTUAL PROPERTY

§ 1.1   What Is Intellectual Property?
§ 1.2   Why Is Intellectual Property Important?
§ 1.3   —Litigation
§ 1.4   —Foreign Competition
§ 1.5   —Valuable Asset
§ 1.6   How to Use This Book

§ 1.1   What Is Intellectual Property?

Intellectual property is a term used in this book to describe the body of legal rights owned by an individual or company in technology, information, products, processes, designs, chemical compounds, forms of expression, slogans, and other intellectual work products. These legal rights are designed to protect innovative endeavors of an individual or company. Intellectual property consists of four distinct types: patents, copyrights, trademarks, and trade secrets. Some people often add to this list a fifth type of property known as *know-how*.

Although the concept of intellectual property may seem complicated at first, keep in mind that it is simply another kind of property. Common forms of property include real property, such as land, and personal property, such as an automobile. Many of the same characteristics associated with real and personal property are also associated with intellectual property. For instance, it can be bought, sold, leased, given away, or exchanged for something else, in the same manner as an automobile or land. In addition, just as a landowner can prevent others from trespassing or an automobile owner can prevent others from joyriding in her automobile, an intellectual property owner can prevent others from making, using, copying, or selling her technology, information, products, and forms of expression.

One difference, however, is that intellectual property is intangible, whereas real and personal property are tangible. Real and personal property are readily defined and identified by their physical parameters, such as the acreage of land or the size and model of an automobile. In contrast, intellectual property cannot be defined in physical terms of acreage or size and model. In some cases, intellectual property is defined by a written description drafted in a legally recognized and acceptable format such as a patent claim. In other cases, it might not be formally defined at all, in the instance of a trade secret or know-how. As a result, intellectual property is often difficult to quantify and define. It is however, no less property than the physically observable land and automobile.

Intellectual property and its value to society have been recognized throughout history. In the fifteenth century, the Republic of Venice in Italy enacted the following statute:

> WE HAVE among us men of great ingenious, apt to invent and discover ingenious devices...
>
> BE IT ENACTED that, by the authority of this Council, every person who shall build any new and ingenious device in this City, not previously made in our Commonwealth, shall give notice of it to the office of our General Welfare Board when it had been reduced to perfection so that it can be used and operated. It being forbidden to every other person in any of our territories and towns to make any further device conforming with and similar to said one, without the consent and license of the author, for the term of 10 years.[1]

The United States patent and copyright laws are rooted in the United States Constitution, which delegates to Congress the power "to promote the Progress of Science and useful Arts, by securing for limited Times to Authors and Inventors the exclusive Right to their respective Writings and Discoveries."[2]

Intellectual property is not a new body of law, nor are its underlying concepts difficult to grasp. **Chapter 2** introduces the various types of intellectual property and the legal hurdles a company must clear to obtain legal rights to them.

§ 1.2 Why Is Intellectual Property Important?

In the last few years, some United States companies have received substantial profits by maintaining strong intellectual property portfolios.

---

[1] R. Choate, W. Francis, & R. Collins, Patent Law (3d ed. 1987).

[2] U.S. Const., art. I, § 8, cl. 8.

§ 1.4 FOREIGN COMPETITION

There is an increasing appreciation of the value of such portfolios. In addition to asset value, the emergence of high-impact intellectual property litigation and large damage awards along with the reality of tough foreign competition have significantly contributed to a renewed focus on the importance of intellectual property.

§ 1.3 —Litigation

In 1991, Johnson & Johnson was ordered to pay 3M an award of $116 million in damages and interest for infringing 3M patents relating to a tape used to set fractures faster than plaster.[3] However, this was not the largest such award in recent patent cases. In 1990, Polaroid was awarded a record-setting $909 million in damages after a court concluded that Kodak had infringed seven of Polaroid's patents relating to instant photography.[4] Hughes Corporation sought an award of approximately $3.3 billion against the United States government in a patent suit relating to Hughes's satellite technology.[5]

Copyright and trademark litigants are also receiving high damage awards. In 1988, Fujitsu agreed to pay approximately $1 billion to IBM to resolve a dispute over copyrights on mainframe operating system software.[6] At the time of this writing, Mirage Studios, creator of the Teenage Mutant Ninja Turtles®, is suing AT&T for $100 million in a trademark suit for using terms such as "turtle power" and "cowabunga" in a 900-number telephone service for children.[7] Headline-making litigation appears to be part of our new competitive world, and it is forcing companies to place more emphasis on intellectual property.

§ 1.4 —Foreign Competition

International competition is another reason why United States companies are focusing on intellectual property. Valid United States intellectual property rights, for example, can restrict infringing goods from being imported

---

[3] T.M. Carroll, "Whose Bright Idea?", Time, June 10, 1991, at 44–46.

[4] Polaroid Corp. v. Eastman Kodak Co., 16 U.S.P.Q.2d (BNA) 1481 (D. Mass. 1990). As a result of calculation error, the award was later reduced to $873 million. Polaroid Corp. v. Eastman Kodak Co., 17 U.S.P.Q. 2d 1711 (D. Mass. 1991).

[5] E. Richards, "Hughes Case Could Send Patent Claims Into Orbit," Wash. Post, Aug. 13, 1989, at H1.

[6] Bus. Wk., May 22, 1989, at 78.

[7] T.M. Carroll, "Whose Bright Idea?", Time, June 10, 1991, at 44–46.

and sold in this country after being produced by overseas competitors at reduced cost.

Foreign companies, particularly Japanese companies, are placing great emphasis on intellectual property. **Table 1-1** lists the top 10 companies to receive United States patents in the years 1986, 1989, and 1991. In 1986, Hitachi replaced General Electric as the top company receiving United States patents. In 1989, the top four companies were Japanese and seven of the top ten were foreign companies. In 1991, the top three companies were Japanese and six of the top ten were foreign companies.

As a measure of United States technological and innovative strength, these statistics send a clear warning. With foreign companies becoming more aggressive in securing United States patents and with United States companies failing to follow suit, it will become increasingly difficult for United States companies to compete even in their own lucrative market. Given the current trend, United States companies could be forced to take more licenses from foreign competitors, or perhaps be forced out of business entirely as a result of poor intellectual property positions.

An example of how important intellectual property considerations have become to American companies in the face of foreign competition was the legal battle between Hitachi and Motorola. Motorola's 68030 microprocessor allegedly infringed a patent owned by Hitachi. Unable to settle the dispute, Hitachi obtained a court injunction to prevent Motorola from producing these microprocessors until a royalty fee was paid. Motorola was faced with a decision to cease production of a highly profitable product, or pay a significant fee to Hitachi.

Motorola was not alone in this battle. Apple Computer also had a large stake in this legal proceeding because the 68030 microprocessor was employed in Apple's personal computers. Apple would have been in significant danger had an injunction been ordered that interfered with production of this vital component. Thus, the single patent owned by Hitachi temporarily crippled two large United States companies. In the end, Motorola was forced to negotiate a cross-license with Hitachi and eventually to redesign the portion of the 68030 that infringed the Hitachi patent.[8]

§ 1.5 —Valuable Asset

Apart from litigation and foreign competition concerns, some United States companies are beginning to appreciate intellectual property as a valuable company asset. Over the past five years, Texas Instruments has earned approximately $900 million simply from patent license royalties. This amount was more than their net income for the same period.[9]

---

[8] 36 Elec. News 1820 (1990).
[9] Wall St. J., Jan. 15, 1992.

Table 1-1
Companies Receiving United States Patents

Rank	1986 Company[1]	Patents	1989 Company[2]	Patents	1991 Company[3]	Patents
1	Hitachi	730	Hitachi	1053	Toshiba	1014
2	GE	713	Toshiba	961	Mitsubishi	936
3	Toshiba	691	Canon	949	Hitachi	927
4	IBM	597	Fuji Photo	884	Kodak	863
5	Canon	522	GE	818	Canon	823
6	Philips	503	Mitsubishi	767	GE	809
7	RCA	484	Philips	745	Fuji Photo	731
8	Fuji Photo	446	Siemens	656	IBM	679
9	Siemens	409	IBM	623	Philips	650
10	Westinghouse	398	Kodak	589	Motorola	613

[1] "The Pitfalls of Patents," The Economist, May 9, 1987, at 82.
[2] Compiled by Intellectual Property Owners.
[3] Pat. Trademark & Copyright J. (BNA) [Vol. 43, Mar.] (1992).

In addition to patents, other forms of intellectual property can also be very valuable to a company. The trademark Coca-Cola® and its trade secret formula are very likely the two most valuable assets owned by the Coca-Cola Corporation. The copyrights pertaining to the computer disk operating system MS DOS® are very valuable to Microsoft.

§ 1.6 How to Use This Book

This book is written in three parts. The first part is intended to help the reader understand intellectual property and appreciate its worth. **Chapter 2** sets forth the legal requirements for obtaining the various types of intellectual property—patents, copyrights, trademarks, and trade secrets—and the scope of protection provided by each type. **Chapter 3** illustrates real-life misfortunes of companies that wrongly considered or entirely failed to consider intellectual property in their business decisions. **Chapter 4** discusses from a business perspective the many benefits that result from intellectual property.

The second part of the book, containing **Chapters 5** through **11,** is entitled "Selecting the Most Appropriate Intellectual Property Protection." It provides a systematic managerial approach to analyzing every intellectual property situation. **Chapter 5** introduces the Protection Analysis Model to help the reader systematically explore each type of intellectual property available for a given innovation. In **Chapters 6** through **11,** the specific decisional steps of the Protection Analysis Model are discussed in more detail. Addressed are such topics as whether innovations should be protected at all (**Chapter 6**), when patent, copyright, or trademark protection is appropriate (**Chapters 8, 10,** and **11**), and what decision-making factors should be weighed when choosing between keeping an innovation a trade secret or patenting it (**Chapter 9**).

Part III, containing **Chapters 12** through **14,** is entitled "Intellectual Property Management Strategies." **Chapter 12** examines why intellectual property policies and procedures are important and necessary. **Chapter 13** provides a number of meaningful policies and procedures that can help prevent a company from unnecessarily or unknowingly losing its intellectual property rights. Finally, in **Chapter 14,** are some general principles for managing an intellectual property portfolio.

CHAPTER 2
LEGAL FRAMEWORK AND REQUIREMENTS

PATENTS

§ 2.1 Patent Definition
§ 2.2 —How to Read Patent Claim
§ 2.3 —Patent Claims Define Patented Subject Matter
§ 2.4 Legal Framework and Requirements of Patent
§ 2.5 —Subject Matter
§ 2.6 —Novelty
§ 2.7 —Nonobviousness
§ 2.8 —Utility
§ 2.9 —Enablement and Best Mode
§ 2.10 Right to Exclude
§ 2.11 Protection Extends to Equivalent Products
§ 2.12 Duration of Patent Protection
§ 2.13 Enforcement Against Patent Infringers
§ 2.14 How Company Secures Patent Protection

DESIGN PATENTS

§ 2.15 Design Patent Definition
§ 2.16 Legal Framework and Requirements of Design Patent
§ 2.17 —Subject Matter
§ 2.18 —Ornamental
§ 2.19 —Originality
§ 2.20 —Novelty and Nonobviousness
§ 2.21 Scope of Design Patent Protection
§ 2.22 How Company Secures Design Patent Protection

COPYRIGHTS

§ 2.23 Copyright Definition
§ 2.24 Legal Framework and Requirements of Copyright
§ 2.25 —Subject Matter

§ 2.26 —Original Authorship
§ 2.27 —Fixation
§ 2.28 Actions Not Necessary but Recommended
§ 2.29 Exclusive Right to Copy and Distribute Work
§ 2.30 Duration of Copyright Protection
§ 2.31 Copyright Protection Very Narrow
§ 2.32 Enforcement Against Copyright Infringers
§ 2.33 How Company Secures Copyright Protection

TRADEMARKS

§ 2.34 Trademark Definition
§ 2.35 Legal Framework and Requirements of Trademark
§ 2.36 —Subject Matter
§ 2.37 —Affixation
§ 2.38 —Use or Intent to Use
§ 2.39 —Distinctiveness
§ 2.40 —Absence of Confusion with Similar Marks
§ 2.41 —Nonfunctionality
§ 2.42 Exclusive Use of Mark
§ 2.43 Duration of Trademark Protection
§ 2.44 Enforcement Against Trademark Infringers
§ 2.45 How Company Secures Federal Trademark Protection

TRADE SECRETS

§ 2.46 Trade Secret Definition
§ 2.47 Legal Framework and Requirements of Trade Secret
§ 2.48 —Subject Matter
§ 2.49 —Secrecy
§ 2.50 —Value
§ 2.51 —Novelty
§ 2.52 —Affirmative Steps
§ 2.53 Rights May Not Be Exclusive
§ 2.54 Trade Secrets Only Protected Against Improper Taking
§ 2.55 Duration of Trade Secret Protection
§ 2.56 Legal Recourse for Theft of Trade Secret
§ 2.57 Others May Patent Technological Trade Secrets
§ 2.58 How Company Secures Trade Secret Protection

KNOW-HOW

§ 2.59 Know-How Definition
§ 2.60 Intellectual Property Rights Checklist

PATENTS

§ 2.1 Patent Definition

A patent provides an ownership right in a new and useful technological innovation. It is perhaps best viewed as an agreement between the inventor and the federal government. The federal government awards the inventor exclusive ownership of an invention in exchange for disclosing the invention to the public. The benefit to the inventor is the right to prevent others from making, using, or selling the invention for a limited period of time. The benefit to the government is the technological advancement to society that is gained from public disclosure of the invention, whereby members of society are immediately able to study and learn from the technological innovation, even during the limited exclusive term of the patent. The patent may also be viewed as a reward for creative innovation and intellectual advancement. The exclusive right gives the inventor the incentive to innovate.

There are three primary types of patents: utility, design, and plant. A *utility patent* covers the useful or functional aspects of innovative technology. A utility patent covers, for example, machines, processes, electrical circuits, chemical compositions, and methods of manufacturing. For convenience, use of the unmodified term *patent* throughout this book will mean *utility patent*. In contrast to a utility patent, a *design patent* protects only the appearance or ornamental aspects of a useful article, not its functional aspects. A design patent covers, for example, the shape of a table, a stylish new car body, or the facial or body features of a toy doll. Design patents are discussed in more detail in §§ **2.15** through **2.22**. The third type of patent, a *plant patent*, can be awarded to anyone who invents or discovers and asexually reproduces a distinct and new variety of plant. Plant patents are rare and will not be referred to often in this book.

Returning to utility patents, the legal patent rights awarded to an inventor are described in a patent document bearing the official seal of the United States Commissioner of Patents and Trademarks. The patent document is a booklet of sorts that includes a description of the invention, illustrative drawings (when necessary or helpful to understand the invention), and at least one claim expressing what the inventor considers to be the legally protected intellectual property. An example of a patent, entitled "Lap Counting System," is found in **Appendix A**.

The description of the invention in the patent document need not be in any particular format. Typically, the description of the invention includes a background statement describing the problem solved by the inventor and how others have previously attempted to solve the same or similar problems. The description also typically includes a brief summary of the invention, a description of the drawings (if any), and a detailed description of the invention.

The description of the invention is followed by one or more patent claims defining the subject matter that is given patent protection. This is a critical concept and deserves emphasis. For utility patents, the *claims*, not the description or the drawings, define the scope of the inventor's intellectual property. The patent in **Appendix A** has 18 claims that define a no-touch, radio-based lap counter for swimmers and runners. Because the claims alone are what define one's patented subject matter, § 2.2 provides a brief lesson on how to read and interpret patent claims. **Section 2.3** follows with a second lesson illustrating how the claims of a patent, rather than the description or drawings, define the invention.

§ 2.2 —How to Read Patent Claim

When interpreting patent claims, all claim limitations are significant and must be considered.[1] For instance, suppose a patent had the following claim to a basketball hoop:

A basketball apparatus, comprising:
 a fan-shaped backboard;
 a circular rim, attached to the backboard, and having six hooks; and
 a net formed of woven cord, the net defining six loops which hang on respective hooks.

As defined by this claim, the protected basketball apparatus must have a "fan-shaped backboard," not a rectangular-shaped backboard. Similarly, the rim must have "six hooks," not four or eight. Moreover, the net must be "woven cord," not molded plastic or chain link.[2] As demonstrated by

---

[1] *See, e.g.*, Becton Dickinson & Co. v. C.R. Bard, 922 F.2d 792, 798, 17 U.S.P.Q.2d (BNA) 1097, 1101 (Fed. Cir. 1990)(noting that "whether necessary or not, after issuance, all limitations in a claim are material"). Interpreting patent claims is both a legal and technical exercise. When interpreting claim language and scope for purposes of validity, infringement, or breadth of property rights, it is advisable to consult a patent attorney.

[2] The courts have developed a doctrine, known as the *doctrine of equivalents*, which provides some leniency in interpreting claim language. Under this doctrine, claims that do not read *literally* on a device may still be met if the device performs substantially the same function, in substantially the same way, to achieve substantially the same result as the claimed invention. Graver Tank Co. v. Linde Air Prod. Co., 339 U.S. 605, 610, 85 U.S.P.Q. (BNA) 328, 330 (1950). For example, under this doctrine, the fan-shaped backboard may be interpreted to cover a rectangular-shaped backboard if the rectangular-shaped backboard performs substantially the same function, in substantially the same way, to achieve substantially the same result as the fan-shaped backboard. See **§ 2.11.**

§ 2.3 CLAIMS DEFINE SUBJECT MATTER

this example, each limitation of the patent claim is closely scrutinized when being interpreted to determine the bounds of one's intellectual property defined by that claim.

§ 2.3 —Patent Claims Define Patented Subject Matter

The patent claims define the patent property and the afforded scope of patent protection. The patent disclosure or the product being sold in the market do not.[3] Consider the following example.

During the course of its normal research and development work, StringThing, Inc., developed a new entertainment device they called a "TwangBoard." Essentially, the TwangBoard was a four-piece wood frame with nails punched into opposing ends. Strings of varying lengths were fastened to the nails and stretched between the two ends. The TwangBoard is shown in **Figure 2-1**.

An employee at StringThing discovered that by plucking the strings of the TwangBoard, the strings vibrated and produced twangs, with different strings producing different twangs. Thinking that others might also find entertainment in twanging the device, StringThing patented and marketed the TwangBoard. In its patent, StringThing disclosed the only design that the inventor knew, that is, the rather rustic-looking frame between which the strings were stretched. StringThing was allowed the following claim, which described its intellectual property:

Claim 1: An apparatus, comprising:
   a frame having two opposing ends; and
   multiple strings having varying lengths attached to the frame between the opposing ends.

Much to the disappointment of StringThing, Inc., the TwangBoard was a marketing flop. In fact, most of those who used the TwangBoard thought the TwangBoard created an exceedingly unpleasant noise.

After conducting many experiments with the TwangBoard, an employee at another company, C-Sharp, Inc., discovered that the length and tension of the TwangBoard strings could be carefully selected to produce musical chords. With this newfound improvement to the TwangBoard, C-Sharp experienced tremendous marketing success. Eventually, C-Sharp, Inc., refined and expanded its instrument line to include harps, guitars, and violins, as shown in **Figure 2-2**.

---

[3] Although it cannot be used to define the patented invention, the patent disclosure can be used to help *interpret* the claims in some situations to give meaning to certain words and phrases used in the claims.

14   LEGAL REQUIREMENTS

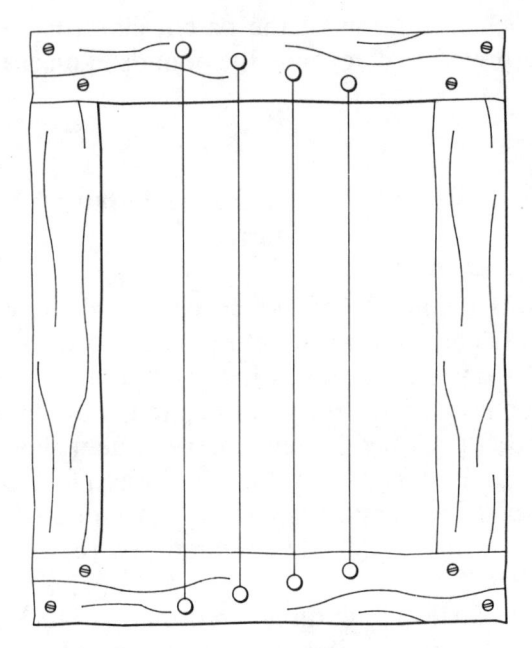

Figure 2-1. The Twangboard.

In this example, StringThing's prudence in obtaining broad patent protection for the TwangBoard may rescue StringThing from a marketing nightmare. Even though StringThing may never have contemplated or built the "tuned" instrument, nor ever disclosed the "tuned" instrument in its patent, the patent claim recited above is infringed by the making, using, or selling of C-Sharp's tuned instruments. Note that, just like StringThing's patent claim, C-Sharp's harps, guitars, and violins include a "frame having two opposing ends" between which "multiple strings having varying lengths" are attached. In patent terminology, the claim of StringThing's patent "reads on" C-Sharp's instruments. That is, the actual words of the claim literally describe the components of C-Sharp's instruments.

Importantly, even though StringThing's patent described only a rustic device and described nothing with respect to "tuned" strings and even though the Twangboard product itself was not a tunable instrument, StringThing's patent claim 1 was not limited to rustic devices and untuned instruments. Indeed, claim 1 encompassed C-Sharp's tuned instruments. C-Sharp's production and sales of tuned instruments thus infringed StringThing's patent because StringThing's patent claim "reads on" C-Sharp's instruments, even though the tuned instruments were quite different from the disclosed or constructed TwangBoard.

A patent is infringed if any one of its claims reads on an accused device in the manner described above. For example, suppose that StringThing's

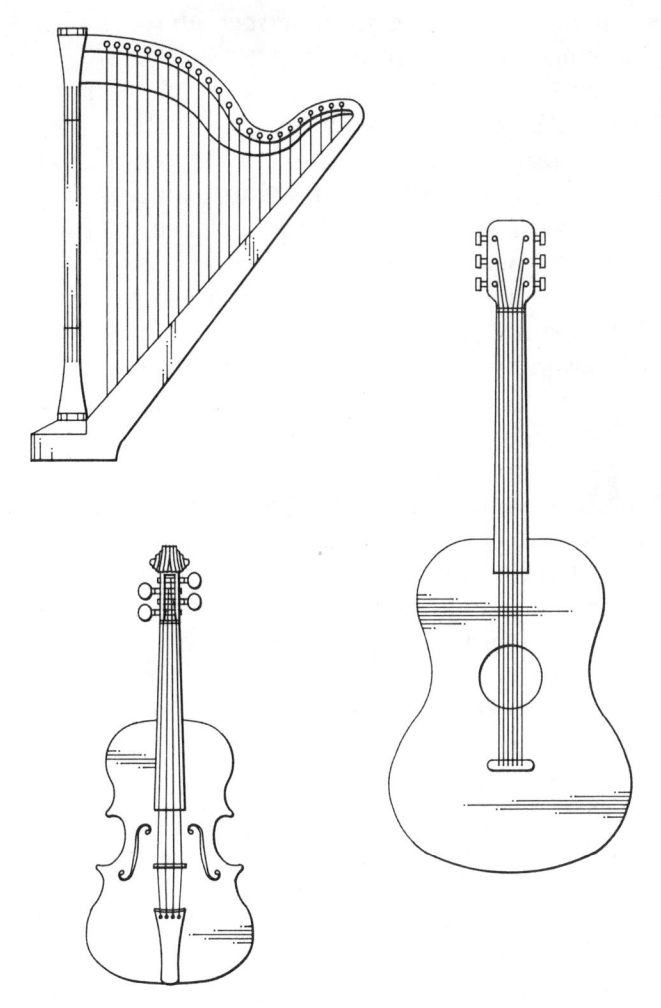

Figure 2-2. C-Sharp's instruments.

patent included two claims, the broad claim 1 above and the following narrower claim:

Claim 2: An apparatus, comprising:
 a frame having four wooden sides nailed together in a rectangular shape; and
 multiple strings having varying lengths attached to the frame between two of the four wooden sides.

Claim 2 does not literally "read on" any of C-Sharp's products because none of the instruments has four sides that are nailed together in a rectangular shape. Nevertheless, C-Sharp's tuned instruments would still infringe StringThing's patent because claim 1 still literally "reads on" C-

Sharp's instruments in the manner described above, and only one claim needs to be infringed to stop an infringer.

Another lesson to be learned from this example is that claims vary in scope and such variance can be very important. Here, both claims 1 and 2 describe the TwangBoard of **Figure 2-1**. However, only the broadly drafted claim 1 reads on C-Sharp's tuned instruments.

In the TwangBoard example, the inventor never considered a stringed instrument with "tuned" strings; but, due to good claim drafting, the patent was valuable. In contrast to that example, suppose that an inventor did consider all features of an invention and described these features in the patent disclosure, but failed to claim the features broadly enough to cover the full scope of his invention. Once again, patent protection extends only to the *claimed* invention, and not to that which is described in the disclosure or to the product itself.

To illustrate this point, suppose C-Sharp, from all of its knowledge in the string instrument field, invented the first piano. C-Sharp discovered that the strings could produce beautiful sounds when struck by soft hammers. These hammers could then be controlled by several keys aligned in a uniform manner to form a keyboard. In fact, the keys could be arranged so that those at one end of the keyboard would produce low tones and those at the opposite end would produce high tones. C-Sharp considered using various numbers of keys in its keyboards, but finally settled on 88 keys, which permits 11 musical octaves.

C-Sharp filed for a patent on the piano. The patent disclosure described the structure of the piano, including the hammers and the keyboard. The disclosure even broadly described that the piano could have a keyboard with any number of keys, from 8 to 108. However, C-Sharp's claim to the piano was much narrower:

Claim 1: An apparatus, comprising:
a frame;
88 strings stretched within the frame;
88 hammers, one for each of the 88 strings, for striking the strings to produce sound; and
a keyboard having 88 keys, one for each of the 88 hammers, for selectively causing the hammers to strike the strings.

Three years later, after reviewing C-Sharp's piano, ShortBoard, Inc., developed a more economical piano with only 40 keys (five octaves). ShortBoard experienced considerable success with its 40-key piano. Unfortunately for C-Sharp, ShortBoard most likely does not infringe claim 1. C-Sharp's patent protection may not extend to ShortBoard's 40-key piano, even though C-Sharp had contemplated small keyboards and had discussed smaller keyboards in the patent disclosure. This is because C-Sharp's *claim* only literally reads on pianos with 88 keys, not pianos having

40 keys.[4] Thus, even though C-Sharp's patent taught the world in its patent disclosure how to make and use smaller keyboards, C-Sharp only owns patent rights to a piano having 88 keys.

In summary, the patent claims, not the patent disclosure or product itself, are what define the patent property owned by the inventor. Every word of the claims will be scrutinized to determine the appropriate bounds of the property rights. For these reasons, it is advisable to have a trained patent attorney or agent draft the patent claims.

§ 2.4 Legal Framework and Requirements of Patent

The United States Constitution empowers Congress to promote the progress of useful arts, by securing for limited times to inventors the exclusive right to their discoveries. Under this authority, Congress has enacted a patent statute, Title 35 of the United States Code. Patent law is governed exclusively by this federal statute. There is no state-governed patent law.

The federal patent statute dictates several requirements for obtaining patent protection, including:

1. Subject matter
2. Novelty
3. Nonobviousness
4. Utility
5. Enablement and best mode.

§ 2.5 —Subject Matter

Some discoveries, however new, are not offered patent protection because the discoveries are not the types or classes of discoveries the patent laws are designed to protect. A classic example of a discovery that falls outside patentable subject matter is a scientific principle, such as Einstein's famous equation, $E=mc^2$. Although Einstein may be hailed a genius for discovering this equation, the equation itself is a law of nature, and as such, falls within a class of subject matter, "laws of nature, physical phenomena and abstract ideas," which is not patentable.[5] Another class of nonpatentable

---

[4] The doctrine of equivalents may or may not save C-Sharp from its poor claim drafting. See § 2.2.
[5] Diamond v. Chakrabarty, 447 U.S. 303, 206 U.S.P.Q. (BNA) 193 (1980).

subject matter includes printed subject matter,[6] such as works of art, literary works, and musical compositions (although this subject matter may be protectable under copyright law, as discussed below).

The patent statute at 35 U.S.C. § 101 defines *patentable subject matter* as "any new and useful process, machine, manufacture, or composition of matter, or any new and useful improvement thereof." Although this list appears limited, the classes of patentable subject matter are broadly interpreted. For example, *machines* includes anything from the largest of machines, such as telephone switching networks and nuclear reactors, to the smallest of machines, such as ballpoint pens and bread clips. *Machines* also includes the components of larger machines, such as bearings or computer chips.

The class *compositions of matter* includes novel chemical compounds such as fertilizers, medicines, plastics, and alloys.

Processes is broadly defined in the patent statute to include any process, art, or method, as well as any new use of a known process, machine, manufacture, composition of matter, or material.[7] Thus, in addition to *new* processes, the term *processes* also includes *old* processes used in new ways. To illustrate this point, consider an inventor who invents a novel machine for manufacturing soda cans. The inventor may be entitled to two sets of patent claims, one set for the novel structural aspects of the machine and a second set for the novel method of manufacturing the soda cans. If, however, the same inventor discovers that an old machine, which is already known and used to make tires, can be used to make soda cans, the inventor may still be entitled to one set of patent claims for a new method of manufacturing soda cans with the old tire machine. This avenue of protection is available even though the inventor would not be entitled to patent claims for the structural aspects of the old machine.

Using the statutory definition as a guide, courts have also found patentable subject matter to include microorganisms produced by genetic engineering,[8] mathematical algorithms applied to otherwise statutory subject matter,[9] circuits operating according to a computer program,[10] and genetically altered animals.[11] In one opinion, the Supreme Court went so far as to state that the Congressional intent in defining patentable subject matter was to "include anything under the sun that is made by man."[12]

---

[6] *In re* Miller, 418 F.2d 1392, 164 U.S.P.Q. (BNA) 46 (C.C.P.A. 1969); *In re* Jones, 373 F.2d 1007, 153 U.S.P.Q. (BNA) 77 (C.C.P.A. 1967).

[7] 35 U.S.C. § 100 (1952).

[8] Diamond v. Chakrabarty, 447 U.S. 303, 206 U.S.P.Q. (BNA) 193 (1980).

[9] *In re* Abele, 684 F.2d 902, 214 U.S.P.Q. (BNA) 682 (C.C.P.A. 1982).

[10] *In re* Iwahashi, 888 F.2d 1370, 12 U.S.P.Q.2d (BNA) 1908 (Fed. Cir. 1989).

[11] *Ex parte* Allen, 2 U.S.P.Q.2d (BNA) 1425 (Bd. Pat. App. & Interferences 1987)(holding animals are patentable if human intervention caused change).

[12] Diamond v. Chakrabarty, 447 U.S. 303, 206 U.S.P.Q. (BNA) 193 (1980).

§ 2.6 —Novelty

The patent statute requires that the subject matter be *novel* or new to receive patent protection. The novelty requirement is defined in § 102 of the patent statute. Instead of defining what is novel, however, § 102 describes several events that dictate when subject matter is *not* novel. When one of these events occur, patentability is prevented for lack of novelty. For this reason, the events of the novelty requirement in § 102 are sometimes referred to in the patent profession as the *§ 102 bars* to patentability. If any one of the events occurs, the event will "bar" (prevent) patentability of the subject matter. Understanding how the § 102 bars operate is critical to understanding how otherwise meritorious inventions can lose their opportunity for patentability. The § 102 bars are thus a cornerstone for understanding which policies a company can and should implement to prevent accidental barring of otherwise patentable inventions. A summary of the § 102 bars is provided in **Table 2–1**.

Each event described in **Table 2–1** precludes patentability. The most common of these bars are Bar #3, the printed publication bar; Bar #4, the public use bar; and Bar #5, the on-sale bar. These more common bars are discussed in detail in **Chapter 8**.

The scope and interpretation of the bars outlined in **Table 2–1** have been the basis for many controversies and much litigation effort. As a result, many subrules and sub-subrules have evolved with respect to the § 102 bars to patentability. How courts interpret § 102 bars is a topic of many legal and scholastic opinions and is beyond the scope of this book.

For our purposes, however, an important aspect of the § 102 bars is that each bar is concerned with "the" invention: the applicant is entitled to a patent unless "the invention" was known, or "the invention" was on sale, or "the invention" was described in a publication. This language leads to an important requirement of § 102. To bar patentability under § 102, the previously invented subject matter must be *identical* to "the" claimed invention. In patent terminology, this means that the previously invented subject matter must "anticipate" the applicant's claimed invention. If your company's invention is not clearly anticipated by somebody else's invention, then § 102 will not bar patentability of your company's invention. To illustrate the operation of § 102, consider the following example involving two ladder companies.

Acme Ladder, Inc., invents and patents a ladder with two parallel and vertical wooden beams and several wooden dowels attached between the beams at spaced intervals. **Figure 2–3** shows Acme's ladder, which would also typically be described in the patent specification. Acme's patent has the following claim:

Table 2-1
Section 102 Bars to Patentability

A person shall be entitled to a patent unless one of the following bars occurs....

Bars	Event	Rationale
Bar #1 35 U.S.C. 102(a)	The patent applicant is not entitled to a patent if the invention was publicly known or used by others in the U.S. before the invention by the patent applicant.	Patent applicant is not the first to invent as evidenced by prior knowledge or use by others in the United States. The "invention" is already in the hands of the public and so the government need not grant protection in return for disclosure of the invention.
Bar #2 35 U.S.C. 102(a)	The patent applicant is not entitled to a patent if the invention was patented or described in a printed publication anywhere in the world before the invention by the patent applicant.	Patent applicant is not the first to invent as evidenced by a prior U.S. or foreign patent or a prior description in a printed publication, such as a professional journal. The "invention" is already in the hands of the public and so the government need not grant protection in return for disclosure of the invention.
Bar #3 Printed Publication Bar 35 U.S.C. 102(b)	The patent applicant is not entitled to a patent if the invention was patented or described in a printed publication anywhere in the world more than one year prior to the date the patent applicant filed for a patent.	Government gives the patent applicant a maximum one-year "grace period" to file a patent application from the time the invention appears in a publication (including patents) written by the patent applicant or another person.
Bar #4 Public Use Bar 35 U.S.C. 102(b)	The patent applicant is not entitled to a patent if the invention was in public use in the U.S. more than one year prior to the date of the application for patent.	Government gives the patent applicant a maximum one-year "grace period" to file a patent application from the time the patent applicant first publicly uses the invention.

Bar #5
On-Sale Bar
35 U.S.C. 102(b)	The patent applicant is not entitled to a patent if the invention was on sale in the U.S. more than one year prior to the date of the application for patent.	Government gives the patent applicant a maximum one-year "grace period" to file a patent application from the time the patent applicant first tries to sell the invention.
Bar #6
35 U.S.C. 102(c)	The patent applicant is not entitled to a patent if the applicant has abandoned the invention.	Patent applicant has willingly given the idea to the public domain.
Bar #7
35 U.S.C. 102(d)	The patent applicant is not entitled to a U.S. patent if the applicant files a foreign patent application more than one year before filing a corresponding U.S. patent application and the invention becomes patented in the foreign country before the applicant files the U.S. application.	This bar prevents the applicant from unreasonably delaying in his or her filing of a U.S. application after having filed a foreign application. Once the applicant has filed a foreign application, the bar proscribes a window of time during which the applicant must file a corresponding U.S. application. The window begins when the applicant files the foreign application and ends when the foreign patent is granted, except that in no event can the window end in less than 12 months.
Bar #8
35 U.S.C. 102(e)	The patent applicant is not entitled to a patent if the invention was described in a U.S. patent granted to someone else and the application for that patent was filed in the U.S. before the applicant's invention.	Patent applicant is not the first to invent because the invention was described by someone else in a granted U.S. patent filed prior to the applicant's invention.
Bar #9
35 U.S.C. 102(f)	The patent applicant is not entitled to a patent if the applicant is not the true inventor.	In the U.S., only the true inventors may file a patent application. Failing to name even one of the inventors can prevent patenting or render an issued patent unenforceable.

Table 2–1
(continued)

A person shall be entitled to a patent unless one of the following bars occurs....

Bars	Event	Rationale
Bar #10 35 U.S.C. 102(g)	The patent applicant is not entitled to a patent if, before the applicant's invention, the invention was made in the U.S. by someone else who had not abandoned, suppressed, or concealed the invention.	Patent applicant is not the first to invent as evidenced by someone else in the U.S. making the invention and not keeping it from the public.

§ 2.6 NOVELTY

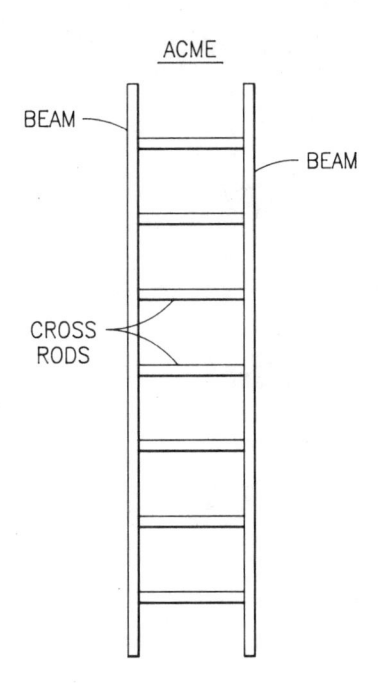

Figure 2–3. Acme's original ladder.

ACME'S BASIC LADDER CLAIM
A ladder, comprising:
  two beams, and
  a plurality of cross-rods attached between the beams at spaced-apart intervals.

Later, a competitor, named Treetop Company, improves Acme's basic ladder by adding a supporting third leg and by spacing the other two beams farther apart at the bottom than at the top. Treetop's structure, shown in **Figure 2–4**, improves stability. In an effort to obtain broad patent protection, Treetop first attempts to make the following patent claim to a ladder structure without the new features:

TREETOP'S PROPOSED CLAIM TO ITS UNIMPROVED LADDER
A device comprising:
  two spaced-apart legs aligned in a first direction; and
  a plurality of dowels aligned in a second direction substantially perpendicular to the first direction and spaced at predetermined distances along the two legs.

Assuming Acme's patent is the only patent in ladder technology, Treetop would not be granted the above patent claim on the basic structure of a ladder (two legs and a plurality of dowels) because Acme's patent already

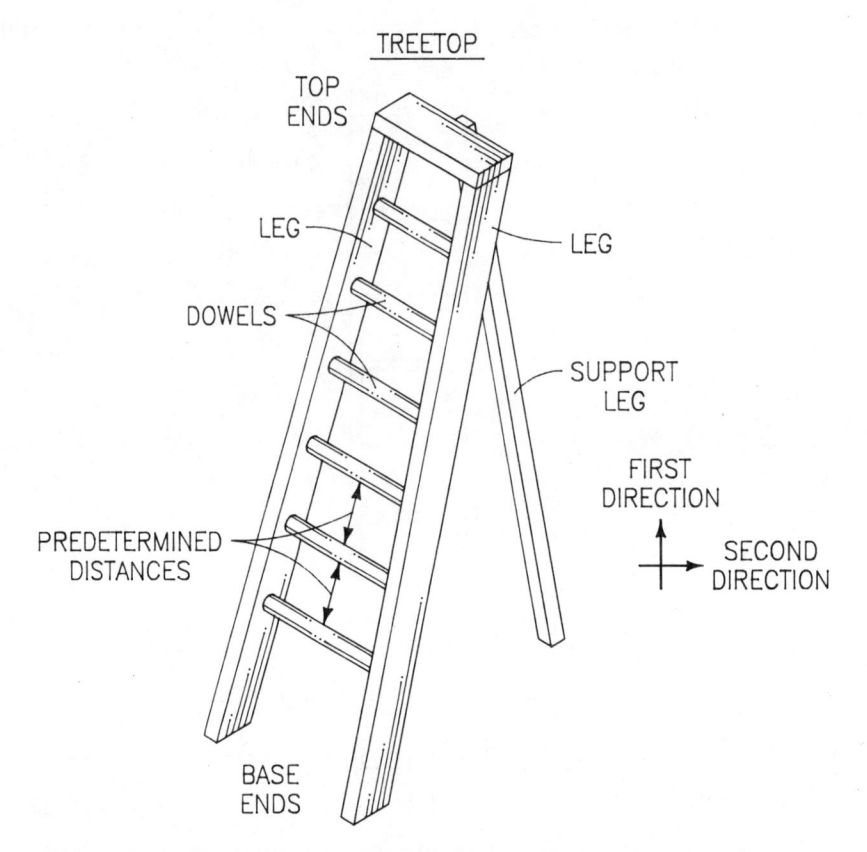

Figure 2-4. Treetop's improved ladder.

described a ladder having "two beams" and a "plurality of cross-rods." Thus, Treetop's attempt to claim the basic, unimproved, ladder structure (which was already introduced by Acme) should be rejected under § 102 in view of Acme's patent because the ladder patented and described by Acme is *identical* to Treetop's claim to the unimproved ladder (see Bars #2 and #7 and possibly Bar #3 of **Table 2–1**).

On the other hand, suppose Treetop made the following claim:

TREETOP'S CLAIM TO ITS IMPROVED LADDER

A device comprising:

    two spaced-apart legs aligned in a first direction, whereby base ends of the legs are spaced apart a distance greater than top ends of the legs;

    a plurality of dowels aligned in a second direction and spaced at predetermined distances along the two beams, each of the dowels being anchored to both of the legs; and

    a support leg, pivotally connected to the top ends of the legs, for supporting the top ends of the legs in an upright position.

Section 102 does not operate to bar this claim because it recites elements, such as the support leg and the widened base, that are not shown by Acme's ladder. The invention defined by Treetop's second claim is not identical to Acme's basic ladder and thus satisfies the novelty requirement.

In summary, § 102 of the patent statute provides the cornerstone for determining whether an invention is sufficiently novel to warrant patent protection. Several bars, including prior uses and offers to sell, prior publications and patents, and prior inventorships, might operate simultaneously to prevent patentability of an invention. To operate as a § 102 bar, however, a prior event must involve *exactly* the same invention as that claimed by the applicant. The § 102 bars to patentability will be discussed again in **Chapter 12**, which addresses common pitfalls that companies should avoid to ensure proper preservation of their patent rights.

§ 2.7 —Nonobviousness

In addition to the subject matter and novelty requirements, an invention must not have been "obvious" at the time the invention was made to someone skilled in the relevant technical field in view of the then-existing knowledge in that technical field. To illustrate the nonobviousness requirement, consider the following scenario.

An upcoming young inventor named Henry Ford invents a new and useful motorized machine for carrying people. Henry calls his invention an automobile and, in prudent business fashion, protects his invention by securing a United States patent. Although paints in a variety of colors are in wide supply, Henry prefers black and thus makes his automobiles available only in black. Additionally, his patent discloses and claims only black cars. Recognizing that consumers will quickly demand more colorful cars, CarCopy, Inc., files for a patent application with a claim to an automobile identical in structure to Henry's patented automobile but with the additional limitation that the automobile is red, yellow, or blue.

If novelty under § 102 were the only criterion for patentability under the patent statute, CarCopy might be entitled to a patent because the automobile claimed by CarCopy is not identical to Henry's automobile. In other words, CarCopy's automobile claim is novel in relation to Henry's automobile because CarCopy's automobile claim requires a new color—red, yellow, or blue—while Henry's automobile and patent concern only black automobiles. Under the patent statute, however, an invention surviving the novelty requirements of § 102 is not guaranteed patent protection.

Instead, § 103 of the patent statute prevents the grant of a patent on an invention that is merely an "obvious" variation of known technology. Specifically, § 103 requires that, even though the claimed invention is novel under § 102, a patent will not be awarded if the difference between the claimed subject matter and the prior teaching is *obvious* to those of ordinary skill in the art to which the subject matter pertains at the time the applicant makes the invention. The procedure for determining nonobviousness includes (1) determining the differences between the claimed invention and the prior teaching, (2) determining what level of knowledge a hypothetical person having ordinary skill in the art would possess, and (3) determining whether such a hypothetical person would consider the differences obvious. In conducting the analysis, the hypothetical, ordinarily skilled person is really quite extraordinary, as this person is presumed to know all of the prior art in the field of endeavor, as though the references were hanging on the walls around them.[13]

In the CarCopy example, CarCopy would not be entitled to a patent if, at the time CarCopy made the colorful cars, ordinarily skilled automobile manufacturers would have considered a change in color as an obvious change. Because a variety of colors were widely available and because Henry Ford simply chose black out of preference, CarCopy's patent application to a colorful car would not likely survive the nonobviousness requirement under § 103.

Consider again Acme's and Treetop's competing ladders discussed in § **2.6**. There, the question under § 103 with respect to Treetop's claim to the ladder with improved stability is whether Treetop's claim to a self-supporting ladder with nonparallel legs and a support leg is obvious in view of Acme's patent on the basic ladder structure. If neither Acme's patent nor other known technology would teach, suggest, or motivate one of ordinary skill in the art of ladder designs to incorporate the advantages of nonparallel legs or the support leg onto Acme's basic ladder, Treetop's claim would survive the nonobvious requirement of § 103.

The courts have also developed several fact patterns relating to patentable inventions, called *secondary considerations*, which assist in considering whether inventions can survive the nonobviousness requirement. These secondary considerations are discretionary in the fact finding process and no one of them should be considered dispositive of the obviousness issue. **Table 2-2** summarizes the secondary considerations of nonobviousness.[14]

Affirmative answers to the secondary considerations suggest that those of ordinary skill in the art did not consider the invention obvious.

In summary, although the § 102 bars require that the barring event involve the identical invention, novel inventions will still be denied pat-

---

[13] Union Carbide Corp. v. American Can Co., 724 F.2d 1567, 220 U.S.P.Q. (BNA) 584 (Fed. Cir. 1984).

[14] Stratoflex, Inc. v. Aeroquip Corp., 713 F.2d 1530, 218 U.S.P.Q. (BNA) 871 (Fed. Cir. 1983).

Table 2-2
Secondary Considerations Concerning Nonobviousness

Has the invention enjoyed commercial success?
Have others failed to solve the problem solved by the inventor?
Has there been a long-felt need in the industry for such an invention?
Did the industry experts express disbelief that the invention would work?
Has your company been successful licensing the invention to other companies?
Have prior patented inventions attempted to solve the problem in a way very different from the invention?

entability if the differences between the novel invention and the prior knowledge are found to have been obvious to those having ordinary skill in the particular art.

§ 2.8 —Utility

As a fourth requirement, § 101 of the patent statute requires that the invention discovery be "new *and* useful." Inventions that have no utility are not patentable. This requirement, however, is almost always satisfied. The classic example of an invention that does not satisfy this requirement is a perpetual motion machine.

§ 2.9 —Enablement and Best Mode

The final patentability requirement is that the patent specification sufficiently describe in clear and complete terms how one of ordinary skill in the technological field would make and use the invention,[15] including the best way to make and use the invention known to the inventor at the time of filing the patent application.[16] Because the goal of the patent process, at least with respect to the government, is to advance society's technological position through disclosure of new inventions, the government understandably requires that the specification teach others in sufficient detail how to best practice the invention.

Technically, *enablement* and *best mode* are two separate requirements. They are designed to prevent inventors from obtaining patent protection for inventions without telling others the best way to practice their inventions. The requirements do not go to the merits of whether an invention

---

[15] 35 U.S.C. § 112, para. 1 (1975).
[16] 35 U.S.C. § 112, para. 1 (1975).

is patentable. The requirements are more of a concern for corporate patent attorneys or counsel because they are typically responsible for writing enabling patent disclosures that disclose the best mode of practicing the invention. However, these requirements are included to make you aware that the patent law requires disclosure of the best way to implement the invention in a clear and enabling text. If this requirement is not met by you and your counsel, the patent will be effectively invalid and unenforceable.

§ 2.10 Right to Exclude

The owner of a patent has the right to exclude others from making, using, or selling the patented invention in the United States.[17] This right is exclusive to the patent owner, preventing even those inventors who subsequently develop the same invention through their own independent research from making, using, and selling the invention.

One point worth emphasizing is that the patent owner only has the right to "exclude others" from making, using, or selling the claimed invention. The patent owner does not have the absolute right to make, use, or sell the invention. This may initially seem odd, but consider the previous example in § 2.6 involving the ladder companies, Acme and Treetop. Treetop's improved self-supporting ladder must use Acme's intellectual property because the self-supporting ladder necessarily includes Acme's basic ladder structure defined in Acme's claim, which recites "two beams" and "a plurality of cross-rods." If the patent laws granted Treetop the positive right to make and use its self-supporting ladder invention, Treetop could make ladders without paying any royalties to Acme for the use of Acme's intellectual property, that is, the basic ladder structure defined by its claim. Under this regime, companies would simply copy their competitors' inventions, add a trivial, but nonetheless nonobvious element, and then obtain a patent to gain the right to make basically the same invention as their competitor.

Fortunately, the patent laws do not grant Treetop the right to make, use, or sell the self-supporting ladder; rather, Treetop only has the right to *exclude* others, including Acme, from making, using, or selling the improved self-supporting ladder. Similarly, Acme has the right to exclude others, including Treetop, from making, using, or selling the basic ladder. Under this structure, a company is forced to compensate others for the use of their patented technology. Treetop must compensate Acme for using

---

[17] 35 U.S.C. § 154 (1988).

the basic ladder technology because Treetop uses Acme's basic ladder concept when producing the self-supporting ladder. Acme, on the other hand, can make and sell the basic ladder without incumbrance because the basic ladder does not infringe Treetop's patent to the self-supporting ladder. However, if Acme added a support beam to its basic ladder and spaced the two beams farther apart at the base for improved stability, Acme would then be required to compensate Treetop for the use of Treetop's patent rights to the self-supporting ladder technology.

§ 2.11 Protection Extends to Equivalent Products

Patent protection is not limited to excluding others from producing products that are identical to the patented invention. Instead, patent protection also excludes competitors from making products that are "equivalent" to the claimed invention. Thus, a competitor will not escape infringing a patent simply by making a trivial change in the patented product from a claimed component to an unclaimed, yet equivalent component.

Suppose Treetop made and sold a ladder that differed from Acme's basic ladder only in that Treetop drilled holes in the two beams and slid the cross rods through the holes without "attaching" the cross rods to the two beams (as required by Acme's claims). This modified Treetop ladder is thus not "identical" to the ladder claimed by Acme. However, Treetop's modified ladder might still infringe Acme's claim because a ladder without attached rods is probably the functional and structural equivalent to Acme's basic ladder having the attached rods as defined by the claim.

The issue of whether a product is equivalent to the claimed invention involves a combination of legal and technical analysis. First, the terms employed in claims must be interpreted and given a proper construction based on how they were used in the specification and during prosecution. Then, after the terms have been interpreted, a product that is believed to be infringing is compared to the properly construed claims. The product is deemed equivalent if it performs substantially the same function, in substantially the same way, to achieve substantially the same result as the claimed invention.[18] This test is known as the *doctrine of equivalents*.

The range of equivalents granted to claims may, however, be cut back if the inventor made representations during patent prosecution to gain patentability. The typical scenario is when the inventor distinguishes the claimed invention from a certain technology during prosecution to gain allowance. The inventor is precluded from later going back during an infringement dispute and arguing that the claimed invention covers this

---

[18] Graver Tank Co. v. Linde Air Prod. Co., 339 U.S. 605, 85 U.S.P.Q. (BNA) 328 (1950).

technology. In this situation, such technology will not be considered equivalent to the claimed invention.

§ 2.12 Duration of Patent Protection

Patent protection extends for 17 years from the date the patent is issued. The 17-year duration was selected as a fair reward for the inventor's agreement to publicly disclose the invention. However, to enjoy the full 17-year term, the patent owner must pay maintenance fees before the 3½-, 7½-, and 11½-year anniversaries to keep the patent in force.[19] Failure to pay these fees will result in the patented technology lapsing into the public domain, and no further protection will be given.

§ 2.13 Enforcement Against Patent Infringers

When a competitor infringes a patent, the patent owner may seek remedy by civil action.[20] All such actions are brought in federal courts. The remedies available to the patent owner include injunctions, monetary damages, and an award of attorneys' fees.[21] In some situations, the patent owner is entitled to all three remedies.

Injunctions are orders by a court instructing a company not to continue acting in a particular manner. In patent litigation, injunctions typically order the defendant company to stop making, using, or selling something that infringes a patent claim. Damages might also be awarded to the patent owner to compensate for losses caused by the infringing activities. If the infringing competitor is determined to have willfully or purposefully infringed, the court can increase these damages up to three times the amount.[22] Attorneys' fees can be awarded to the victor (either party) in exceptional cases.

§ 2.14 How Company Secures Patent Protection

To obtain patent protection, a patent application is filed in the United States Patent and Trademark Office (PTO) in Washington, D.C. The PTO has examiners with technical degrees in engineering and science. These

---

[19] 35 U.S.C. § 154 (1988).
[20] 35 U.S.C. § 281 (1952).
[21] 35 U.S.C. §§ 283–285 (1952).
[22] 35 U.S.C. § 284 (1952).

examiners review the patent application to determine if the invention satisfies the legal requirements of patentability, including whether the invention is novel and nonobvious.

United States patents are filed by individual inventors and not their company. For a company to gain title to the patents, the inventors must assign their legal rights in the patent to their company. Thus, most companies require that their employees, as a condition for employment, agree to assign all future rights to any patents related to the company business that are secured during their employment.

The law also provides some relief for those few companies that do not have assignment agreements. Such companies are given a "shop right" in any patent issued to an employee who used the company's facilities and resources to develop the patented invention. The shop right is a nonexclusive right for the company to practice the invention without paying royalties to the inventor.

DESIGN PATENTS

§ 2.15 Design Patent Definition

A design patent protects the appearance or ornamental aspects of an article of manufacture. It does not protect the functionality of that article. A design patent document includes one or more drawings or pictures illustrating the design and a single claim directed to the illustrated design features. An example of a design patent is in **Appendix B**. This design patent illustrates a computer mouse and has a standard claim reciting: "The ornamental design for computer mouse, as shown and described."

§ 2.16 Legal Framework and Requirements of Design Patent

A design patent is granted to "[w]hoever invents any new, original and ornamental design for an article of manufacturing."[23] Design patent protection has five primary legal requirements:

1. Subject matter
2. Ornamental

---

[23] 35 U.S.C. § 171 (1952).

3. Originality
4. Novelty
5. Nonobviousness.

§ 2.17 —Subject Matter

Design patent protection extends only to manufactured articles. Examples of subject matter protected by design patents include:

1. Facial or body features of a toy doll
2. Shapes of car fenders
3. Decorative designs in furniture
4. Fabric prints.

§ 2.18 —Ornamental

The ornamental requirement limits design patent protection to only those aspects of the article that are ornamental or aesthetic. For instance, a design patent for a table covers a new shape or the decorative woodworking, but does not cover the functional aspects of the table, such as a platform supported by four legs. The functional aspects are protectable, if at all, through utility patent protection. See §§ 2.4 through 2.9. In fact, if the design of an object is necessary to achieve a particular function, the design cannot be protected by a design patent.

§ 2.19 —Originality

Because design patents protect the artistic appearance of a manufactured product, the design must be original. This requirement is very similar to the "original work of authorship" requirement in copyright law. See § 2.26.

§ 2.20 —Novelty and Nonobviousness

The final two requirements, novelty and nonobviousness, are the same as those considered in relation to utility patents. The design novelty and nonobviousness requirements are also governed by §§ 102 and 103 of the

§ 2.21 Scope of Design Patent Protection

The owner of a design patent has the right to *exclude* others from making, using, or selling the patented design in the United States.[25] Design patent protection extends for 14 years from the grant of the patent.[26] The patent owner is not required to pay any maintenance fees to keep a design patent in force.

§ 2.22 How Company Secures Design Patent Protection

Your company can secure design patents in the same manner as it secures utility patents, specifically by filing a design patent application in the PTO. Again, because patent rights vest in the inventor rather than a company, your company must require the inventor to assign his rights in these patents if your company is to gain any legal title to the designs.

COPYRIGHTS

§ 2.23 Copyright Definition

A copyright is an exclusive ownership right in a form of expression. Copyright protection subsists in original works of authorship fixed in any tangible medium of expression, from which the works may be perceived, reproduced, or otherwise communicated.[27] For instance, words fixed to a page, voices fixed to a compact disc, and images fixed to a videotape are all eligible for copyright protection. It is important to note, however, that copyright protection does not extend to the ideas or concepts themselves, but only to the expression of ideas.

---

[24] Design patents are governed under § 102, with one exception. The time period for Bar #6 (**Table 2-1**) is six months rather than one year. 35 U.S.C. § 172 (1952).

[25] 35 U.S.C. § 154 (1988); 35 U.S.C. § 171 (1952).

[26] 35 U.S.C. § 173 (1982).

[27] 17 U.S.C. § 102(a) (1990).

You will notice a change in terminology from patents to copyrights regarding the term used to describe the underlying subject matter. In patents, the patentable subject matter is referred to as an *invention*. In copyrights, the copyrightable subject matter is called a *work*.

§ 2.24 Legal Framework and Requirements of Copyright

The United States Constitution grants Congress the power to promote the progress of science by securing for limited times to authors, the exclusive right to their writings.[28] Under this power, Congress enacted a copyright statute, now Title 17 of the United States Code. Copyright law is governed exclusively by this federal statute. There is no state copyright law.

Copyright protection involves three general requirements:

1. subject matter
2. original authorship
3. fixation.

§ 2.25 —Subject Matter

Proper subject matter for copyright protection includes literary works, musical works, dramatic works, choreographic works, pictorial and sculptural works, motion pictures, sound recordings, and architectural works.[29] These categories are construed very broadly. For example, computer programs, both high level software and low level operational codes, are registrable as "literary works." In addition to the categories listed above, you may also register compilations of data.[30]

Copyright protection does not extend to an idea, procedure, process, system, method of operation, concept, principle, or discovery, regardless of the form in which it is described.[31] Copyright protection extends only to the form of expression itself. Additionally, copyright protection does not cover titles, names, short phrases, and slogans (although this subject matter might be protectable under trademark law).

---

[28] U.S. Const., art. I, § 8, cl. 8.
[29] 17 U.S.C. § 102(a) (1990).
[30] 17 U.S.C. § 103 (1976).
[31] 17 U.S.C. § 102(b) (1990).

§ 2.26 —Original Authorship

Subject matter eligible for copyright protection must be original. Works that consist entirely of information that is common property of the public and that do not contain original authorship are not eligible for copyright protection. For example, standard calendars, height and weight charts, tape measures and rulers, and lists or tables taken from public documents or other common sources are not capable of being copyrighted due to lack of originality.[32]

§ 2.27 —Fixation

All works must be "fixed" in a tangible form of expression to be protected by copyright law.[33] This simply means that the subject matter must be expressed in some medium, such as paper, a computer disc, or a cassette tape. Copyright protection does not extend to "unfixed" works, such as a contemporaneous speech.

§ 2.28 Actions Not Necessary but Recommended

Copyright laws were historically very formalistic and contained rigid procedural requirements that, if not meticulously followed, could result in loss of copyright protection. Fortunately, the copyright laws were changed in 1988 (effective March 1989) and the acquisition of copyright protection was greatly simplified.

The first major change under the new copyright laws was that copyright protection can now be secured *automatically* when a work is created and fixed in a tangible medium. Thus, as soon as the words in this sentence were written, the words received copyright protection.

A second major change was that a work no longer needed to be registered with the Copyright Office to receive copyright protection.[34] Registration still remains desirable, however, because it provides proof that a valid copyright exists. Further, registration is required to bring an infringement action under federal statute.[35]

A third significant change was that copyright protection cannot be forfeited for failure to place a copyright notice (© plus year of publication or

---

[32] United States Copyright Office, Circular 1, Copyright Basics (1989).
[33] 17 U.S.C. § 101 (1990).
[34] 17 U.S.C. § 408(a) (1988).
[35] 17 U.S.C. §§ 411, 412 (1990).

creation plus name of copyright owner) on the work. Notice is still recommended because it aids in the collection of damages in an infringement suit.[36] If the work carries a copyright notice, the defendant cannot legitimately claim that it innocently copied the work, not knowing that the work was intended to be protected. Therefore, prudence still dictates placing a copyright notice on all works.

§ 2.29 Exclusive Right to Copy and Distribute Work

Copyright protection provides basically what the name implies, a "right" to "copy" the work. Under the copyright statute, a copyright owner is granted five exclusive rights:

1. A right to reproduce the work
2. A right to prepare a derivative work (for example, a sequel to a book)
3. A right to distribute copies of the work
4. A right to perform the work publicly (this right applies mainly to musical and dramatic works)
5. A right to display the work publicly.[37]

The rights to reproduce and distribute copies of the work may be the most valuable for business purposes. These rights allow companies to produce and distribute such works as software, promotional brochures, and packaging label designs and thus protect them by preventing others from copying such materials.

Although these rights are exclusive to the copyright owner, the rights are subject to certain limitations known collectively as *fair use*. The fair use doctrine permits others to use portions of a copyrighted work without permission from the copyright owner for certain limited purposes, such as news reporting, classroom instruction, and research, as long as the use does not adversely affect the value of the copyrighted work.[38]

§ 2.30 Duration of Copyright Protection

Copyright protection for companies is generally obtained under the *work made for hire* doctrine. See § 2.33. Under this doctrine, the term of copyright protection held by the company extends for 75 years from the date

---

[36] 17 U.S.C. § 401(d) (1988).
[37] 17 U.S.C. § 106 (1990).
[38] 17 U.S.C. § 107 (1990).

of publication, or 100 years from the date of creation, whichever expires first.[39]

§ 2.31 Copyright Protection Very Narrow

Copyright protection is very narrow in comparison to patent protection. Copyright protection only prevents others from copying that particular work protected under the copyright. It does not prevent others from using the same underlying idea or concept. Thus, others may take the same idea and create their own expressive work and avoid copyright infringement.

Although narrow, copyright protection can still have considerable value. For example, a copyrighted computer program that provides an efficient method of operation can be more marketable than a competitor's program that, to escape copyright infringement, must be altered to a less efficient method.

§ 2.32 Enforcement Against Copyright Infringers

When a competitor infringes a copyright, the copyright owner can seek an injunction to stop the competitor from copying or selling the copyrighted work. The copyright owner can also seek damages, court costs, and attorneys' fees.[40] The copyright owner is entitled to actual damages plus any additional profits made by the infringing competitor that are attributable to the copyrighted work.[41] Alternatively, the copyright holder can elect statutory damages as an award for infringement.[42] However, to qualify for statutory damages, the work must be registered with the United States Copyright Office. In addition to these civil remedies, criminal remedies are sometimes available against very blatant, willful infringers.[43]

§ 2.33 How Company Secures Copyright Protection

Copyright protection is automatically secured when the work is created and fixed in a tangible medium. This might occur when it is written down

---

[39] 17 U.S.C. § 302(c) (1976).

[40] 17 U.S.C. § 502 (1976); 17 U.S.C. § 504 (1988); 17 U.S.C. § 505 (1976).

[41] 17 U.S.C. § 504(b) (1988).

[42] 17 U.S.C. § 504(c) (1988). Currently, statutory damages are set at $500 to $20,000 as compensation for all infringement of any one work.

[43] 17 U.S.C. § 506(a) (1990).

on paper or stored on a computer disc. Copyright registration is normally secured in the name of the author. However, in the employer/employee relationship, copyright registrations can be issued to a company, in lieu of the author/employee, when the employee prepared the work "within the scope of his or her employment."[44] This situation is known as a *work made for hire*. For example, a company will own the copyright in a marketing brochure produced by a graphic designer who was hired to produce such marketing brochures. Alternatively, it is common for companies to require employees to agree to assign all future rights in works created during employment with the company as part of their initial employment contract.

TRADEMARKS

§ 2.34 Trademark Definition

A trademark is any word, name, symbol, device, or combination of such elements used or intended to be used by a company to identify and distinguish its products from those manufactured and sold by others. The classic purpose of a trademark is to indicate the source of the marked products.[45] A trademark should not be the name of the goods themselves; rather, it should be used as an indication of the source of particular products. For instance, KODAK, NIKON, and POLAROID are trademarks for a generic product—a camera. The KODAK trademark indicates that Kodak Corporation is the source of the cameras bearing its trademark and distinguishes its cameras from those manufactured and sold by Nikon or Polaroid. When used properly, a trademark is an identifying adjective for a product noun. Kodak Corporation sells KODAK cameras; *KODAK* is the identifying adjective that modifies the product noun *cameras*.

Technically, *trademarks* are those marks used to identify the source of *products*. A *service mark*, on the other hand, is a mark used to identify the source of *services*. However, because trademarks and service marks effectively perform the same function (identifying and distinguishing one company's products or services from those of another company), we will refer to both types of marks generally as trademarks.

A trademark registration issued by the PTO shows the mark, provides the date when the mark was first used, and lists the classes and identity of the products and/or services covered by the mark. A sample trademark

---

[44] 17 U.S.C. § 201(a) (1978).
[45] 15 U.S.C. § 1127 (1988); Lanham Act § 45.

§ 2.35 LEGAL REQUIREMENTS 39

registration for the trademark BUCKAROO BAGEL is shown in **Appendix C**. Words that appear in all capital letters throughout this book designate trademarks.

§ 2.35 Legal Framework and Requirements of Trademark

Trademarks are governed principally under a dual system of state and federal laws.[46] The federal trademark laws are rooted in the commerce clause of the United States Constitution, which gives Congress the exclusive power to regulate interstate commerce.[47] From this power, Congress enacted a federal trademark statute known as the Lanham Act, or Title 15 of the United States Code.

To qualify for federal trademark protection, products or services must be traded in foreign commerce or across state lines. Because of current liberal interpretation of the term *interstate commerce* in other legal contexts, this is a fairly easy requirement for most companies to meet. Trademark protection under federal law extends throughout the United States.

In addition to federal registration, each state has a trademark registration process. Protection under state trademark law extends only to the state's territorial boundaries. Both federal and state protection may be obtained concurrently. In a clash between federal trademark law and state trademark law, federal trademark law preempts state trademark law.[48]

In the United States, rights in a trademark are established primarily through using the trademark. Some rights may be established in trademarks regardless of whether your company federally registers the mark in the PTO or registers the mark in a particular state, but federal registration is far more desirable. Unregistered trademarks are termed *common law trademarks*. They are enforceable in the market area in which they are actually used.

Federal trademark protection is preferable over state trademark protection if a company intends to trade in interstate commerce. As noted, federal trademark protection extends nationwide. Once a mark is federally registered, no other company can acquire any additional rights superior to those obtained by the federal trademark owner.[49] Additionally, federal

---

[46] Federal or state registration of a trademark is not mandatory. Common law protects marks that are being publicly used. However, common law protection is geographically limited to the region of actual use.

[47] U.S. Const., art. I, § 8, cl. 3.

[48] Burger King of Fla., Inc. v. Hoots, 403 F.2d 904, 159 U.S.P.Q. (BNA) 706 (7th Cir. 1968).

[49] Burger King of Fla., Inc. v. Hoots, 403 F.2d 904, 159 U.S.P.Q. (BNA) 706 (7th Cir. 1968).

registration may deter other companies from selecting a similar trademark. Other companies are more likely to search the federal trademark databases (as opposed to all 50 states) before selecting a trademark.

Federal trademark protection involves six primary requirements:

1. Subject matter
2. Affixation
3. Use
4. Distinctiveness
5. Similarity
6. Nonfunctionality.

§ 2.36 —Subject Matter

Proper trademark subject matter includes fanciful words, some geographic terms and personal names, slogans, symbols, shapes, colors, scents, or visual appearances. **Table 2–3** lists well-known examples for each of these types of subject matter.

§ 2.37 —Affixation

The Lanham Act requires that the trademark be displayed on the products or containers for the products so that the customers can view the marks in the marketplace. This requirement makes sense because the purpose of a trademark is to assist the consumer in identifying and distinguishing one company's products from those of another company. If the consumer does not see the trademark relation to the products, then he cannot identify the company that serves as the source for the products in question.

§ 2.38 —Use or Intent to Use

The Lanham Act requires that a company actually use the trademark in interstate commerce before registering for trademark protection, or at least have a bona fide intent to use the trademark within a period of time after filing for federal trademark protection. For an intent to use registration, the company must still eventually use the mark in interstate commerce to secure the requested registration. Actual use is therefore very important.

Table 2–3
Examples of Trademark Subject Matter

Fanciful Words	EXXON or KODAK
Geographic Terms	"Washington State" Apples
Personal Names	Hewlett/Packard
Slogans	"The Real Thing" of Coca-Cola
	"The Good Hands People" of Allstate
Symbols	McDonald's Golden Arches
	Mouse ears of Disney
Shapes	"Mrs. Butterworth" syrup bottle
	Mercedes car fender
Colors	The color pink in Owings Corning's fiberglass insulation
Visual Appearance	TIME Magazine's cover
Scent	Embroidery yarn having distinctive floral fragrance

§ 2.39 —Distinctiveness

A distinctive mark is one that is unique or nonordinary when used with a particular type of goods. Some marks are inherently distinctive and are registrable immediately. Other marks are not distinctive and are not registrable immediately. For federal registration, a trademark must either be distinctive at the time of registration or become distinctive over time.

The degree of distinctiveness among particular marks is often difficult to determine. It is useful to think of distinctiveness as a spectrum ranging from inherently distinctive marks to nondistinctive marks. This spectrum may be segmented into five categories: fanciful, arbitrary, suggestive, descriptive, and generic. **Table 2–4** illustrates these categories and provides examples for each.

Fanciful, arbitrary, and suggestive marks are inherently distinctive and can be registered immediately (assuming there is no confusion with another's mark). Descriptive marks are not inherently distinctive, but can satisfy the distinctiveness requirement once they acquire *secondary meaning* in the marketplace. A mark acquires secondary meaning when over time consumers have grown to recognize the mark as identifying a particular company's products. Marks that have been in exclusive and continuous use for five years are generally considered to have attained secondary meaning and thus are distinctive.[50]

---

[50] 15 U.S.C. § 1052(f) (1988); Lanham Act § 2(f).

Table 2–4
Distinctiveness Spectrum

Category	Definition	Examples
Fanciful	Words that are made up	EXXON or KODAK
Arbitrary	Marks that are real words, but have no relation to the goods	APPLE for computers TIDE for clothes detergent
Suggestive	Words that tend to reveal or hint at an attribute of the goods	COPPERTONE for suntan lotion RAPID-SHAVE for shaving cream
Descriptive	Marks that describe an attribute or characteristic of the goods	HOLIDAY INN for motels YELLOW PAGES for phone directory
Generic	Not really marks, but rather words that are the name of the goods themselves	*Tennis shoes* for tennis shoes *Watches* for watches

A company attempting to prove distinctiveness through secondary meaning must provide evidence showing that consumers have, over time, come to recognize the mark as identifying products or services of the company. Factors evidencing secondary meaning include:

1. Consumers' testimony that they identify the mark with the registering company
2. Consumer surveys
3. Manner of advertising and quantity of sales
4. Length and manner of use of the mark
5. Whether the mark was exclusively used or whether others used the same or confusingly similar marks
6. Proof that others intentionally copied the mark.[51]

A mark cannot be merely descriptive.[52] For example, a Florida orange grower could not register the trademark JUICY for the oranges. A mark cannot be deceptively misdescriptive.[53] For instance, the PTO might prevent a Pennsylvania potato chip producer from registering the mark IDAHO for potato chips if consumers would mistakenly identify Idaho

---

[51] J. Gilson, Trademark Protection and Practice § 2.09[5] (1990).
[52] 15 U.S.C. § 1052(e) (1988); Lanham Act § 2(e).
[53] 15 U.S.C. § 1052(e) (1988); Lanham Act § 2(e).

State as their source. However, merely descriptive or deceptively misdescriptive marks might qualify for federal trademark protection if they attain secondary meaning. The Pennsylvania company could, for example, register the mark IDAHO for potato chips if it could show that through extensive advertising and sales, consumers have come to recognize IDAHO brand potato chips as those chips made by the Pennsylvania company.

Generic marks cannot be registered. Additionally, trademarks that were once distinctive can become generic if the consuming public begins to assume that the mark is the name of the product as opposed to identifying the company that manufactures the product, and the company acquiesces in this public assumption. Trademarks that have become generic include *aspirin, cola, nylon,* and *cellophane.*

§ 2.40 —Absence of Confusion with Similar Marks

Trademark protection will not be given to a mark that is likely to cause confusion with another registered mark.[54] Permitting confusingly similar marks in the marketplace would negate the purpose of trademarks, which is to assist the consumer in identifying and distinguishing one company's products or services from those of another.

This *likelihood of confusion* standard necessarily requires inquiry as to whether the two marks will be used in the same market and for related products or services. The more similar the marks, products or services, and the market, the less likely that trademark protection will be granted. On the other hand, trademarks on products that are very different from one another may indicate a small likelihood of confusion. For example, the mark CADILLAC is registered by one company for automobiles and by another company for dog food. Because automobiles and dog food are such different classes of goods, there is essentially no confusion.

Factors that are considered in determining whether two marks are confusingly similar include:

1. The similarity of the marks with respect to appearance, sound, connotation, and impression
2. The similarity and nature of the products or services
3. The similarity of established trade channels for the products or services
4. The conditions of the sale (impulse purchase versus sophisticated purchase)

---

[54] 15 U.S.C. § 1052(d) (1988); Lanham Act § 2(d).

5. Fame of the prior mark
6. The number and nature of similar marks in use on similar products or services
7. The nature and extent of any actual confusion
8. The variety of products and services with which the mark is used.[55]

§ 2.41 —Nonfunctionality

The nonfunctionality requirement is a court created policy that considers whether a shape or feature has some utilitarian purpose or contributes to the ease or economy of manufacture. Functional features are typically not available for trademark protection. The rationale for this is to avoid a clash with patent laws that are designed to protect functional aspects.

The fact that a product having a distinctive shape performs a utilitarian function does not necessarily prevent the shape from receiving trademark protection. For example, all bottles are functional in that they can hold liquid. However, some bottles can be designed with a distinctive shape that sets them apart from other bottles, such as the old Coca-Cola bottle, the Mrs. Butterworth syrup bottle, or the Listerine bottle. Each of these bottles might qualify for trademark protection even though they have a utilitarian purpose of holding liquid.

§ 2.42 Exclusive Use of Mark

A federal trademark owner has the right to use the mark for specified products or services exclusively throughout the United States.[56] In addition, others are prevented from using a mark that is a reproduction or a colorable imitation of a registered mark, or is likely to cause confusion with it.

---

[55] *In re* E.I. Du Pont de Nemours & Co., 476 F.2d 1357, 177 U.S.P.Q. (BNA) 563 (C.C.P.A. 1973).

[56] Minor exceptions to this rule of exclusive ownership do exist. One exception is that a prior user of the same mark who had not registered the mark may be permitted to continue using the mark, but will be restricted to the geographical area within which the mark is actually used. The registered trademark owner would have rights to the mark throughout the remaining portion of the country. *See, e.g.*, Weiner King, Inc. v. Weiner King Corp., 615 F.2d 512, 204 U.S.P.Q. (BNA) 820 (C.C.P.A. 1980).

§ 2.43 Duration of Trademark Protection

Trademark protection exists as long as the mark is being used or until it becomes generic. Federal registration of the trademark must be renewed every 10 years.

§ 2.44 Enforcement Against Trademark Infringers

When a competitor infringes a federally registered trademark by using the same or a confusingly similar mark, the trademark owner can seek an injunction to stop the competitor's use of the infringing mark. The trademark owner can also sue for damages, the infringing competitor's profits, court costs, and attorneys' fees.[57]

§ 2.45 How Company Secures Federal Trademark Protection

To secure federal trademark protection, an applicant must file a trademark application with the PTO. Trademark examiners review the application to determine if the legal requirements have been satisfied. Unlike patents, the company itself, rather than the trademark designer, can register the trademark and all resulting rights will vest in the company itself.

It bears reemphasizing, however, that rights in a trademark are established through using the mark in conjunction with the products or services. Federal registration helps establish the rights nationwide and gives constructive notice of your company's ownership rights in the mark. However, *use* is the main criterion for establishing trademark rights.

TRADE SECRETS

§ 2.46 Trade Secret Definition

The Uniform Trade Secret Act (UTSA) defines a *trade secret* as follows:

> "Trade secret" means information, including a formula, pattern, compilation, program, device, method, technique, or process, that:

---

[57] 15 U.S.C. §§ 1116, 1117 (1988); Lanham Act §§ 34, 35.

(i) derives independent economic value, actual or potential, from not being generally known to, and not being readily ascertainable by proper means by other persons who can obtain economic value from its disclosure or use, and
(ii) is subject of efforts that are reasonable under the circumstances to maintain its secrecy.[58]

In simpler words, a trade secret is confidential information that is valuable to a company by providing an advantage in the marketplace over those who do not know the secret.

§ 2.47 Legal Framework and Requirements of Trade Secret

Trade secrets are governed solely by state law. There is no federal trade secret law. The UTSA is one attempt to provide uniform treatment of trade secrets among the states. Accordingly, we will refer to the UTSA for legal guidance in trade secret matters. However, the states need not adopt this Act, and many states that have adopted it have made changes in its content. Thus, each state has slightly different trade secret laws.

The creation and maintenance of trade secrets include several legal requirements:

1. Subject matter
2. Secrecy
3. Value
4. Novelty
5. Affirmative steps.

However, secrecy and affirmative steps are the more restrictive requirements.

§ 2.48 —Subject Matter

Trade secret protection has practically *no* subject matter requirement.[59] The UTSA defines proper trade secret subject matter as information "including a formula, pattern, compilation, program, device, method, technique, or process."

---

[58] Unif. Trade Secrets Act § 1.
[59] *See, e.g.*, CVD, Inc. v. Raytheon Co., 769 F.2d 842, 227 U.S.P.Q. (BNA) 7 (1st Cir. 1985), *cert. denied*, 475 U.S. 1016 (1986).

The scope of subject matter that is protectable as a trade secret is considerably broader than and includes the subject matter protectable by patents, copyrights, and trademarks. Thus, trade secret protection includes patentable subject matter (such as machines, processes, articles of manufacture, and compositions of matter), copyrightable subject matter (such as company literature, compilations, and software), and subject matter registrable as a trademark (such as names for future products and future campaign slogans). Examples of subject matter that may be protected by trade secrets include:

1. Engineering blueprints and patterns[60]
2. Drawings and data[61]
3. Computer software[62]
4. Market research studies[63]
5. Operating and pricing policies[64]
6. Processes[65]
7. Customer lists[66]
8. Sources for raw materials.[67]

§ 2.49 —Secrecy

The subject matter must be generally unknown in the industry. The UTSA requires that the subject matter not be "generally known" or "readily ascertainable by proper means." Absolute secrecy is not required.[68]

---

[60] Schulenburg v. Signatrol, 33 Ill. 2d 379, 212 N.E.2d 865, 147 U.S.P.Q. (BNA) 167 (1965).

[61] A.H. Emery Co. v. Marcan Prod. Corp., 389 F.2d 11, 156 U.S.P.Q. (BNA) 529 (2d Cir. 1968), *cert. denied*, 159 U.S.P.Q. (BNA) 799 (1968).

[62] Telex Corp. v. International Bus. Mach. Corp., 510 F.2d 894, 184 U.S.P.Q. (BNA) 521 (10th Cir. 1974), *cert. denied*, 423 U.S. 802 (1975).

[63] Western Electro-plating Co. v. Henness, 180 Cal. App. 2d 442, 4 Cal Rptr. 434 (1960).

[64] Black, Sivalls & Bryson, Inc. v. Keystone Steel Fabrication, 584 F.2d 946, 199 U.S.P.Q. (BNA) 385 (10th Cir. 1978).

[65] Syntex Ophthalmics, Inc. v. Novicky, 745 F.2d 1423, 223 U.S.P.Q. (BNA) 695 (Fed. Cir. 1984).

[66] Kewanee Oil Co. v. Bicron Corp., 416 U.S. 470, 181 U.S.P.Q. (BNA) 673 (1974).

[67] Water Serv., Inc. v. Tesco Chem., 410 F.2d 163, 162 U.S.P.Q. (BNA) 321 (5th Cir. 1969).

[68] Clark v. Bunker, 453 F.2d 1006, 172 U.S.P.Q. (BNA) 420 (9th Cir. 1972); A.H. Emery Co. v. Marcan Prod. Corp., 389 F.2d 11, 156 U.S.P.Q. (BNA) 529 (2d Cir. 1968), *cert. denied*, 159 U.S.P.Q. (BNA) 799 (1968).

§ 2.50 —Value

The subject matter must generate some independent economic value from not being generally known to competitors. The subject matter is said to have value if competitors could obtain economic value from knowledge of it.

§ 2.51 —Novelty

Courts often require at least some minimum level of novelty before the subject matter is given trade secret protection. To satisfy the trade secret novelty requirement, subject matter must not be readily available in the industry. The level of trade secret novelty does not, however, rise to the level of novelty required by the patent laws.

§ 2.52 —Affirmative Steps

A company must take conscious, affirmative steps to keep the subject matter secret. The UTSA requires a company to make "efforts that are reasonable under the circumstances to maintain secrecy." However, the phrase "efforts reasonable under the circumstances" does not adequately impart the importance of acting positively to protect trade secrets. The descriptive phrase "affirmative steps" is more useful because it emphasizes that positive action should be taken to ensure secrecy.

Affirmative steps are defined as implementing extra precautions above and beyond normal operating procedures. Subject matter will not be deemed a trade secret if no affirmative steps are taken, even though the subject matter is secret to the rest of the world.

Affirmative steps include restricting access to facilities, protecting confidential records, restricting access to proprietary documents, and forbidding employees from disclosing proprietary information. Some policies and procedures that are designed to satisfy this legal requirement are discussed in **Chapter 13**.

§ 2.53 Rights May Not Be Exclusive

Unlike patents, copyrights, and trademarks, trade secrets do not provide "exclusive" rights. Under some circumstances, more than one company can possess the same trade secret at the same time. For example, consider the following scenario involving two cookie makers in the cookie industry. To this cookie industry, the known and widely used recipe for making chocolate chip cookies calls for baking the cookies for 15 minutes at 400° F. Unknown to the other, each cookie maker independently discovered that chocolate chip cookies have a longer shelf life in stores if these cookies are baked for 18 minutes at 350° F. Both cookie makers derive value from the baking improvement, and both take affirmative steps to keep the baking improvement secret. Because the baking improvement is not generally known to the cookie industry, both cookie makers may legitimately have rights to the same trade secret.

§ 2.54 Trade Secrets Only Protected Against Improper Taking

Trade secret protection only protects against those who acquire the trade secret through "improper means." Improper means includes (1) unlawful conduct and (2) otherwise lawful conduct that is improper under the circumstances. Acquiring a trade secret through unlawful conduct includes theft of trade secrets, bribing an employee to disclose his company's trade secrets, fraud, breach of contract, and electronically surveying a competitor's operation.[69]

With respect to the second category of improper means, the *DuPont* case exemplifies a situation in which the conduct was otherwise lawful, but improper under the circumstances. DuPont was constructing a new plant to manufacture methanol. Part of the trade secret was the plant layout, which was important to the efficient production of methanol. DuPont went to great lengths to prevent observers from witnessing the new construction, including the construction of a high fence about the facility. Unable to view the plant from the ground, a competitor hired a photographer to take aerial photographs of the plant during construction. These photographs showed the structural layout of the plant, and from them the competitor could determine how methanol was being manufactured. Although taking pictures from an airplane is not ordinarily unlawful, doing so over a competitor's new plant solely for the purpose of discerning the competitor's trade secrets was found to be improper under these circumstances.[70]

On the other hand, trade secret protection does not prevent a competitor from discovering the trade secret through proper means. For example, a competitor may purchase your company's product and "reverse engineer" that product by disassembling the product to determine how it works. The competitor may then legally use any of your company's trade secrets

---

[69] Unif. Trade Secrets Act § 1, commissioners' cmt.
[70] E.I. Du Pont de Nemours & Co. v. Christopher, 431 F.2d 1012, 166 U.S.P.Q. (BNA) 421 (5th Cir. 1970), *cert. denied*, 400 U.S. 1024, 168 U.S.P.Q. (BNA) 385 (1970).

learned from this reverse engineering. Proper means to acquire trade secrets includes independently discovering the secret by one's own research and development, reverse engineering a competitor's product, observing the product in public use or on public display, and obtaining the secret from published literature.[71]

§ 2.55 Duration of Trade Secret Protection

Trade secret protection exists until the secret becomes generally known in the industry. Therefore, a trade secret may exist in perpetuity as long as it remains secret. Possibly the most famous trade secret is the recipe for Coca-Cola.® It has remained secret for over 100 years.

Once a trade secret is publicly disclosed, however, it is lost forever.[72] The once-trade secret information passes into the public domain and other companies can then use it.

§ 2.56 Legal Recourse for Theft of Trade Secret

When a competitor steals a trade secret, the trade secret owner may seek an injunction to prevent the competitor from using it. The trade secret owner may also sue for actual damages, punitive damages, the competitor's profits, and attorneys' fees. During trade secret litigation, courts often impose a secrecy order in an effort to prevent the trade secret from being leaked to the public. Unfortunately, there is a risk that the trade secret owner may lose the trade secret, despite efforts by a court to protect its secrecy during trial.

§ 2.57 Others May Patent Technological Trade Secrets

The trade secret laws do not prevent others from independently "inventing" the secret technology and then securing a patent on that technology. Someone's secret use of a novel innovation does not prevent another from obtaining patent protection on that innovation. Accordingly, there is a risk that your company could be excluded from using technology that it once kept as a trade secret.

---

[71] Unif. Trade Secrets Act § 1, commissioners' cmt.
[72] *See, e.g.*, Cadillac Gage Co. v. Verne Eng'g Corp., 203 U.S.P.Q. (BNA) 473 (Mich Cir. Ct. 1978).

§ 2.58 How Company Secures Trade Secret Protection

Unlike patent, copyright, and trademark protection, no formal procedure exists for filing an application or registration for a trade secret with some branch of the government. Instead, your company must take "affirmative steps" to keep it secret (or, as the UTSA states, make "efforts that are reasonable under the circumstances" to maintain secrecy). This requires implementation of specific policies and procedures designed to prevent loss of trade secrets. Mere "intent" by a company to maintain subject matter as a trade secret is not sufficient without a showing that the company implemented specific precautions to protect the subject matter.[73]

KNOW-HOW

§ 2.59 Know-How Definition

In addition to the intellectual properties defined in this chapter—patents, copyrights, trademarks, and trade secrets—some people include a fifth intellectual property called *know-how*. As the name aptly describes, know-how is simply knowing how to do something, or knowing how not to do something. Know-how includes all of the information developed by a company through its successes and failures, which assists in operating the company.

Know-how is the genesis of ascertainable ideas, innovations, and discoveries. It is the foundation upon which companies build intellectual property portfolios of patents, copyrights, trademarks, and trade secrets. Know-how is broader than and encompasses all subject matter that may be protected by patents, copyrights, trademarks, and trade secrets. Know-how includes technological innovations, ideas, processes, concepts, formulations, best guesses, experimental results, on-going research and development efforts, the selection of one design over another, and choices of materials. Know-how also includes failed experiments and unexpected results of experiments. It includes employee experience, product team experience, management policies, accounting methods, and internal procedures for improved efficiency.

We have purposely defined know-how very broadly. We will return to this definition in later chapters as it becomes important for our analysis of which type of protection is most suitable for a particular subject matter.

---

[73] *See, e.g.*, Arco Indus. Corp. v. Chemcast Corp., 633 F.2d 435, 443, 208 U.S.P.Q. (BNA) 190, 197 (6th Cir. 1980).

§ 2.60 Intellectual Property Rights Checklist

The following checklist summarizes the key aspects of the various types of intellectual property rights:

PATENTS:
  Legal requirements:

  1. Subject matter
  2. Novelty—Bars to patentability (**Table 2-1**)
  3. Nonobviousness
  4. Utility
  5. Enablement and best mode.

  The claims define the patent rights. The patent disclosure and the marketed product do not.

  A patent provides the right to *exclude* others from making, using, and selling the invention. It does not give one the right to make, use, and sell.

  Patents are governed exclusively by federal law.

DESIGN PATENTS:
  Legal requirements:

  1. Subject matter
  2. Ornamental
  3. Originality
  4. Novelty
  5. Nonobviousness.

  Design patents only protect ornamental or aesthetic aspects of manufactured product.

  Design patents are governed exclusively by federal law.

COPYRIGHTS:
  Legal requirements:

  1. Subject matter
  2. Original authorship
  3. Fixed in a tangible medium.

Not required, but recommended:

1. Placing copyright notice (© + year + owner) on work
2. Registering the work in the Copyright Office.

Copyright protection is secured immediately upon fixing the expression in a tangible medium.

Copyrights only protect the form of expression, not the concept or idea underlying the expression.

Copyrights are governed exclusively by federal law.

TRADEMARKS:

Legal requirements for federal protection:

1. Subject matter
2. Affixation
3. Use or intent to use
4. Distinctiveness
5. Absence of confusion with similar marks
6. Nonfunctional.

Trademark rights are created and established simply through *use* of the trademark.

Trademarks are governed by federal, state, and common laws.

TRADE SECRETS:

Legal requirements:

1. Subject matter
2. Secrecy
3. Value
4. Novelty
5. Affirmative steps.

Trade secret rights may not be exclusive to a single company.

Trade secret protection does not protect against reverse engineering or other innocent techniques of discovering the trade secret. Inadvertent public disclosure by an employee may cause irreversible loss of trade secret rights.

Trade secrets are governed under state and common laws.

KNOW-HOW:

Know-how is the genesis of ascertainable ideas, innovations, and discoveries. It is the foundation upon which companies build intellectual property portfolios of patents, copyrights, trademarks, and trade secrets.

CHAPTER 3

DANGERS OF FAILING TO CONSIDER INTELLECTUAL PROPERTY ISSUES

§ 3.1 Lessons from Real-Life Cases
§ 3.2 Case 1: Loss of Patent Rights as a Result of Patent Holder's Marketing Activity
§ 3.3 Case 2: Loss of Patent Rights Caused by Business Partner's Sales Activities
§ 3.4 Case 3: Loss of Patent Rights as a Result of Prior Public Use
§ 3.5 Case 4: Loss of Trade Secret Rights as a Result of Inadvertent Disclosure
§ 3.6 Case 5: Loss of Trade Secret Rights as a Result of Failing to Adequately Identify Confidential Information
§ 3.7 Case 6: Loss of Trade Secret Rights as a Result of Failing to Take Affirmative Steps to Maintain Secrecy
§ 3.8 Case 7: Monetary Loss for Patent Infringement
§ 3.9 Case 8: Monetary Loss for Patent Infringement
§ 3.10 Case 9: Monetary Loss for Willful Patent Infringement
§ 3.11 Case 10: Monetary Loss for Trademark Infringement

§ 3.1 Lessons from Real-Life Cases

Chapter 2 outlined some of the more significant intellectual property areas. This chapter shows how the various rules might affect a company's everyday business decisions. Case histories illustrate the impact of intellectual property laws on real decisions made by real businesses.

These case histories convincingly show the dangers of inadequately considering intellectual property issues or drawing inaccurate conclusions when making strategic, managerial, and routine decisions during the course of business. Some of the businesses examined were devastated and forced to leave otherwise lucrative markets because of their failure to comply with intellectual property laws. Other businesses lost profitable opportunities. If this chapter creates anxiety over whether your business choices could damage your company, take heart because **Chapters 5 through 11** describe, step-by-step, how to analyze business decisions to maximize rewards and avoid dangers under the intellectual property laws.

Recognize that the cases described are not unusual. There are thousands of cases similar to the ones presented here. Employee decisions made without proper regard for the impact of the intellectual property laws have restricted or eliminated company opportunities more frequently than one might believe. In addition to the loss of companies' own intellectual property opportunities, failing to monitor and appreciate the intellectual property rights of others has frequently cost companies large dollar damages and elimination from otherwise profitable markets. The cases in §§ 3.2 through 3.11 thus illustrate how the operation of intellectual property laws can make seemingly good business decisions ultimately very disappointing.

§ 3.2 Case 1: Loss of Patent Rights as a Result of Patent Holder's Marketing Activity

CASE 1: RCA v. DATA GENERAL

October 8, 1962: Proposal covering displays is submitted to FAA.

October 8, 1963: One year from the sales activity. Section 102 provides a one-year grace period from the date of the sales activity to file a patent application.

October 16, 1963: RCA filed a U.S. patent application on the displays.

RESULT: RCA's U.S. patent is invalidated because of the premature marketing activity.

New product introductions are exciting for company salespersons who are anxious to reap new sales of the products to their regular customers. On occasion, such overanxious salespersons have unwittingly started the "on sale" bar to patentability by offering the new products for sale during a sales presentation. This "on sale" bar will preclude United States patent rights in the product that a salesperson offered, unless a patent application is filed within one year of the offer date. A company that is unaware that the offer was even made may let the one year pass and miss out on its patent opportunity. Furthermore, such sales activity will most likely immediately preclude the company from securing foreign patent protection in many foreign countries of interest, including European countries and Japan. Unlike in the United States, there is no one-year grace period in these foreign countries.

§ 3.3 PARTNER'S SALES ACTIVITIES

Marketing products that a company has not yet released for sale can be detrimental to the company's intellectual property opportunities, especially when the company was relying on what it considered to be valid patents to secure a better market position against its competitors. Often the sales activity is not discovered until after a patent has proven valuable and is being enforced in court against an infringing competitor. Imagine the reaction of company executives when, in the midst of a trial to enforce a patent against the accused infringer, they first learn that an overzealous salesperson from their own company offered the patented product for sale to a customer more than a year before the United States patent filing date. The patent, of course, would be rendered invalid and the otherwise possible infringer might then be free to make, use, and sell the other company's valuable invention without any compensation.

In 1989, the "on sale" bar rendered invalid a patent for computer displays held by RCA Corporation.[1] The Federal Aviation Administration (FAA) needed displays for its air traffic control centers. On October 8, 1962, RCA submitted a proposal for its displays to the FAA. On October 16, 1963, just eight days more than a year after the proposal was sent to the FAA, RCA filed a United States patent application covering the displays.

When RCA later sued another party, Data General, alleging patent infringement, Data General learned of RCA's proposal to the FAA and argued that the proposal amounted to an offer to sell the patented displays more than a year before the patent filing date. The trial and appellate courts agreed. The courts rejected RCA's arguments that (1) the display it proposed to the FAA was not the same as that covered by the patent, (2) the sale was only for experimentation, and (3) the display was not sufficiently developed as of the date of the proposal as to amount to an offer of sale. RCA's patent was held invalid.

§ 3.3 Case 2: Loss of Patent Rights Caused By Business Partner's Sales Activities

CASE 2: *In re* HAMILTON

Hamilton invented a machine for perforating paper to produce business forms.

In mid-1980, Hamilton and business partner Uarco tested the invention.

First tests proved satisfactory.

July 25, 1980: Business partner Uarco solicits Christ for the World to purchase over 300,000 form lengths for further "testing" of the invention.

---

[1] RCA Corp. v. Data Gen. Corp., 887 F.2d 1056, 12 U.S.P.Q.2d (BNA) 1449 (Fed. Cir. 1989). The material throughout the remainder of this section is derived from material included in the above-cited opinion.

Hamilton was not involved in this second set of "tests."

July 25, 1981: One year from sale activity.

Sept. 15, 1981: Hamilton filed a U.S. patent application.

Court found that the sale was for commercial purpose, and not further experimentation, as evidenced by the fact that Hamilton did not participate in the second set of tests conducted by the business partner.

RESULT: Patent denied by the U.S. Patent and Trademark Office.

Western Printing Machinery lost the patent rights for an invention of its employee, James Hamilton, as a result of its business partner's sales activity.[2] Mr. Hamilton invented perforated business forms and machinery for making the forms. The machinery perforated a roll of paper with perforations small enough to weaken the paper so that it could be easily separated into individual form lengths, yet strong enough that the paper could be processed continuously without breaking apart. Apparently, the perforations were so small and so close together that the forms, once separated, were indistinguishable from precut stationary. Mr. Hamilton presented his invention to a business partner, Mr. Schnitzer, of Uarco, a Chicago manufacturer of business forms. After a test run of 10,000 to 20,000 form lengths under Hamilton's supervision, Mr. Schnitzer concluded that the test run was satisfactory and that testing should proceed on a commercial-scale run.

Apparently, employees of both Western and Uarco had questions concerning the ability of the perforating cutter to perform for large-scale runs amounting to hundreds of thousands of cuts. Mr. Schnitzer mentioned this fact to a Uarco salesperson, who then solicited an order of 309,000 form lengths from Christ for the World, Inc. The order was obtained on July 25, 1980.

Mr. Schnitzer and the Uarco salesperson may well have intended that the offer to Christ for the World would simply continue the "testing" of Mr. Hamilton's invention because both Western and Uarco were curious about the ability of the perforating machinery to perform on large orders. In fact, Christ for the World did have some problems in folding and "bursting" some of the forms it received. The attempt to classify this activity as experimentation is important because such testing does not invoke the "on sale" or "public use" bars to patentability associated with the novelty requirement of patent law. See **Chapters 2 and 12.**

Nevertheless, while "testing" the invention at Christ for the World, Western made one critical mistake that cost it the patent rights to the

---

[2] *In re* Hamilton, 882 F.2d 1576, 11 U.S.P.Q.2d (BNA) 1890 (Fed. Cir. 1989). The material throughout the remainder of this section is derived from material included in the above-cited opinion.

perforated business forms: neither Western nor Mr. Hamilton significantly participated in the "testing" process being conducted by Uarco. The appellate court said: "What is remarkable about the tale of experimental use which has been placed before us in this case is the lack of involvement of either the inventor, James Hamilton, or his employer and assignee, Western Printing Machinery."

Despite the appearance that Uarco was selling the invention for further testing, the court determined that the business partner was selling the invention for commercial purposes. This commercial purpose was borne out by the fact that neither Mr. Hamilton nor someone under his control participated in the experimentation. If the purpose of the experimentation was to improve the product, and not for commercial gain, one would naturally expect the inventor to be involved in these tests. Yet, the court noted that neither Hamilton nor Western knew or cared what, if anything, Mr. Schnitzer of Uarco was doing to sell or test the forms. Indeed, neither Hamilton nor Western even knew of the Christ for the World order, and they never received reports concerning the so-called "testing."

The court ruled that Mr. Hamilton's United States patent application for the perforated forms was properly rejected by the Patent and Trademark Office (PTO) as having claimed subject matter that was on sale in this country more than a year before the application was filed, in violation of the novelty requirement of patent law.

§ 3.4 Case 3: Loss of Patent Rights as a Result of Prior Public Use

CASE 3: *In re* SMITH & McLAUGHLIN

August 1976: Airwick has 76 consumers "test" CARPET FRESH product.

August 1977: One year from public "test."

Sept. 2, 1977: Airwick filed its patent application on the formula.

Court concluded that consumer "test" was primarily for testing the *marketability* of product and not for testing the product itself.

RESULT: Patent denied by the U.S. Patent and Trademark Office because of premature public use of invention.

Public use of an invention can prevent patentability of a company's invention. The United States patent statute grants a one-year grace period from the time of public use in which to file a patent application on the publicly disclosed technology. Unfortunately, public use of an invention will most likely immediately prevent patentability in most foreign countries.

In 1983, Airwick Industries lost the opportunity to patent its CARPET FRESH formula as a result of its own public use of that formula.[3] Airwick's director of research and development, Mr. Smith, together with a co-inventor, developed a vacuumable powder that exhibited deodorizing, antistatic, and antisoil characteristics when applied to a carpet.

In August 1976, more than one year before the inventors filed a United States patent application for the formula, Airwick conducted a consumer test in St. Louis involving 76 consumers. The consumers were divided into two groups, with 40 of the consumers receiving a granular formula and 36 receiving a powdered formula. The consumers were allowed to use the products in their homes for two weeks. Their use of the product was unrestricted during the two weeks and none of the consumers entered into confidentiality or secrecy agreements with Airwick.

At the conclusion of the testing, Airwick instructed the consumers to return unused portions of the products. Airwick then interviewed 68 of the 76 consumers regarding the fragrance and vacuumability of the products they had used.

After reviewing these facts, an appellate court ruled that Airwick was not entitled to a patent on the claimed CARPET FRESH formula because Airwick's St. Louis testing amounted to a public use of that formula. The court was persuaded that Airwick's St. Louis experiment was *market* testing, not *product* testing. That is, Airwick was gauging consumer demand for the product, rather than gauging whether the product would work. Although the inventors claimed that their intentions during the St. Louis experiment were to test the fragrance levels and vacuumability of the product, the court disclaimed their subjective intent as "of minimal value" and looked instead to objective evidence.

Specifically, the court noted that the fragrance levels and vacuumability could have been tested in a laboratory. Instead, Airwick tested the product using "typical housewives," that is, consumers. The purpose behind this choice, the court rationalized, was to determine whether potential consumers would buy the product and how much they would pay for it, not whether the product would work. Further, the testing of the products was not conducted in the presence of the inventors or their representatives. Nor were the consumers restricted in their use of the product. The consumers, instead, were free to use the products as they wished for two weeks. The appellate court was convinced by the objective evidence suggesting Airwick's dominant purpose was to test the commercial acceptability of the CARPET FRESH product.

---

[3] *In re* Smith, 714 F.2d 1127, 218 U.S.P.Q. (BNA) 976 (Fed. Cir. 1983). The material throughout the remainder of this section is derived from material included in the above-cited opinion.

Typically, when "users" are under an obligation to maintain secrecy, their use will not invalidate potential patent rights. However, Airwick did not require its users to sign confidentiality agreements. Instead, it gave the product to the test group without restriction. Accordingly, Airwick could not avail itself of this exception.

Airwick's consumer test invalidated its potential patent rights to the CARPET FRESH formula by violating the public use rule in the patent laws.

§ 3.5 Case 4: Loss of Trade Secret Rights as a Result of Inadvertent Disclosure

CASE 4: DEFIANCE BUTTON MACHINE v. C&C METAL PRODUCTS

Defiance had trade secret rights in its customer lists.

Defiance sold a computer having customers lists stored therein to C&C.

Defiance employee showed C&C how to operate the computer and printed out the customer list for C&C.

Defiance did not erase customer lists from the computer prior to C&C taking possession.

RESULT: Defiance lost trade secret rights in customer lists for failure to take reasonable steps to protect these lists.

Trade secret rights, like patent rights, can also be lost through carelessness of the property holder. Defiance Button Machine Company lost its trade secret rights in its customer lists as a result of an inadvertent disclosure.[4]

Due to slowing sales, Defiance Button defaulted on a bank loan and an auction sale was held to sell some of Defiance's assets to meet the loan obligation. At the auction, C&C Metal Products Corporation purchased some of Defiance's office equipment, including a computer. Shortly after the auction sale, Defiance temporarily ceased operation, leaving its general manager in charge of its premises. The computer purchased by C&C was on the premises, together with customer lists and customer files loaded in the memory of the computer and in backup disks.

When an employee of C&C arrived at Defiance's premises to pick up the computer, the C&C employee asked a Defiance computer operator

---

[4] Defiance Button Mach. Co. v. C&C Metal Prod. Corp., 759 F.2d 1053, 225 U.S.P.Q. (BNA) 797 (2d Cir. 1985). The material throughout the remainder of this section is derived from material included in the above-cited opinion.

how the computer functioned. Without authorization from Defiance, the computer operator demonstrated the use of the computer and, possibly at the request of a C&C employee, printed out Defiance's customer lists. The customer lists could be accessed either through disks kept in a locked room or through the memory of the computer sold to C&C with the use of a password readily available in source books to which C&C had access.

The court held that Defiance had lost its trade secret rights to the customer lists because Defiance had not taken adequate steps to ensure the secrecy of the lists by failing to deny C&C access to the source books and by failing to erase the lists from the computer that C&C purchased. Thus, even though C&C may have obtained the lists by improperly extracting information from the Defiance computer operator, Defiance had not adequately protected the lists from access by C&C. Defiance lost trade secret protection in its customer lists.

§ 3.6 Case 5: Loss of Trade Secret Rights as a Result of Failing to Adequately Identify Confidential Information

CASE 5: JOSTENS v. NATIONAL COMPUTER SYSTEMS

Jostens developed a computer system used for making class ring molds.

Computer system offered advantage over competitors.

No policy was implemented at Jostens to keep computer system secret.

Jostens's engineer, Mr. Titus, gave public presentations of the computer system.

Jostens never identified for its employees what parts of the computer system were considered to be confidential.

Mr. Titus was encouraged to continue work on such systems after departing from Jostens.

RESULT: Jostens lost any potential trade secret rights in the computer system by failing to adequately identify confidential information and failing to keep the system secret.

Jostens, Inc. lost any potential trade secret rights that it held in a computer system used in making ring molds for class rings as a result of its failure to identify and protect its confidential information.[5] In 1974, Jostens began successfully operating the computer system and enjoyed a competitive

---

[5] Jostens, Inc. v. National Computer Sys., Inc., 318 N.W.2d 691, 214 U.S.P.Q. (BNA) 918 (Minn. 1982). The material throughout the remainder of this section is derived from material included in the above-cited opinion.

advantage over its competitors as a result. Jostens's engineer, Mr. Titus, who was responsible for putting the system into operation, left Jostens in 1975 and began working at National Computer Systems, Inc. In 1978, National Computer Systems, Inc. designed and sold a similar computer system to a competitor of Jostens, and Jostens sued National Computer over the sale.

In determining whether a trade secret existed, the court looked in part to whether Jostens kept its computer system secret. When Jostens installed its system, no consideration was given or policy established to keep the system secret. The court noted that Jostens allowed customers into its facility and allowed Mr. Titus to give a public presentation regarding the system. Such activities did not constitute the affirmative steps required to maintain a trade secret.

The court then noted that Mr. Titus did not misappropriate the information concerning Jostens's computer system because Jostens did not take reasonable steps to identify which information it considered to be confidential. The court found that Jostens itself did not even know which parts of the system it intended to protect as confidential information and that it thus never relayed its intentions to its engineer, Mr. Titus. At best, the facts suggest that the company gave Mr. Titus mixed signals about the confidentiality of its system. First, Jostens allowed customers to view the system at work; later, it retracted this opportunity. Second, Mr. Titus asked, and was given permission by Jostens, to give the oral presentation concerning the computer system project. Third, in lieu of an "exit interview," Jostens' president told Mr. Titus that his continued work on such computer systems after his departure would be "fine with us."

If the subject matter of Jostens's computer system could have been a trade secret, Jostens failed to make it so by failing to communicate what it considered to be secret and by failing to maintain its secrecy.

§ 3.7 Case 6: Loss of Trade Secret Rights as a Result of Failing to Take Affirmative Steps to Maintain Secrecy

CASE 6: MOTOROLA v. FAIRCHILD

Motorola developed a production line for plastic- or aluminum-encapsulated semiconductors.

Motorola conducted regular public tours of production line and answered any questions concerning the technology.

Motorola posted no signs and gave no verbal warnings that the production line was confidential and proprietary.

Motorola allowed a trade magazine to photograph the production line for one of its issues.

Motorola never identified for present or departing employees what it considered to be proprietary information.

Motorola disclosed trade secrets in foreign patent applications.

RESULT: Motorola lost trade secret rights in the production line by failing to take affirmative steps to maintain its secrecy.

Motorola lost potential trade secret rights in its production line for plastic- or aluminum-encapsulated semiconductors as a result of its failure to take affirmative steps to maintain the technology as a secret.[6] As a result, Fairchild Camera and Instrument Corporation was free to use what Motorola considered to be its trade secret information. The dispute between Motorola and Fairchild arose when seven Motorola employees (including Motorola's general manager for its semiconductor division) transferred to Fairchild. After this transfer, Fairchild implemented its own semiconductor production line.

Motorola sued Fairchild, claiming that the employees took and disclosed trade secrets associated with Motorola's production line. The court disagreed. Motorola apparently did not take sufficient steps to keep the information secret. For instance, Motorola never advised the seven employees during their employment what technology it considered confidential. Upon their termination, Motorola conducted an exit interview to point out the employees' general obligations of not disclosing trade secrets, but did not present the employees with a list, either orally or in writing, of what it considered to be proprietary trade secrets.

Motorola also failed to take sufficient steps to maintain the secrecy of its production line because it gave the public the opportunity to view the line technology. Motorola regularly conducted tours of its facility for customers and, at times, employees of competitors. On at least one tour, an employee of the ultimate builder of Fairchild's production line toured Motorola's facility. No signs were posted warning of trade secrets. No verbal warnings were given. Persons taking the tour could observe and time the processes. They could present questions to the Motorola system operators and receive honest answers. Little was left unknown following such a tour.

During one such tour, Motorola permitted a magazine's employees to photograph the production line. The photos were then published in a picture article describing the general nature of the production line.

---

[6] Motorola, Inc. v. Fairchild Camera & Instrument Corp., 366 F. Supp. 1173, 177 U.S.P.Q. (BNA) 614 (D. Ariz. 1973). The material throughout the remainder of this section is derived from material included in the above-cited opinion.

§ 3.8 PATENT INFRINGEMENT

In addition, Motorola produced and distributed movies that described some of its alleged trade secrets. Most convincing for the court, however, was Motorola's disclosure of its trade secrets in its own patents. Apparently, four of Motorola's foreign patents disclosed most of the trade secrets that it later claimed to be protectable. The court concluded that Motorola had not taken reasonable steps to protect its trade secrets from disclosure and may not even have known at the time what it was intending to claim as proprietary information. Fairchild was therefore not liable to Motorola for use of the production line.

§ 3.8 Case 7: Monetary Loss for Patent Infringement

CASE 7: HONEYWELL v. MINOLTA

Honeywell developed and patented auto-focus technology.

Minolta reviewed Honeywell patents, but did not take a license.

Minolta produced auto-focusing cameras in violation of Honeywell's patent rights.

RESULT: Minolta ordered to pay $96 million in damages to Honeywell.

Protecting and exploiting its own intellectual property rights is not the only intellectual property concern a company faces. Liability for inadequately considering the intellectual property rights of others is also of great concern. In February 1992, a jury awarded Honeywell, Inc., an award of $96 million as damages for Minolta's infringement of Honeywell's patents to automatic focus systems.[7]

In the mid-1970s, Honeywell opted not to enter the automatic focus camera market, but it did retain its patents on auto-focus technology. It also allowed Minolta and 13 other companies to review the auto-focus technology, although it never licensed the patents. Instead, Honeywell waited. Then, in the mid-1980s, sales of single-lens reflex cameras grew and Minolta capitalized on the demand by selling auto-focus cameras. In 1987, Honeywell sued Minolta for infringement of its auto-focus patents and won a $96 million judgment.

---

[7] *From the Mind of Minolta—Oops, Make That Honeywell*, Bus. Wk., Feb. 24, 1992, at 34. The material throughout the remainder of this section is derived from material included in the above-cited article.

The $96 million award from Minolta is apparently only the beginning. Honeywell might now take legal action against 15 other camera manufacturers and may collect a total of $300 million in past royalties. Thus, Honeywell's diligence in monitoring the commercial markets and its own patent portfolio, even in markets in which it was not competing, paid off for Honeywell in patent infringement damages.

For Minolta, its inadequate consideration of Honeywell's patent rights resulted in an enormous monetary fine.

§ 3.9 Case 8: Monetary Loss for Patent Infringement

CASE 8: POLAROID v. KODAK

Pre-1972: Polaroid developed and patented instant photography technology.

1972: Polaroid began selling instant cameras.

1976: Kodak entered instant photography market.

1976: Polaroid sued Kodak.

1985: Polaroid wins liability portion of suit. Kodak found to have infringed 20 claims of seven valid patents.

1986: Kodak enjoined from further infringement of five patents that had not yet expired.

1987: Kodak left the instant photography market. Kodak lost $600 million during its tenure in market.

1990: Damages portion of the suit is completed.

RESULT: Polaroid awarded $873 million for damages and royalties.

Eastman Kodak Company was ordered to pay a staggering $873 million in patent infringement damages to Polaroid Corporation for use of instant photography technology covered by Polaroid's patents.[8] In 1972, Polaroid introduced its first instant photography camera, the SX-70. In 1976, Kodak responded by selling the EK-4 and EK-6 instant photography cameras. In the late 1970s, sales of instant cameras grew rapidly, and Kodak and Polaroid fought for market share by lowering prices. As a result, Kodak's instant photography business had lost $600 million by the time it was

---

[8] Polaroid Corp. v. Eastman Kodak Co., 16 U.S.P.Q.2d (BNA) 1481 (D. Mass. 1990). The material throughout the remainder of this section is derived from material included in the above-cited opinion. *See* Polaroid Corp. v. Eastman Kodak Co., 17 U.S.P.Q. 2d 1711 (D. Mass. 1991) (modifying award from $909 million to $873 million due to clerical errors in initial calculation).

forced to leave the instant market camera market in 1987. Polaroid lost $82 million from 1976 to 1985.

Polaroid argued that Kodak had infringed its instant photography patents and that, if Kodak had not done so, it would have enjoyed growth and profitability. Polaroid further argued that the profits it lost on infringing sales that Kodak made should be recoverable from Kodak.

The court found that without Kodak in the market, Polaroid would have made a portion of Kodak's camera and film sales and that Polaroid would have profited from those sales. The court awarded Polaroid its lost profits on the Kodak sales that Polaroid would have made and, for the portion of sales that Polaroid would not have made, the court awarded Polaroid a royalty of 10 percent on each unit sold by Kodak. After computing interest on the award from the time of infringement to the entry of the judgment, Polaroid's total award was more than $873 million.

§ 3.10 Case 9: Monetary Loss for Willful Patent Infringement

CASE 9: GREAT NORTHERN v. DAVIS CORE & PAD

Great Northern developed and patented shipping pallets.

Supplier told Davis Core & Pad that Great Northern has patent on shipping pallet, but thought the patent may be invalid. Davis Core & Pad was therefore aware of Great Northern's patent.

Davis Core & Pad did not verify supplier's information.

Davis Core & Pad began manufacturing infringing pallets.

Davis Core & Pad did not seek any infringement or validity opinion from patent attorney.

Great Northern sued Davis Core & Pad and asserted willful infringement.

RESULT: Davis Core & Pad ordered to pay three times Great Northern's actual damages plus attorneys' fees for willfully disregarding Great Northern's patent rights.

In the two cases in §§ 3.8 and 3.9, neither Minolta nor Kodak was found to have willfully infringed patents. When a court finds that an infringer acted with willful disregard of the patent holder's rights, damages can be tripled, and the infringer may be forced to pay the patent holders attorneys' fees. Davis Core & Pad Co. was held to have willfully infringed a patent on shipping pallets held by Great Northern Corporation. As a result, Davis

Core faced an assessment of damages for infringing and a tripling of that amount as damages for infringing willfully.[9]

The trial and appellate court agreed that Davis Core knew of Great Northern's patents before it began manufacturing its infringing pallets. Before Davis Core's manufacturing, an employee of Davis Core heard from a supplier that a patent existed, but the supplier claimed that it was invalid. Davis Core did not verify the information, nor did it seek any infringement and validity opinions of a patent attorney. Instead, Davis Core began manufacturing infringing pallets.

The court held that Davis Core had a duty to obtain validity and infringement opinions from its patent attorney. By failing to do so, its conduct could be considered willful infringement of Great Northern's patent, and thus Great Northern's damages could be tripled. Then, as an additional award for Davis's failure to secure the validity and infringement opinion, Davis Core was ordered to pay Great Northern's attorneys' fees.

§ 3.11 Case 10: Monetary Loss for Trademark Infringement

CASE 10: SANDS, TAYLOR & WOOD v. QUAKER OATS

STW federally registered mark THIRST AID for beverages.

Quaker Oats released advertising slogan "GATORADE is THIRST AID, for that deep down body thirst."

Quaker Oats legal review of commercial campaign did not include trademark issues.

Quaker Oats did not review others trademarks until after campaign began.

STW sued Quaker Oats for trademark infringement.

Court found use of THIRST AID trademark accounted for 10 percent of Quaker Oats's profit on GATORADE sales during campaign.

Court found Quaker Oats's lack of regard for others' trademark rights may suggest bad faith.

RESULT: Quaker Oats ordered to pay STW $24,730,000 in damages plus attorneys' fees.

---

[9] Great N. Corp. v. Davis Core & Pad Co., 782 F.2d 159, 228 U.S.P.Q. (BNA) 356 (Fed. Cir. 1986). The material throughout the remainder of this section is derived from material included in the above-cited opinion.

§ 3.11 TRADEMARK INFRINGEMENT

The Quaker Oats Company was ordered to pay damages of more than $24 million to Sands, Taylor and Wood (STW) as a result of its infringement of STW's trademark, THIRST AID.[10] The Quaker Oats Company manufactures the beverage GATORADE and had used the advertising slogan, "Gatorade is thirst aid, for that deep down body thirst." STW is the owner of the registered trademark THIRST-AID for (1) nonalcoholic maltless beverages, (2) sundae toppings, and (3) soda fountain syrups. STW sued Quaker Oats over its use of the "thirst aid" slogan to advertise its GATORADE product.

The court concluded that Quaker Oats's mark and STW's mark were confusingly similar, in sight, sound, and meaning. In the GATORADE campaign, the words *THIRST AID* were printed in large bold letters that could not be ignored. Further, the court noted that both parties used THIRST AID on drinks for retail sale. Surveys showed that a substantial percentage of consumers associated GATORADE with THIRST AID, again suggesting consumers could confuse Quaker Oats's use of THIRST AID with the trademark owner's use of that mark.

The court concluded that Quaker Oats's use of THIRST AID infringed STW's mark, and that it accounted for 10 percent of Quaker Oats's profit on its GATORADE product. The award to STW was $24,730,000.

The court then looked at Quaker Oats's willfulness in infringing. The court noted that Quaker Oats's legal department reviewed the THIRST AID campaign around the time its commercials were being produced. The review did *not* include a discussion of trademark issues, nor did Quaker Oats at that time request a trademark search. A trademark search was requested several months later, one week before the commercials were to be aired. After the commercial had aired, Quaker Oats's in-house trademark attorney received the results from the trademark search and learned of STW's trademark rights. The court concluded that Quaker Oats had a duty to ensure through a proper and timely trademark search that its campaign would not infringe the trademark rights of another. Instead, Quaker Oats never seriously considered its trademark liability for use of the THIRST AID slogan until faced with the prospect of a lawsuit. The conduct suggested that Quaker Oats acted in bad faith. STW was thus held to be entitled to receive its attorneys' fees from Quaker Oats in addition to the $24,730,000 damage award.

On appeal, the enormous award of over $24 million was reversed and remanded to the district court for a new damage calculation, although one

---

[10] Sands, Taylor & Wood v. Quaker Oats Co., 18 U.S.P.Q.2d (BNA) 1457 (N.D. Ill. 1990). The amount of the award was later reversed and remanded for modification. Sands, Taylor & Wood v. Quaker Oats Co., 24 U.S.P.Q.2d (BNA) 1001 (7th Cir. 1992). The material throughout the remainder of this section is derived from material included in the above-cited opinion.

of the three judges believed the award to be justified. The appellate court did, however, affirm the finding that Quaker Oats acted in bad faith and thus permitted STW to collect attorneys' fees.[11] This case therefore continues to serve as an example of what problems can be encountered by a company that does not appropriately consider the intellectual property rights of others.

---

[11] 24 U.S.P.Q.2d (BNA) at 1001.

CHAPTER 4

VALUE AND BENEFITS OF INTELLECTUAL PROPERTY

§ 4.1   Introduction
§ 4.2   Exclusive Rights
§ 4.3   Remedies for Infringement of Intellectual Property
§ 4.4   —Patent Remedies
§ 4.5   —Copyright Remedies
§ 4.6   —Trademark Remedies
§ 4.7   —Trade Secret Remedies
§ 4.8   Ability to Assign Rights
§ 4.9   Ability to License Rights
§ 4.10 —Royalty Revenue
§ 4.11 —Technology Exchanges
§ 4.12 —Grantbacks
§ 4.13 —Second Sources
§ 4.14 —Exploiting in Closed Markets
§ 4.15 —Prevent or Settle Lawsuit
§ 4.16 —Testing of Technology
§ 4.17 —Establishing Industry Standard
§ 4.18 Recoupment of Research and Development Expenditures
§ 4.19 Control Market Share
§ 4.20 Enter New Markets
§ 4.21 Secure Interest in Foreign Market
§ 4.22 Extend Product Life Cycle
§ 4.23 Valuable Intangibles
§ 4.24 Asset Value
§ 4.25 Increasing Strength of Patents
§ 4.26 —Creation of Federal Circuit
§ 4.27 —International Trade Commission

§ 4.1 Introduction

Chapter 3 examined real-life examples of misfortunes caused by incorrect or inadequate considerations of intellectual property issues in business decision-making. Turning now to the positive side, this chapter explores the value companies can derive from a strong intellectual property portfolio.

§ 4.2 Exclusive Rights

Intellectual property ownership generally offers certain rights to exploit the intellectual property. Often, these rights are exclusive to the owners, permitting them to exclude all others from exploiting the protected technology. A patent owner has the right to exclude others from making, using, or selling its patented products or using its patented process in the United States for 17 years. A patent excludes production of both identical and functionally equivalent products.

A corporate copyright owner has the exclusive rights to reproduce and distribute copies of a copyrighted work for 75 years. A federal trademark owner has the generally exclusive right to use its mark on the goods for which it is registered in the United States for an indefinite period of time, so long as the mark is used in interstate commerce and does not become generic.

A trade secret owner has the right to benefit from secret proprietary information until this information is inadvertently disclosed to the public or independently discovered by another company. However, unlike patent, copyright, and trademark rights, which are exclusive to the owner, trade secret rights might not be exclusive. Rather, two or more companies can have the same trade secret rights.

Intellectual property rights can be very valuable to a company. Consider, for example, the value of the following intellectual property: Polaroid's patents on instant photography cameras and film and Xerox's patents on photocopying devices; Microsoft's copyrights on MS-DOS and Lotus's copyrights on the 1-2-3 spreadsheet; the CADILLAC trademark and McDonald's Golden Arches logo; and Coca-Cola's formula trade secret.

§ 4.3 Remedies for Infringement of Intellectual Property

An intellectual property owner may enforce its exclusive rights in court. The federal patent, copyright, and trademark statutes provide remedies

§ 4.4 —Patent Remedies

A patent owner has numerous remedies available for recourse against an infringer. The patent owner may seek an injunction to stop the infringing activity[1] and/or may recover damages adequate to compensate for injury caused by the infringement.[2] At the very least, the patent owner will recover a reasonable royalty from the infringer.[3]

In general, a patent owner may attempt to prove damages based upon his lost profits. This is the amount of profits that the patent owner would have made had it not been for the infringing activity.[4] Lost profits are computed by multiplying the number of units sold by the infringer times the patent owner's profit margin on its units. This computation is shown in **Table 4–1.**

To help evaluate the profit margin element of lost profits, the courts may also take into consideration whether there was any price erosion or any lost sales of accompanying products by virtue of the infringement. The first element, *price erosion,* is the amount of revenue that the patent owner loses as a result of having to lower his prices to compete with the infringer's product. The second element, lost sales of accompanying products, is the amount of profits that the patent owner would have made on nonpatented goods that would normally accompany a sale of the patented item. **Table 4–2** summarizes these elements.

If a court determines that the patent infringer's conduct was willful, it may increase the damage award up to three times the amount found.[5] In exceptional cases, the court may also award reasonable attorneys' fees.[6]

In situations in which it cannot prove lost profits, a patent owner is at least entitled to a reasonable royalty from the infringer. This reasonable royalty is a theoretical amount that would result from hypothetical negotiations between a willing licensor and a willing licensee.[7] The factors

---

[1] 35 U.S.C. § 283 (1952).

[2] 35 U.S.C. § 284 (1952).

[3] 35 U.S.C. § 284 (1952).

[4] King Instrument Corp. v. Otari Corp., 767 F.2d 853, 226 U.S.P.Q. (BNA) 402 (Fed. Cir. 1985).

[5] 35 U.S.C. § 284 (1952).

[6] 35 U.S.C. § 285 (1952).

[7] Panduit Corp. v. Stahlin Bros. Fibre Works, Inc., 575 F.2d 1152, 197 U.S.P.Q. (BNA) 726 (6th Cir. 1978).

Table 4-1

Lost Profits Formula

$$\text{Lost profits} = \text{Patent owner's profit margin} \times \text{Number of units sold by the infringer}$$

Table 4-2

Factors to Consider in Determining Lost Profit

$$\text{Price erosion} = \left(\begin{array}{c} \text{Price absent} \\ \text{infringer's} \\ \text{product} \end{array} - \begin{array}{c} \text{Lower price} \\ \text{to compete} \\ \text{w/ infringer} \end{array} \right) \times \begin{array}{c} \text{Number of} \\ \text{units sold} \\ \text{by patent owner} \end{array}$$

$$\begin{array}{c} \text{Lost sales of} \\ \text{accompanying} \\ \text{products} \end{array} = \begin{array}{c} \text{Patent owner's profit} \\ \text{margin on related} \\ \text{products} \end{array} \times \begin{array}{c} \text{Number of} \\ \text{units sold by the} \\ \text{infringer} \end{array}$$

a court can use in determining a reasonable royalty are listed in **Table 4-3**.[8]

One significant advantage a patent owner has in infringement litigation is that the patent is presumed valid by the courts.[9] Under this presumption, an accused infringer has the burden of proving to the court by clear and convincing evidence that the patent is not valid. This "clear and convincing evidence" burden is a higher standard than the common legal burden of "preponderance of the evidence" used in many civil lawsuits.

§ 4.5 —Copyright Remedies

A copyright owner also has an assortment of remedies in copyright infringement cases. First, a copyright owner can obtain an injunction to stop the infringing activity.[10] Second, a copyright owner can seek actual damages caused by the infringement and the profits of the infringer.[11] Third, a copyright owner of a federally registered work can recover statutory damages (presently, $500 to $20,000 per infringement) *regardless* of

---

[8] Georgia-Pacific Corp. v. U.S. Plywood-Champion Papers, Inc., 318 F. Supp. 1116, 166 U.S.P.Q. (BNA) 235 (S.D.N.Y. 1970).

[9] 35 U.S.C. § 282 (1984).

[10] 17 U.S.C. § 502(a) (1976).

[11] 17 U.S.C. § 504 (1988).

§ 4.5 COPYRIGHT REMEDIES

Table 4-3

Reasonable Royalty Guidelines

Royalties received by the licensor from other licensees.

Royalty paid by a licensee for other similar intellectual property.

Nature and scope of the license with respect to whether the license is exclusive or nonexclusive, or whether sale or territory restrictions are imposed.

Licensor's established policy and marketing program to maintain its exclusive rights by refusing to license its intellectual property.

Commercial relationship between licensor and licensee.

Effect the intellectual property has on the sale of the licensee's other related, but nonprotected products.

Duration of the license.

Established profitability, success, and current popularity of products made under the intellectual property.

Utility and advantages of the intellectual property over old products.

Nature and benefits of the product protected by the intellectual property.

Extent to which others have infringed the intellectual property.

Customary royalties in the particular industry.

Portion of profit credited to the intellectual property as distinguished from nonprotected elements of the product.

Opinion of experts.

---

whether the copyright owner was actually damaged or can prove the damage caused by the infringement. This statutory award can be increased upon a finding of willful copyright infringement (presently, up to $100,000). However, these statutory damages are not available for copyrights that are not federally registered.

A fourth remedy available to a copyright owner is that he can obtain a court order to have all infringing copies, including the machinery used to produce the infringing copies, impounded and destroyed.[12] Fifth, a copyright owner may receive full costs and reasonable attorneys' fees for litigating the infringement action.[13] Sixth, though rather rare, the act of copyright infringement may be deemed a criminal offense if the infringement was found to be blatantly willful,[14] resulting in fines and imprisonment for the willful infringer.

---

[12] 17 U.S.C. § 503 (1976).
[13] 17 U.S.C. § 505 (1976).
[14] 17 U.S.C. § 506 (1990).

§ 4.6 —Trademark Remedies

In trademark infringement cases, a trademark owner may seek several remedies. The trademark owner may obtain an injunction to prevent further violation of his trademark rights.[15] The trademark owner may also recover any damages that he sustained, the infringer's profits, and costs of the infringement action.[16] The court may increase the amount of profits or damages, whichever is greater, up to three times for willful infringement.[17] In exceptional cases, the trademark owner may receive reasonable attorneys' fees.[18] Finally, a trademark owner may obtain a court order to have all labels, signs, prints, packages, wrappers, receptacles, and advertisements bearing the infringing mark, including the machinery used to produce such a mark, delivered up and destroyed.[19]

§ 4.7 —Trade Secret Remedies

When a trade secret is stolen or "misappropriated" by another company, the trade secret owner has two general types of remedies. First, the trade secret owner may obtain injunctive relief against any actual or threatened misappropriation.[20] An injunction is awarded for "threatened" misappropriation in an attempt to prevent the irrevocable loss of the trade secrets that may occur when the other company does, in fact, misappropriate the trade secret. After a trade secret is misappropriated, the trade secret owner may still obtain an injunction to stop the other company from using the trade secret for a "head-start" period of time. The *head-start period* is typically estimated as the period of time necessary for the other company to discover the trade secret lawfully through either independent discovery or reverse engineering.[21]

The second remedy available to the trade secret owner is the recovery of damages caused by the actual loss of the misappropriated trade secret.[22] A damage award may also include an amount that the misappropriating company was unjustly enriched by stealing the trade secret. The court may double the damages if the misappropriation was willful or malicious.[23] In

---

[15] 15 U.S.C. § 1116 (1988); Lanham Act § 34.
[16] 15 U.S.C. § 1117 (1988); Lanham Act § 35.
[17] 15 U.S.C. 1117(b) (1988); Lanham Act § 35(b).
[18] 15 U.S.C. § 1117(a) (1988); Lanham Act § 35(a).
[19] 15 U.S.C. § 1118 (1988); Lanham Act § 36.
[20] Unif. Trade Secrets Act § 2.
[21] K-2 Ski Co. v. Head Ski Co., 506 F.2d 471, 182 U.S.P.Q. (BNA) 724 (9th Cir. 1974).
[22] Unif. Trade Secrets Act § 3.
[23] Unif. Trade Secrets Act § 3(b).

addition, the trade secret owner may recover reasonable attorneys' fees for bringing the suit.[24]

§ 4.8 Ability to Assign Rights

The intellectual property owner may assign his rights to others. An *assignment* is the transfer of rights in the intellectual property from the *assignor* to the *assignee*. **Figure 4–1** illustrates the process.

In an assignment, the assignor may transfer all rights, or an undivided interest in the property, or all rights within a particular geographical territory.[25] The intellectual property owner may wish to assign the rights for numerous reasons. For example, he may lack the capacity or financing to exploit the intellectual property, or may have no economic interest in exploiting the intellectual property.

§ 4.9 Ability to License Rights

An intellectual property owner may license the intellectual property rights. A *license* is the transfer of rights from a *licensor* to a *licensee*. A license may be thought of as granting permission to the licensee to use the intellectual property without any fear of being sued for infringement. In contrast to an assignment, in which all intellectual property rights are conveyed, a license does not necessarily convey all rights to the other party. Rather, a license is a special contract that transfers some or all rights in the intellectual property, subject to specific limitations. For instance, in a patent license, the licensor may convey the right to make, use, and sell the patented invention or may convey only the right to use the patented invention. In either case, the patent licensor may condition the license upon payment of royalties for the right to use the invention. **Figure 4–2** illustrates the licensing relationship.

There are two categories of licenses: exclusive and nonexclusive. An exclusive license conveys the intellectual property rights to only one licensee, whereas several nonexclusive licenses can convey rights to several licensees.

There are many reasons why a company would want to license its intellectual property. Several of these reasons are discussed in **§§ 4.10** through **4.17**.

---

[24] Unif. Trade Secrets Act § 4.
[25] Waterman v. McKenzie, 138 U.S. 252 (1891).

```
                    All Rights
  ┌──────────┐  - - - - - - - →  ┌──────────┐
  │ ASSIGNOR │                    │ ASSIGNEE │
  └──────────┘  ← - - - - - - -   └──────────┘
                   Consideration
```

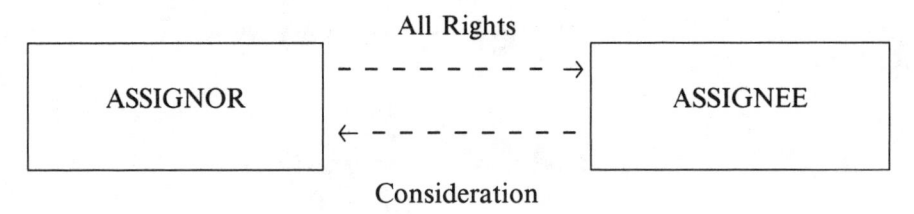

Figure 4-1. Assignment of intellectual property rights.

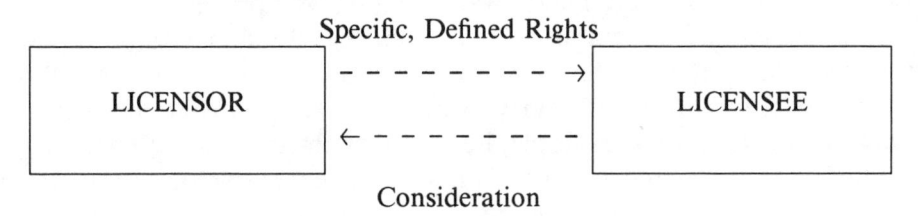

```
                Specific, Defined Rights
  ┌──────────┐  - - - - - - - →  ┌──────────┐
  │ LICENSOR │                    │ LICENSEE │
  └──────────┘  ← - - - - - - -   └──────────┘
                   Consideration
```

Figure 4-2. Licensing of intellectual property rights.

§ 4.10 —Royalty Revenue

One reason to license intellectual property is to generate revenue by way of royalty payments. A *royalty* is the fee paid by the licensee for use of the licensor's intellectual property under the license. Royalties may be (1) paid in one lump sum or in periodic installments; (2) computed as a percentage of the sale price or as a straight fee for each patented product sold; (3) computed at a flat rate or at a graduated rate that varies according to the volume sold; or (4) any other contractual arrangement between the licensee and the licensor.

Royalty revenue is relatively cost free to the licensor, requiring only the expense of negotiating and drafting the license, and the expense of policing the license. Moreover, royalty revenue may provide a significant amount of income. One company that presently receives substantial income from its patent royalties is Texas Instruments (TI). TI has adopted a very aggressive licensing posture in an attempt to earn significant revenue from its intellectual property portfolio. Since TI began this posture in 1986 to the end of 1991, it generated more than $900 million in royalties, which exceeded its net income during this same period.[26]

As a guideline to setting a royalty in licensing agreements, attorneys use the reasonable royalty guidelines set forth in **Table 4-3** of **§ 4.4.**

---

[26] Wall St. J., Jan. 15, 1992.

§ 4.11 —Technology Exchanges

A company may license its intellectual property in exchange for receiving a license to use another company's intellectual property. This reciprocal licensing, known as *cross-licensing,* enables companies to exchange technological expertise in the hope of strengthening their respective market positions. Cross-licensing is illustrated in **Figure 4-3**.

To illustrate the advantage of cross-licensing, suppose Bike-Frames, Inc., and G&B Systems Co. were among several competitors in the 10-speed bicycle market. Bike-Frames had several patents on kevlar-reinforced frames and the methods for manufacturing these frames. G&B Systems had several patents on state-of-the-art gear and brake systems for 10-speed bicycles. Without a cross-licensing arrangement, G&B Systems could only sell 10-speed bicycles with second-rate frames because Bike-Frames could exclude its competitors, including G&B Systems, from making and selling its patented kevlar-reinforced frames. Likewise, because of G&B Systems's patents on gears and brakes, Bike-Frames could only sell bicycles with second-rate gear and brake systems.

If, on the other hand, Bike-Frames and G&B Systems were to cross-license their respective patents, both companies could manufacture and sell 10-speed bicycles with first-rate frames and gear-and-brake systems. As a result, both companies would have a stronger position in the 10-speed bicycle market.

As shown in this example, both companies can strengthen their market positions and enjoy the benefits of state-of-the-art technology without expending large amounts of capital. Bike-Frames did not spend money developing a first-rate gear-and-brake system and G&B Systems did not spend money developing a better bike frame. Yet, the cross-license enabled each company to incorporate the other's superior technology into its own bicycles. Accordingly, each company's patent portfolio was the catalyst for this very significant business opportunity. Had either company not had a strong patent portfolio in its technology, the cross-license would not have occurred.

§ 4.12 —Grantbacks

On some occasions, a company may license today's intellectual property to acquire an interest in future technology to be developed by the licensee. Such a license has a provision requiring the licensee to grant a license back to the company (the licensor) on any improved technology developed from the originally licensed technology. This type of licensing provision is known as a *grantback* and is illustrated in **Figure 4-4**.

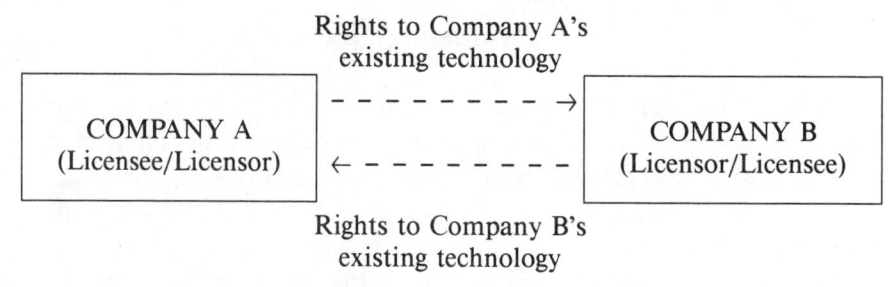

```
                    Rights to Company A's
                     existing technology
  ┌─────────────────┐ - - - - - - - →  ┌─────────────────┐
  │    COMPANY A    │                  │    COMPANY B    │
  │(Licensee/Licensor)│ ← - - - - - - - │(Licensor/Licensee)│
  └─────────────────┘                  └─────────────────┘
                    Rights to Company B's
                     existing technology
```

Figure 4-3. Technology exchanges.

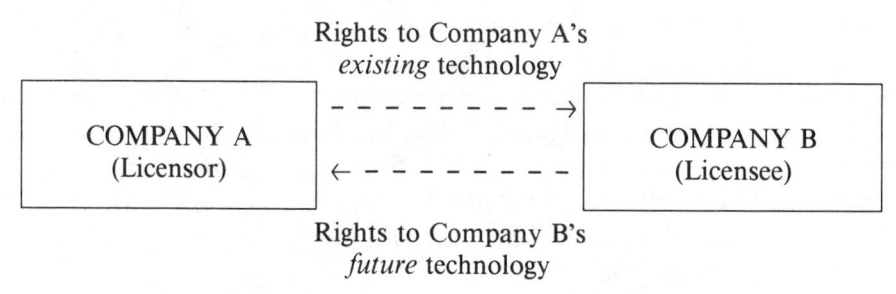

```
                    Rights to Company A's
                     *existing* technology
  ┌─────────────────┐ - - - - - - - →  ┌─────────────────┐
  │    COMPANY A    │                  │    COMPANY B    │
  │   (Licensor)    │ ← - - - - - - -  │   (Licensee)    │
  └─────────────────┘                  └─────────────────┘
                    Rights to Company B's
                      *future* technology
```

Figure 4-4. Grantbacks.

In the bicycle scenario in § **4.11,** an example of a grantback provision would be to require G&B Systems to grant some future license to Bike-Frames on any technology developed by G&B Systems in the kevlar-reinforced bicycle frame field that was derived from the frame technology originally conveyed by Bike-Frames.

A grantback provision helps the licensor stay current with the state-of-the-art innovations in a particular technology the licensor helped pioneer. Additionally, a grantback arrangement prevents the licensee from developing and patenting the next generation technology and then excluding the licensor from this improved technology. A third advantage of a grantback provision is that the licensor benefits from the research and development efforts of all licensees. As a result, many companies are working to develop a common technology in which the licensor owns the fundamental rights.

A grantback of future technology, however, should only occur through a nonexclusive license. For instance, Bike-Frames should not require G&B Systems to grantback all future technology exclusively to Bike-Frames and no other 10-speed bicycle company. Exclusive grantbacks have a taint of antitrust wrongdoing and may be found to be illegal. Courts often infer that a company is using its patents to maintain a monopoly position by forcing licensees to grantback exclusive licenses only to that company. Thus, nonexclusive grantback licenses are preferred.

§ 4.13 —Second Sources

Another common reason why a company might grant a license is to provide a customer with a second source for the patented products in the event that the company cannot supply the products. The government, for example, routinely requires that the contracting company (licensor) have arrangements with a second supplier (licensee) to fulfill any obligations or satisfy any excess demand that cannot be met by the contracting company.

§ 4.14 —Exploiting in Closed Markets

A company may license its intellectual property to gain entry into domestic or foreign markets that would otherwise be unavailable to that company. Smaller companies, for example, may not be able to exploit their intellectual property in certain regional domestic markets because they lack the capacity and resources to do so. To reach these markets, the smaller companies may wish to license their technology to companies located in those regions. For instance, a small Massachusetts company that is unable to supply its patented goods to potential markets on the West Coast may desire to license its patents to a California manufacturer in return for a royalty. This arrangement allows the Massachusetts company to gain additional return on its patents that it otherwise would not have made absent the license.

Licensing also helps a company penetrate foreign markets protected by tariffs and other such barriers. An example of a licensing strategy being used to enter foreign markets occurred in the semiconductor industry in the 1960s and 1970s when penetration into the Japanese market was very difficult. The Japanese government tightly controlled access to the Japanese market. It forbid United States and other foreign companies from controlling wholly or majority-owned subsidiaries within Japan and limited imports to the Japanese markets with tariffs and quotas. As a result, United States companies began licensing their semiconductor technology to Japanese companies to generate some revenue from the Japanese market. At one point, Japanese companies were paying at least 10 percent of their semiconductor sales revenues as royalties to United States companies.[27]

---

[27] M. Borrus, Competing for Control: America's Stake in Microelectronics 120 (1988).

§ 4.15 —Prevent or Settle Lawsuit

A company may license its intellectual property to prevent or settle a lawsuit. When an infringing company is discovered, the intellectual property owner typically makes an initial inquiry as to whether the infringer is interested in taking a license.[28] When it appears that neither company can benefit from the litigation or when the outcome of the litigation is too unpredictable, litigation may be avoided by the allegedly infringing company's taking a license. If the allegedly infringing company refuses to take a license, the intellectual property owner may then enforce its rights through an infringement action.

Licensing agreements may also be made after litigation has begun. In every lawsuit, certain events, such as the exchanging of documents and the taking of depositions, provide insight into the probable result of the litigation. Upon reaching these events, companies may elect to settle the lawsuit to avoid any further costs and to minimize their losses. Licensing issues are almost always a part of the settlement negotiations.

§ 4.16 —Testing of Technology

A company may license its technological intellectual property to foreign companies to allow these foreign companies to test market the new technology in foreign markets before sale in the United States. Such practice, for example, is prevalent in the drug industry. Food and Drug Administration (FDA) approval of new drugs often requires a tremendous amount of time. Drug companies therefore license companies in foreign countries with a more relaxed regulatory environment to make and sell the new drugs before introducing them in the United States. Once FDA approval is obtained, the new drug can be marketed in the United States and the companies have the benefit of the earlier market experience gained in foreign countries.

§ 4.17 —Establishing Industry Standard

A company that pioneers a new technology may wish to license its intellectual property rights in this new technology in an attempt to establish it as the industry standard. The value of the pioneering technology, although important, should not prevent a company from licensing it. As one author explains:

---

[28] Of course, some companies make it their policy not to license their intellectual property.

If the invention represents a technological breakthrough of major significance, the company, realizing that an attempt to exclude others from exploiting the innovation will definitely mean expensive litigation, the risk of invalidity, and major industry-wide efforts to design around the statutory protection covering the innovation, may decide to license on a nonexclusive basis thereby following in the footsteps of Bell, which licensed the transistor patent, and Westinghouse, which has offered to license its laser patent.[29]

A good example of a missed opportunity to establish the industry standard is the story of Sony and the videocassette recorder (VCR) industry. Sony pioneered VCR technology with the Beta type VCR. Sony obtained many patents on the Beta VCR, but refused to license these patents. As a result, other companies interested in the VCR industry were forced to develop a different technology. Thus, the VHS technology was developed and has since become the industry standard. By not licensing the Beta technology to other companies, Sony very likely missed a golden opportunity to set the VCR standard with Beta technology.

§ 4.18 Recoupment of Research and Development Expenditures

Intellectual property, and particularly patents, allows a company to recoup its research and development expenditures. A patent permits a company to exclude others from making, using, or selling a new invention for 17 years. During this exclusive duration, the company can attain above-average profits on the product because others cannot legally make the same or an equivalent product and sell it at a reduced price. Moreover, licensing the patent can provide additional revenue from royalties. Therefore, the above-average profits and/or royalty revenue available to a patent owner allows for recoupment of initial research and development expenditures.

§ 4.19 Control Market Share

Intellectual property may help a company control market share. For instance, patented products are usually unique in the market because patents prevent others from making and selling equivalent products. If a company owns a patent on a preferred technology, it has a significant advantage over competitors because its competitors are prevented from incorporating the patented technology into their product line. The competitors are therefore necessarily limited in the kinds of technology they can offer to the

---

[29] P. Sherber, Intellectual Property Management § 7.01.

market. If the marketplace favors the company's protected technology, that company has better control of its market position.

In addition, as a company continues to research and improve each patented technology, it can continue to obtain patents on improvements and next generation products. Thus, the company's improving product line may be continuously protected over a long period of time. This too gives a company better control over its market position.

A company may also "buffer" its market niche from competitors by obtaining patents on technology similar to the primary technology employed in its products. Even if the similar technology is not as efficient or effective as the primary technology, patenting the similar technology still prevents competitors from using it. The buffering technique is illustrated in **Figure 4–5.** Suppose a company's product is based upon technology Z and that this technology is protected by patent A. Patent A prevents competitors from making, using, or selling a product using technology Z. By obtaining patents B, C, D, and E on similar technology Y, the company can prevent competitors from making, using, or selling the similar technology Y. Thus, competitors are forced to manufacture products based upon technology X, which may be inferior to both technologies Y and Z. According to this buffering technique, the company's product is buffered from the competitors' products, thereby highlighting the company's product in the marketplace as superior to competitors' products.

Trademarks also help control and maintain market share. Loyal consumers will often purchase only a certain name brand they have come to prefer over time. For example, some cola drinkers prefer to drink only Coca-Cola®, while others prefer to drink only Pepsi®. Over time, these consumers associate a particular taste with the Coca-Cola or Pepsi trademark and the corresponding soda can design. Due to the exclusiveness of trademark rights, other cola companies are prevented from selling a cola in a red-and-white can marked *Coca-Cola* or a red, white, and blue can marked *Pepsi*. Accordingly, the Coca-Cola and Pepsi trademarks help maintain a strong market position.

§ 4.20 Enter New Markets

Intellectual property helps a company enter new markets. Intellectual property protects products in the new environment until the company has become more acclimated to the new market. Companies already in this market will have more experience in the new market and presumably lower production costs, established distribution networks, and better customer relations. As a result, these companies are most likely able to supply products at a lower price.

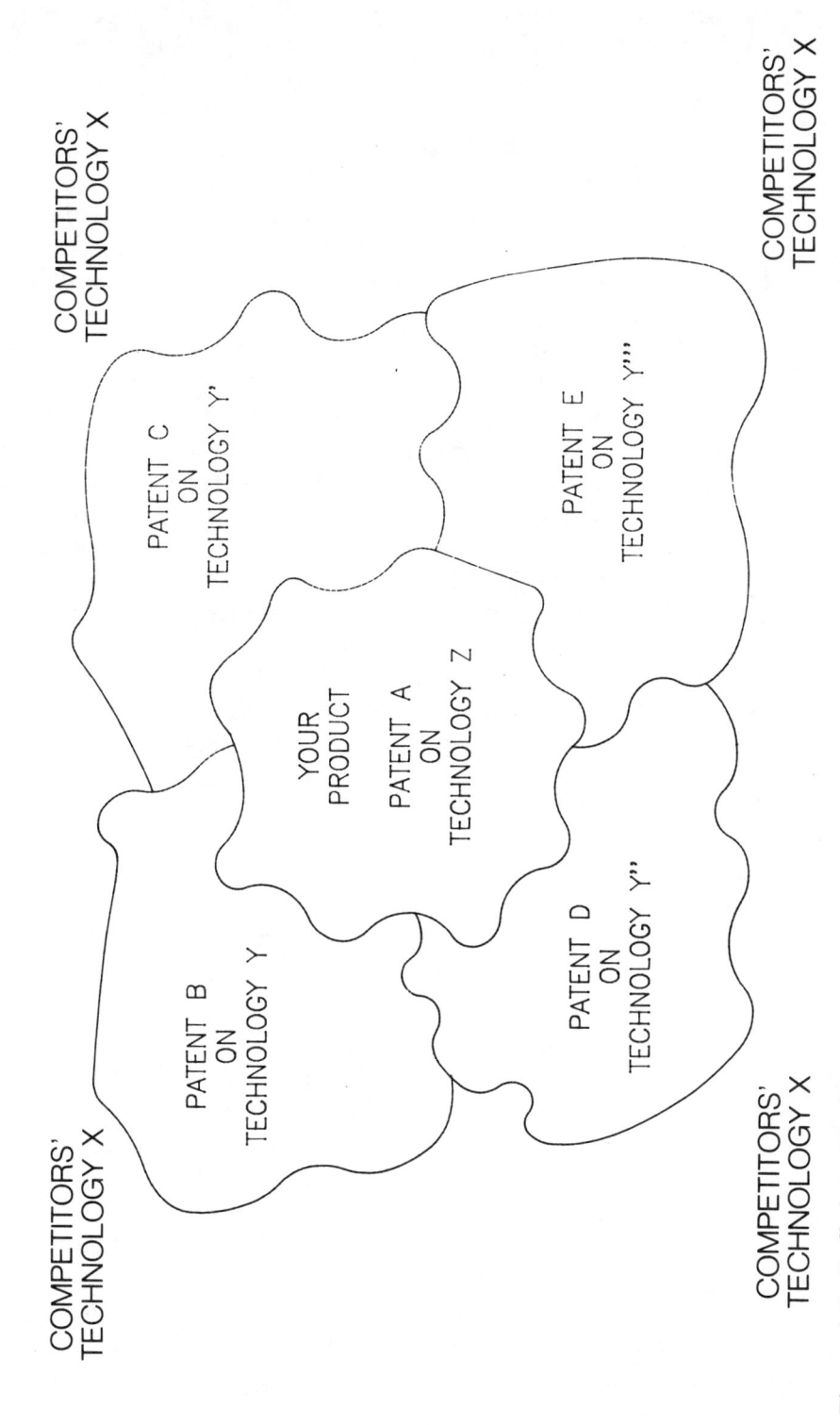

Figure 4-5. Buffering technique.

A company attempting to enter a new market would have to contend with these disadvantages. Protecting its new product provides a means for the new company to compete initially. Without protection, existing companies can copy the new company's unprotected product, if that product proves successful, and possibly produce it more efficiently and profitably due to their experience in the market.

Strong trademarks also help a company enter a new market, particularly those markets related to the company's primary market. When a company wishes to enter a new market, the company may simply use a familiar trademark with the new product. Because the company has already used the trademark with its primary product, consumers can easily associate the qualities perceived in the mark with the new product. Therefore, if the company has built up goodwill in a familiar trademark, a new product sold under it will more likely experience quicker success in the new market.

For example, Procter & Gamble initially introduced IVORY brand hand soap. Subsequently, Procter & Gamble has extended the IVORY trademark to cover such products as IVORY brand shampoo and conditioner, IVORY brand dish soap, IVORY SNOW detergent, and IVORY brand liquid hand soap. By using a familiar trademark, Procter & Gamble was able to convey the goodwill built up with the trademark IVORY in the hand soap market to the detergent, dish soap, and shampoo markets. Procter & Gamble might not have experienced success as quickly had it decided to employ new trademarks with each new product.

In a new market that is created by pioneering technology, intellectual property helps the pioneering company maintain a dominating market share.

§ 4.21 Secure Interest in Foreign Market

A company may use its intellectual property to secure an interest in a foreign-based company. Foreign companies, particularly in countries that are evolving technically, often look to United States companies for technological guidance. These companies are interested in obtaining licenses from United States companies. As noted in § 4.14, United States companies may license their technology to foreign companies in return for royalties. As an alternative, however, a company may wish to license its technology to a foreign company in exchange for an equity position in a joint subsidiary in the foreign country. In this manner, the United States company can secure a corporate interest in a foreign country, thereby providing better access to this foreign country's domestic market. It may then operate in the foreign country with less concern about import tariffs and quotas.

Texas Instruments employed this strategy very effectively to access the Japanese markets in the 1960s. In an attempt to protect its domestic semiconductor market, Japan prohibited foreign companies from owning subsidiaries in Japan. Texas Instruments petitioned the Japanese government for a wholly owned subsidiary in Japan. As its bargaining chip, Texas Instruments refused to license its industry-leading integrated circuit patents to Japanese companies unless TI received a substantial interest in a production subsidiary in Japan. The Japanese government finally consented to this request and allowed TI to own a 50-percent share in a joint venture with Sony.[30] In 1972, TI purchased Sony's 50-percent share. Therefore, based primarily on the strength of its patent portfolio, TI was able to establish a wholly owned subsidiary in a protected Japanese integrated circuit market.

§ 4.22 Extend Product Life Cycle

Intellectual property may help extend the life cycle of a company's product. **Figure 4–6** illustrates a typical product life cycle. When a product is first introduced, the sales volume is low. The product is new to the market and the customers do not yet recognize or appreciate its advantages. In addition, the company is probably still working out the kinks of manufacturing and marketing the new product. In the growth stage, sales volume increases as product marketing, manufacturing, and sales all come together and customers begin to buy the new product. In the maturity stage, sales begin to plateau. Then, during the decline stage, sales volume drops off as competitors introduce new and more advanced products.

A patent may help extend this normal product life cycle. During the introduction and growth stages, a patent helps a company earn above-average profit margins due to the exclusive rights associated with a patent. These profit margins would be unavailable in the absence of a patent due to fierce pricing pressures from competitors. Additionally, the patent can help to insolate the product from pricing pressures during the maturity stage.[31]

Figure 4–7 shows another advantage of protecting products. Suppose that the product illustrated by the life cycle curve 1 is protected by a patent. As discussed, the patent allows the company to earn above-average profit margins during the introduction and growth stages of curve 1. While this product is on the market, the company continues to research and improve the product. The company can then patent these improvements.

---

[30] M. Borrus, Competing for Control: America's Stake in Microelectronics 120–21 (1988).

[31] *See* G. Smith & R. Parr, Valuation of Intellectual Property and Intangible Assets 270–71 (John Wiley & Sons 1989).

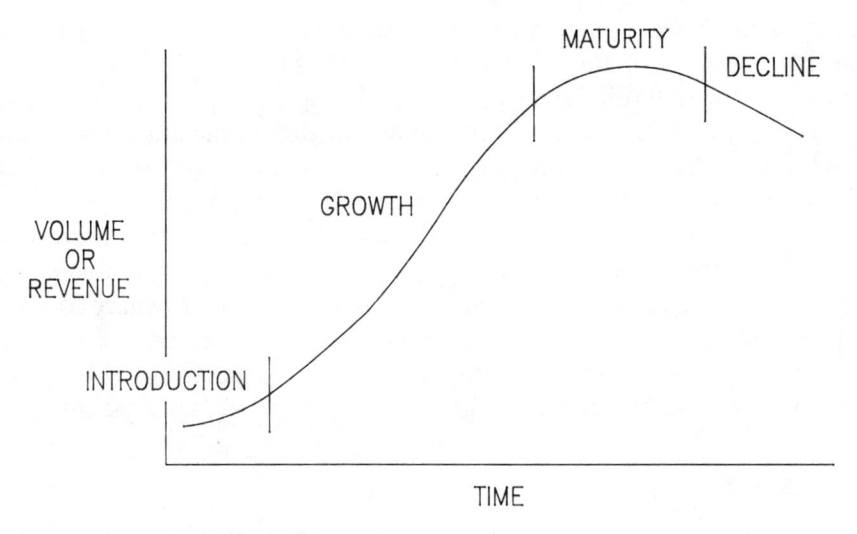

Figure 4-6. Product life cycle.

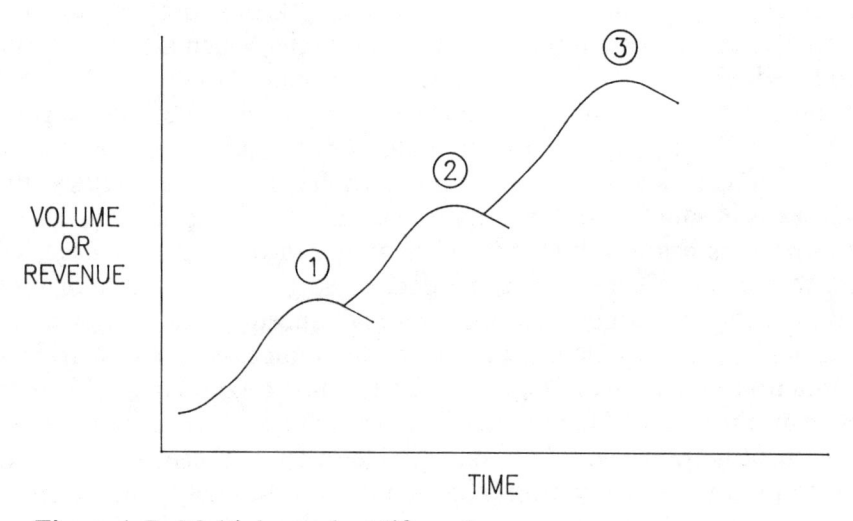

Figure 4-7. Multiple product life cycles.

When the first product matures, the company introduces the patented, improved product. Curve 2 represents the life cycle of the improved product. Because the first product already developed a customer base and the marketing and manufacturing groups are now more experienced, the sales volume of the improved product may begin substantially where the first product left off. When the improved product matures, the company can introduce an even more improved product, which of course is patented. Curve 3 represents this third product. The company is therefore able to earn above-average profit margins and increase sales volume for a longer period of time and over several different product lifetimes.

§ 4.23 Valuable Intangibles

Intellectual property provides valuable intangibles that are not readily measurable, but that most certainly help make a product more competitive. A strong trademark can increase the value, and thus profit margin, of a product. For instance, the trademarks CADILLAC or MERCEDES add a premium to the list price of an automobile sold under these names. Consider the value added to the products sold under the following trademarks: LIZ CLAIBORNE clothing for women, ROLEX watches, NIKE AIR JORDAN basketball shoes, and HAGEN DAAS ice cream.

Simply having a registered trademark may discourage others from using a similar mark. Most companies will shy away from using a mark that is already registered in a related class of goods because these companies want a distinctive mark that can be registered immediately. Companies do not want the trouble associated with fighting for registration against a similarly registered mark. Further, companies may not wish to invest in advertising simply to establish the necessary secondary meaning to meet the distinctiveness requirement and secure registration.

Turning to patents, a patent application filed on a product provides some market value by virtue of being able to claim *patent pending* on its product. Even if a patent does not ever issue, the patent pending status may provide a competitive edge by stalling the efforts of a competitor, who will be hesitant to copy the product with this warning for fear of infringing a resultant patent. In addition, the patent pending label does not precisely disclose the claimed invention. The label therefore keeps competitors in the dark as to what features the company is claiming as its intellectual property. Moreover, competitors cannot discover the scope of the claims because the patent process is kept confidential within the Patent and Trademark Office (PTO). Such information is not accessible under the Freedom of Information Act.

It is important to remember, however, that *patent pending* should not be used if a United States patent application is not pending. Criminal sanctions are provided by the patent statute for offenders of this labeling privilege.

§ 4.24 Asset Value

Intellectual property is an asset, and as such is valuable to a company. For example, under Article 9 of the Uniform Commercial Code, intellectual property may be used as a source of collateral in secured business transactions.[32] Intellectual property is often the main asset of a high-tech

---

[32] T. Bahrick, *Security Interests in Intellectual Property*, 15 AIPLA Q. J. 30–49 (1987).

start-up company. In the early stages, a start-up company may only have ideas and concepts of a revolutionary technology. Upon these ideas and concepts, banks and venture capitalists are often willing to lend large sums of money. Such situations demonstrate that intellectual property can have tremendous value.

When accounting for intellectual property, some companies have a special balance sheet entry, while other companies lump intellectual property into a category headed "intangible assets." A few companies make no entry at all. Some companies attempt to value their intellectual property, while others show an asset value of one dollar to indicate that the asset exists, but there is no way to quantify it. Regardless of the accounting formalities, however, intellectual property is an asset and has value.[33]

A strong intellectual property portfolio also portrays a strong image to financial investors and shareholders. The portfolio signals technical strength and competitiveness, and thus, longevity in the marketplace. The portfolio also implies that the company will be more effective competing in the short run simply because of the protection afforded its products.

§ 4.25 Increasing Strength of Patents

Over the past century, United States patents have not been treated kindly in the courts. In an era of trust busting, the courts viewed patents as a "legal monopoly" that furthered the interests of big business and undesirably restricted competition. As a result, courts often held patents invalid. For example, the Court of Appeals for the Third Circuit invalidated 77 percent of all patents that it reviewed during the 1950s and early 1960s. Not to be outdone, the Court of Appeals for the Eighth Circuit invalidated *every* patent it reviewed between 1950 and 1970.

The hostility toward patents was encouraged many times by the Supreme Court. Between 1930 to 1950, in 20 significant cases, the Supreme Court struck down patents on the ground of lack of invention. In only five significant cases were patents upheld, but only because the Supreme Court did not review the question of validity when both the district court and the court of appeals had the same findings on this question.[34] Perhaps the lowest point in United States patent history was the blunt yet telling assertion by dissenting Supreme Court Justice Robert Jackson that "the

---

[33] *See generally* G. Smith & R. Parr, Valuation of Intellectual Property and Intangible Assets (John Wiley & Sons 1989).

[34] D. Chisum, Patents § 5.02[3] (1992).

only patent that is valid is one which this Court has not been able to get its hands on."[35]

With the increase of formidable foreign competition in the 1970s, many people began rethinking the usefulness of patents. The United States had been for the past century the world leader in technology. To maintain leadership status and defend against foreign competition, companies decided to increase research and development spending. Patents were thus rediscovered as a valuable means for protecting the fruits of that spending. Patent holders began turning to the courts, more than ever before, for enforcement of these valuable properties. In 1990, United States companies filed more than 5,700 intellectual property lawsuits, compared to 3,800 in 1980.[36]

§ 4.26 —Creation of Federal Circuit

In October 1982, the Court of Appeals for the Federal Circuit (Federal Circuit) was created and given exclusive jurisdiction over all patent appeal cases. The Federal Circuit immediately began reversing the view that patents were undesirable legal monopolies. In the past 10 years, the Federal Circuit has attempted to unify interpretations of the patent laws and eliminate the discrepancies existing throughout the federal circuits. The court has consistently applied the law as Congress intended, rather than the encrusted, judge-created doctrine established during the previous 50 years. Moreover, because the Supreme Court rarely accepts patent cases, the Federal Circuit is now considered *the* voice in patent law.

Since its creation, the Federal Circuit has been generally favorable to patent holders. One study conducted on the Federal Circuit's patent decisions between 1982 and 1988 demonstrated the court's favorable bent toward patents.[37] As shown in **Table 4-4,** the Federal Circuit upheld findings of patent claim validity in virtually every case (25 to 3) and often reversed decisions finding invalidity (19 to 18). When the lower court found the claims of a patent infringed by another, the Federal Circuit upheld infringement nearly seven times as often as it reversed such a finding (67 to 10).

---

[35] Jungersen v. Ostby & Barton Co., 335 U.S. 560, 572, 80 U.S.P.Q. (BNA) 32, 36 (1949). *See also* Reiner v. I. Leon Co., 285 F.2d 501, 503, 128 U.S.P.Q. (BNA) 25, 27 (2d Cir. 1960).

[36] T. McCarroll, *Whose Bright Idea?*, Time, June 10, 1991, at 44–46.

[37] R. Cooley, *What the Federal Circuit Has Done and How Often: Statistical Study of the CAFC Patent Decisions—1982 to 1988*, 71 J. Pat. Off. Soc'y 385–410 (1989).

Table 4–4

Federal Circuit Rulings Involving Patents

Ruling of Lower Court	Number of times Federal Circuit ... Affirmed	Reversed
Claims valid	25	3
Claims invalid	18	19
Claims infringed	67	10
Claims not infringed	44	12
Patent valid	42	10
Patent invalid	33	25

§ 4.27 —International Trade Commission

The International Trade Commission (ITC) has a special court that handles patent infringement actions initiated by domestic companies against foreign companies. Under § 337 of the Tariff Act of 1930, as amended, products that infringe United States patents may be excluded from importation into the United States because such importation is unfair competition. Patent owners may therefore seek relief against such unfair competition by bringing an action in the ITC to have the foreign goods stopped from entering the country.

To initiate an action in the ITC, a patent owner only needs to show (1) the import, or sale after import, of an infringing article, and (2) existence of a domestic industry. The action requires approval of the ITC, which remains a party throughout the proceedings. In recent years, these preliminary requisites have become easier to prove. Additionally, unlike typical infringement actions brought in district courts that can go on for many years, infringement actions brought in the ITC must be completed in one year. Thus, patent owners sometimes favor the ITC action because the relief is more immediate.[38] There are, however, no damage awards in the ITC.

---

[38] *See* Krosin & Kozlowski, *Patent-Based Suits at the International Trade Commission Following the 1988 Amendments to Section 337*, 17 AIPLA Q. J. 47–68 (1989).

PART II
SELECTING MOST APPROPRIATE INTELLECTUAL PROPERTY PROTECTION

CHAPTER 5
INTRODUCTION TO PROTECTION ANALYSIS MODEL

§ 5.1   What Is Best Protection?
§ 5.2   Common Scenario
§ 5.3   Protection Analysis Model
§ 5.4   —Know-How and Trade Secret Phases
§ 5.5   —Patent Phase
§ 5.6   —Copyright Phase
§ 5.7   —Trademark Phase
§ 5.8   —More Than One Type of Protection May Be Available

§ 5.1   What Is Best Protection?

A question confronting every manager or engineer who handles intellectual property issues, or the attorney working with this person, is: What is the most appropriate intellectual property protection for a particular technology, concept, or idea? **Part I** introduced the types of intellectual property and the legal requirements for obtaining each type. Unfortunately, simply knowing that different types of protection exist does not necessarily help you select appropriate intellectual property protection for real-life products, services, methods, and works encountered on the job.

Part II introduces a process for selecting the most appropriate type of intellectual property protection for your company's technology, concepts, and ideas. This process guides the user through each type of protection and the competing factors and trade-offs of selecting one type of protection over another.

This chapter provides an overview of the process. **Chapters 6** through **11** then examine specific aspects of that process in more detail.

§ 5.2 Common Scenario

Consider the following scenario: your company manufactures measuring instruments. An engineer in your company comes to you and says, "Guess what? I've just discovered that we can replace the bimetallic strips in our pressure gauges with polyvinyl-this-and-that. The gauges will have faster response and are so much simpler that we can reduce our pressure gauge manufacturing costs." This discovery sounds great to you! A better product produced at less cost.

You must now decide whether this new technology should be protected. But how do you do that? If you decide to protect it, what protection do you choose? Should you patent this new technology? Should you keep it a trade secret? Are you going to market it under a new trademark? Should you register the trademark? Will you set up a new sales campaign with television and radio commercials and sales brochures? Should you register the copyrights on these commercials and sales brochures?

Selecting an appropriate form of intellectual property protection is very important for maximizing the legal protection afforded to your company's innovations and ideas. In one situation, a trade secret may provide better protection than a patent, even though both types of protection are available. In another situation, a patent may provide better protection than a trade secret. Although many of these protection questions can, and should, be answered by your company's intellectual property department or counsel, they are generally not in a position *initially* to identify and analyze the intellectual property opportunities. As a practical matter, the intellectual property department or counsel cannot actively and continuously search the company's engineering and marketing departments for technological innovations and ideas warranting intellectual property protection. The opportunity to preliminarily identify available intellectual property rights within the company is entrusted to those who are most deeply involved with the company's technological innovations. That is, the responsibility rests with the engineers and managers.

Recognize, then, that you who can identify intellectual property opportunities that a company can obtain and commercialize are valuable contributors to the company's overall profitability. However, to be a contributor, you must be able to identify the types of intellectual property that are legally available for innovations and which types offer the most appropriate protection. Each type of intellectual property provides fundamentally different legal rights, with distinct advantages and limitations. Each type has its own set of legal requirements that must be satisfied before a company is entitled to the intellectual property rights. Additionally, many competing business factors must be evaluated to determine the appropriate protection.

To assist you in selecting intellectual property protection, an analytical framework for approaching each intellectual property situation is necessary. This framework facilitates consideration of the legal requirements of the different types of intellectual property and the competing factors in acquiring one type of protection as opposed to another type.

Sections 5.3 through **5.8** introduce an analytical framework called the *Protection Analysis Model*. The specific steps of the model are discussed in depth in subsequent chapters.

§ 5.3 Protection Analysis Model

The Protection Analysis Model, as illustrated in **Figure 5–1**, diagrams the fundamental decision-making analysis necessary to determine the appropriate type of intellectual property. The Protection Analysis Model serves two important purposes. First, the model provides a systematic approach to each intellectual property situation. Second, the model ensures that all types of intellectual property are considered in each situation.

Note that the model is necessarily circular, meaning that to understand and appreciate certain steps, you must understand and appreciate later steps. For example, to fully appreciate the decision of whether a certain know-how warrants protection, you must already have an understanding of the requirements and rights of trade secret, patent, design patent, copyright, and trademark protection. You should also be familiar with the benefits provided by these different intellectual properties. For this reason, a brief summary of the entire Protection Analysis Model is provided first, with a more detailed discussion of each decision in the model following in subsequent chapters. The intent is to identify the interrelationship among the various decisions before discussing the decisions themselves. This way, your appreciation of the interrelationship will be complete when the more intricate aspects of the decision-making process are explored.

§ 5.4 —Know-How and Trade Secret Phases

The Protection Analysis Model begins in the top left corner with your company's continuously growing know-how foundation. Every daily endeavor adds to this know-how base. Eventually, certain identifiable ideas, concepts, or subject matters evolve from the know-how. Such subject matters may be a product innovation, a new artistic packaging design, or a new advertising slogan. We use the term *subject matter* throughout this book as the generic name for any underlying concept, innovation, idea, or expression that might possibly qualify for trade secret, patent, copyright,

98 PROTECTION ANALYSIS MODEL

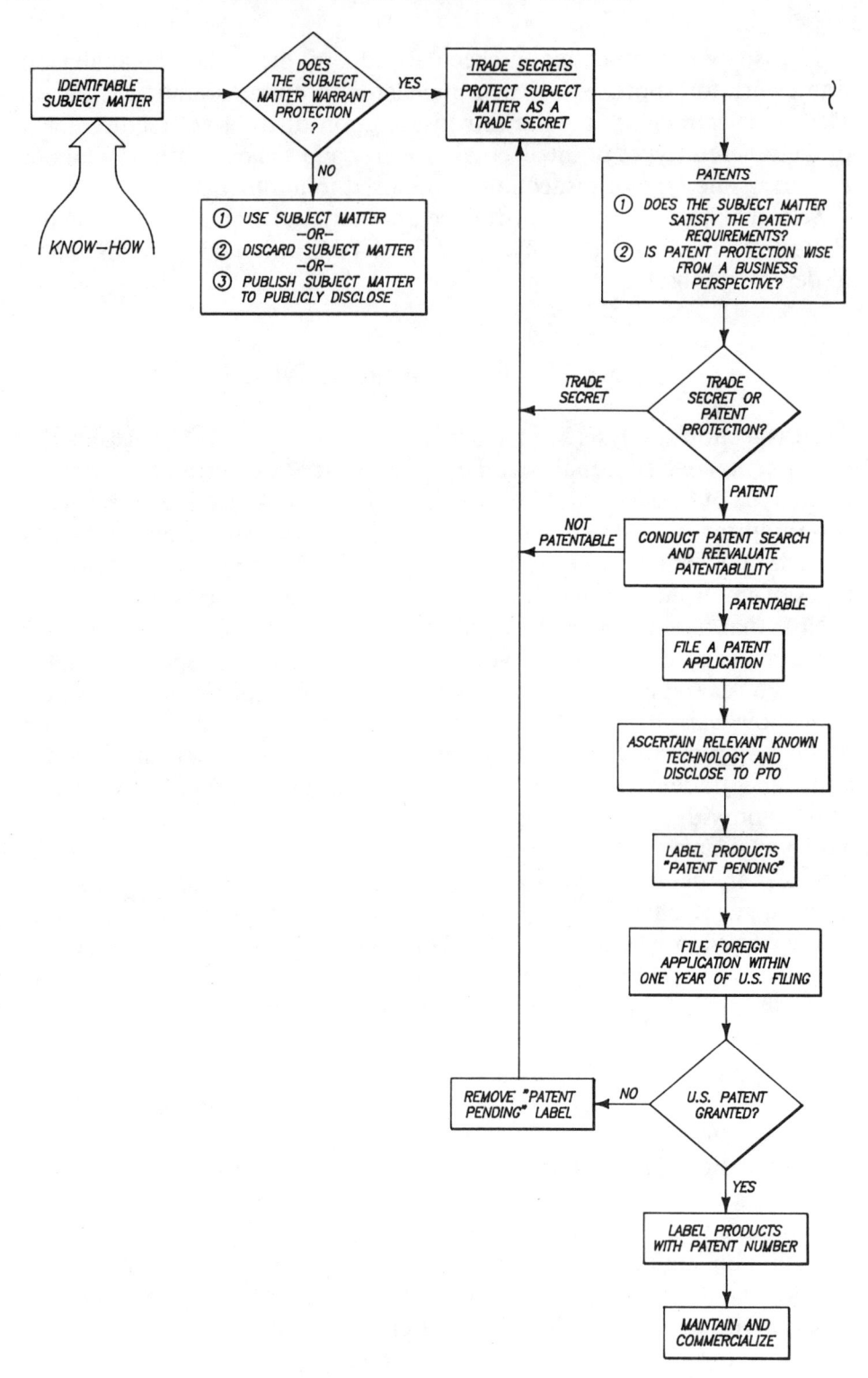

Figure 5-1. Protection Analysis Model.

§ 5.4 KNOW-HOW 99

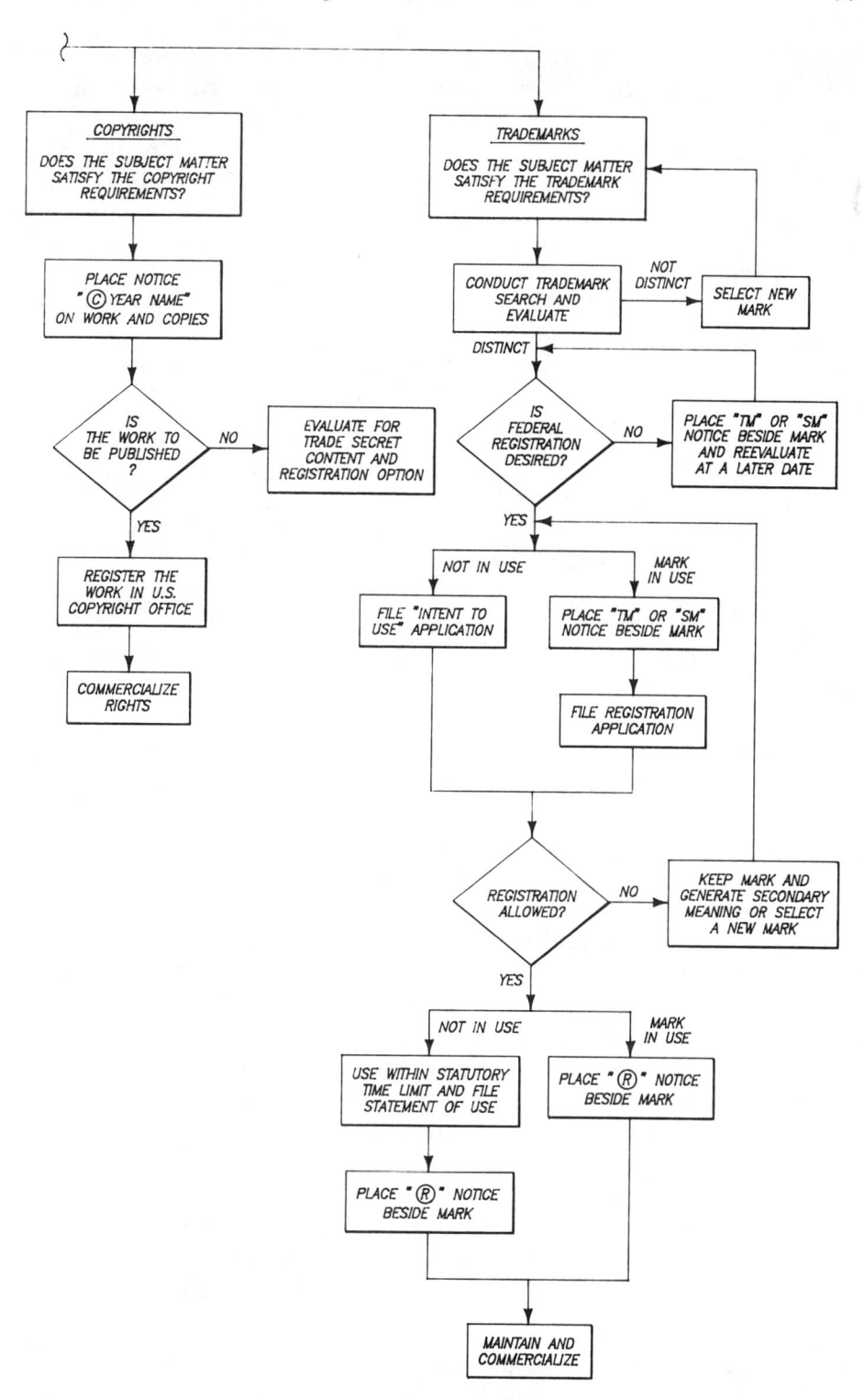

Figure 5-1. Protection Analysis Model *continued*

or trademark protection. It is these identifiable subject matters that can then undergo evaluation for potential intellectual property protection.

According to the Protection Analysis Model, the first step is to determine whether the identifiable subject matter created by your company is sufficiently valuable to warrant some kind of protection. The initial protection decision is very important, as all other protection decisions turn on the result. The decision is influenced by many factors and is discussed in depth in **Chapter 6**.

If the identifiable subject matter is not sufficiently valuable, obviously you need not protect it. Instead, your company can simply use the subject matter or discard it. Alternatively, your company may wish to publish the matter to place it in the public domain and thereby prevent someone else from claiming it as their own intellectual property.

If, on the other hand, the subject matter is sufficiently valuable to your company and protection is deemed necessary, the next step in the model is to treat the subject matter as a trade secret. Trade secret law imposes practically no subject matter limitations, and thus you should have little concern that an innovation or concept will qualify for trade secret protection. This step is therefore relatively simple because it merely requires a conscious and affirmative effort on the part of your company to keep the subject matter a secret.

The first two steps of the Protection Analysis Model ((1) deciding whether protection is warranted and (2) protecting valuable subject matter as a trade secret) are very important for trade secret protection. One of the legal requirements of trade secret protection is that a company take "affirmative steps" to maintain the subject matter in secrecy. In this model, a company takes its first affirmative step by distinguishing the valuable subject matter to be protected from the nonvaluable subject matter that is left unprotected. This move establishes that the company is consciously making an effort to maintain specific subject matter as a trade secret. Furthermore, by consciously excluding the nonvaluable subject matter from trade secret protection, and perhaps publishing this nonvaluable subject matter, the company emphasizes the "affirmativeness" of treating the valuable subject matter as a trade secret. In this manner, the company will prevent the appearance of overprotection, which might tend to diminish the effectiveness of its trade secret program.[1] Trade secret protection is discussed in more detail in **Chapter 7**.

As shown in **Figure 5-1**, the next set of phases in the Protection Analysis Model is to determine whether the subject matter (now classified as a trade secret) should be protected by a patent, copyright, and/or trademark

---

[1] Some courts look dimly on companies that overprotect their technology by classifying most of it as a trade secret. Epstein & Levi, *Protecting Trade Secret Information: A Plan for Proactive Strategy*, 43 Bus. Law. 887, 902 (1988).

in lieu of trade secret protection. As you become familiar with the various types of intellectual property, you will become more comfortable with selecting one type over another. With a little experience, you may even be able to immediately identify the preferred protection for a particular subject matter. Until then, however, it is best if you consider each type of intellectual property independently of the others to ensure that an available form of protection is not inadvertently overlooked.

This portion of the Protection Analysis Model offers a flexible approach to decision making. Decision paths concerning patents, copyrights, and trademarks are arranged vertically and adjacent to one another, with each path flowing directly from the trade secret box. This arrangement affords the flexibility of going directly from trade secret considerations to any one of the other intellectual property types. The flexibility is useful to the experienced manager who can immediately discern the optimum form of protection and can proceed directly to the relevant steps relating to that optimum intellectual property type. For the less experienced manager, the vertical column design enables a sequential approach to the model in which the manager simply considers each type of intellectual property—patents, copyrights, and trademarks—independently of the other and in sequential order beginning with patents.

§ 5.5 —Patent Phase

The kind of subject matter considered for utility patent protection is purely technical. It relates to functional or utilitarian aspects of an innovation. Alternatively, design patents protect the ornamental features of a manufactured product. The initial patent determination involves two inquiries: (1) Does the subject matter satisfy the legal requirements for patent protection? and (2) Is patent protection wise from a business perspective? If the answer to either inquiry is no, patent protection should not be pursued for this particular subject matter.

On the other hand, if the answers to both inquiries are yes, you should next decide whether patent protection is more desirable than trade secret protection. This is one of the most important decisions in the Protection Analysis Model. Subject matter protected by a trade secret must be kept secret, whereas subject matter protected by a patent must be disclosed to the public. The two types of protection are mutually exclusive, and the same subject matter cannot be protected simultaneously by both a patent and a trade secret. There are many competing factors in choosing between trade secret and patent protection, including whether the subject matter is capable of being kept secret, the scope of intellectual property rights afforded by each type, and the enforceability of those rights. Each type has distinct advantages and disadvantages that must be weighed. **Chapter 9** specifically examines this decision.

Assuming that patent protection is preferable over trade secret protection, your company should take appropriate steps to secure patent protection. The Protection Analysis Model identifies the more critical steps in this process. First, your company should conduct a patentability search of prior and known technology to determine if patentability remains viable and to gain an understanding of the potential scope of any resulting patent protection. Such a patentability search is typically performed by examining relevant existing patents on file in the Patent and Trademark Office (PTO). Often, the patentability search will change your perspective as to whether the invention is sufficiently novel or nonobvious (two of the patent legal requirements) to qualify for patent protection.

If you determine, based upon the results of the search, that patent protection does not satisfy the legal requirements, your company can simply maintain the subject matter as a trade secret. If the search yields positive results, however, your company should file a patent application covering the subject matter. As part of the application process, the inventors, the patent attorneys or agents, and any other person involved with the invention have a duty to disclose to the PTO any information material to the patentability of the invention.

Once a patent application has been filed, a "patent pending" label should be placed on all products embodying the subject matter in the patent application. During the first year that the patent application is pending in the PTO, your company should also consider whether to file patent applications in foreign countries. As a general rule, your company has one year from the filing date of its United States patent application to file an equivalent foreign patent application on the same subject matter, assuming that the subject matter was not publicly disclosed before the United States filing date.

After the United States patent application is filed, the PTO will examine it to discern whether the legal requirements of patent protection are met. This examination is conducted in secrecy, thereby preventing public disclosure of the valuable technological subject matter. If a patent is granted by the PTO, your company now has patent rights on the subject matter and should mark its products with the issued patent number. Your company should then maintain and commercialize its new patent rights.

Conversely, if the PTO does not grant a patent (for example, for failure to satisfy the legal requirements of patent protection), your company should continue to protect the subject matter as a trade secret. The subject matter is still secret, and thus still protectable as a trade secret, because the patent procurement process is conducted in privacy. In this situation, be sure to remove the "patent pending" label because there is no longer any application pending.

The patent phase of the Protection Analysis Model is discussed in more detail in **Chapter 8**.

§ 5.6 —Copyright Phase

The next phase in the Protection Analysis Model is to determine whether the subject matter should be protected by copyright. This is done by evaluating the subject matter against the legal requirements for copyright protection. The kind of subject matter to be considered for copyright protection can be technical, such as computer software, or nontechnical, such as promotional brochures.

If the subject matter is not copyrightable, analysis for the copyright phase is completed. Conversely, if the subject matter is copyrightable, copyright protection is instantly available. It attaches immediately upon creation of the subject matter or work. For such works, you should place a copyright notice (© plus year of publication or creation plus name of copyright owner) on the work.

The next step is to determine whether the work is to be *published*, which means unrestricted distribution of copies of the work to the public. Your company should register all published works at the United States Copyright Office to ensure maximum protection and remedy for the copyrighted work. Registration is also available for works to be left unpublished (such as engineering drawings). However, there is some incentive to keep such works secret so that they might also qualify for trade secret protection.

Upon registration, the Copyright Office will examine the work in a very cursory manner to determine whether the work contains copyrightable subject matter. The Copyright Office rejects approximately only 3 percent of the copyright applications on the grounds that the work is not copyrightable subject matter.[2]

The last step in the copyright phase of the Protection Analysis Model is to commercialize the rights provided by copyright protection. The copyright phase is explored in more detail in **Chapter 10**.

§ 5.7 —Trademark Phase

The final phase in the Protection Analysis Model is to determine whether the subject matter can be protected as a trademark or service mark. This is accomplished by evaluating the subject matter under the legal requirements for federal trademark protection. The kind of subject matter considered for trademark protection is strictly nontechnical in nature, such

---

[2] I. Koenigsberg & W. Patry, How to Handle Basic Copyright and Trademark Problems (1991).

as a name to identify a new product, an advertising campaign slogan, or a new packaging shape. The procedure for trademarks and service marks is the same; for simplicity, we use the term *trademark* to refer generically to both trademarks and service marks.

The initial analysis for purposes of federal registration essentially comes down to whether the new mark or slogan is sufficiently distinctive to qualify for protection. If you conclude that the subject matter is not registrable, trademark protection is not available and no more analysis under the trademark phase is necessary. If you conclude that the subject matter might be registrable, your company should conduct a trademark search. The purpose of a trademark search is twofold. First, a trademark search reveals whether your company can register this particular mark for its goods or whether someone else is already using the same or a similar mark for similar goods. Second, a search helps to identify situations in which your company, by using a particular mark, might be infringing someone else's trademark rights. If the search reveals the existence of a confusingly similar mark used on similar goods or that your proposed mark might infringe another's rights, your company should select a new mark and return to step one of the trademark phase.

If the trademark search indicates that the mark is unique and that your company is not violating another's rights, you must decide whether to seek federal registration for the mark. Although trademark rights in the United States are established simply through using the mark, and not through registration, there are compelling advantages to federal registration, and it is much preferred to state registration or no registration.

If you determine that federal registration is not desired at this time, your company should place a trademark notice, "TM" (for products) or "SM" (for services), beside the mark. This notice informs others that your company intends to claim the new mark as its own. At this point, you may wish to contemplate state registration as an alternative. After a period of time, you should reevaluate whether federal protection has become desirable. Federal registration can be sought at any time. The risk of delay is that another party may obtain federal registration on the same or similar mark and thereby preclude your company from ever obtaining federal trademark protection.

On the other hand, if you decide that federal registration is desirable from a business perspective, your company has two avenues, depending upon whether the mark is presently in use. If the mark has *not* been used, your company can file an *intent to use* application to reserve the mark. This application allows you to save the mark until your company actually uses the mark. Presently, your company can reserve a mark for up to three years. However, if the mark is presently in use, your company should begin placing the trademark notice beside the mark, wherever the mark appears, and file a federal registration application.

The PTO will examine the intent to use application or the regular registration application to discern whether the proposed mark satisfies the trademark legal requirements. If the PTO rejects the mark despite efforts by your legal counsel, your company will not be granted a registered trademark at this time. The rejection commonly falls into one of two categories: (1) the mark was too close to an existing mark, or (2) the mark was too descriptive of the product or service with which it is to be used. For either rejection, it is most advisable to select a new mark.

As an alternative, however, your company can keep the same mark (assuming it is not infringing the rights of another) and attempt to create secondary meaning in the mark. *Secondary meaning* is the process of educating the public to recognize that a particular trademark designates your company as the source of a particular product or service and is not merely descriptive of the product or service. This is achieved through advertising and continuous interstate use of the mark. The process usually takes several years. After acquiring secondary meaning, your company can then reapply for federal registration.

If the PTO grants registration of your company's trademark, you again have two avenues depending upon whether the mark is actually in use. If your company has *not* yet used the mark, it must do so within the statutory time period and file a document entitled "Statement of Use" to declare that it has actually used the registered mark in commerce. Your company can also begin placing the "®" symbol beside the mark to indicate that it is federally registered. If the mark was already in use, your company must simply replace the "TM" or "SM" symbol with the "®" symbol.

As the final step in the model, your company should take measures to commercialize its rights established in the mark. It must also take precautions to maintain its federal registration. This primarily involves the timely filing of legal documents at the end of five years and the payment of maintenance every ten years following the date of federal registration. The trademark analysis is explored in more detail in **Chapter 11**.

§ 5.8 —More Than One Type of Protection May Be Available

Certain subject matter qualifies for more than one type of protection. Subject matter satisfying the legal requirements for both design patent protection and trademark protection can be protected under both laws. In the *Mogen David Wine* case, Mogen David Wine Corporation attempted to federally register the shape of its bottle for trademark protection for wine. The corporation already had a design patent on the bottle. The Court of Customs and Patent Appeals (a predecessor court to the Court of Appeals for the Federal Circuit) held that the existence of the design patent did not preclude Mogen David's right to register the bottle's shape as a trademark for wine.[3]

Subject matter satisfying both the legal requirements for design patent protection and copyright protection may be protected under both laws. In a Supreme Court case, a female dancer statuette was mass produced and used as bases for table lamps.[4] The statuette qualified for copyright protection and the ornamental features of the mass-produced table lamp bases (manufactured goods) qualified for design patent protection. The Supreme Court concluded that the same subject matter could be protected with a copyright and a design patent.

There is also some overlap in copyright protection and trademark protection. Certain subject matter may therefore be protectable under both copyright and trademark.

The lesson to be learned from the possibility of overlapping protection is that you must be careful to consider each type of protection under the Protection Analysis Model. For instance, if you determine that design patent protection is available and worthwhile, do not stop your analysis. You should continue to analyze whether copyright and/or trademark protection is also available.

---

[3] *In re* Mogen David Wine Corp., 372 F.2d 539, 152 U.S.P.Q. (BNA) 593 (C.C.P.A. 1967).
[4] Mazer v. Stein, 347 U.S. 201, 100 U.S.P.Q. (BNA) 325 (1954).

CHAPTER 6

DECIDING WHETHER PROTECTION IS WARRANTED

§ 6.1   Everything Begins as Know-How
§ 6.2   Weighing the Factors
§ 6.3   —Is Subject Matter Already Known?
§ 6.4   —Exclusive Ownership of Subject Matter
§ 6.5   —Preventing Competitors from Owning Subject Matter
§ 6.6   —Does Subject Matter Make Company's Products More Competitive?
§ 6.7   —Is Subject Matter Economically Practical?
§ 6.8   —Does Subject Matter Help Reduce Company's Costs?
§ 6.9   —Does Subject Matter Help Satisfy Customer Preference?
§ 6.10 —Company Goals
§ 6.11 —Company Market Position and Strategy
§ 6.12 —Is Market Mature and Ready to Accept Technology?
§ 6.13 —Company Profile
§ 6.14 —Does Subject Matter Have Licensing Potential?
§ 6.15 —Does Subject Matter Improve Corporate Bargaining Posture?
§ 6.16 —Is Subject Matter Sufficiently Valuable to Warrant Expenditure of Limited Resources?
§ 6.17 —Is Asset Value Important?
§ 6.18 Protection Factors Checklist
§ 6.19 All Things Being Equal, Favor Protection
§ 6.20 Protection Alternatives

§ 6.1   Everything Begins as Know-How

The initial premise of the Protection Analysis Model (see **Chapter 5**) is that everything created by your company begins as know-how. This is

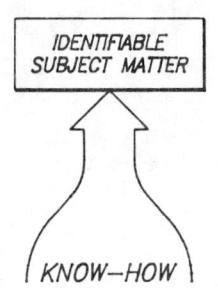

Figure 6–1. Know-how phase of Protection Analysis Model.

graphically illustrated in the upper left-hand corner of the model in **Figure 5–1**, the key section of which is reproduced as **Figure 6–1**. Out of the know-how environment springs forth specific identifiable subject matter that might qualify for protection under the intellectual property laws. It is this identifiable subject matter you should then evaluate for protection.

Know-how is difficult to define. It is an "I know it when I see it" phenomenon. In an attempt to describe know-how, one team of writers defined it as including

> inventions, processes, formulae, or designs which are either unpatented or unpatentable; it may be evidenced by some form of physical matter, such as blue-prints, specifications, or drawings; ... and it may involve accumulated technical experience and skills which can best, or perhaps only, be communicated through the medium of personal services.[1]

Know-how is the genesis of ascertainable ideas, innovations, and discoveries. It consists of the background or underlying foundation from which all creative activity evolves. It includes facilities, employees, experience, and teamwork, as well as experiments, engineering plans, sketches, brainstorming sessions, plant layouts, inventory scheduling, distribution routes, and processing methods. Know-how also includes "know-not-how." That is, know-how includes past failures, failed experiments, and any other unexpected or undesired events that contribute to valuable information gained by your company through daily trials of operation.

The accumulation of know-how over a period of time creates an incubating environment that gives birth to distinct ideas, concepts, or innovations. With additional research and development, the ideas, concepts, or innovations become more defined and bits of know-how aggregate to form identifiable subject matter that might qualify for protection under trade secret, patent, design patent, copyright, or trademark laws.

This process might take years, or it might happen overnight. For instance, after years of research, a scientist might finally derive an optimum

---

[1] Creed & Bangs, *Know-How Licensing and Capital Gains*, 4 Patent, Trademark & Copyright J. of Res. & Educ. 93 (1960).

chemical process that can be protectable by trade secret or patent law. An engineering team, after struggling for months, might come up with a new product that is protectable under patent law. A marketer, after days of brainstorming, might select a new campaign slogan that is protectable under trademark law. Although the genesis and timing of each protectable subject matter is different, each springs forth from the underlying know-how foundation.

Know-how is therefore the foundation upon which companies build intellectual property portfolios of patents, copyrights, trademarks, and trade secrets. A subject matter diagram shown in **Figure 6–2** illustrates the relationship between know-how and other intellectual properties. Subject matter that qualifies for patent, copyright, trademark, or trade secret protection is contained within the know-how universe. Outside of this universe is unprotectable information, such as items that are clearly within the public domain. The space exterior to the intellectual property spheres represents protectable know-how that might not otherwise rise to a level of formal protection under one of the intellectual properties.

The trade secret sphere is comparatively large. Trade secret law has practically no subject matter requirement and so almost any subject matter will qualify as long as it is secret and kept secret. The subject matter exterior to the trade secret sphere but contained within the know-how universe represents ideas that are still protectable, yet are no longer secret and thus not protectable under trade secret laws.

The patent sphere contains patentable subject matter, which includes machines, products, processes, and compositions. Part of this sphere is dedicated to subject matter suitable for design patent protection. This includes ornamental aspects of manufactured products. The copyright sphere represents copyrightable subject matter, which includes advertisements, labels, brochures, software, and manuals. Finally, the trademark sphere contains subject matter that is registrable for trademark protection and includes words, slogans, logos, and shapes.

The trade secret sphere overlaps with the patent, copyright, and trademark spheres because certain secret subject matter can qualify for trade secret protection for these other forms of intellectual property. A secret innovation could be protected by either a patent or a trade secret. Works such as computer programs could be protected by copyrights and/or trade secrets. A new slogan for an upcoming sales campaign that has not yet been made public might be considered a trade secret before it is later registered as a trademark.

The diagram also demonstrates the overlap in subject matters that can qualify for design patent, copyright, and trademark protection. That is, a manufactured product might have ornamental aspects protectable by design patents; might be an original, artistic, three-dimensional work protectable by copyright; and the overall shape might become identifiable,

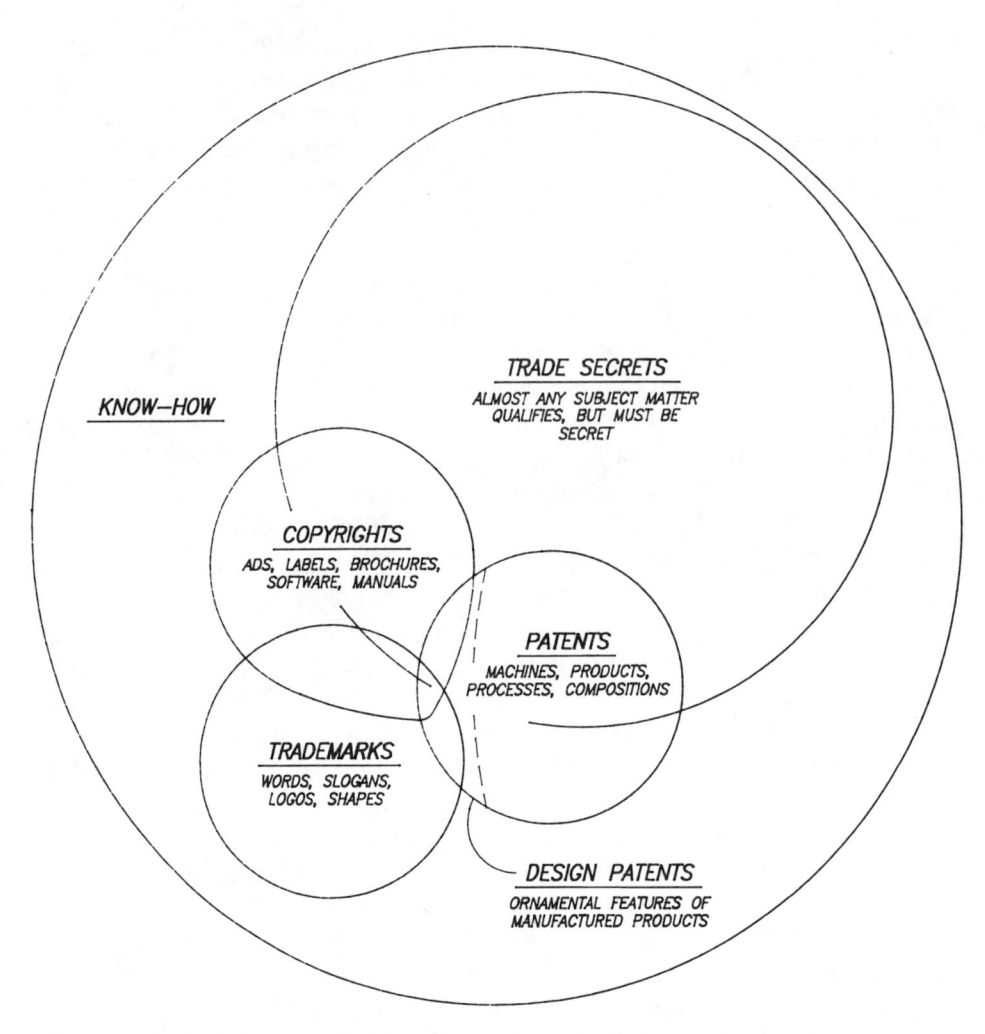

Figure 6–2. Relationship between know-how and other intellectual properties.

over time, as representing the company that manufactures the product and thus qualify for trademark protection. This overlap is discussed in **Chapter 5**.

§ 6.2 Weighing the Factors

The first important decision of the Protection Analysis Model is to determine whether a particular subject matter should be protected. Ideally, your company should protect a subject matter if the value gained from protecting it outweighs the cost of obtaining protection. Unfortunately, it is often very difficult to determine today whether the subject matter will be valuable to your company in the future. Moreover, your company has

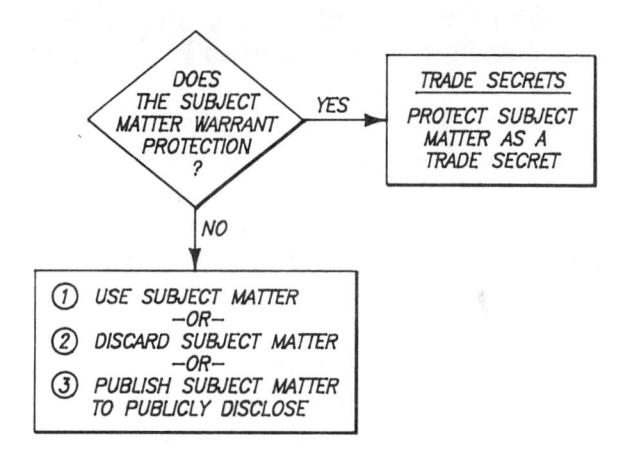

Figure 6-3. Protection decision of Protection Analysis Model.

limited resources. Protecting all new innovations or concepts developed by your company is economically impractical, even though most of them might have some value.

The portion of the Protection Analysis Model that is the focus of this chapter is illustrated in **Figure 6-3**. You might also wish to refer to **Figure 5-1** in **Chapter 5**, which shows the entire model. **Sections 6.3** through **6.17** explore many competing factors to consider in determining whether certain subject matters should be protected. These factors provide guidance in making the protection decision. Not all factors are necessarily applicable in all intellectual property situations. In some situations, any one of the factors may be determinative. In other situations, several factors will weigh in the decision. No precise formula exists.

If the decision is *not* to protect the subject matter, your company can simply use it without any formal protection or discard it. Your company might also consider "publishing" the subject matter (publicly disclosing the technology or concept in a technical or trade magazine) to prevent others from subsequently "discovering" the same concept and claiming it as their own intellectual property. On the other hand, if the decision favors protection, the subject matter should initially be protected as a trade secret. This chapter examines the protection decision and possible alternatives to protection. **Chapter 7** then addresses the use of trade secret protection as a threshold level of protection.

§ 6.3 —Is Subject Matter Already Known?

Although this may be stating the obvious, your company generally cannot protect subject matter that is already known to others throughout the industry. Known subject matter will not qualify for trade secret protection for failure to satisfy the secrecy requirement (the requirement that trade secrets not be generally known to others). The subject matter will not qualify for patent protection if it was already known and being used by others before the time your company developed and identified it. The subject matter will not qualify for trademark protection if the trademark is already registered and/or being used by another. It might qualify for copyright protection, provided that it is an original work of authorship and not a copy of another's work.

§ 6.4 —Exclusive Ownership of Subject Matter

Your company should protect the subject matter that it wants to own exclusively. This is typically the primary reason for securing intellectual property rights and is unfortunately often the only factor considered by companies in determining whether to protect certain ideas. A patent owner has the right to exclude others from making, using, or selling the invention, or its equivalent, throughout the United States for a period of 17 years after the patent issues. A copyright owner has the exclusive right to copy and distribute the copyrighted work. A trademark owner has the right to use a federally registered mark virtually exclusively throughout the United States. A trade secret owner has the right to prevent others from stealing his trade secrets (although this right is not necessarily exclusive).

Exclusive rights to intellectual property may be used defensively to prevent a competitor from legally using your company's intellectual property. For instance, when your company patents its technology, competitors are prevented from using the patented technology absent a license. Intellectual property rights also provide an offensive weapon to (1) stop infringing competitors from making or using your intellectual property, and (2) recover monetary damages caused to your company by the infringing activities.

§ 6.5 —Preventing Competitors from Owning Subject Matter

As the converse to the factor in § 6.4, your company should protect subject matter if it wants to prevent a competitor from owning the subject matter. Even if your company does not intend to incorporate the new concept into its products, your company might still wish to prevent its competitors from securing exclusive rights in the subject matter. A competitor may, for example, derive a significant market advantage from the technology, even though the same technology would not significantly benefit your company. Additionally, your company may wish to buffer its products from competitors by protecting similar technology. This buffering technique is discussed in **Chapter 4**.

Two alternatives to prevent a competitor from owning the subject matter are to (1) acquire intellectual property rights to it or (2) publicly disclose the subject matter in a publication. With respect to the first alternative, acquiring the intellectual property rights prevents your competitor from acquiring similar intellectual property rights in that subject matter. Your company should choose the first alternative if it wishes to commercialize the protected subject matter or to buffer its products from competitors' products.

On the other hand, your company should pursue the publication alternative if it has absolutely no commercial interest in the technology and is not overly concerned if its competitors gain access to the technology. By publishing the subject matter, no company, including your company and its competitors, will be allowed to own the intellectual property rights (unless a competitor had conceived of the technology before your company and was in the process of securing its own intellectual property rights unknown to you). Anyone will be permitted to use the subject matter. Once the concept has been publicly disclosed in a publication, trade secret protection is no longer available because secrecy has been lost. Utility and design patent protection are most likely no longer available for competitors because the publication evidences that your company had knowledge of the invention before any discovery by competitors.[2]

§ 6.6 —Does Subject Matter Make Company's Products More Competitive?

A particular innovation that makes your company's products technologically more competitive in comparison to products presently available in the market should be protected. Product competitiveness can be measured in many ways. The subject matter may, for example, be a new technology that outperforms present technology. Such subject matter would warrant patent protection. Perhaps the subject matter is a more efficient method of manufacturing or a cost saving accounting scheme. A company may wish to keep these innovations as trade secrets.

---

[2] Technically, publishing the innovation does not automatically preclude others from securing rights in the innovation. A printed publication only triggers a one-year period within which any patent claim to the same innovation must be placed on file in the Patent and Trademark Office. If a competitor had arrived at a particular innovation before your company, but had not yet sought patent protection before your company published the innovation in a trade journal, this competitor would have one year from the publication date to file a patent application.

§ 6.7 —Is Subject Matter Economically Practical?

Economics plays an important role in determining whether to protect certain subject matter. Some innovations clearly make a product technologically better in comparison to existing products. However, these innovations may never be incorporated into product lines due to the prohibitive costs of adding the superior technology. Consumers may not be willing to pay for the technology. Innovations that are too expensive to incorporate into a product line may not be sufficiently valuable to protect.

To illustrate this factor, consider the following invention concerning a fully automatic lawn mower. Once programmed, the lawn mower automatically opens a garage door, mows the lawn, and then returns to the garage. The lawn mower is equipped with sensors to detect and avoid children, animals, and other objects and a horn to warn children and animals. The lawn mower also has a rain sensor so that if rain begins to fall during mowing, the lawn mower will temporarily backtrack to the garage and wait for a period of time. The lawn mower will then return to where it left off before the rain began and finish mowing the lawn. The lawn mower can also be programmed to mow the lawn at the same time every week. It requires absolutely no supervision.

This invention is clearly superior to presently available lawn mowers. Unfortunately, most consumers would not be willing to pay the price for this fully automatic lawn mower. Many of these innovations may simply not be worth it. If the producer of this lawn mower is interested in competing in the manual lawn mower market, money set aside for intellectual property protection of these advanced innovations may be better spent protecting ideas that will actually be incorporated into manual lawn mowers, and not ideas that are economically impractical.

In considering this factor, keep in mind that economic considerations can change quickly. Technologies once thought too expensive may become economically feasible. Patent protection lasts a long 17 years. Thus, if an invention may become economically feasible within the life of the patent, protection may be warranted.

§ 6.8 —Does Subject Matter Help Reduce Company's Costs?

Subject matter that helps reduce your company's costs in some manner should be protected. For instance, a new production method that reduces manufacturing costs should be protected by a trade secret or a patent. A new accounting procedure that reduces administrative costs should be protected as a trade secret.

§ 6.9 —Does Subject Matter Help Satisfy Customer Preference?

Subject matter that assists in satisfying customer preference should be protected. Both your company and its competitors are constantly listening to customers in a concentrated effort to better serve their needs. Any new concept that may give your company an edge over its competitor by satisfying a particular customer preference warrants protection. For instance, a product designed in response to customer suggestions or surveys should be protected via patents. A more efficient distribution plan to better serve customers' inventory needs should be protected as a trade secret.

§ 6.10 —Company Goals

Your company's market and technological goals are important factors in determining whether to protect a certain subject matter. Innovations generated from research efforts pertaining to your company's primary technology should be protected. On the other hand, innovations that do not further your company's technological goals may not be sufficiently important to warrant protection.

§ 6.11 —Company Market Position and Strategy

Your company's market position and strategy for increasing market share play an important role in determining whether to protect a certain subject matter. If a new concept can positively influence your company's market posture, that concept should be protected as intellectual property.

Intellectual property is often beneficial to your company's market competitiveness. It can help you control market share and facilitate entry into new markets, foreign or domestic. Intellectual property can also discourage or prevent market entry by potential competitors. It might also assist in extending the market life of your company's products. See **Chapter 4.**

§ 6.12 —Is Market Mature and Ready to Accept Technology?

Protecting innovations is less critical when the market for the new technology is not mature and is not expected to mature during the lifetime of the protection. Similarly, if the market is not ready to accept the technology, the capital spent to protect it can be wasted. Consider, for example, whether a company ought to patent an idea for a complete mass transit system. Under the idea, all major roads would be equipped with imbedded magnetic tracks for automobiles to follow according to a predefined flow rate and pattern. Deciding whether to protect this idea will likely turn on the fact that implementation of the idea would occur so remotely in time that patent protection would expire before the idea even left the governmental review boards.

As another example, consider the value of a patent on a revolutionary new automobile engine to a small, undercapitalized company if the major automobile manufacturers were not willing to accept the engine and incorporate it into their cars. Unable to fund its own automobile manufacturing plant to produce cars using the patented engine, the value of the patent to the small company could be nil.

§ 6.13 —Company Profile

A company's profile and the competitive posture of the industry have an impact on whether to protect a new subject matter. Protecting innovations is very important for new or small companies because it offers them a better chance of competing against larger and more established companies. Whereas large companies have well-established product lines, sales and distribution networks, and long-standing customer relations, newer and smaller companies must rely on their technological superiority. Failure to protect the superior technology could contribute to a short life for the new or small company. When Xerox was a new company, its patent portfolio on plain paper copy machines insulated it from established companies that might have easily seized the plain paper photocopying industry in the absence of such patent protection. In addition, the unique trademark XEROX provided a significant market advantage as it became universally recognized. Xerox's intellectual property proved immensely valuable in the early stages of that company's growth.

A company that invests heavily in research and development should favor protection. Research and development expenses are more readily recouped when the resulting product is both commercially successful and protected.

Intellectual property protection is more important in certain industries than others. A company that operates in a fiercely competitive industry should favor protection. A strong intellectual property portfolio may supply the needed competitive edge over competitors in the industry. A good indication as to whether your company should build an intellectual property portfolio is whether its competitors are actively acquiring intellectual property. However, even if they are not, your company can gain a sizable advantage over them by protecting its innovations.

§ 6.14 —Does Subject Matter Have Licensing Potential?

Subject matter that has a potential of being licensed should be protected. Licensed subject matter can (1) generate revenue by way of royalty payments, (2) be used in exchange for technology from another company by way of cross-licensing, or (3) establish a foundation upon which rights in future technology of another company are transferred back to your company by way of grantback provisions. The advantages to licensing are explained in some detail in **Chapter 4**.

§ 6.15 —Does Subject Matter Improve Corporate Bargaining Posture?

Innovations that improve your company's bargaining posture with other companies should be protected. Companies often enter into agreements to exchange technological ideas or to embark on a joint venture to develop future technologies. A large intellectual property portfolio helps strengthen your company's bargaining posture during negotiations. If your company has no intellectual property to bring to the table, it has little or no negotiating leverage to strike mutually beneficial deals with the other company.

Intellectual property portfolios also play an important role in potential business relationships between two or more companies. The strength of their respective portfolios may provide the necessary incentive for the companies to sit down to negotiations.

Consider the following scenario involving Lens, Inc., and Camera, Inc. Lens has a portfolio of patents and trade secrets covering camera lenses and Camera has a portfolio of patents and trade secrets covering cameras. According to the market situation, both companies conclude that they could profit from cross-licensing their patented technology or by entering into a joint venture. Because both Lens and Camera have protected technologies, each company brings substantive bargaining strength to the table and, as a result, a mutually beneficial agreement can be drafted.

On the other hand, if Lens only possessed unprotected know-how on camera lenses, without a portfolio of patents and trade secrets protecting the lens products, Lens may have no real bargaining power in comparison to Camera. Thus, Camera would be in a position to request a more unilaterally beneficial package than it might otherwise. Moreover, Lens may not even possess sufficient power to entice Camera to the bargaining table because Camera can simply manufacture, or have another company manufacture, camera lenses identical to those made by Lens without any legal obligation to Lens. Thus, Lens misses an opportunity to benefit from a relationship with Camera simply because it did not adequately protect its lens innovations.

A strong intellectual property portfolio for improving bargaining posture is particularly important for a small company. One of the best ways to entice larger companies into serious business negotiations is to possess protected property that would be advantageous to the larger company. If the smaller company has no protection, however, the larger company has no impetus to conduct business negotiations with it.

§ 6.16 —Is Subject Matter Sufficiently Valuable to Warrant Expenditure of Limited Resources?

Unfortunately, companies do not have limitless resources to dedicate to intellectual property protection. Most companies have relatively small budgets for intellectual property protection. As a result, companies must maximize their intellectual property protection within their limited economic boundaries. Protecting all know-how is not feasible. Yet, failing to protect valuable innovations can prove significantly detrimental to a company.

For gauging how much to protect, you may wish to establish a rule of thumb in which your company will protect a similar number of technological innovations as other companies in the industry. This ensures that you are at least not underprotecting. Further, your company will not appear to be overprotecting every idea or concept, thereby diluting its affirmative steps toward protecting trade secrets. The result of overprotecting know-how is that courts will have difficulty separating know-how that your company takes affirmative steps to protect from know-how that your company does not care much about, yet still classifies as a trade secret.

§ 6.17 —Is Asset Value Important?

Intellectual property has more asset value than unprotected know-how. Intellectual property is identifiable and possesses significant legal rights and remedies against theft or infringement. It is much easier to quantify in licensing negotiations or other business agreements than is unprotected know-how. Additionally, intellectual property can be more readily used as collateral for secured financing arrangements.

In contrast, the legal rights and remedies for theft of know-how are much more limited and tremendously difficult to prove. Furthermore, banks are less willing to secure a loan with concepts that are difficult to define and difficult to protect. Banks prefer concrete property, such as intellectual property. Thus, determining the asset value for unprotected know-how is significantly more tenuous than for protected intellectual property.

§ 6.18 Protection Factors Checklist

Table 6–1 summarizes some of the basic factors to be considered when determining whether the identifiable subject matter warrants any protection at all. Consult this table when you are weighing whether protection is appropriate for a particular idea or innovation.

§ 6.19 All Things Being Equal, Favor Protection

The factors discussed in this chapter are provided to assist you in determining whether an identifiable subject matter is sufficiently valuable to justify the expense of obtaining protection. If you conclude after considering the relevant factors in favor of and against protection that the scale balances, you should choose to protect the new subject matter. It is better to err on the side of protection. Innovations or ideas can be protected initially as a trade secret with very little capital outlay. You can always decide at a later time that these ideas should no longer be protected.

Protecting innovations temporarily as trade secrets provides additional evaluation time to determine whether the new technology is valuable to your company. As consumer demands change, technology once thought to be of little or no value might suddenly become valuable to your company. Therefore, protecting innovations as trade secrets, at least temporarily, allows you to make a more informed decision at a later time.

Conversely, choosing not to protect new ideas initially raises a significant risk that these ideas will not be protectable in the future. If in the initial instance, the new ideas are not classified as trade secrets, company employees may not take reasonable precautions to keep them secret and thus preserve them.

§ 6.20 Protection Alternatives

If you decide, after carefully considering the factors influencing the protection decision, that the subject matter does *not* warrant protection, you effectively have three choices: (1) use the subject matter, (2) discard it, or (3) publish the subject matter to place it in the public domain.

The first two protection choices are rather obvious. Most, if not all, innovations naturally fall into one of these two categories every day.

Table 6-1

Factors Influencing Protection Decision

Favoring Protection	Favoring Nonprotection
Subject matter not yet widely known	Subject matter already widely known
Want exclusive rights to subject matter	Exclusive rights to subject matter are not important
Prevent competitors from owning and using the subject matter	Competitor use is not important
Subject matter makes your company's products more competitive	Subject matter fails to enhance your company's products in any manner
Subject matter is economically practical and may be priced competitively	Subject matter is too costly to incorporate into products
Subject matter reduces your company's costs	Subject matter increases your company's costs
Subject matter satisfies customer preferences	Subject matter fails to meet customer preferences
Subject matter helps achieve company goals	Subject matter is unrelated to company goals
Subject matter improves market posture	Subject matter has no impact on market posture
Company profile encourages protection	Company profile suggests that protection is not important
Market is mature and ready to accept technology	Market is either not mature or not ready to accept the technology
Subject matter improves your company's bargaining posture	Subject matter fails to enhance your company's bargaining posture
Subject matter has licensing potential	Subject matter has no licensing potential
Subject matter is sufficiently valuable to warrant expenditure of limited capital	Subject matter is not worth investment of limited capital which may be better spent on other innovations
Protected subject matter has quantifiable asset value	Unprotected subject matter may not have quantifiable asset value

§ 6.20 PROTECTION ALTERNATIVES

As a word of warning, however, be cautious before using innovations. Innovations you might think are "new," could in fact be innovations to which someone else has intellectual property rights. Therefore, it is wise to determine the extent that a new idea is available for your use before your company ignorantly uses or infringes another person's property right. Accordingly, before blindly incorporating an innovation into a product, you should consult your intellectual property counsel to assist you in determining whether the innovation infringes another's rights.

The third choice might not be so obvious. Your company can publish the subject matter in a technical or trade journal to place it irretrievably in the public domain. The main reason for publication is to prevent a competitor from "discovering" the same subject matter and claiming it as its own to your exclusion.

Consider the following scenario involving Analog Filters, Inc., a company that makes and sells analog filters for use in televisions, radios, and microwave communication systems. The analog filter industry is very competitive. One day, Dr. R.C. Circuit, an analog engineer for Analog Filters, discovered a way to improve his filter's performance. He discovered that by spacing the circuit elements farther apart, and by placing all capacitive elements on the opposite side of the circuit board, the filter unexpectedly reduced undesired noise by 5 percent. Analog Filters carefully considered whether to protect Dr. Circuit's improvement, but decided that the improvement was not sufficiently valuable to protect. The company's reasoning was twofold.

First, Analog Filters believed, correctly or incorrectly, that the improvement might not satisfy the requirements for patent protection. For instance, Dr. Circuit's improvement may not be sufficiently novel or nonobvious. Therefore, in the company's opinion, the probability of failing to qualify for patent protection did not warrant the expense of pursuing patent protection. Second, Analog Filters believed that trade secret protection would not adequately protect the improvement. If the improvement was incorporated into any products, it could be easily discovered by competitors through reverse engineering and, as a result, trade secret protection would most likely be lost.

Although Analog Filters decided not to protect Dr. Circuit's improvement, Analog Filters knew that its competitors could decide that the improvement was worth the risk of investing in patent protection. These competitors could independently discover the improvement, or a similar variation of the improvement, and claim the improvement as their own.

To prevent its competitors from laying claim to Dr. Circuit's improvement, Analog Filters should publish the improvement to describe for the world how spacing the elements farther apart and placing the capacitive elements on the opposite side of the circuit board would improve performance by 5 percent. Such a publication will likely prevent competitors from obtaining patent rights by establishing a prior publication bar under § 102 of the patent statute (see Bars #2 or #3 of **Table 2–1** in **Chapter 2**) or by evidencing a prior invention bar under § 102 (Bar #10 of **Table 2–1**). Also, a publication to the public will preclude any trade secret rights to the improvement.

Publishing is therefore an effective and inexpensive defensive measure that, except in unusual instances, prevents a competitor from obtaining intellectual property rights to the same subject matter and then enforcing those rights against your company.

There are three general methods of publishing technological innovations. A first method is to present a discussion of the subject matter in a professional or trade journal, such as the IEEE publication for electronic inventions. A second method is to describe the innovation in a company-sponsored bulletin. IBM, for example, periodically publishes its know-how in the *IBM Technical Disclosure*. Because engineers usually maintain daily records, drafting a short description of the technology is easy and involves relatively little engineering downtime.

A third method is to submit a statutory invention registration to the Patent Office.[3] This method requires submitting a document with a disclosure and drawings, as in a patent application, but without a claim to specific subject matter. The Patent and Trademark Office will publish the invention registration.

For any of the three methods, the published description of the innovation, as in a patent application, must teach the ordinarily skilled practitioner how to make and use the innovation.[4] Otherwise, the innovation is not sufficiently disclosed to the world. Therefore, if you intend to publish the technology to prevent others from claiming title to it to your exclusion, you must ensure that the technology is sufficiently disclosed in the publication to teach others how to practice it.

---

[3] 35 U.S.C. §157.
[4] *In re* Spada, 911 F.2d 705, 15 U.S.P.Q.2d (BNA) 1655 (Fed. Cir. 1990).

CHAPTER 7

TRADE SECRET PROTECTION: A THRESHOLD LEVEL OF PROTECTION

§ 7.1   Legal Requirements for Trade Secret Protection

§ 7.2   Attributes of Trade Secrets

§ 7.3   Maintaining Trade Secret Rights

§ 7.1   Legal Requirements for Trade Secret Protection

If you decide that certain subject matter should be protected in some manner, the next step in the Protection Analysis Model is initially to protect that subject matter as a trade secret. (The model is illustrated in **Figure 5-1** in **Chapter 5**.) This step essentially requires that your company make an assertive effort to keep the subject matter a secret. More specifically, subject matter can be properly maintained as a trade secret if it satisfies the legal requirements listed in **Table 7-1**.

The step of protecting innovations as a trade secret follows very logically from the initial protection decision step. It is natural to assume that innovations, concepts, and ideas generated by your company through research and development efforts and other planning environments are initially secret and confidential to your company. Trade secret protection has practically no subject matter requirement, so almost all new ideas can qualify. The remaining requirements are easy to meet. The subject matter need only be secret, a little novel, valuable to your company, and the subject of affirmative efforts by your company to keep it secret.

Table 7-1
Trade Secret Requirements

1. The subject matter must be kept secret.
2. The subject matter must be valuable to your company.
3. The subject matter must be at least minimally novel.
4. Your company must take affirmative steps to keep the subject matter a secret.

§ 7.2 Attributes of Trade Secrets

Trade secrets provide a threshold level of protection by preventing others from stealing innovations or ideas. However, unlike patent, copyright, and trademark rights, trade secret protection does not provide exclusive rights to exploit the subject matter. In fact, trade secret protection does not even prevent others from copying the innovations, independently discovering them, or reverse engineering your product to learn about them (assuming they obtain lawful access to the information).

Although trade secret protection may not guard as well as other types of protection, it can be valuable. A trade secret can, for example, last forever. It is forfeited only upon public disclosure, independent discovery by another, or through reverse engineering by a competitor. In addition, trade secret laws provide legal recourse against a party that has improperly acquired another's trade secret. Such laws guard against theft, bribery of employees, hiring of employees with the intent to steal trade secrets, and other improper actions. When another company improperly acquires your company's trade secret, your company may seek injunctive relief, damages, punitive awards, costs, and attorneys' fees.[1]

Protecting innovations initially as a trade secret also provides some basic protection while you analyze the other steps of the Protection Analysis Model. The subject matter is therefore being guarded while you determine whether it can qualify for patent, copyright, or trademark protection. If it fails to qualify for other types of protection, it can remain a trade secret.

§ 7.3 Maintaining Trade Secret Rights

As noted, to maintain a trade secret, your company must take appropriate steps to keep the subject matter a secret. Typically, companies develop

---

[1] Unif. Trade Secrets Act §§ 3, 4.

§ 7.3 MAINTAINING RIGHTS

their own trade secret programs suitable for their own needs. The number of precautions or corporate procedures that a company should or must take varies dramatically from company to company depending upon many factors, including its size, the type of technology it produces, and its capital resources. The following list provides general topical areas that all corporate programs should contain. These policies indicate that a company's trade secrets are subject to corporate efforts to keep them secret.

1. **Employee-related procedures.** Corporate procedures directed to protecting company trade secrets should include employee-related procedures involving recruiting practices, programs for current employees, and programs for departing employees. All employees should be continuously educated as to the proprietary nature of trade secret subject matter. Potential new employees should be informed of their expected participation in such procedures and departing employees should be reminded of their obligations to the company.
2. **Security procedures.** Plant facilities should be regulated and access to certain sensitive areas should be restricted. Additionally, employee access to computers, files, and photocopiers, and visitor access in general, should be supervised.
3. **Release review procedures.** Information to be disclosed publicly (via advertisements, brochures, and publications) should be cleared through your legal department or designated committee to prevent accidental disclosure of confidential information. Such disclosure, if left unchecked, might result in an irreversible loss of trade secret rights.
4. **Technological relationships with other companies.** Your company must take appropriate precautions when dealing with other companies to ensure that its proprietary information is correctly handled. These precautions include entering into confidentiality agreements, stamping all documents *CONFIDENTIAL* or with a proprietary label, and recording the type and content of information passed to an outside company. Policies concerning joint development of new products with another company should also be established.

A more detailed examination of corporate policies, and the reasons such policies are necessary, are provided in **Chapters 12** and **13**. Review these chapters before attempting to implement any policy or procedure directed to maintaining trade secrets.

CHAPTER 8

IS PATENT PROTECTION APPROPRIATE?

§ 8.1 Patent Phase of Protection Analysis Model
§ 8.2 Does Subject Matter Satisfy Legal Requirements for Patent Protection?
§ 8.3 Is Patent Protection Economically Desirable?
§ 8.4 —Patent Value Formula
§ 8.5 —Factors Affecting Value Variable V
§ 8.6 —Factors Affecting Value Probability Variable Pv
§ 8.7 —Factors Affecting Cost Variable C
§ 8.8 —Checklist of Factors for Patent Value Formula
§ 8.9 Is Design Patent Protection Appropriate?
§ 8.10 —Does Subject Matter Satisfy Design Patent Requirements?
§ 8.11 —Is Design Patent Protection Desirable from Business Perspective?
§ 8.12 Trade Secret or Patent Protection?
§ 8.13 Conduct Patent Search and Reevaluate Patentability
§ 8.14 File for Patent Protection
§ 8.15 Duty to Disclose Information Known to Be "Material to Patentability"
§ 8.16 Label Products with *Patent Pending*
§ 8.17 Foreign Patent Applications
§ 8.18 Is Patent Granted?
§ 8.19 Maintain and Commercialize Patent Rights

§ 8.1 Patent Phase of Protection Analysis Model

The next phase of the Protection Analysis Model concerns whether a specific subject matter should be protected by a patent. This determination involves two fundamental inquiries: (1) Does the subject matter legally qualify for patent protection? and (2) Is patent protection sufficiently beneficial from a business perspective?

Obviously, if the legal requirements are not met or protection is not feasible from a business perspective, your company should not seek patent protection. This chapter examines the factors used to answer these two inquiries. The discussion corresponds to the boxes in the Protection Analysis Model of **Figure 5-1** in **Chapter 5**. The patent phase of the model is reproduced here as **Figure 8-1**.

§ 8.2 Does Subject Matter Satisfy Legal Requirements for Patent Protection?

Subject matter is patentable if it satisfies the requirements listed in **Table 8-1**.

Failure to satisfy any one of the requirements precludes patent protection. For those innovations that are deemed to be "unpatentable," the reason is usually a failure to satisfy one of the last two requirements, novelty or nonobviousness. See **Chapter 2** for a more in-depth discussion of these requirements.

The following preliminary questions should always be addressed before patent protection is further considered:

1. Has the subject matter been publicly used more than one year ago?
2. Has the subject matter been offered for sale or sold more than one year ago?
3. Has the subject matter been described in a printed publication more than one year ago?

If the answer to any one of these questions is yes, then patent protection is most likely not available to your company. Be sure to bring such facts, and all other public disclosures, to the attention of your intellectual property counsel.

§ 8.3 Is Patent Protection Economically Desirable?

Assuming that the subject matter satisfies the legal requirements for patent protection, the next inquiry is whether obtaining a patent on the subject matter is economically desirable. This inquiry is very important! Obtaining patent protection can be a relatively expensive process. Thus, companies should first make sure that the benefits to be derived from the patent justify the expense of obtaining it.

§ 8.3 ECONOMICALLY DESIRABLE?

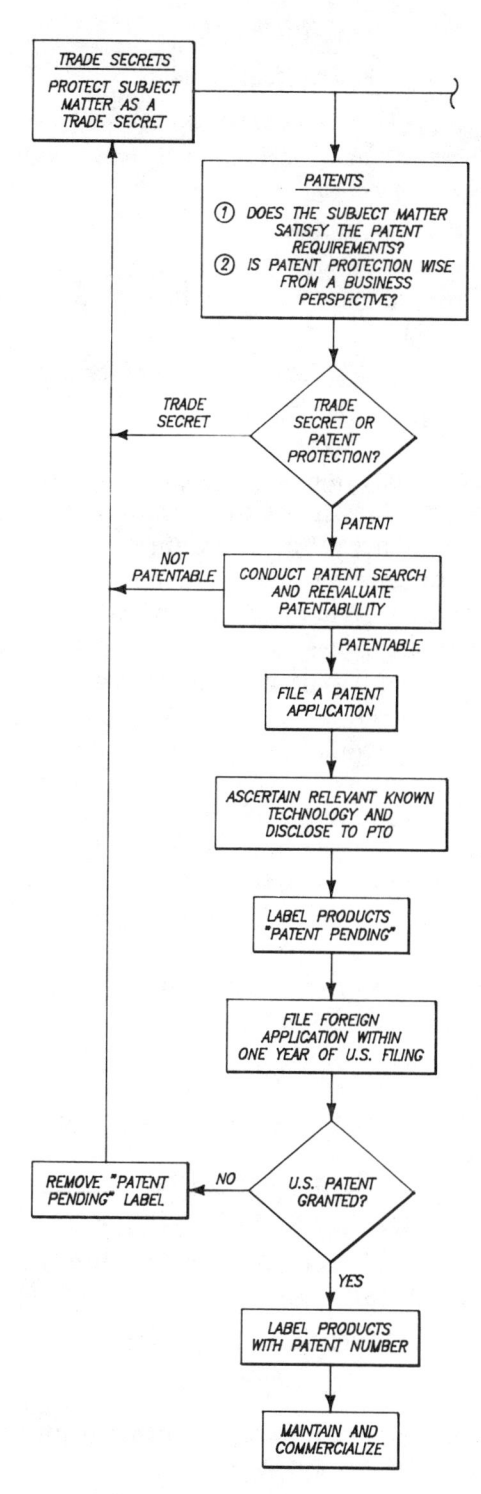

Figure 8–1. Patent phase of Protection Analysis Model.

Table 8-1

Patent Requirements

1. The subject matter must be "patentable" subject matter. Patentable subject matter includes processes, machines, products, compositions of matter, and improvements thereof.
2. The subject matter must be useful.
3. The subject matter must be novel. This requires that the subject matter survive the bars to patentability described in § 102 of the patent statute (**Table 2-1** in **Chapter 2**).
4. The subject matter must not be obvious to those of ordinary skill in the technological area.

Simply obtaining a patent does not necessarily ensure meaningful protection of a product, nor does it ensure that the patented product will be successful in the marketplace. Protection afforded by patents varies considerably in breadth, depending upon how narrowly or how broadly the patent claims are written. When at least minimum inventive effort is present, skilled patent attorneys normally can get some kind of patent claim allowed. However, this patent claim may be so narrow that it does not provide adequate protection in the marketplace, allowing competitors to design around the narrow claims with little effort.

In some instances, however, narrow patent claims can be very valuable if they cover the most advantageous way to do things. There are often many competing patents covering inventions directed to the same problem. Yet, only one of the patents may cover the best invention for solving the problem. This patent may be valuable even though it may have narrow claims.

In general, the second inquiry involves a weighing of the potential value of a patent against the cost of obtaining it.

§ 8.4 —Patent Value Formula

The patent value formula provides a process for deciding whether to patent subject matter that qualifies for patent protection. According to the formula, your company should seek patent protection if the potential value derived from the patent outweighs the cost of obtaining it. In variable terms, your company should seek patent protection if:

$$V \times P_v > C$$

V = Value to your company resulting from the patent
P_v = Probability of realizing value
C = Cost of obtaining the patent

§ 8.5 —Factors Affecting Value Variable V

The formula is not intended to be an exact calculus.[1] The patent value formula is designed to convey an understanding of the variables involved in determining whether obtaining a patent is economically desirable. The formula, therefore, provides a conceptual business approach to discerning whether the subject matter is sufficiently valuable to warrant patent protection. **Sections 8.5** through **8.7** examine the factors affecting each variable.

§ 8.5 —Factors Affecting Value Variable V

The value variable V of the patent value formula represents the value derived from a patent. The value of patents and other intellectual property was examined in detail in **Chapter 4**. The factors set forth below are therefore listed without extensive discussion or example:

VALUE FACTOR 1: Exclusive rights. A patent gives your company the right to exclude competitors from making, using, or selling the patented invention, or an equivalent product, in the United States for 17 years.

VALUE FACTOR 2: Enforcement against infringers. A patent may be enforced in a court against an infringing competitor. Upon a finding of infringement, the court can issue an injunction to stop the competitor from making the infringing products. The court can also award damages and attorneys' fees to the patent holder.

VALUE FACTOR 3: Assignment or license for revenue. A patent may be assigned or licensed to another company in return for consideration. The patent is like a piece of land or a car in that it may be sold for a lump-sum price. Alternatively, a patent can also generate substantially cost-free income in the way of licensing royalties.

VALUE FACTOR 4: Cross-licensing. A patent may be licensed to another company in exchange for a license from the other company's patented technology. This licensing arrangement allows your company to expand its technology base, without expending large amounts of capital in research and development.

VALUE FACTOR 5: Grantback licenses. A patent on a specific technology may be licensed to another company in exchange for future

---

[1] The formula may be used, however, as an approximation after the variables have been estimated. For example, if you estimate that there is a 25 percent probability that a patent covering a certain subject matter would command a licensing royalty of an after-tax present value of $50,000, your company should obtain a patent if the cost to obtain this patent is less than $12,500.

licenses from that company on improvement patents covering technology spawned by the initially conveyed technology.

VALUE FACTOR 6: Improved bargaining posture. Companies with larger patent portfolios may enjoy a better bargaining position than those companies with smaller patent portfolios. As a result, the company with the better patent portfolio may be able to force another company to concede more in a contractual agreement.

VALUE FACTOR 7: Recoupment of research and development expenditures. A patent may allow your company to recoup its research and development expenses because it provides protection for 17 years.

VALUE FACTOR 8: Use of patent pending label. Upon filing a patent application, your company can use the label *patent pending* on its products to be covered by the patent. The patent pending label often provides a market advantage. To consumers, the label implies that the product must be special in some way and therefore better than the unpatented competing product. To the competitor, the label announces that a patent application has been filed on some aspect of the product. Because the competitor does not know which aspect, nor how broadly the claims are written to cover that aspect, the label helps discourage a competitor from copying or designing similar products.

VALUE FACTOR 9: Effect on competitive designs. Your patent may force a competitor to change its initial design, or to seek a license from you, rather than risk a claim of patent infringement.

VALUE FACTOR 10: Enhanced market control. A patent may help your company control its share of the market. Because it excludes competitors from making, using, or selling your company's patented products, a patent may limit the kinds of products your competitors can make available to the customer. Additionally, a patent may help your company enter a new market, secure an interest in a foreign market, or create a new market.

VALUE FACTOR 11: Buffer products. A patent can buffer your company's products from those of a competitor's. This strategy helps distinguish your company's products in the marketplace. Patents obtained on your company's primary technology, and on technology similar to the primary technology (yet nonobvious in view of the primary technology), prevent competitors from using the primary technology and the similar technology. As a result, competitors must use technology that is considerably different from the primary technology used by your company. See **Figure 4–5** of **Chapter 4**.

VALUE FACTOR 12: Extend product life. A patent may extend the life of your company's product. Normally, products mature and decline after a period of time. Patent protection helps isolate your company's products from pricing pressures experienced in the maturing stage of a product life, and thereby extends the product life.

VALUE FACTOR 13: Collateral for secured financing. A patent may act as collateral to secure financing, as banks or other lenders recognize patents as property that has value. The ability to borrow against patents is often very valuable to newer companies in which patents are their primary asset.

VALUE FACTOR 14: Strong technological appearance. A strong patent portfolio can portray a technically strong image for consumers, financial investors, and shareholders. Such an appearance may indirectly help your company's product and stock performance.

§ 8.6 —Factors Affecting Value Probability Variable Pv

The value probability variable Pv represents the probability of realizing the value generated by the patent. This variable must be considered simultaneously with the value variable V discussed in § 8.5. A patent with a low probability of realizing value may not be worth the expenditure of filing for a patent.

Your intellectual property counsel can help you analyze the probability of realizing value on a particular patent by analyzing the scope of the patent claims, the scope of the prior art, and the current (or expected) commercialized products. The value probability variable Pv is affected by at least the following factors:

PROBABILITY FACTOR 1: Current customer demand for similar products in the market. A patent on a product that is in high demand will be more likely to generate value than a patent on a product that is in low demand.

PROBABILITY FACTOR 2: Customer receptiveness to a new technology. A patent on a technology that is marketable now is more likely to generate value than a patent on a technology that may be marketable in the future. Creating a better product does not necessarily ensure that the product will be successful in the market. Consumers must be willing and able to buy the better product today or within the foreseeable future. Consider an automobile company that produces a fuel-efficient car with an aluminum lightweight body and a small, fuel-efficient engine. If this car was marketed today, it would probably be commercially successful. What if, however, the automobile company introduced the new car back in the 1940s, when consumers wanted big, bold cars? The car would have been a commercial flop. Consumers in the 1940s were not ready for aluminum bodies and smaller, fuel-efficient engines and would not have been receptive to this new technology.

PROBABILITY FACTOR 3: Availability of commercially acceptable alternatives. A patent covering a product that is essentially the dominating or primary product in a market has a high probability of realizing its value. Additionally, a patent covering the best product in a particular market is likely to be valuable. This is because consumers have no commercially acceptable alternatives to which they can turn. On the other hand, the patent is less likely to be valuable if the patented product is only one of several commercially acceptable alternatives.

PROBABILITY FACTOR 4: Solution to a long-felt need in the industry. An invention that solves a problem that has been plaguing the industry for some time and thereby achieves the next technological milestone has a high probability of realizing value. For many years, camera companies recognized a market for instant cameras and film. However, for many years, numerous camera companies were unsuccessful in producing the technology. Polaroid finally developed a product that met the long-standing need and its patents have realized tremendous value through the years.

PROBABILITY FACTOR 5: Pricing considerations. A patent covering a new and superior technology is more likely to generate value if this technology can be produced at a price competitive with other products currently available in the market.

PROBABILITY FACTOR 6: Profit margin. A patent covering a product with a large profit margin has a high probability of realizing value. Large profit margins earn high rates of return for the research and development investment and provide a cushion for price reduction in the face of competition.

PROBABILITY FACTOR 7: Costs to practice the invention. A customer may not want to purchase a patented technology if the cost to practice it is higher than the cost that the customer is currently expending to operate present technology. A patent covering a new technology that requires the customer to buy new or more accessories, or to consume more fuel or power, has less probability of realizing value.

PROBABILITY FACTOR 8: Potential customer base. A patent covering a product that is marketable to a broad customer base is more likely to be valuable than a patent on a product that may be marketed to only a few customers.

PROBABILITY FACTOR 9: Range of customer worth. A patent is more likely to realize value if the targeted customer base is willing and able to pay for the new technology.

PROBABILITY FACTOR 10: Scope of protection. In general, a patent with claims of broad scope is more likely to realize value than a patent with claims of narrow scope. Consider the two extremes: pioneering patents and improvement patents. *Pioneering patents* are those patents covering a breakthrough in technology. The transistor, the light bulb, the television, the laser, and the microwave oven may be considered pioneering breakthroughs. Patents covering these breakthroughs are termed *pioneering* and, as a result, typically have very broad patent claims.

Improvement patents cover technological advancements. A more efficient stove, a safer lawn mower, and a stronger door lock would all be covered by improvement patents. Improvement patents make up the majority of patents. Patent claims in an improvement patent are necessarily narrower compared to claims in a pioneering patent. For instance, the patent claims to a more efficient stove may be directed solely to the improved feature that makes the stove more efficient.

In general, a patent with broadly written claims is more likely to realize value than a patent with narrow claims. In rare cases, however, this generalization may not hold true because a narrow claim tailored specifically to a particular feature of a product may realize considerable value if that feature is the best way to implement the product.

PROBABILITY FACTOR 11: Identifiable licensees. A patent is more likely to realize value if there are presently identifiable companies that are interested in the patented technology.

PROBABILITY FACTOR 12: Gut feeling. What is your gut feeling about the commercial success of the patented product? Gut feelings have powered many great ideas. Based upon your experience and market knowledge, you may sense when a product will succeed or fail and thus whether a patent covering the product will have value.

§ 8.7 —Factors Affecting Cost Variable C

The cost variable C involves the expenses associated with patents. This variable includes three factors: (1) the cost of securing a patent, (2) the cost of enforcing the patent, and (3) the cost of exploiting the patent. In the purest sense, this cost should also include the opportunity cost of patenting certain ideas over others because of limited resources. However, estimating opportunity costs in this context is very difficult.

The cost of securing a patent includes Patent Office fees, attorney time to prepare an application, and engineering time necessary to initially educate the attorney and review the patent application. The cost of preparing an application varies considerably. If the subject matter is complex, the cost can be quite high. On the other hand, the cost can be very low if the subject matter is relatively simple. The cost for patent protection is magnified if additional foreign applications are desired. Indeed, obtaining foreign patent protection is substantially more expensive than obtaining patent protection in the United States, depending upon the countries selected for patent protection.

The cost of enforcing the patent includes the cost of policing the market for potential abuses of your intellectual property rights. Included in these costs are attorneys' fees and litigation expenses.

The cost of exploiting the patent may include the cost of management, engineer, and attorney time for negotiating and drafting a license. Exploitation costs also include bookkeeping and other accounting procedures for monitoring licensing arrangements.

§ 8.8 —Checklist of Factors for Patent Value Formula

The patent value formula, $V \times Pv > C$, provides a conceptual approach to determining whether subject matter that qualifies for patent protection is sufficiently valuable to warrant the expense of obtaining the patent protection. **Table 8–2** summarizes the factors to be weighed in this analysis. After you have become familiar with these factors, this table may be useful as a quick reference when you are faced with a patentability issue. The presence and absence of various factors will help you make an informed decision.

§ 8.9 Is Design Patent Protection Appropriate?

Design patent protection is distinct from regular or utility patent protection discussed thus far. Unlike utility patent protection, design patents do not protect the functional aspects of a device. Design patents only protect the aesthetic features of the device, such as shape, appearance, and decoration. The same two initial inquiries for utility patents are also involved here.

§ 8.10 —Does Subject Matter Satisfy Design Patent Requirements?

The subject matter qualifies for design patent protection if it satisfies the requirements listed in **Table 8–3**.

§ 8.10 DESIGN PATENT REQUIREMENTS

Table 8–2
Patent Value Formula Factors

V Potential value of the patent	×	Pv Probability of realizing that value	>	C Cost of obtaining the patent
Exclusive rights		Current customer demand		Cost to secure patent
Enforcement against infringers		Customer receptiveness to new technology		Cost to enforce patent
Assignment or license for revenue		Availability of commercially acceptable alternatives		Cost to maintain and exploit patent
Cross-licensing		Solution to long-felt need in industry?		
Grantback licensing		Pricing considerations		
Improved bargaining posture		Profit margin		
Recoup R&D		Additional cost to practice invention?		
Use of patent pending label		Potential customer base		
Effect on competitive designs		Range of customer worth		
Enhance market control		Scope of protection		
Buffer your company's products		Identifiable licensees?		
Extend product life		Gut feeling		
Collateral for secured financing				
Strong technological appearance for shareholders				

Design patent protection is not available if any one of these requirements is not satisfied. **Chapter 2** should be consulted for a better understanding of these requirements.

The ornamental requirement is unique to design patents. A feature that was added or arranged on a device for aesthetic purposes is protectable under design patents. However, a feature of the device having purely functional purposes will not be protected under a design patent, no matter

Table 8–3

Design Patent Requirements

---

1. The subject matter must be a manufactured product.
2. The subject matter must be original.
3. The subject matter must have some ornamental aspect that was created for the purpose of aesthetic appearance and not for a functional purpose.
4. The design must be novel.
5. The design must not be obvious in view of other designs.

---

how beautiful the feature appears. You must ask yourself, "Why is this feature shaped or arranged in this design?" If the feature is shaped in a certain manner for artistic reasons, the feature is protectable under a design patent. However, a feature that is shaped solely due to functional concerns is not protectable with a design patent.

§ 8.11 —Is Design Patent Protection Desirable from Business Perspective?

If the legal requirements for design patent protection are met, the next consideration is whether obtaining design patent protection is wise from a business standpoint. The following factors provide useful insight to the practicality and scope of protection provided by design patents:

DP FACTOR 1: Basic protection. Design patents prevent others from making, using, or selling the protected design of a manufactured product for 14 years.

DP FACTOR 2: Scope of protection. Design patent protection is limited to the ornamental or aesthetic aspects and not the functional aspects. The protection afforded by design patents is therefore not as comprehensive as the protection afforded by utility patents.

DP FACTOR 3: Expense. Design patents are typically less expensive to obtain than utility patents. Applications for design patents include several drawings and a standard claim. There is no detailed disclosure as in the utility patents, and thus the cost of preparation is less. An example of a design patent for a computer mouse is found in **Appendix B**.

DP FACTOR 4: Design and utility patents both available. Products can be protectable by both design patents and utility patents. An invention may have functional aspects that are protectable by a utility patent and aesthetic aspects that are protectable by a design patent. Design patents thereby provide a secondary level of protection along with utility patent protection.

DP FACTOR 5: Backup protection. In some situations, a product may be functionally equivalent to prior technology and thus may not be entitled to utility patent protection. However, if the product possesses new ornamental features that are not present in prior devices, the product may still qualify for design patent protection.

DP FACTOR 6: Use of patent pending label. Once your company has a design patent application on file, it can put this label on the products with the aesthetic features that are the subject of the design application. The label is identical to that used for utility patents. This label is therefore particularly important in this situation because competitors will not know whether the label refers to the functional aspects of the product or to the ornamental features of it.

DP FACTOR 7: Creating distinctiveness. Design patents are useful for interim protection of distinctive shapes that may become a company trademark in the future. Companies often have trademark or trade dress rights in distinctive shapes. For example, McDonald's has a trademark on the shape of its container for large french fries. Ferrari has trade dress rights in the shape of its cars.[2] To build up these rights, companies must be exclusive users of the shapes. Design patents can provide a period of exclusivity by protecting the shape for 14 years. Accordingly, a company wishing to create trademark or trade dress rights in a distinctive shape might first obtain a design patent to secure exclusive ownership of the shape for 14 years. The trademark or trade dress rights can then develop and strengthen during this period of exclusivity.

These factors to be considered when deciding whether to seek design patent protection in addition to, or instead of, utility patent protection are summarized in **Table 8–4**.

§ 8.12 Trade Secret or Patent Protection?

Assuming patent protection is available and desirable, the next step in the patent phase of the model is to determine whether the subject matter is better protected under patent protection or trade secret protection. This question is very important, and **Chapter 9** examines the factors affecting this determination.

---

[2] Ferrari S.p.A. Esercizio Fabriche Automobile E Corse v. Roberts, 944 F.2d 1235, 20 U.S.P.Q.2d (BNA) 1001 (6th Cir. 1991), *appeal pending,* 60 U.S.L.W. 878 (U.S. 1992).

Table 8–4

Factors to Consider When Determining Whether Design Patent Protection Is Appropriate

1. Protection: Prevent others from making, using, or selling the design for 14 years.
2. Scope of protection: Design patents protect aesthetic features, not functional aspects.
3. Less expensive to obtain in comparison to utility patents.
4. Design patent protection for aesthetic features may be obtained in addition to utility patent protection for functional aspects of the same product.
5. Design patent can be a useful form of protection when utility patent protection is not available.
6. Can use the patent pending label once a design patent application is filed.
7. Design patent protection may help create distinctiveness in a design that may later be used as a trademark or trade dress.

If you conclude that the subject matter is better suited for patent protection, you simply continue on in the patent phase. If trade secret protection appears more appropriate, your analysis under the patent phase is complete, and your company should maintain the subject matter as a trade secret.

§ 8.13 Conduct Patent Search and Reevaluate Patentability

A patent search is a hunt to find issued patents or technical publications (collectively called *prior art*) that are most relevant to and predate your company's invention. The patent search is typically conducted by experienced searchers at the United States Patent and Trademark Office (PTO). These searchers look at indexed patents and publications maintained on file in a public search room at the PTO.

Patents and publications obtained during a patentability search are useful in two ways. First, they provide an initial indication as to whether an invention is novel and nonobvious. Patent examiners in the PTO who will ultimately examine the patent application typically use many of the same patents and technical publications to determine whether your company's invention is patentable.

Second, this prior art provides an indication of the patent activity in a particular technology. The search reveals which companies are actively patenting in a particular technology, the number of patents in that technology, how narrow or broad the patent claims tend to be, and how broad the claims of your company's patent are likely to be. Therefore, conducting a patent search is often advisable before your company spends money filing a patent application.

The down side to conducting a patent search is that your company may not obtain its earliest possible filing date. Companies typically delay in filing a patent application for a few weeks or months until the results of the patent search have been examined. In some highly competitive industries, in which many companies are developing similar technology almost simultaneously, obtaining the earliest filing date may be important in obtaining a patent over other companies in the industry and may be important in avoiding a statutory bar.

When time is critical, you might consider filing an application on a rushed basis and conduct a patent search after the application is filed. If required by the search results, you can refile the application and refine the invention description and claims after reviewing the search report, yet maintain the earlier filing date as to that information contained in the first application.

After conducting a patent search and evaluating your company's new technology in view of patents and documents uncovered during the search, you should consider the issue of whether the technology is still patentable. If the patent search uncovers prior art that describes the same or very similar technology, you might conclude that patent protection is not available because the technology is not novel or is obvious in view of other patents. In this situation, your company may wish to forgo patent protection and instead keep the invention as a trade secret.

On the other hand, the search may not reveal any technology similar to that of your company. Thus, patent protection may be available.

§ 8.14 File for Patent Protection

Assuming the patent search did not uncover prior art that would prevent your company's invention from being patented, the next step in the Protection Analysis Model is to seek patent protection. To do this, your company must file a patent application with the PTO. The patent application contains a detailed technical description and related drawings of the invention, followed by the patent claims that define the scope of your protected invention. An example of a utility patent document is provided in **Appendix A** and a design patent document is in **Appendix B**.

The PTO employs patent examiners, each having a science or technical background, to examine the applications. The examiner evaluates the patent application to determine whether the invention is sufficiently inventive to justify the granting of a patent. The examiner will conduct a search of the prior patents and technical publications (typically the same documents that were discovered during your patent search). The examiner will also review any documents submitted by your company (which are those that your company found in its patent search). The examiner then determines whether the invention is novel and nonobvious over the prior patents and technical publications.

The examiner and your corporate patent counsel "negotiate" the proper scope of protection during this examination period. The examiner's job is to protect the public interest, and thus he negotiates for narrow patent protection so as not to unduly burden public activity. The patent attorney's or agent's interests lie with the client, and thus he negotiates for broad patent claims. Through this process, the patent claims can change considerably from their original form when the patent application was first filed to the final form when a patent is actually granted.

§ 8.15 Duty to Disclose Information Known to Be "Material to Patentability"

Everyone at your company involved in preparation or prosecution of a patent application has a duty of candor and good faith in dealing with the PTO, which includes a duty to disclose to the PTO all information known to that individual to be "material to patentability."[3] The rationale for this is that the public interest is best served, and the most effective patent examination occurs, when the PTO is made aware of all information material to patentability.

Typical information submitted to the PTO includes patents issued before the application filing date, articles published before that date, and any information concerning public use and sale activities. Information is said to be "material to patentability" when (1) a patent examiner could use it to establish that a patent claim is unpatentable (for example, on the basis that the invention lacks novelty or is obvious), or (2) the information is inconsistent with assertions made to the PTO during prosecution. Many of the relevant patents and articles that satisfy this duty are uncovered as a result of the patent search discussed in § 8.13.

Failure to disclose material information that you are aware of at the time of filing, or become aware of during prosecution, will most likely cause your patent to be invalid. The patent regulations clearly state that no patent will be granted on an application for which the duty of disclosure was violated through bad faith or intentional misconduct.

---

[3] 37 C.F.R. § 1.56 (1991).

§ 8.16 Label Products with *Patent Pending*

Once a patent application is filed, your company may label its products with *patent pending*, provided that the products are covered by the subject matter in the patent application. This label provides notice to the world that patent rights in the technology are currently being sought by your company. Labeling products with *patent pending* provides a significant market advantage by keeping competitors guessing as to what features or aspects of the product your company is attempting to protect. Because patent applications are examined in secrecy in the PTO, competitors are precluded from viewing the patent specification and claims to determine the breadth of your company's rights. Competitors are therefore more hesitant to copy a product bearing the patent pending label.

§ 8.17 Foreign Patent Applications

Once your company has filed a United States patent application, it should consider foreign patent protection for the same invention. There is no "international" patent that grants exclusive worldwide rights to an invention. Patent rights are registered and enforced on a nation-by-nation basis. They typically control making, using, or selling of the invention within the borders of the country issuing a patent. These patent rights do not extend outside the country itself. However, because the exclusive rights usually include the right to use and sell an invention, one cannot produce the invention elsewhere and import it into a country where the invention is protected by a patent.

For maximum flexibility in selecting countries within which you wish to file, it is necessary to file your United States application before any public disclosure of the invention details. The reason for emphasizing prompt filing is that almost all foreign countries bar filing of applications on inventions that have been publicly introduced.

The United States and most other countries are members of an international treaty known as the *Paris Convention*. Under this treaty, your company can use its United States filing date for a foreign application so long as the foreign application is filed within one year of the United States filing date. In practice, this allows your company one year to determine whether foreign patent rights are desirable given the market conditions in the foreign countries, without loss of the earliest priority date.

The Paris Convention rules do not, however, trump the patent laws in the individual countries. For many countries, their novelty requirements preclude patentability if there has been a public disclosure, offer of sale, or public use of a product embodying the invention before the United States filing date. Accordingly, if your company has committed any of these acts before its United States filing date, most foreign patent rights will be forfeited. The one-year grace period provided by the Paris Convention will not save a premature, publicly disclosed invention.

Countries that are not a part of the Paris Convention require that their novelty requirements be met at the time the application is filed in their countries, regardless of whether there has been any filing in the applicant's home country (such as the United States). One notable non-Paris Convention country is Taiwan. To file in Taiwan, the Taiwan application must be filed before there has been any sale or public disclosure of the invention anywhere, or the opportunity for patent in Taiwan is lost.

Therefore, when foreign protection is desired, the only safe approach is to (1) file in the United States and in any desired non-Paris Convention countries before any public activity regarding the invention, and (2) complete all foreign filings (for Paris Convention countries) before one year after your United States filing date.

There are three basic methods for initiating foreign filing efforts. The timing associated with each method of filing is illustrated in **Figure 8–2**.[4]

1. File individual national patent applications in selected countries of prime interest. This option involves the greatest immediate effort and expense, but results in more prompt issuance of foreign patents. A disadvantage is that the application will be independently searched and examined in several patent offices, and the results of these procedures might be inconsistent with one another.
2. File a patent application in the European Patent Office (EPO) if patent protection in several of its member nations is desired. Under this method, your company files one application in the EPO (the lower time line in **Figure 8–2**). After being searched and examined, the approved European patent is then translated and registered in those European countries you elect. This step is basically procedural as each country accepts the results of the EPO examination. The advantages of EPO filing are that the application is subjected to only one examination on its merits, all procedures can be conducted in English, and your company can delay the larger expenses of translating the application until examination results are confirmed as positive.
3. File a patent application under the Patent Cooperation Treaty (PCT). The PCT approach (middle time line in **Figure 8–2**) requires a single international application filed through the United States PTO or EPO in the English language. The application is then subjected to an in-depth international search and examination on the merits. This route

---

[4] The explanatory chart in **Figure 8–2** and portions of this section on foreign filing are adapted from works created by Richard St. John. Reprinted with permission.

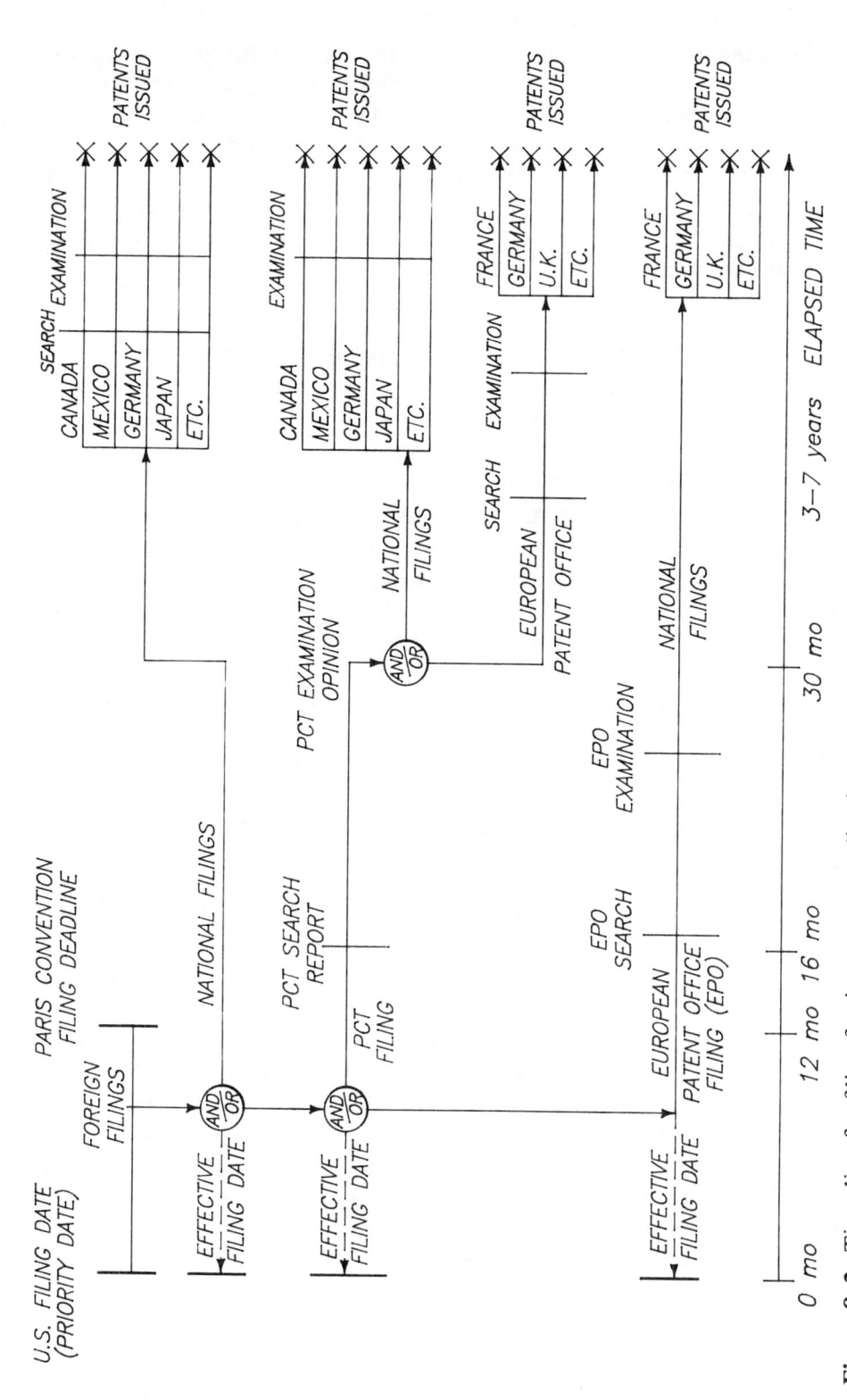

Figure 8-2. Time line for filing foreign patent applications.

buys the most options for subsequent filing. The primary advantage of filing a PCT application is to minimize immediate expense and maintain your options for subsequent foreign filing decisions. These decisions can be postponed for a period up to 30 months from the United States filing date. In the meantime, you can review the search and examination results. The PCT application can then lead to subsequent EPO or national filings after it has been subjected to the international search and examination.

§ 8.18 Is Patent Granted?

After a patent application has been filed, the next step is to wait and see if a patent is granted. This may take several months to several years. If a patent is *not* granted, your company must remove the patent pending label from its products. The subject matter that did not qualify for patent protection should then be maintained as a trade secret if this is practical. The subject matter is still secret and can therefore still qualify as a trade secret because the patent process in the PTO is conducted in confidentiality. Furthermore, you have already decided that the subject matter is valuable and warrants protection. Trade secret protection is the only remaining protection available for the technologically related subject matter.

On the other hand, if a patent is granted, your company should then label its patented products with the new patent number. For example, an appropriate label would be "U.S. Patent No. 5,125,010." This designation provides public notice that your company has patent rights to the technology employed in the product. Marking a product with the patent number notifies a competitor that any unauthorized making, using, or selling of this product is an infringement of your company's rights. Such a marking is not, however, necessary for process patents.

Patent marking is important for infringement purposes. If the product is marked, your company need not actually notify a competitor of its infringing activity to collect damages against it.[5] The patent number label serves as *constructive notice* and the infringing company is presumed to know of your company's patent rights simply because your patent number appears on your product. If infringement litigation ensues, money damages accrue against each manufacture, use, or sale of an infringing competitor, if your own products have been marked with your patent number. Further, if the competitor continues to make, use, or sell the product, it may become (or remain) a "willful infringer," which may result in an assessment of treble damages in an infringement action.

---

[5] 35 U.S.C. § 287 (1988).

More important, however, failure to mark products can result in loss of money damages from an infringing competitor for all infringing sales that occurred before filing your suit. The patent laws state that if your company fails to mark its product with the patent number, no damages shall be recovered by your company in any action for infringement, unless your company can prove that the infringing company was expressly notified of the existence of your patent through some other means and still continued to infringe.[6] If the competitor was never expressly notified and your product was not marked, your company cannot collect money damages for that period of time before the actual notice received by the infringing competitor.

§ 8.19 Maintain and Commercialize Patent Rights

If a patent is granted, your company should then maintain and commercialize its patent rights. To keep a United States patent enforceable for the entire 17-year duration, your company must pay maintenance fees before the 3½-, 7½-, and 11½-year anniversaries after the issue date of the patent.[7]

With a newly granted patent, your attention should be turned toward commercializing the patent. This includes building products under the patent protection, licensing the patent rights, using the patent to bargain for business concessions, and policing for potential infringers. There are many other exploitive practices that take advantage of patent rights. Some of the practices are discussed in **Chapter 4**.

---

[6] 35 U.S.C. § 287 (1988).

[7] 35 U.S.C. § 41 (1991), 35 U.S.C. § 154 (1988); 37 C.F.R. § 1.17 (1991).

CHAPTER 9
CHOOSING BETWEEN TRADE SECRET AND PATENT PROTECTION

§ 9.1   Introductory Story
§ 9.2   Weighing the Factors
§ 9.3   —Is Patent Protection Available?
§ 9.4   —Nature of Subject Matter: Can It Be Kept Secret?
§ 9.5   —Life Expectancy of Technology
§ 9.6   —Patent Protection Has Stricter Legal Requirements
§ 9.7   —Scope of Intellectual Property Rights
§ 9.8   —Subsequent and Independent Discovery by Another
§ 9.9   —Duration of Protection
§ 9.10 —Cost of Obtaining and Maintaining Protection
§ 9.11 —Preservation of Intellectual Property Rights
§ 9.12 —Breadth of Intellectual Property
§ 9.13 —Policing
§ 9.14 —Risk of Losing Intellectual Property Rights
§ 9.15 —Enforcement and Burden in Court
§ 9.16 —Cost of Enforcing
§ 9.17 —Remedies
§ 9.18 —Is Technology Pioneering?
§ 9.19 —Is Market Ready?
§ 9.20 —Licensing
§ 9.21 Checklist of Trade Secret versus Patent Protection Factors

§ 9.1   Introductory Story

In the late nineteenth century, a small company discovered a very novel formula. This discovery posed a major decision for the small company.

Should it patent the new formula or keep the formula a trade secret? The small company guessed right and kept the formula a trade secret. To this day, 100 years later, the public still does not know the ingredients of Coca-Cola®. As a result, Coca-Cola Corporation has become a megacompany with sales all over the world. Had Coca-Cola patented this formula, however, many companies would have been able to copy the formula many decades ago, after the expiration of the patent. The decision to keep the Coca-Cola formula as a trade secret has been invaluable, arguably making it one of the greatest business decisions of all time.

Deciding between patent protection and trade secret protection will rarely, if ever, be as commercially significant as the Coca-Cola decision. Yet, it is important to know the differences between the two types of protection and the advantages of each type.

This chapter focuses on the critical decision of whether to maintain a certain subject matter as a trade secret or to patent it. Subject matter protected by a trade secret must be kept secret, whereas subject matter protected by a patent must be disclosed to the public. The protections are not compatible, and only one type of protection, trade secret or patent, can be selected.

§ 9.2 Weighing the Factors

This chapter examines factors involved in selecting between patent protection and trade secret protection. These factors should familiarize you with the trade-offs between the two types of protections and the advantages and disadvantages of each. Analysis of these factors should also help reveal which type of protection is best suited for a specific situation.

§ 9.3 —Is Patent Protection Available?

Obviously, your company must first determine whether patent protection is available for the subject matter before proceeding through the remaining factors. If it does not satisfy the legal requirements (type of subject matter, novelty, nonobviousness, and utility), the subject matter is not patentable. It might, however, be maintained as a trade secret.

Subject matter that has been used publicly, offered for sale, or described in a printed publication more than one year before your company can file for a patent will no longer qualify for patent protection. Such activity prevents the granting of a patent under § 102 of the patent statute. See **Table 2-1** in **Chapter 2**. If the activity has occurred less than one year before the filing date, your company's foreign patent rights have most likely been lost.

Public use, offers for sale, and publications might not, however, preclude trade secret protection if the activity did not expose the subject matter to the public. For instance, Kentucky Fried Chicken sells chicken made from a secret recipe of 11 herbs and spices every day of the year without exposing Colonel Sanders's trade secret to the world.

§ 9.4 —Nature of Subject Matter: Can It Be Kept Secret?

Often, the nature of the subject matter dictates whether patent protection or trade secret protection should be used. Subject matter that may be easily discovered from examination of the product, or easily reverse engineered, would not fair well under trade secret protection. Competitors could simply purchase the product and quickly discover and expose the new subject matter. Such products should be protected, if at all, with a patent.

On the other hand, inventions that are not easily discoverable or reverse engineered may be better protected as a trade secret. For instance, process inventions may be better protected under trade secret laws because they are difficult to reverse engineer. The process may be used secretly for periods longer than the 17-year patent grant.

§ 9.5 —Life Expectancy of Technology

Rapidly evolving technology may be better suited for trade secret protection than patent protection. Technology that will become obsolete within a period of less than 18 months will not live to see an issued patent due to the relatively long delay in securing protection through the Patent and Trademark Office (PTO). If broad patent claims cannot be drafted to cover both this technology and the improved evolving technology, keeping the technology as a trade secret may be a better use of capital than investing in a patent.

Consider, for example, the rapidly evolving semiconductor memory field. Memory arrangements and processes change very quickly as technology improves. If the subject matter to be protected is something that may be broadly protected, such as a new, high-density memory array arrangement, the subject matter might be better protected with patents. On the other hand, if the subject matter is a new fabrication process for one specific memory layout that will be rendered obsolete in 12 months, the subject matter might be more suited for trade secret protection.

§ 9.6 —Patent Protection Has Stricter Legal Requirements

Patent protection has stricter legal requirements than trade secret protection. **Table 9-1** compares the legal requirements for the two types of protection.

Patent protection has a more limited subject matter requirement and the subject matter must be novel and nonobvious. The combined standards of novelty and nonobviousness are sometimes difficult to satisfy and are the more common reasons given for patent applications being denied. When reviewing subject matter for patent protection, the patent examiner *objectively* applies the novelty and nonobvious requirements, often making those requirements difficult to achieve.

With respect to the legal requirements for trade secret protection, practically all subject matter qualifies for trade secret protection. The subject matter must be minimally novel, but the trade secret novelty requirement is not nearly as strict as the patent novelty requirement. For trade secret protection, the subject matter must also be secret, valuable to the company, and the focus of efforts to maintain its secrecy. Unlike the patent requirements, the trade secret requirements may be *subjectively* defined by the company as to what is secret, valuable, and the subject of affirmative steps. A company can more easily define its own trade secrets and satisfy the trade secret legal requirements than it can satisfy the objective judgment of the patent examiner to meet the patent legal requirements.

§ 9.7 —Scope of Intellectual Property Rights

Patents provide exclusive protection, whereas trade secret protection does not. A patent carries with it the right to exclude others from making, using, or selling the invention in the United States.[1] This right prevents even those who subsequently and independently invent the same invention from making, using, or selling it. In contrast, a trade secret only provides the right to prevent others from stealing a company's proprietary secrets. A trade secret does not prevent others from independently discovering the invention or reverse engineering the product to learn the trade secret.

---

[1] 35 U.S.C. § 154 (1988).

Table 9-1

Comparison of Legal Requirements of Trade Secrets and Patents

Trade Secrets	Patents
Subject matter: Very nonrestrictive. Almost any subject matter qualifies	Subject matter: More restrictive. Only processes, machines, compositions of matter, and improvements thereof
Trade secret novelty: Minimal novelty required	Patent novelty: Higher degree of novelty required
Secrecy	No equivalent requirement
Valuable to your company	No equivalent requirement
Your company must take affirmative steps to keep subject matter secret	No equivalent requirement
No equivalent requirement	Nonobviousness: Very high legal standard
No equivalent requirement	Utility: Almost always satisfied
Company may *subjectively* define its own trade secrets	Patent examiners *objectively* apply standards to determine patentability

§ 9.8 —Subsequent and Independent Discovery by Another

A patent prevents even other would-be "inventors" who have subsequently and independently discovered the same invention from making, using, or selling it. A trade secret, however, does not preclude other independent "inventors" from using the innovation. If fact, a subsequent inventor may be able to obtain patent protection on the innovation and stop the original trade secret owner from making, using, or selling the previously secret innovation.

§ 9.9 —Duration of Protection

A patent has a 17-year life. A trade secret, on the other hand, may last indefinitely, so long as it remains secret. Unfortunately, once a trade secret is released to the public, through accidental disclosure or reverse engineering, trade secret protection terminates. Although the life of an average trade secret is very difficult to approximate (if not impossible), one commentator has estimated that the average life of a trade secret is only approximately three years.[2]

§ 9.10 —Cost of Obtaining and Maintaining Protection

Patents are more expensive to obtain and maintain than trade secrets. To secure a patent, your company's expenses include PTO fees, attorneys' fees, and engineering time (as engineers take time to document the invention and to meet with patent attorneys during preparation of a patent application). Once a patent application is allowed, your company must pay an initial issue fee and maintenance fees before the $3\frac{1}{2}$-, $7\frac{1}{2}$-, and $11\frac{1}{2}$-year anniversaries following the issue date to keep the patent in force.

The expenses involved in obtaining and maintaining trade secret protection are simply the cost of establishing and implementing company policies to guard trade secret information. Trade secrets can therefore be less expensive if the company is organized properly to take affirmative steps to keep the subject matter a secret. Proper company policies and procedures are outlined in **Chapter 13**.

§ 9.11 —Preservation of Intellectual Property Rights

A patent is preserved for its 17-year duration by payment of maintenance payments. A trade secret is preserved by implementing appropriate precautions to keep the subject matter a secret and by a little luck that the trade secret is not legally discovered and exposed.

§ 9.12 —Breadth of Intellectual Property

A patent has a set of claims that specifically define the intellectual property. Your company is entitled to nothing more than the subject matter defined in these claims and its equivalents. In contrast, a trade secret is not specifically limited to a set of claims. A company may claim practically anything as a trade secret so long as the trade secret is valuable to the company, is not generally known to the public, and is conscientiously guarded by

---

[2] P. Leuzzi, *Process Inventions: Trade Secret or Patent Protection*, 66 J. Pat. Off. Soc'y 159, 166 (1984).

the company to keep it secret. This gives the trade secret owner a little more latitude in defining its intellectual property than do the patent requirements.

§ 9.13 —Policing

In general, patent rights are easier to police than trade secret rights. Each patent expressly sets forth in its claims the intellectual property to be protected. For patents on a specific product or component, the patent owner may simply examine products on the market to discern whether the product infringes the claim. For patents on a particular process, policing is a little more difficult because often you are unable to discern what process produced the final product in the market. Yet, the patent statute assists the patent holder in policing process patents. The law presumes that the patented process is infringed if the court finds that the product was likely to be made by the patented process and that the patent holder has made a reasonable effort to determine what process was actually used in the production of the product.[3] Additionally, a process patent can be asserted against a manufacturer of a product sold in the United States, regardless of whether the infringing production occurred in the United States or a foreign country.

A trade secret is usually not defined in any detail. Thus, analyzing products in the market to determine if trade secrets are being used by another company is more difficult. Even if trade secrets are being used, proving that the other company misappropriated the trade secrets from your company is often even more difficult.

§ 9.14 —Risk of Losing Intellectual Property Rights

The risk of losing trade secret rights is much higher than the risk of losing patent rights. Trade secret rights may be lost simply through inadvertent disclosure. One employee's accidental disclosure can irrevocably release a company trade secret to the public. A trade secret may also be lost through independent discovery or reverse engineering.

A patent may be lost only if it is later found to be invalid, or is rendered unenforceable as a matter of law. Once granted, a patent is presumed valid.[4] This presumption, however, may be rebutted in court or through special reexamination proceedings in the PTO.

---

[3] 35 U.S.C. § 295 (1988).
[4] 35 U.S.C. § 282 (1984).

Patent validity is most commonly attacked in three situations: an infringement action, a declaratory judgment action, or a reexamination proceeding. In the infringement action, the party being sued for patent infringement almost always defends on the ground that the patent is invalid. This defense is made independent of an argument that no infringement exists. In the declaratory judgment action, a party accused of infringement may offensively attack the validity of a patent by suing the patent holder to have a court declare the patent invalid. In the reexamination proceeding, a party may attack the validity of a patent by initiating proceedings within the PTO to have a patent reexamined for validity in view of some newly discovered prior art (such as a patent or publication) that was not available to the examiner when the patent was initially examined.[5]

In all three situations, validity is attacked on the theory that the body of knowledge available to the public before the patent was filed would have made the invention covered by the patent known or obvious to those people of ordinary skill in the field of the endeavor. Validity may also be attacked, however, for failure to comply with specific statutory requirements imposed during the patent procurement process, such as a failure to provide an enabling disclosure.

Apart from validity, a patent may be rendered unenforceable as a matter of law. For example, a patent may be unenforceable for misusing the patent in some manner or for failure to enforce the patent rights against a known infringer for a period of time.

§ 9.15 —Enforcement and Burden in Court

Patent law is governed by federal statute and is fairly uniform throughout the United States. In patent litigation, the patent is presumed valid. The patent owner is not required initially to prove that the patent is valid. Instead, the accused infringer has the burden of proving that a patent is *in*valid. The patent owner only needs to prove that the patent has been infringed.

Trade secrets are governed by state common law, which is not nationally uniform but varies from state to state. Trade secret owners have the initial, added burden of proving that a trade secret exists. Once they overcome this threshold burden, they must then prove that the trade secret was improperly taken or misappropriated.

---

[5] Technically, the "presumption of patent validity" does not attach during the reexamination proceeding in the PTO. *In re* Yamamoto, 740 F.2d 1569, 222 U.S.P.Q. (BNA) 934 (Fed. Cir. 1984). The rationale is that the patentee has the opportunity to amend or change the claims, and thus, no presumption should be afforded to the claims.

§ 9.16 —Cost of Enforcing

If an infringing company refuses to take a license, or the patent owner chooses not to license, enforcement against an infringer usually involves litigation. Enforcement of patent rights is generally expensive. The complexities of the technology, the intricacies of patent law, and the enormous amount of discovery necessary to uncover the relevant facts all contribute to a long and expensive litigation. Litigation can take years, and a party may incur substantial expense to argue whether the patent is valid and whether the infringer's product infringes the patent.

Trade secrets are generally cheaper to enforce. One writer estimated that litigation for a complex technological trade secret action is one-third to two-thirds less costly than a similar complex technological case involving a patent.[6]

§ 9.17 —Remedies

A patent owner may obtain an injunction to stop infringing activity.[7] The patent holder may also sue for damages to compensate for lost profits and, at the very least, is entitled to damages amounting to a reasonable royalty.[8] Furthermore, if the infringing company is found to have knowingly and willfully infringed the patent, the court may require this company to pay attorneys' fees and up to three times the actual damages.

For trade secret remedies, once the trade secret owner demonstrates the existence of a trade secret, actual or, in some circumstances, threatened theft of the trade secret may be enjoined.[9] In addition, the trade secret owner may sue for damages resulting from the actual loss caused by theft of the trade secret. Unlike patent owners who are guaranteed a reasonable royalty award against infringers, however, trade secret owners are generally not statutorily guaranteed a damage minimum.

§ 9.18 —Is Technology Pioneering?

If the innovation constitutes a pioneering technology, you should lean toward patent protection. Patent claims can be considerably broad, covering basic features of this pioneering technology. With broad claims, technology developed by others based upon your company's patented pioneering technology will most likely infringe your company's patent rights.

---

[6] 12A R. Milgrim, Business Organizations: Milgrim on Trade Secrets § 9.03[7] (1990).

[7] 35 U.S.C. § 283 (1952).

[8] 35 U.S.C. § 284 (1952).

[9] Unif. Trade Secrets Act § 2.

Consider, for example, the value of obtaining the initial patent on the first television picture tube, or the basic transistor structure, or aspartame (a sugar substitute).

On the other hand, if the innovation is merely an improvement in a crowded technological field, patent protection may not be as valuable. Hence, trade secret protection may be a more economical route in this instance.

§ 9.19 —Is Market Ready?

If the market is not ready for the technology, you may not wish to seek patent protection immediately. Technological innovations that are far superior to current market products may outlive the 17-year patent life before the market catches up. There are many reasons why the market lags technology. For instance, the new technology may initially be too expensive, and cheaper alternatives are available. Products (new or old) that are necessary to support the new technology may not be adaptable to it. The end user may not be sufficiently educated to use the new technology without additional instruction.

If the market is not ready, your company may wish to maintain the new technology as a trade secret and continue to develop and improve the technology. When the market catches up, your company can then seek patent protection. The danger of waiting is that others might be able to secure patent rights ahead of you because your "secret" invention may not preclude the patentability of someone else's "reinvention."

§ 9.20 —Licensing

Both trade secrets and patents may be licensed to other companies. A brief review of **Chapter 4** will remind you of the many reasons for licensing intellectual property. There is, however, one notable difference between trade secret licenses and patent licenses. Patents may be licensed for a duration that cannot extend past the 17-year life of the patent.[10] On the other hand, trade secrets may be licensed for an indefinite duration, even if the secret is later exposed to the world.

The Listerine case[11] illustrates the distinction. In this case, Dr. J.J. Lawrence, the inventor of Listerine®, licensed the secret formula to Warner-

---

[10] Brulotte v. Thys Co., 379 U.S. 29, 143 U.S.P.Q. (BNA) 264 (1964).

[11] Warner-Lambert Pharmaceutical Co. v. John J. Reynolds, Inc., 178 F. Supp. 655, 123 U.S.P.Q. (BNA) 431 (S.D.N.Y. 1959).

Lambert Pharmaceutical Company in 1881 in exchange for a royalty from the sales of Listerine. By 1949, the formula was common knowledge to the public, as it had been published in many professional journals. Warner-Lambert sued the heirs of J.J. Lawrence for a judgment, declaring that it was no longer obligated to pay royalties for a trade secret that had become known to the public. The court held in favor of Lawrence's heirs and ordered Warner-Lambert to continue paying for the use of Listerine so long as it markets the product. The court stated:

> The parties are free to contract with respect to a secret formula or trade secret in any manner which they determine for their own best interests. A secret formula or trade secret may remain secret indefinitely. It may be discovered by someone else almost immediately after the agreement is entered into. Whoever discovers it for himself by legitimate means is entitled to its use.
>
> But that does not mean that one who acquires a secret formula or a trade secret through a valid and binding contract is then enabled to escape from an obligation to which he bound himself simply because the secret is discovered by a third party or by the general public.... One who acquires a trade secret or secret formula takes it subject to the risk that there be a disclosure.[12]

We can assume from the court's decision that, today, over 100 years after the trade secret license was entered into, Warner-Lambert is still paying for the use of Listerine. Therefore, trade secret licenses need not be limited in duration as are patent licenses.

As a practical matter, most licensees of trade secrets (the companies who take a license in the secret technology) are aware of the consequences imposed by the Listerine case. Therefore, modern licensees are most assuredly not going to allow an indefinite term on the licenses they take. Nevertheless, that term may be longer than the 17-year term of a patent.

§ 9.21 Checklist of Trade Secret versus Patent Protection Factors

Choosing between trade secret protection and patent protection is often very difficult. Each affords a different type of protection, and each has its own advantages. We have examined numerous factors that should assist you in selecting one type over the other. **Table 9–2** summarizes these factors. You may quickly reference this chart when considering the trade-offs between patent and trade secret protection.

---

[12] Warner-Lambert Pharmaceutical Co. v. John J. Reynolds, Inc., 178 F. Supp. 655, 665–66, 123 U.S.P.Q. (BNA) 431, 439 (S.D.N.Y. 1959).

Table 9-2
Trade Secret Protection versus Patent Protection

Is Patent Protection Available?

Factors: If invention was on sale, described in printed publication, or used publicly more than one year before a patent application is to be filed, patent protection is *NOT* available. Review Chapter 2 and check with your patent attorney for additional prohibitions against patentability.

If patent protection is available, weigh the following factors:

Trade Secret	Patent
Subject matter can be publicly used or sold so long as not exposed to public without loss of trade secret rights.	Public use or sale of subject matter may bar patentability and preclude patent rights.
The subject matter is capable of being kept secret.	The subject matter is capable of being discovered or reverse engineered.
Life expectancy of technology is very short.	Technology is expected to be around for a reasonable length of time.
Easier to satisfy the legal requirements for trade secret protection.	More difficult to satisfy the legal requirements for patent protection.
Protects against others who improperly acquire the trade secret. Does *not* protect against independent discovery or reverse engineering.	A patent excludes others from making, using, or selling the invention in the U.S.
A trade secret does not preclude a subsequent inventor from obtaining a patent on the secret innovation and enforcing it against the original trade secret owner.	A patent prevents even a subsequent independent inventor from making, using, or selling the invention in the U.S.
A trade secret can last indefinitely.	A patent extends for 17 years.
Trade secret rights are less expensive to obtain and maintain.	Patent rights are more expensive to obtain and maintain.
Must take affirmative steps to preserve trade secrets.	Must pay maintenance fees to preserve patent.
Intellectual property not easily defined.	Patent claims define the scope of intellectual property.
Difficult to police for theft of trade secrets.	Easier to police for infringers.

(continued)

Table 9–2

continued

Trade Secret	Patent
Trade secret rights can be lost more easily through inadvertent disclosure or independent discovery.	Patent rights are lost only when the patent is held invalid or unenforceable by a federal court, or the patent owner fails to pay maintenance fees.
A trade secret owner has both the burden of proving that the trade secret exists and that it was stolen.	A patent owner does not have to prove validity because the patent is presumed to be valid. The patent owner only has to prove infringement.
Less expensive to enforce trade secret rights.	More expensive to enforce patent rights.
A trade secret owner may seek an injunction, or recover damages and attorneys' fees.	A patent owner may seek an injunction, or recover damages (not less than a reasonable royalty) and attorneys' fees.
Innovation is in crowded technological field.	Innovation is pioneering technology.
Market is not ready for new technology.	Market is ready for new technology.
Trade secrets can be licensed for any time duration.	Patents cannot be licensed beyond 17 years.

CHAPTER 10

IS COPYRIGHT PROTECTION APPROPRIATE?

§ 10.1 Copyright Phase of Protection Analysis Model
§ 10.2 Does Subject Matter Satisfy Legal Requirements for Copyright Protection?
§ 10.3 Place Copyright Notice on the Work
§ 10.4 Is Work to Be Published?
§ 10.5 Advantages of Registration
§ 10.6 Commercialize Rights Afforded by Copyright

§ 10.1 Copyright Phase of Protection Analysis Model

The next phase in the Protection Analysis Model is to determine whether the subject matter qualifies for copyright protection. The model is illustrated in full in **Figure 5–1** in **Chapter 5**, and the copyright phase is reproduced as **Figure 10–1**. **Sections 10.2** through **10.6** correspond to the flowchart boxes in the copyright phase of the model.

§ 10.2 Does Subject Matter Satisfy Legal Requirements for Copyright Protection?

Subject matter is protectable under copyright law if the requirements listed in **Table 10–1** are met.

The kind of subject matter qualifying for copyright protection may be technical, such as computer software, or nontechnical, such as a promotional brochure or an instruction manual. Other examples of copyrightable subject matter include package labeling and appearance, newspaper or radio advertisements, newsletters, engineering drawings, warranties, and catalogs. The requirements of **Table 10–1** are discussed in greater depth in **Chapter 2**.

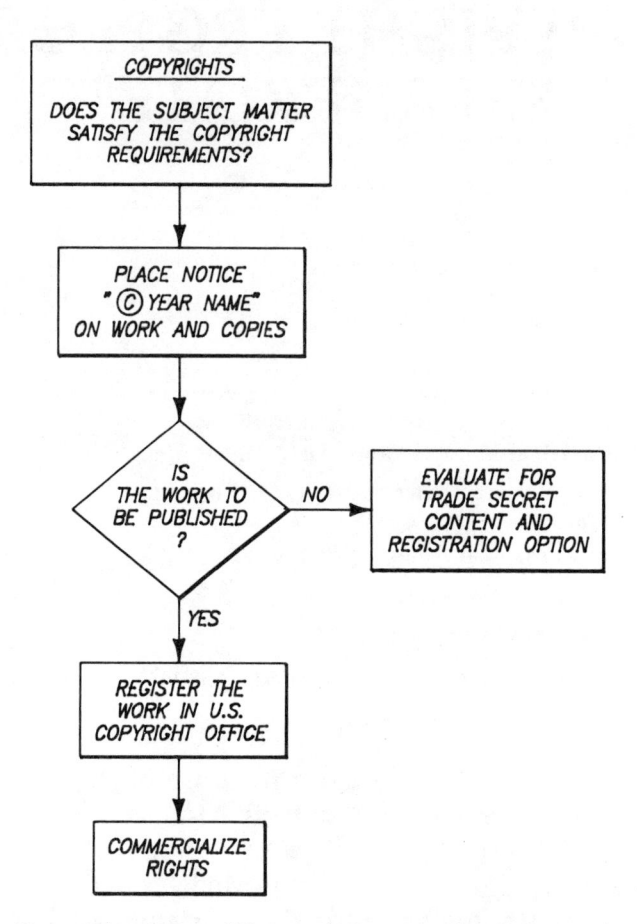

Figure 10–1. Copyright phase of Protection Analysis Model.

Table 10–1

Copyright Requirements

---

1. The subject matter must be proper "copyrightable" subject matter, which includes literary works, pictorial, graphic and sculptural works, audiovisual works, and sound recordings.
2. The subject matter must be an original work.
3. The subject matter must be fixed in some tangible form of expression, such as written down on paper or recorded on a cassette tape.

---

§ 10.3 Place Copyright Notice on the Work

If the subject matter satisfies the copyright legal requirements, your company should put a copyright notice on the work and any copies thereof regardless of whether your company eventually registers the work at the United States Copyright Office. A copyright notice informs the public that your company has rights in the work. Two common forms of copyright notice include:

© 1991 COMPANY, INC.

or

Copyright 1991 COMPANY, INC.

Under the copyright laws that became effective in 1989, copyright notice is not required by law to preserve the copyright.[1] However, placing the notice on works and copies is highly advisable. The notice helps a copyright owner in litigation by preventing a defendant from mitigating damages by claiming that he "innocently infringed" the work because he was not aware that the work was copyrighted. Accordingly, notice should appear on every company document created, including engineering drawings, pamphlets, catalogs, product descriptions, newsletters, art work, advertisements, packaging designs, labeling, and manuals.

Notice is also important if the works are to be disclosed to third parties during business negotiations. During the negotiations, one company may need to disclose its engineering drawings and documentation to a partner company. All such documents should carry a copyright notice along with a written notice of the proprietary or trade secret status of the information contained within them.

§ 10.4 Is Work to Be Published?

A copyrighted work is "published" when it is freely disseminated to the world without restrictions. The kinds of works that are commonly published include software, operational manuals, instruction manuals, warranties, promotional brochures, packaging design and labeling, television commercials, and newspaper advertisements. If the work is to be published, it should be registered in the United States Copyright Office for the reasons set forth in § 10.5.

Some works are not intended for publication. Such works include engineering drawings, manuals on corporate procedures, and internal reports. Although each work is "copyrightable," your company most likely does not want the world to see its drawings, manuals, and reports. Accordingly, you should reevaluate the work for trade secret content. Engineering drawings, for example, might contain information that is also protectable as a trade secret.

---

[1] 17 U.S.C. § 401(a) (1988).

The fact that a work is not published does not preclude it from being registered in the United States Copyright Office. Unpublished works are registrable. It is prudent, however, not to register any materials that might disclose valuable trade secret information.

§ 10.5 Advantages of Registration

Copyright protection is secured immediately upon fixing the expression in some form of medium, such as writing words on paper. Registration of the copyrighted work is a separate and distinct procedure. It is not a condition for copyright protection.[2] There are, however, many advantages to registering a copyright:

1. Registration is required to bring an infringement suit in a federal court under the copyright statute.[3] Registration may, however, be made immediately before commencement of the infringement suit.
2. A certificate of registration constitutes evidence that the copyright is valid so long as registration is made within five years of the first publication.[4] This means that in a copyright infringement suit, your copyright will be presumed valid by the court and the infringing party will then have the burden of demonstrating that your copyright is not valid. This is often an impossible task. Placing the burden on the infringing party is a significant procedural advantage during litigation.
3. Registration enables copyright owners to seek certain remedies for infringement. An owner of a registered copyright can seek discretionary statutory damages and attorneys' fees in addition to normal proven damages.[5] In fact, statutory damages are available even if the registered copyright owner was not damaged or cannot prove damage by sale of the infringing copies. Such statutory damages and fees are not available to an owner of an unregistered work.
4. Registration is very inexpensive and easy. It is nearly impossible to err by registering your company's more important original works.

As a general rule, your company might wish to avoid registering documents or software that contain any significant trade secret information because that information will be publicly disclosed and thus voided of its

---

[2] 17 U.S.C. § 408(a) (1988).
[3] 17 U.S.C. § 411(a) (1990).
[4] 17 U.S.C. § 410(c) (1976).
[5] 17 U.S.C. § 412 (1990).

trade secret protection. The Copyright Office does make some provisions for works that contain trade secret subject matter. For instance, your company can register a computer program containing trade secrets by simply omitting the portions of code containing trade secrets.[6]

To register a copyrighted work, you or your legal counsel must simply fill out a form provided by the United States Copyright Office, a branch of the Library of Congress in Washington, D.C. Different forms are available for different types of works. For example, a form for literary works is different from a form for sound recordings. One such form for a literary work is shown in **Appendix D**. To register the work, you submit the appropriate completed form along with a minimal registration fee and one or two copies of the protected material to the Copyright Office.

§ 10.6 Commercialize Rights Afforded by Copyright

As the final step of the copyright phase, your company should seek to commercialize its copyright property. Copyrighted works can be assigned, licensed, and used in negotiations, as discussed generally in **Chapter 4**. Copyrighted works are another integral part in a portfolio of intellectual property that enhances the economic strength of your company.

---

[6] United States Copyright Office, Circular 61 (1989).

CHAPTER 11
IS TRADEMARK PROTECTION APPROPRIATE?

§ 11.1 Trademark Phase of Protection Analysis Model
§ 11.2 Does Subject Matter Satisfy Legal Requirements for Trademark Protection?
§ 11.3 Conduct Trademark Search
§ 11.4 Is Trademark Registration Desirable?
§ 11.5 Checklist of Registration Factors
§ 11.6 Registering Trademark
§ 11.7 —Intent to Use Application
§ 11.8 —Regular Application for Mark in Use
§ 11.9 When Trademark Registration Is Not Allowed
§ 11.10 —Select New Mark
§ 11.11 —Keep Mark and Generate Secondary Meaning
§ 11.12 Trademark Registration Is Allowed
§ 11.13 —Intent to Use
§ 11.14 —Mark Is in Use
§ 11.15 Maintain, Properly Use, and Commercialize Trademark

§ 11.1 Trademark Phase of Protection Analysis Model

The last phase in the Protection Analysis Model is to determine whether the subject matter is suitable for trademark protection. The model is illustrated in **Figure 5–1** in **Chapter 5**, with the trademark phase reproduced as **Figure 11–1**. Sections 11.2 through 11.15 correspond to the flowchart boxes in the trademark phase of the model.

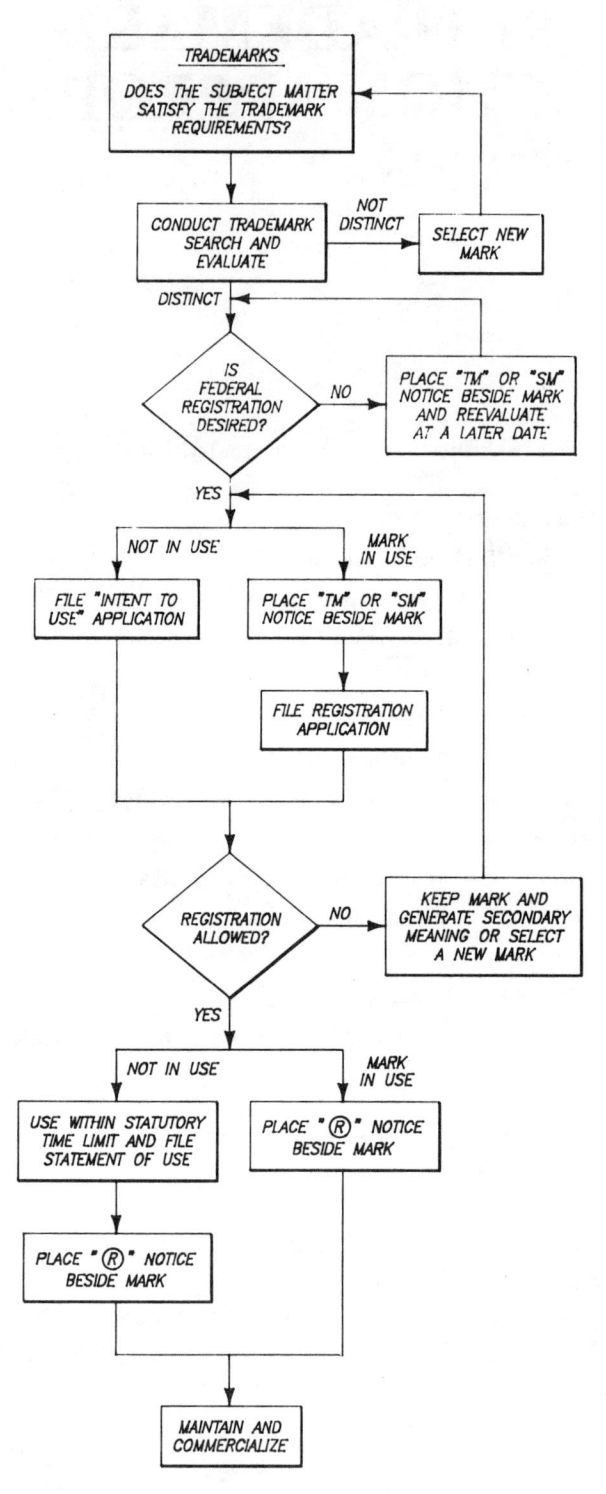

Figure 11-1. Trademark phase of Protection Analysis Model.

§ 11.2 Does Subject Matter Satisfy Legal Requirements for Trademark Protection?

Subject matter qualifies for trademark protection if it satisfies the requirements listed in **Table 11-1**.

When you are initially reviewing a new word, slogan, or logo for potential use as a trademark, consider first the requirements numbered 4 and 5. With respect to requirement 5, you should not seek federal registration on a mark that is identical or confusingly similar to another registered mark for the same product or service. The United States Patent and Trademark Office (PTO) and the owner of the other mark will most certainly oppose this registration.

With respect to requirement 4, a distinctive mark is one that is unique with respect to a particular product or service. **Table 11-2**, a reprint of **Table 2-4** in **Chapter 2**, illustrates the "spectrum of distinctiveness."

If your proposed mark falls into the fanciful, arbitrary, or suggestive category, it is inherently distinctive and immediately registrable (assuming there is no confusion with another's mark). If your mark is merely descriptive of the product or service, it is not inherently distinctive and must acquire *secondary meaning* in the marketplace before it can satisfy the distinctiveness requirement. A mark acquires secondary meaning when, over time, consumers have grown to recognize the mark as identifying a particular company's products.

A full discussion of each trademark requirement is provided in **Chapter 2**.

§ 11.3 Conduct Trademark Search

If you determine that a mark satisfies the legal requirements for trademark protection, your company should then conduct a trademark search to discover whether the mark is already being used by another party. Trademark searches typically cover federal and state registered marks and should be extended when possible to encompass marks that are in use but not registered. Such searches usually comprise electronic searching on a computer database listing registered, pending, and abandoned trademarks. Alternatively, the trademark records at the PTO can be examined by an experienced trademark searcher.

Trademark searches seek to uncover identical or similar marks with respect to spelling, phonetics, and appearance. They also reveal who owns the marks and the class and nature of goods or services in which the marks are being used. Trademark searches, therefore, provide a good indication

Table 11-1

Trademark Requirements

1. The subject matter must be "registrable." Words, slogans, packaging designs and shapes, and logos are proper subject matter.
2. The mark must be used, or intended to be used in the near future, in interstate commerce.
3. When used in interstate commerce, the words, slogans, or symbols must be affixed to the goods in such a manner that the consumer can easily view the mark. This requirement is inherently met when the shape itself is the trademark.
4. The mark must be either inherently distinctive or have acquired distinctiveness through secondary meaning.
5. The mark must not be identical or confusingly similar to another mark used on similar types of goods or services.
6. The mark must be nonfunctional.

Table 11-2

Distinctiveness Spectrum

Category	Definition	Examples
Fanciful	Words that are made up	EXXON or KODAK
Arbitrary	Marks that are real words, but have no relation to the goods	APPLE for computers TIDE for clothes detergent
Suggestive	Words that tend to reveal or hint at an attribute of the goods	COPPERTONE for sun-tan lotion RAPID-SHAVE for shaving cream
Descriptive	Marks that describe an attribute or characteristic of the goods	HOLIDAY INN for motels YELLOW PAGES for phone directory
Generic	Not really marks, but rather words that are the name of the goods themselves	*Tennis shoes* for tennis shoes *Watches* for watches

of whether your company can register its new mark for a particular product line or service area.

It is advisable to conduct a trademark search before using the mark. In this manner, you can determine whether the mark is likely to receive registration before your company spends a large amount of money on marketing efforts using the particular mark. By conducting a search at this early stage, your company will have flexibility to switch to another mark

§ 11.4 IS REGISTRATION DESIRABLE?

if this becomes advisable. Additionally, your company will not begin building customer recognition and goodwill in a particular mark only to switch to a different mark after determining that the first mark is not registrable.

If a trademark search uncovers very similar marks in the same class of goods, your company should consider selecting an alternative mark. Very similar marks registered with respect to related products or services will most likely preclude registration of your mark.

§ 11.4 Is Trademark Registration Desirable?

Federally registered trademarks provide companies with the most comprehensive protection. However, trademarks need not be federally registered. State registration, or simply no registration at all (so-called common law protection), are available alternatives. State trademark protection is bounded by the state lines and will not protect your company's mark in other states. Common law (unregistered) trademarks are protected only within the market area in which you are using your mark before the public.

Federal registration is therefore the preferred avenue of protection because nationwide rights attach to this registration. The following factors should be considered to determine whether federal registration is beneficial to your company:

1. Exclusive use. A federal trademark gives your company the exclusive right to use the protected name or symbol throughout the entire United States. This right to the entire United States exists even though your company sells its products or services only in a small geographical region of the United States. Registration also provides constructive notice to all other companies of these exclusive, nationwide rights. The only exception to these rights is a situation in which a regional company has been using the mark continuously before the time you register. The PTO or the courts will place a boundary around this regional company and permit it to keep using the mark within this boundary, but give your company exclusive rights within the remaining territory in the United States.[1]

2. Ownership evidence. A federally registered trademark is evidence that the registrant owns the mark and has an exclusive right to use the mark in commerce.[2] This means that in any trademark litigation, your company is presumed to be the owner of the registered trademark, and the opposing party has the burden to prove otherwise.

---

[1] 15 U.S.C. § 1115(b)(5) (1988); Lanham Act § 33(b)(5).
[2] 15 U.S.C. § 1057(b) (1988); Lanham Act § 7(b).

3. Validity evidence. A federally registered trademark that has been used in interstate commerce for five consecutive years is "conclusive" evidence that (1) the mark is valid, (2) the registrant owns the mark, and (3) the registrant has the exclusive right to use the mark in commerce.[3]

4. Effect on other companies' selection of trademarks. A registered trademark often deters other companies from using the same or a confusingly similar mark. Other companies wish to own distinctive marks for the same reasons that you do. One advantage to distinctive marks is that they can be registered more quickly. When another company is considering the use of a new mark for a product or campaign, it typically conducts a trademark search to see if the mark can be registered. If relevant, your company's registered mark should be uncovered during the search. The other company might then conclude that your mark is too similar and that it should choose an alternative mark to avoid problems with registration, opposition by your company, or infringement concerns.

    A federally registered trademark, therefore, deters another company from using your company's mark. This is an intangible benefit that can never be fully measured because your company will rarely know that another company has contemplated and then rejected the use of a similar mark.

5. Reserve mark for later use. Under present federal trademark laws, your company can reserve a mark for future use by filing an *intent to use* application in the PTO. The mark can be reserved for up to three years. This allows your company sufficient time to determine the feasibility of a mark, and to coordinate announcement activities before a launch of a new product under the reserved trademark. Indeed, companies commonly reserve several potential marks for the same product, and then later select the desired mark.

6. Extending a company mark. As your company develops goodwill in a federally registered mark for a particular product, it might be able to extend the mark to cover a new product or service in lieu of developing and registering a new mark. This technique saves money by profiting from the goodwill that is already established in an old mark. For example, the trademark ARM & HAMMER has been extended from baking soda products to detergents.

7. Intended duration of using the mark. If you intend to use a mark indefinitely, trademark registration is advisable. Over time, trademarks may become very valuable in terms of customer goodwill.

---

[3] 15 U.S.C. § 1115(b) (1988); Lanham Act § 33(b).

For example, the trademark CADILLAC, by itself, may add a premium to the price tag of any automobile or related products sold under that name. On the other hand, if the mark is intended to identify fad products that are to be manufactured for a single season, your company may choose to forgo the expense of registration. In this situation, your company can simply use a TM notice beside the mark.

A trademark should be obtained for new campaign themes or slogans that are expected to be the framework for a series of advertising spots. For instance, American Express Company has registered the familiar campaign slogan, "Don't Leave Home Without It."

8. Intended region of use. As discussed, your company can obtain state registration or rely on common law trademark rights instead of federal registration. State or common law rights are not as comprehensive as federal registration, but do sometimes afford adequate protection for a small business whose region of use is geographically small. If, for instance, your company intends to use a slogan only within a particular state (for example, to take advantage of a state university motto or mascot known primarily by state residents), then it may wish to forgo federal registration in favor of state registration or common law rights.

§ 11.5 Checklist of Registration Factors

Federal trademark registration maximizes your company's rights in a mark. **Table 11–3** summarizes the factors to be considered when determining whether federal trademark protection makes sense from a business perspective.

If you decide that federal registration is not appropriate at this time, but you still wish to use the mark for your products or services, a trademark notice, TM (for products) or SM (for services), should be placed beside the mark at all times, beginning with the very first use of the mark. Your company establishes rights in the mark simply by using it. The trademark notice TM or SM informs the public that your company is using the mark as its own and warns others that your company intends to protect its rights in the mark.

To use the TM notice, your company simply places TM beside the mark on the product or package in the same location that the federal registration notice ® will eventually go, such as COMPANY MARK™. If the trademark is for services, the SM notice should be used and similarly placed.

As your company continues to use the mark, you should reevaluate at a later date whether federal registration has become appropriate. For the reasons listed, federal registration provides the most comprehensive form

Table 11-3
Factors to Be Considered When Determining Whether to Federally Register a Trademark

1. Federal registration provides exclusive use of the mark throughout the United States.
2. Federal registration is evidence of ownership of the trademark.
3. Federal registration is evidence that the trademark is valid.
4. Federal registration affects the selection of trademarks by other companies.
5. Your company can reserve federal trademarks for future use through an *intent to use* application process.
6. Can your company extend an existing trademark in lieu of creating and registering a new mark?
7. Does your company intend to use the mark for a long time, or for a minimal time?
8. Does your company intend to use the mark in a large or small geographical region?

of trademark protection. There is, however, a risk in waiting to seek federal registration. While you wait, another party may attempt to register the same or a similar mark before you do. The federal trademark laws award rights to the first party to register the mark, even though that party might not have been the first to use the mark. Accordingly, be careful that you do not delay too long before seeking federal protection.

§ 11.6 Registering Trademark

To secure federal trademark protection, an applicant must file a trademark application with the PTO. Trademark examiners employed by the PTO compare the mark with registered trademarks to determine if the mark is already registered or if the mark is confusingly similar to a registered mark. The examiner also makes a determination as to whether the mark is too descriptive to be registered as a distinctive trademark.

If the examiner approves the mark for registration, it is published in the *Official Gazette* (a book published by the PTO) for opposition by other members of the public, such as prior trademark owners, who may feel that they would be damaged by the proposed registration. These parties have 30 days from the publication date to file for opposition. If no opposition is made, a certificate of registration is issued to the applicant, thereby giving the applicant trademark protection in the mark. The application process differs slightly depending upon whether your company has already begun using the trademark.

§ 11.7 —Intent to Use Application

If the mark is not in use, you should file an *intent to use* application that will allow you to reserve the mark until your company actually uses it. This application contains (1) a statement of an intent to use the mark in the future, (2) a description of the goods or services with which the mark will be used, (3) a drawing of the mark, and (4) a registration fee. Assuming the mark is registrable, this intent to use process will reserve the mark for a period of six months, which can be extended up to three years upon payment of extension charges.

§ 11.8 —Regular Application for Mark in Use

A regular trademark application is submitted if the mark is already in use. This application contains (1) a date when the mark was first used, (2) a description of the goods or services with which the mark will be used, (3) a drawing of the mark, and (4) a registration fee.

Your company should also begin placing a trademark notice, TM (for products) or SM (for services), beside the mark once it begins using the mark, while awaiting federal registration. The waiting period can vary in length depending upon the similarity of existing registered marks and the distinctiveness of the mark your company is seeking to register.

§ 11.9 When Trademark Registration Is Not Allowed

The trademark examiner evaluates the mark for registration. Typically, a registration is rejected on one of two grounds: (1) the proposed mark was too descriptive of the goods or services (the mark was not sufficiently distinctive), or (2) the proposed mark was too similar to an existing registered mark.

If the examiner determines that the mark is not registrable for either of these reasons, your company has two general options. First, it can select an entirely new mark. Second, it can develop evidence that the mark is distinctive as having acquired secondary meaning. A mark acquires secondary meaning when, over time, consumers have grown to recognize the mark as identifying a particular company's goods.

§ 11.10 —Select New Mark

Selecting a new mark is often the less expensive option. Presumably, with the results of a search and a failed registration attempt in hand, the next selected mark will be more distinctive and more different than the existing registered marks. Sidney Diamond, a former United States Commissioner of Patents and Trademarks, offers the following tips for selecting a trademark:

1. Do not copy another's mark, even innocently.
2. Do not be too obvious; rather, be distinctive.
3. Do not be descriptive.
4. Do not use a family name.
5. Do not use a geographically descriptive name.
6. Try to coin a new word.[4]

After selecting a new mark, you should again attempt to federally register it, presumably with more success.

§ 11.11 —Keep Mark and Generate Secondary Meaning

If you decide to keep the mark, your objective is to generate secondary meaning to make the mark distinctive. Your company must continue to use the mark and advertise and promote its products or services under this mark until consumers identify the products or services as originating from your company. Once you feel that the mark has achieved secondary meaning, you can reapply for federal registration. The factors that the PTO or a court will use to determine whether your mark has acquired secondary meaning include:

1. Direct consumer testimony of distinctiveness
2. Consumer surveys
3. Advertising and sales expenditures
4. Length and manner of use of the trademark
5. Exclusivity of use.[5]

The process of generating secondary meaning can be very expensive and time consuming.

---

[4] S. Diamond, Trademark Problems and How to Avoid Them 31–43 (rev. ed. 1981).

[5] J. Gilson, Trademark Protection and Practice § 2.09[5] (1990).

§ 11.12 Trademark Registration Is Allowed

Once a trademark examiner allows the federal registration, and you survive the opposition period, your remaining duties again differ slightly depending upon whether your company has already begun using the trademark.

§ 11.13 —Intent to Use

If the mark has yet to be used, you must use the mark within a prescribed statutory period. Presently, you have six months from the date that the mark is indicated as allowed by the PTO,[6] but this period can be extended up to three years.[7] Once your company begins using the mark, you must file a Statement of Use and submit actual labels or photographs demonstrating that the mark is being used in interstate commerce. Your company can then use the federal trademark notice ® beside the mark, as discussed in § 11.14.

§ 11.14 —Mark Is in Use

Once your company receives federal registration of a mark that it has been using, it should begin placing the federal registration notice ® beside the mark. For example, the mark would look like COMPANY MARK®. The federal registration notice ® informs the public that your company has a federally registered mark and the rights that attach to such a mark.

§ 11.15 Maintain, Properly Use, and Commercialize Trademark

Once your company begins using a mark, it must take proper precautions to maintain rights in the trademark. Your company must continue to *use* the mark. A long lapse in using the mark may weaken your company's rights in the mark, or worse, may indicate that your company has abandoned its mark. Another company can then take the unused abandoned mark as its own.

Proper use of the trademark entails using the mark as an adjective when describing your company's goods. *Never* let the trademark describe the

---

[6] 15 U.S.C. § 1051(d)(1) (1988); Lanham Act § 1(d)(1).
[7] 15 U.S.C. § 1051(d)(2) (1988); Lanham Act § 1 (d)(2).

goods themselves. This practice helps prevent your company's trademarks from becoming generic, a fate that has victimized previously strong trademarks such as *aspirin, zipper,* and *shredded wheat.*

To illustrate how to use a trademark as an adjective, Nike Corporation makes and sells NIKE® brand basketball shoes. It does not make "NIKES." Here, Nike Corporation uses the trademark NIKE as an adjective to describe the generic goods, basketball shoes. The trademark does not become the noun (the name for the generic goods).

Your company should follow this practice in its promotional brochures, advertising, and other company literature. Your company must also monitor other media spots (such as magazine articles regarding your company's products) to ensure that others properly use your company's mark.

If your company receives federal registration, it must pay maintenance fees to maintain the federal registration. Five years after a federal registration is issued, your company must pay a fee and file a declaration of continued use. Additionally, trademark registrations must be renewed every 10 years. A fee is required for each renewal.

Once your company selects a mark, it must actively exploit the mark. First and foremost, your company must *use* the trademark. Second, your company must actively oppose marks that are similar to your company's marks. As mentioned with reference to filing a trademark application, each mark is published in the *Official Gazette* for a 30 day opposition period during which other parties may oppose it. Your company must continually scan each edition of the *Official Gazette* for similar marks and oppose the registration of such marks.

A third way to exploit your company's trademark rights is to police for trademark infringers. Your company must ensure that other companies do not use identical or similar marks on similar goods. Allowing other companies to use even similar marks might diminish the strength of your company's marks.

Trademarks may also be exploited through licensing agreements or other business arrangements, as discussed in **Chapter 4**.

PART III
INTELLECTUAL PROPERTY MANAGEMENT STRATEGIES

CHAPTER 12

WHY COMPANY INTELLECTUAL PROPERTY POLICIES AND PROCEDURES ARE NECESSARY

§ 12.1   Introduction
§ 12.2   Trade Secret Laws
§ 12.3   Satisfying Secrecy and Affirmative Steps Requirements
§ 12.4   Preventing Unnecessary Loss of Trade Secrets
§ 12.5   —Inadvertent Disclosure
§ 12.6   —Former Employee and Innocent New Employer
§ 12.7   —Trade Secret Matters in Business Relationships
§ 12.8   Patent Laws
§ 12.9   Failing to Satisfy Novelty Requirement: Self-inflicted Bars to Patentability
§ 12.10 —Printed Publication Bar
§ 12.11 —Public Use Bar
§ 12.12 —On-Sale Bar
§ 12.13 —Experimentation Incident to Public Use or Sale Activity
§ 12.14 —Loss of Foreign Patent Rights
§ 12.15 First Inventorship
§ 12.16 Checklist

§ 12.1   Introduction

Each type of intellectual property has specific legal requirements defining subject matters that are protectable. Associated with each type of intellectual property are also certain procedures necessary to secure protective rights. Failure to comply with the legal requirements and procedures can result in irrevocable loss of intellectual property rights. Some types of intellectual property also define certain events that, if they occur, will bar or terminate rights. For instance, public disclosure of a trade secret can result in irrevocable loss of trade secret rights, or selling an invention before filing a patent application may cause irrevocable loss of patent rights.

Corporate-wide policies and procedures are important to ensure that the specific legal requirements for intellectual property are met. These policies and procedures also help companies prevent the occurrence of critical events that terminate their rights.

Carefully drafted and well-communicated policies and procedures are also useful to identify for your employees what is and is not acceptable behavior regarding your company's proprietary information. In many cases, your company's intellectual property rights can be severely compromised by a *single* employee. For example, one employee may disclose a trade secret to your competitor, resulting in a complete loss of that trade secret for your entire company. Another employee may use or sell an invention more than one year before your company files a patent on the invention, thereby barring all patent rights to that invention. Uniform and well-communicated policies and procedures are therefore necessary to reduce the risk that an uninformed employee will accidentally destroy your company's intellectual property rights.

Finally, your company's establishment of uniform policies and procedures provides good evidence in intellectual property litigation that your company has taken measures to comply with legal requirements. A formal strategy shows, for example, that your company is taking affirmative steps to maintain a trade secret.

The best instruction for devising future prevention is to study historical failures. Therefore, to best understand why intellectual property policies and procedures are necessary, this chapter examines some of the intellectual property problems experienced by companies in the past and then addresses potential dangers that, if unchecked, cause companies to lose intellectual property rights. The discussion also provides some insight as to how courts have traditionally treated situations often encountered in these danger areas.

§ 12.2 Trade Secret Laws

In trade secret cases, the courts make two general inquiries: (1) Did a trade secret exist? and (2) Did another company steal, or misappropriate, the trade secret? In protecting its trade secrets, your company must anticipate these two inquiries. Intellectual property policies and procedures, carefully drafted for your company, are necessary to ensure that your company's trade secrets legally exist, and to prevent other companies from learning of your company's trade secrets through legal means.

§ 12.3 Satisfying Secrecy and Affirmative Steps Requirements

With respect to the first inquiry in § 12.2, a trade secret is found to exist when the subject matter is secret, novel, valuable to the company, and the company has taken affirmatives steps to keep it secret. See **Chapter 2**. The courts have traditionally employed the following criteria to determine whether these legal requirements are met:

1. The extent to which the subject matter is known outside the company
2. The extent to which the subject matter is known by employees and others involved in the company
3. The extent of preventive measures taken by the company to guard the secrecy of the subject matter
4. The value of the subject matter to the company and its competitors
5. The amount of effort or money expended by the company in developing the subject matter
6. The ease or difficulty with which the subject matter could be properly acquired or duplicated by others.[1]

Trade secret litigation usually involves a dispute as to whether the subject matter was secret, and whether the company took affirmative steps to effectively keep it a secret. Accordingly, the secrecy and affirmative steps legal requirements are most critical.

The subject matter is considered secret if it is not generally known outside your company and is not readily ascertainable by competitors through proper means. Absolute secrecy, however, is not required.[2] On the other hand, the subject matter can be secret to the rest of the world and still not qualify for trade secret protection. Affirmative steps must be taken by your company to keep the subject matter secret.

What constitutes affirmative steps? The answer is unclear. Mere "intent" by a company to maintain the subject matter as a trade secret is not

---

[1] Restatement of Torts § 757 cmt. b (1939).
[2] Clark v. Bunker, 453 F.2d 1006, 172 U.S.P.Q. (BNA) 420 (9th Cir. 1972); A.H. Emery Co. v. Marcan Prod. Corp., 389 F.2d 11, 156 U.S.P.Q. (BNA) 529 (2d Cir. 1968).

186 WHY POLICIES ARE NECESSARY

sufficient.[3] Moreover, failure to follow procedures established for protecting trade secrets is sometimes found to be worse than having no procedures at all.[4] Therefore, affirmative steps must be at least the implementation of extra precautions above and beyond normal operating procedures, combined with a dedication to following the extra precautions. Examples of affirmative steps include:

1. Restricting access to key facilities
2. Educating employees of the existence of trade secrets
3. Identifying for each employee which portions of the projects they are working on are trade secrets
4. Warning employees of disclosing trade secrets
5. Locking up engineering notebooks and other confidential information
6. Requiring employees to sign nondisclosure agreements
7. Requiring other companies to sign nondisclosure agreements before disclosure of trade secrets
8. Implementing visitor policies.

Implementing multiple procedures designed to prevent loss of trade secrets is perhaps the best affirmative step that a company can take. In one case, a company was found to have taken sufficient affirmative steps to protect its trade secrets by having employees sign employment agreements, implementing strict plant security, and restricting computer access.[5]

Although it is difficult to determine what constitutes affirmative steps, failing to take any steps will almost guarantee a loss of trade secrets. Failure to take affirmative steps to keep trade secrets secret is best exemplified in *Motorola, Inc. v. Fairchild Camera & Instrument Corp.*[6] In this case, Motorola sued Fairchild and its former employees then working for Fairchild for misappropriation of trade secrets. Motorola originally claimed that 140 trade secrets were stolen, but later reduced that number to 10. The 10 trade secrets related to the manufacture of two discrete transistor devices, the plastic-encapsulated TO-92 and the aluminum-packaged TO-3.

The evidence revealed that Motorola allowed plant tours of the entire TO-92 production line. There were no signs in the area warning of trade secrets and no warnings given to people taking the tours. Motorola did

---

[3] *See, e.g.*, Arco Indus. Corp. v. Chemcast Corp., 633 F.2d 435, 443, 208 U.S.P.Q. (BNA) 190, 196 (6th Cir. 1980).

[4] J. Pooley, Trade Secrets 38 (1982).

[5] Schalk v. Texas, 823 S.W.2d 633, 21 U.S.P.Q.2d (BNA) 1838 (Tex. Crim. App. 1991).

[6] 366 F. Supp. 1173, 177 U.S.P.Q. (BNA) 614 (D. Ariz. 1973).

not require anyone to sign or acknowledge statements regarding nondisclosure of trade secrets. Motorola employees would even explain the operation of the production line to its visitors.

Other evidence showed that Motorola allowed reporters from a technology magazine to photograph the TO-92 production line for an article. Motorola showed movies of the production line at trade shows. Many of the trade secrets were also disclosed in patents and publications.

Perhaps most damaging to Motorola's case was the fact that Motorola did not even know what it considered to be its trade secrets. Motorola had never established a record, list, or index of what it considered to be trade secrets.

Based on this evidence, the court denied Motorola's claim of misappropriation because the court concluded that Motorola had made no real effort to define its trade secrets and keep them secret.

Policies and procedures are therefore necessary to ensure that your company properly establishes and documents its trade secrets. This primarily includes ensuring that your company is taking affirmative steps to keep its trade secrets secret. Moreover, established and documented policies and procedures are useful for proving that your company is taking affirmative steps, which is very helpful in trade secret litigation.

§ 12.4 Preventing Unnecessary Loss of Trade Secrets

After determining whether a trade secret exists, the next inquiry made by a court is whether another company misappropriated the trade secret. A company *misappropriates* a trade secret if that company uses *improper* means to acquire the trade secret.[7] Acquisition of a trade secret through improper means includes such actions as theft, bribing an employee to disclose a trade secret, fraud, electronic surveillance, and other actions (such as breach of contract) that are improper under the circumstances. On the other hand, courts will not impose liability for misappropriation on a company that uses *proper* means to acquire the trade secret. Proper means to discover a trade secret include such actions as reverse engineering, independent discovery, or discovery after public disclosure (inadvertent or otherwise) by the trade secret owner.

In determining whether a company used proper or improper means, courts have looked at how the accused company *did in fact* learn of the trade secret, and not how it *could* have learned of the trade secret.[8] In one

---

[7] Unif. Trade Secrets Act § 1.

[8] Sikes v. McGraw-Edison, 671 F.2d 150, 217 U.S.P.Q. (BNA) 1086 (5th Cir. 1982), *cert. denied*, 458 U.S. 1108 (1982); Smith v. Dravo Corp., 203 F.2d 369, 97 U.S.P.Q. (BNA) 98 (7th Cir. 1953).

case, an inventor named Charles Sikes made a significant improvement to a powered trimming tool used to cut grass and weeds. Sikes's invention replaced the metal blade, which was being used at the time of Sikes's invention, with a nylon monofilament line. Sikes agreed to show the invention to McGraw-Edison, a manufacturer of such trimming tools. Before he did so, Sikes had McGraw-Edison sign a confidential disclosure agreement prohibiting public disclosure for a two-year period. McGraw-Edison expressed interest and enthusiasm over the trimmer because its own model was not scheduled for market for another two years. Just two weeks later, however, McGraw-Edison informed Sikes that its own product was now going to be ready for market within a few months. McGraw-Edison offered Sikes a small royalty for his contribution, but Sikes declined.

A few months later, McGraw-Edison marketed a trimmer using a nylon monofilament like Sikes's device. Sikes sued McGraw-Edison for using his trade secret to construct the trimmer in violation of their confidential disclosure agreement. As a defense, McGraw-Edison asserted that it did not use Sikes' idea, and that the trade secret was already public knowledge at the time of Sikes's disclosure to McGraw-Edison. The court saw things differently. The court found that McGraw-Edison learned of the nylon concept from Sikes and used this concept in breach of their agreement, even though McGraw-Edison *could* have independently learned of the concept without too much effort. The evidence showed that no one at McGraw-Edison, before Sikes's disclosure, thought about replacing the metal blade of the powered trimmer with a spool of nylon line. Furthermore, it was irrelevant that Sikes's trade secret, once implemented, would be exposed to the world and could be legally imitated. Sikes was awarded $900,000 in damages.[9]

McGraw-Edison asked that the case be heard a second time. On rehearing, the court emphasized that McGraw-Edison's legal wrong was in using improper means to acquire and exploit Sikes's trade secret. McGraw-Edison had signed a confidential disclosure agreement to learn of the secret and then breached the agreement. The court concluded that "one who acquires knowledge of this sort in confidence may not turn it to his own use in breach of that confidence even though subsequent events make it available to the rest of the world."[10] From the *Sikes* case, we learn that the courts will determine that a company misappropriates another's trade secrets by employing improper conduct, even though the company might have achieved the same end through proper conduct. Company policies

---

[9] Sikes v. McGraw-Edison, 665 F.2d 731, 213 U.S.P.Q. (BNA) 983 (5th Cir. 1982), *cert. denied*, 458 U.S. 1108 (1982).

[10] Sikes v. McGraw-Edison, 671 F.2d 150, 217 U.S.P.Q. (BNA) 1086 (5th Cir. 1982), *cert. denied*, 458 U.S. 1108 (1982).

and procedures are necessary to ensure that your company only learns of another's trade secrets through proper conduct to prevent any appearance of trade secret theft. Additionally, a corporate policy may help mitigate the opportunity of another to learn of your company's trade secret through proper means.

§ 12.5 —Inadvertent Disclosure

Still perhaps the biggest threat to loss of trade secret rights are the actions of the trade secret owner, and not the actions of a competitor. A company can legally lose its trade secrets to a competitor, without any regard to the appropriateness of the competitor's conduct, through its own conduct, such as when an employee accidentally discloses a trade secret, publishes an article that describes the trade secret, or boasts about the trade secret at a trade show. In each case, the employee's carelessness in publicly disclosing the trade secret can lead to immediate loss of trade secret protection for the company, irrespective of a competitor's conduct.

Company-wide policies and procedures are necessary to prevent employees from accidentally disclosing trade secrets to the public. The policies and procedures should define trade secret subject matter and establish a routine for obtaining clearance before any secret information is released to the world.

§ 12.6 —Former Employee and Innocent New Employer

Another key area in protecting trade secrets involves a departing employee. In many industries, employees migrate from one competitor to another, taking with them a baggage full of proprietary information. New employees often disclose, accidentally or purposefully, their former employers' trade secrets to their new employers. When an employee leaves your company, you may find preventing the disclosure of trade secrets to be a difficult task. Enforcing your trade secret rights against a new employer who is simply an innocent recipient of the trade secrets can be even more difficult.

The general rule is that an innocent new employer who unknowingly acquires trade secrets of its employee's former employer is not liable to that former employer.[11] The *Conmar* case exemplifies this point. In this case, employees left Conmar Products to work for a competitor company, Universal Slide Fasteners Company. Conmar and Universal Slide Fasteners were competitors in the zipper industry. Conmar accused its former

---

[11] Milgrim, R. Business Organizations: Milgrim on Trade Secrets § 5.04[2][a] (1990).

employees of stealing its trade secrets relating to methods of making zippers. While employed at Conmar, these employees had signed employment agreements promising not to disclose Conmar's trade secrets. After leaving Conmar, the employees used these trade secrets at their new jobs with Universal Slide Fasteners in violation of these agreements. However, Universal Slide Fasteners itself did not know the employees had signed such employment agreements, nor did it know that their new employees were using Conmar's trade secrets. The court held Universal Slide Fasteners *not* liable to Conmar for acquisition of these trade secrets because Universal Slide Fasteners was an innocent party to the trade secret theft.[12]

Company policies and procedures must be established that alert both the former employee and the new employer that the former employee has knowledge of your company's trade secrets. Such policies and procedures are aimed at defusing the innocent recipient defense by laying a foundation showing that every accused party knew of the existence of the trade secret status of the information you wished to protect.

§ 12.7 —Trade Secret Matters in Business Relationships

One final area of concern when considering trade secrets is the necessity to ensure that any disclosure to a third party in a business venture is done so under a veil of confidentiality. This is typically handled by requesting that the other company sign a confidentiality agreement.

Failure to impose any type of secrecy requirement on a prospective business partner could result in a loss of your company's trade secret rights. In one case, a company installed a prototype unit and provided engineering drawings of the unit for one of its customers. The company did not warn the customer that the prototype and drawings were confidential, nor did the company mark the drawings confidential. Additionally, other people not involved in the business relationship were allowed to see the prototype without restriction. The court concluded from this evidence that the company did not own any trade secret rights in the technology embodied in the prototype and drawings because the company never treated them as trade secrets and took no steps to guard their confidentiality.[13]

Intellectual property policies and procedures are necessary to ensure that an appropriate confidential arrangement has been reached before any disclosure of trade secret materials.

---

[12] Conmar Prod. Corp. v. Universal Slide Fasteners Co., 172 F.2d 150, 80 U.S.P.Q. (BNA) 108 (2d Cir. 1949).

[13] Palin Mfg. Co. v. Water Technology, Inc., 221 U.S.P.Q. (BNA) 640 (Ill. App. Ct. 1982).

§ 12.8 Patent Laws

When companies lose patent rights, the loss typically occurs in one of two ways. First, companies lose patent rights because they fail to satisfy the legal requirements of patentability. This is covered in §§ 12.9 through 12.14. Second, companies lose rights because they fail to establish first inventorship. This is discussed in § 12.15. Many companies have unnecessarily forfeited patent rights simply because they did not institute proper policies and procedures designed to address these two legal areas.

§ 12.9 Failing to Satisfy Novelty Requirement: Self-inflicted Bars to Patentability

The novelty requirement for obtaining a patent, defined in § 102 of the patent statute, specifies numerous bars to patentability. See **Table 2–1** in **Chapter 2**, which lists and describes the § 102 bars. These bars are fatal to efforts to patent an invention, preventing the grant of a patent or invalidating a patent that was erroneously issued by the PTO because it was unaware of the barring activity.

The bars to patentability defined in § 102 may be divided into two groups: (1) bars caused by others and (2) bars caused by your company, or *self-inflicted bars*. The first group of bars will operate despite your company's preventive policies and procedures because they are the result of activities by others. Your company cannot prevent them. For instance, § 102(a) prohibits the grant of a patent if the invention was already publicly known or used by others in the United States before your company conceived of the invention. This bar prevents your company from obtaining a patent because the invention had already been discovered and was being used by another. Nothing on the part of your company can alter or reverse that "barring" event.

Your company can, however, prevent the second group of bars referred to as the self-inflicted bars to patentability. Self-inflicted bars are within your company's direct control and might arise due to carelessness or a lack of knowledge about how the patent laws operate. For example, § 102(b) bars a company from obtaining a patent when that company tries to sell the invention in the United States more than one year before filing a patent application on the invention. The company itself creates this *on-sale bar* to patentability to its own detriment.

Your company should establish intellectual property policies and procedures to prevent the self-inflicted bars to patentability. The policies and procedures should be circulated to all employees and strict compliance demanded. Just as your company would not willingly allow employees to throw away tangible company property (such as computers, desks, and office supplies), so too should your company safeguard against careless employees throwing away valuable intellectual property rights. Preventing the unintentional operation of the self-inflicted bars is a primary safeguard.

The three most frequent self-inflicted bars to patentability are the *printed publication bar*, the *public use bar*, and the *on-sale bar*. In full, § 102(b) of the patent statute states:

> A person shall be entitled to a patent unless—
>
> (b) the invention was patented or described in a *printed publication* in this or a foreign country or in *public use* or *on sale* in this country, more than one year prior to the date of the application for patent in the United States. [Emphasis added.]

Before examining the intricacies of these three patentability bars, notice that § 102(b) allows a one-year period between the barring activity and the filing deadline for a United States patent application. This one year period is strictly enforced. The courts are inflexible and unforgiving to companies forgetting or neglecting to file a patent application within this one-year period.

The one-year period is selected as a compromise between the interests of the inventor and the interests of the public. In the inventor's interests, the one-year period provides the inventor sufficient time to decide whether the invention warrants patent protection. In the public's interests, the one-year period encourages prompt public disclosure of new and useful information and prevents the inventor from unreasonably reaping benefits from the invention for more than the legally allotted 17-year patent duration.[14]

The one-year grace period applies only to United States applications. Most foreign countries do not have this grace period and thus, any public disclosure—including public use, offer to sell, or publication—might destroy foreign patent rights.

Sections 12.10 through **12.14** examine the intricacies of the three most frequent bars and how the courts interpret this important paragraph of the patent statute.

§ 12.10 —Printed Publication Bar

The first bar to patentability that can be self-inflicted is the printed publication bar, as interpreted by the courts, a *printed publication* is a pub-

---

[14] T.P. Lab., Inc. v. Professional Positioners, Inc., 724 F.2d 965, 220 U.S.P.Q. (BNA) 577 (Fed. Cir. 1984), *cert. denied*, 469 U.S. 826 (1984).

§ 12.10 PRINTED PUBLICATION BAR

lished paper or article that describes a technology and is sufficiently accessible to the public interested in the technology.[15] If members of the relevant public could obtain the information in the reference through reasonable efforts, the reference is said to be sufficiently accessible.[16] The reference can be accessible even though members of the public did not actually receive the information.

Printed publication consists of more than what a literal interpretation suggests, that is, a printed and published document. A printed publication includes computer disc storage and other ongoing advances in the technologies of data storage, retrieval, and dissemination.[17] Examples of printed publications include:

1. Articles in professional or trade journals
2. Graduate or doctoral theses[18]
3. Newspaper articles[19]
4. Brochures[20]
5. Microfilm[21]
6. Photographs[22]
7. Computer disc storage[23]
8. Manufacturers' catalogs.

The reference may be published in the United States or in a foreign country. Additionally, the reference, to prevent a patent grant under § 102(b), must sufficiently describe the invention to the ordinary practitioner to enable the practitioner to use the invention.[24] However, even if not sufficiently enabling, the information disclosed in the reference can

---

[15] Constant v. Advanced Micro-Devices, Inc., 848 F.2d 1560, 7 U.S.P.Q.2d (BNA) 1057 (Fed. Cir. 1988), *cert. denied*, 488 U.S. 892 (1988).

[16] Constant v. Advanced Micro-Devices, Inc., 848 F.2d 1560, 7 U.S.P.Q.2d (BNA) 1057 (Fed. Cir. 1988), *cert. denied*, 488 U.S. 892 (1988).

[17] *In re* Hall, 781 F.2d 897, 228 U.S.P.Q. (BNA) 453 (Fed. Cir. 1986).

[18] *In re* Hall, 781 F.2d 897, 228 U.S.P.Q. (BNA) 453 (Fed. Cir. 1986).

[19] Harrington Mfg. Co. v. Powell Mfg. Co., 815 F.2d 1478, 2 U.S.P.Q.2d (BNA) 1364 (Fed. Cir. 1986), *cert. denied*, 479 U.S. 1030 (1987).

[20] Preemption Devices, Inc. v. Minnesota Mining & Mfg. Co., 732 F.2d 903, 221 U.S.P.Q. (BNA) 841 (Fed. Cir. 1984).

[21] Regents of the Univ. of Cal., Inc. v. Howmedica, Inc., 530 F. Supp. 846, 210 U.S.P.Q. (BNA) 727 (D.N.J. 1981), *aff'd*, 676 F.2d 687 (3d Cir. 1982).

[22] Universal Athletic Sales Co. v. American Gym Recreational & Athletic Equip. Corp., 546 F.2d 530, 192 U.S.P.Q. (BNA) 193 (3d Cir. 1976), *cert. denied*, 430 U.S. 984 (1977).

[23] *In re* Hall, 781 F.2d 897, 228 U.S.P.Q. (BNA) 453 (Fed. Cir. 1986).

[24] *In re* Spada, 911 F.2d 705, 15 U.S.P.Q. (BNA) 1655 (Fed. Cir. 1990).

be combined with common knowledge and technical information contained in other references for purposes of evidencing that the invention is obvious under a § 103 analysis.

The courts have had difficulty pinning down when a reference is sufficiently accessible to the public to constitute a printed publication. On the one hand, references that courts have found to be sufficiently accessible to the public include one copy of a doctoral thesis deposited in a German library,[25] and a paper delivered at a conference attended by interested members of the public, where the speaker handed out only six copies of the paper to those who requested a copy.[26] On the other hand, references that courts have found not to be sufficiently accessible to the public include six copies of a brochure given to a person to help obtain financing,[27] and an undergraduate thesis that was deposited in a college library open to the public, but not cataloged or indexed.[28]

The printed publication bar becomes a self-inflicted bar when your company publishes the invention more than one year before filing a patent application. As you can see from the examples, very little is required to trigger the printed publication bar. If an employee describes your company's technology in a document and disseminates this document to some outside audience (no matter how small), the printed publication bar may become effective. Therefore, an engineer who publishes an article on an invention in a professional journal more than one year before filing for a patent on the invention may cause a loss of patent rights in the invention. Likewise, a marketer who prematurely releases a brochure describing the invention more than one year before filing for a patent on the invention may cause a loss of patent rights in the invention.

Properly implemented intellectual property policies and procedures can prevent loss of patent rights due to the printed publication bar. First, established policies can prevent employees of your company from publishing or releasing articles describing the invention before your company has fully considered its patent rights in the invention. Second, if your company or another company does publish the technology, then procedures can ensure that your company considers all United States patent options before the one-year bar period expires.

---

[25] *In re* Hall, 781 F.2d 897, 228 U.S.P.Q. (BNA) 453 (Fed. Cir. 1986).

[26] Massachusetts Inst. of Technology v. AB Fortia, 774 F.2d 1104, 227 U.S.P.Q. (BNA) 428 (Fed. Cir. 1984).

[27] Preemption Devices, Inc. v. Minnesota Mining & Mfg. Co., 732 F.2d 903, 221 U.S.P.Q. (BNA) 841 (Fed. Cir. 1984).

[28] *In re* Cronyn, 890 F.2d 1158, 13 U.S.P.Q.2d (BNA) 1070 (Fed. Cir. 1989).

§ 12.11 —Public Use Bar

The second bar to patentability that can be self-inflicted is the public use bar. *Public use* is defined as any use of an invention that is under no limitation, restriction, or obligation of secrecy to the inventor.[29] Your company forfeits patent rights to a new technology if it publicly uses the new technology, or allows another company to use the technology without restriction, more than one year before filing for a patent. On the other hand, your company may use the new technology in secret, or allow another company to use the technology after imposing secrecy restrictions, without invoking the public use bar. However, a secret "commercial" use will create a bar under the on-sale bar. See § 12.12.

The fact that an invention is hidden from the public within a machine does not prevent a finding of public use.[30] In addition, only one use is necessary to invoke the public use bar.[31] To trigger this bar, however, the use must be in the United States. Examples of public use situations include:

1. Demonstrating a prototype to a public group[32]
2. Giving samples of the new product to customers[33]
3. Consumer testing of a new product[34]
4. Displaying the invention at a trade show.[35]

Your company's intellectual property policies and procedures are important to safeguard against public use bars. First, established policies can prevent the use of the technology in public before your company has fully considered its potential patent rights. Second, set procedures can ensure that your company considers secrecy agreements in business dealings with other companies to ensure that the other companies do not prematurely use the invention in public. Third, if your company or another company does use the technology publicly, then procedures can ensure that your

---

[29] *In re* Smith, 714 F.2d 1127, 218 U.S.P.Q. (BNA) 976 (Fed. Cir. 1983).

[30] Koerhring Co. v. National Automatic Tool Co., 362 F.2d 100, 149 U.S.P.Q. (BNA) 887 (7th Cir. 1966).

[31] Molecular Research Corp. v. CBS, Inc., 793 F.2d 1261, 229 U.S.P.Q. (BNA) 805 (Fed. Cir. 1986), *cert. denied*, 479 U.S. 1030 (1987).

[32] Harrington Mfg. Co. v. Powell Mfg. Co., 815 F.2d 1478, 2 U.S.P.Q.2d (BNA) 1364 (Fed. Cir. 1986), *cert. denied*, 479 U.S. 1030 (1987).

[33] Milliken Research Corp. v. Dan River, Inc., 739 F.2d 587, 222 U.S.P.Q. (BNA) 571 (Fed. Cir. 1984).

[34] *In re* Smith, 714 F.2d 1127, 218 U.S.P.Q. (BNA) 976 (Fed. Cir. 1983) (having 76 consumers test a new carpet treatment method is public use).

[35] *In re* Mann, 861 F.2d 1581, 8 U.S.P.Q.2d (BNA) 2030 (Fed. Cir. 1988).

company considers potential United States patent rights before the one-year bar period expires.

§ 12.12 —On-Sale Bar

The third potentially self-inflicted bar to patentability is the on-sale bar. The *on-sale* requirement of § 102(b) is satisfied by a single sale or even a single *offer* to sell.[36] The offer need not be formal, nor accepted.[37] The sale or offer must occur in the United States but need not be public, as even a sale or offer under a confidentiality agreement will invoke the bar. The on-sale bar begins tolling the one-year period when an enforceable contract is executed by seller and purchaser,[38] or when the basic terms of an offer (such as price and delivery schedules) have been communicated to a potential customer.[39] Examples of on-sale activity include:

1. Attempts to sell the product to be covered by a patent
2. Distributing advertising brochures that describe the invention[40]
3. Showing blueprints or photographs to prospective purchasers
4. Discussing in detail the invention during a trade show[41]
5. A contract bid that details the invention[42]
6. Distributing samples
7. Sale of a product made by a patentable process, even if the process is not publicly known.[43]

One critical issue in the on-sale bar analysis is whether the invention being sold or offered for sale by the inventor was sufficiently developed at the time of the sales activity. In general, if the invention is not very well developed, there is really no invention to bar from patentability. On

---

[36] *In re* Caveney, 761 F.2d 671, 226 U.S.P.Q. (BNA) 1 (Fed. Cir. 1985).

[37] A.B. Chance Co. v. RTE Corp., 854 F.2d 1307, 1311, 7 U.S.P.Q.2d (BNA) 1881, 1884 (Fed. Cir. 1988); *In re* Caveney, 761 F.2d 671, 676, 226 U.S.P.Q. (BNA) 1, 4 (Fed. Cir. 1985).

[38] *In re* Caveney, 761 F.2d 671, 677, 226 U.S.P.Q. (BNA) 1, 4 (Fed. Cir. 1985).

[39] *In re* Caveney, 761 F.2d 671, 675, 226 U.S.P.Q. (BNA) 1, 3 (Fed. Cir. 1985).

[40] *In re* Brigance, 792 F.2d 1103, 1107, 229 U.S.P.Q. (BNA) 988, 990 (Fed. Cir. 1986).

[41] *In re* Mann, 861 F.2d 1581, 8 U.S.P.Q.2d (BNA) 2030 (Fed. Cir. 1988).

[42] RCA Corp. v. Data Gen. Corp., 887 F.2d 1056, 12 U.S.P.Q.2d (BNA) 1449 (Fed. Cir. 1989).

[43] D.L. Auld Co. v. Chroma Graphics Corp., 714 F.2d 1144, 1147, 219 U.S.P.Q. (BNA) 13, 15 (Fed. Cir. 1983); Metallizing Eng'g Co. v. Kenyon Bearing & Auto Parts Co., 153 F.2d 516, 68 U.S.P.Q. (BNA) 54 (2d Cir. 1946).

§ 12.12 ON-SALE BAR

the other hand, if the inventor offers for sale an experimentally proven invention, the on-sale bar will prevent patentability.

Many courts have attempted to construct comprehensive tests indicating the stage of development required to invoke the on-sale bar. An early legal test, known as the *on-hand doctrine*, required that the invention be in working order, delivered to the purchaser, and accepted by the purchaser.[44] This test has since been rejected.[45] Another legal test required that the invention be "reduced to practice" before the on-sale bar was triggered.[46] Reduction to practice required that the invention be embodied in some tangible form,[47] such as a prototype, and that it be tested to demonstrate that it would work for its intended purpose.[48] The reduction to practice standard, however, has also been rejected.[49]

Today it is unclear at what point an invention is sufficiently developed to invoke the on-sale bar. The courts have simply determined that an invention that has been built and tested will invoke the bar, while a mere conception of an invention will not invoke the bar.[50] One important lesson to be learned is that the courts are increasingly intolerant of a company's attempt to commercialize its inventions beyond the one-year statutory period, *even if the invention is not yet fully built or functional*. Therefore, intellectual property policies and procedures are necessary to ensure that inventions are not prematurely sold or offered for sale, resulting in an unnecessary loss of patent rights.

---

[44] *See, e.g.*, B.F. Sturtevant v. Massachusetts Hair & Felt Co., 124 F.2d 95, 97, 51 U.S.P.Q. 420, 422 (1st Cir. 1941); Burke Elec. Co. v. Independent Pneumatic Tool Co., 234 F. 93 (2d Cir.), *cert. denied*, 241 U.S. 682 (1916); McCreery Eng'g Co. v. Massachusetts Fan Co., 195 F. 498 (1st Cir. 1912).

[45] Timely Prod. Corp. v. Arron, 523 F.2d 288, 187 U.S.P.Q. (BNA) 257 (2d Cir. 1975); Barmag Barmer Maschinenfabrik AG v. Murata Mach., Ltd., 731 F.2d 831, 221 U.S.P.Q. (BNA) 561 (Fed. Cir. 1984).

[46] Timely Prod. Corp. v. Arron, 523 F.2d 288, 187 U.S.P.Q. (BNA) 257 (2d Cir. 1975).

[47] Shatterproof Glass Corp. v. Libbey-Owens Ford Co., 758 F.2d 613, 225 U.S.P.Q. (BNA) 634 (Fed. Cir. 1985) (approving a jury instruction that there could be no on-sale bar if the offer did not involve "functional machines and processes"), *cert. denied*, 474 U.S. 976 (1985); CTS Corp. v. Piher Int'l Corp., 527 F.2d 95, 188 U.S.P.Q. (BNA) 419 (7th Cir. 1975) (the statute might better have specified "a device embodying or disclosing the invention"), *cert. denied*, 424 U.S. 978 (1976).

[48] Great N. Corp. v. Davis Core & Pad Co., 782 F.2d 159, 165, 228 U.S.P.Q. (BNA) 356, 358 (Fed. Cir. 1986); Shatterproof Glass Corp. v. Libbey-Owens Ford Co., 758 F.2d 613, 225 U.S.P.Q. (BNA) 634, 640 (Fed. Cir. 1985), *cert. denied*, 474 U.S. 976 (1985); Barmag Barmer Maschinenfabrik AG v. Murata Mach., Ltd., 731 F.2d 831, 838, 221 U.S.P.Q. (BNA) 561, 567 (Fed. Cir. 1984).

[49] UMC Elec. Co. v. United States, 816 F.2d 647, 2 U.S.P.Q.2d (BNA) 1465 (Fed. Cir. 1987), *cert. denied*, 484 U.S. 1025 (1988).

[50] UMC Elec. Co. v. United States, 816 F.2d 647, 657, 2 U.S.P.Q.2d (BNA) 1465, 1472 (Fed. Cir. 1987), *cert. denied*, 484 U.S. 1025 (1988).

§ 12.13 —Experimentation Incident to Public Use or Sale Activity

Legitimate experimental activity does not give rise to a public use bar and provides an exception to the on-sale bar. The Supreme Court established in 1878 that the use of an invention for experimental purposes does not violate the public use bar of § 102(b).[51] This principle is sometimes known, and will be referred to throughout this book, as the *experimental use exception*.[52] Although the experimental use exception was established for the public use bar, most courts extend its application to the on-sale bar.[53]

In determining whether the experimental use exception applies, the courts focus on the underlying purpose of the use or sale of the invention. When the sole purpose of a company's public use is to test the utility or operability of its invention, a public use might be excused.[54] Likewise, when a company's sale of an invention was primarily for experimental purposes, the on-sale bar might be avoided.[55] However, if the company is commercially motivated to make the public use or sale, then the experimental use exception does not save the invention from the public use and on-sale bars.[56]

Factors that a court may consider when determining whether the use of the invention was experimental include:

1. Whether the user pays for the invention and how much (suggesting that the inventor is motivated more by profit than experimentation)
2. Whether the user agrees to use the invention secretly (suggesting that the inventor is interested more in experimentation than public attention)
3. Whether the user and inventor keep progress records or test reports (suggesting that experimentation is a primary motive of the public use or sale)

---

[51] Elizabeth v. Nicholson Pavement Co., 97 U.S. 126 (1878).

[52] Recent case law states that experimentation is not an exception to the public use bar, but simply negates public use. TP Lab., Inc. v. Professional Positioners, Inc., 724 F.2d 965, 220 U.S.P.Q. (BNA) 577 (Fed. Cir. 1984), *cert. denied*, 469 U.S. 826 (1984).

[53] *See, e.g.*, UMC Elec. Co. v. United States, 816 F.2d 647, 657, 2 U.S.P.Q.2d (BNA) 1465, 1472 (Fed. Cir. 1987) (a sale made to a purchaser participating in experimental testing creates no on-sale bar), *cert. denied*, 484 U.S. 1025 (1988).

[54] *See, e.g.*, TP Lab., Inc. v. Professional Positioners, Inc., 724 F.2d 965, 220 U.S.P.Q. (BNA) 577 (Fed. Cir. 1984), *cert. denied*, 469 U.S. 826 (1984).

[55] *In re* Dybel, 524 F.2d 1393, 187 U.S.P.Q. (BNA) 593 (C.C.P.A. 1975); *In re* Theis, 610 F.2d 786, 204 U.S.P.Q. (BNA) 188 (C.C.P.A. 1979).

[56] West & Linck, *The Law of "Public Use" and "On Sale": Past, Present and Future*, J. Proprietary Rights, Feb. 1990.

4. Whether the inventor participates in the experiments (suggesting that the inventor is using the use or sale to ascertain whether the invention is functional)
5. Whether the inventor or user conducts a reasonable number of experiments (suggesting that experimentation is a primary motive of the public use or sale)
6. Whether the testing period is lengthy compared to tests of similar devices (a reasonable time period suggesting that the experiments were not simply token experiments but were designed to ascertain the functionality of the invention; a large time period suggesting that the experimentation may be a subterfuge for commercialization)
7. Whether the inventor retains control over the tests conducted by the user (suggesting that the inventor questions the utility of the invention and that experimentation is thus warranted).[57]

Implementing carefully tailored intellectual property policies and procedures may convince a court that any use or sale of an invention before filing a patent application was for experimental purposes and not for commercial gain.

§ 12.14 —Loss of Foreign Patent Rights

Most foreign countries have a strict novelty requirement that precludes patentability if *any* public disclosure was made before filing a patent application. Unlike United States patent laws, which give an inventor a one-year grace period after a public use or sale to file for a patent, foreign countries do not offer a grace period. Any public disclosure before filing a United States or foreign patent application automatically kills foreign patent rights in most foreign countries. To preserve foreign patent rights, a United States patent application must be filed before any public disclosure of the invention in any manner.

§ 12.15 First Inventorship

Occasionally, a situation arises in which two companies independently develop the same new area of technology. If neither company knows about the other's developments, each company might file a patent application on its technology, claiming this technology as its own. The patent laws,

---

[57] TP Lab., Inc. v. Professional Positioners, Inc., 724 F.2d 965, 220 U.S.P.Q. (BNA) 577 (Fed. Cir. 1984), *cert. denied*, 469 U.S. 826 (1984).

however, permit only one patent per invention. Thus, only one company is entitled to a patent. When two companies both claim patent rights to the same technology, the Patent and Trademark Office (PTO) must decide which company was first to invent the new technology. The PTO awards first inventorship to the company that proves the earliest, legally recognized date on which the new invention existed. The process for resolving such issues is called an *interference*.

Figure 12-1 follows a first inventorship contest (interference) between two hypothetical companies, Pharmteck and Trimmit, Inc., which compete in the pharmaceutical industry. **Figure 12-1** illustrates the time lines of each company's research and development of a new weight-reduction drug, known generically as SLIM-X.

The PTO initially presumes that the inventor who was first to file for a patent is the legal first inventor. It makes this presumption because the patent application, if sufficiently enabling, teaches the ordinary artisan how to practice the invention and thus constitutes good evidence that the inventor(s) had invented the subject matter of the application at least as early as the date of filing the patent application.

As illustrated in **Figure 12-1**, Pharmteck filed a patent application for SLIM-X on November 15, 1990. Trimmit, Inc., filed a patent application for SLIM-X on January 9, 1991. Because Pharmteck's filing date preceded Trimmit's filing date, Pharmteck is initially presumed by the PTO to be the first to invent SLIM-X. If no other evidence is presented, the PTO would resolve the question of first inventorship in favor of Pharmteck by virtue of its earlier filing date.

Despite having a later filing date, however, Trimmit has an opportunity to present evidence showing that it invented SLIM-X before Pharmteck's filing date. In other words, even though Trimmit has a later filing date, Trimmit can still try to establish an earlier invention date. If Trimmit is successful, Pharmteck must then prove an invention date earlier than the invention date established by Trimmit. The PTO will then grant first inventorship to the company that proves the earliest invention date.

To be entitled to an invention date earlier than its filing date, a company must show three elements: conception, diligence, and reduction to practice. An inventor *conceives* of an invention when he has completely performed the mental part of the inventive act.[58] This means that the inventor must have in mind every feature that is set forth in the claimed invention at the date of conception.[59] A mere suggestion that a thing of practical utility could be done does not constitute a conception.[60]

---

[58] *In re* Tansel, 253 F.2d 241, 117 U.S.P.Q. (BNA) 188 (C.C.P.A. 1958).
[59] Coleman v. Dines, 754 F.2d 353, 359, 224 U.S.P.Q. (BNA) 857, 862 (Fed. Cir. 1985).
[60] Willis v. Suppa, 209 U.S.P.Q. (BNA) 406, 417 (Bd. Pat. Int. 1980).

PHARMTECK

12/4/89   Diligence   9/17/90   11/15/90
|—————————————————————|——————————|
Conception   Actual   Filed Patent
                              Reduction   Application
                              to Practice

TRIMMIT

7/22/89   Diligence   1/9/91
|———|
Conception   Filed Patent Application
                                                (Constructive Reduction
                                                     to Practice)

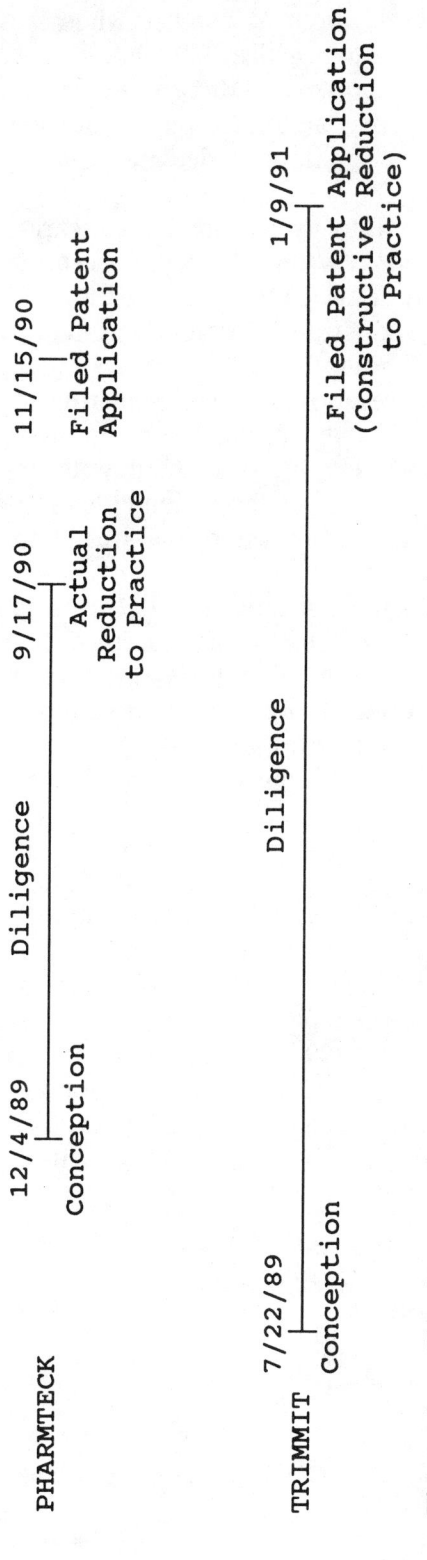

Figure 12-1. First inventorship rules.

The invention is then *reduced to practice* when it is built and tested (known as *actual* reduction to practice)[61] or when it is described in a patent application (known as *constructive* reduction to practice).[62] Actual reduction to practice requires that an invention be sufficiently tested to demonstrate that it will work for its intended purpose in its intended environment.[63]

Finally, to benefit from an invention date as early as the conception date, an inventor must *diligently* work on the invention between the time of conception and the time the invention is reduced to practice. All three elements—conception, reduction to practice, and diligence—must have been performed in the United States.

Companies generally use laboratory or engineering notebooks, or similar written and dated records of new projects, which were contemporaneously maintained during the development of the new technology, to establish the three requisite elements. If all three elements are proven, a company is awarded an invention date as of the date of the conception of its invention.[64]

The evidence used to show conception, diligence, and reduction to practice must be corroborated.[65] This means that another person (usually another employee), apart from the inventor(s), must verify by signature and present recollection an understanding of the invention as described in the notebook. In practice, companies generally require that each page of a laboratory notebook be signed and dated regularly by the inventor and an additional employee.

Returning to **Figure 12-1**, Pharmteck established a conception date of December 4, 1989, and an actual reduction to practice date of September 17, 1990. That is, Pharmteck was able to prove that SLIM-X worked for its intended purpose in its intended environment by September 17, 1990. Pharmteck established diligence between conception and reduction to practice, and all three elements were corroborated. Trimmit established a conception date of July 22, 1989, and filed a patent application on January 9, 1991, thereby receiving a constructive reduction to practice date as of this filing date. Trimmit also established diligence and all three elements were corroborated. Accordingly, Pharmteck's earliest invention date is

---

[61] UMC Elec. Co. v. United States, 816 F.2d 647, 2 U.S.P.Q.2d (BNA) 1465 (Fed. Cir. 1987), *cert. denied*, 484 U.S. 1025 (1988).

[62] Hazeltine Corp. v. United States, 820 F.2d 1190, 1196, 2 U.S.P.Q.2d (BNA) 1744, 1749 (Fed. Cir. 1987).

[63] Shatterproof Glass Corp. v. Libbey-Owens Ford Co., 758 F.2d 613, 225 U.S.P.Q. (BNA) 634 (Fed. Cir. 1985), *cert. denied*, 474 U.S. 976 (1985).

[64] Marconi Wireless Tel. Co. v. United States, 320 U.S. 1 (1943).

[65] Minnesota Mining & Mfg. Co. v. General Elec. Co., 167 F. Supp. 37, 40, 119 U.S.P.Q. (BNA) 65, 67 (D.D.C. 1958).

December 4, 1989, and Trimmit's earliest invention date is July 22, 1989. Based upon this evidence, Trimmit would be awarded first inventorship.

Therefore, even though Trimmit was second to file a patent application on SLIM-X, and Trimmit took longer to develop SLIM-X, Trimmit is still awarded first inventorship.

There are two lessons to be learned from this discussion. First, for every invention, companies should be able to provide sufficient evidence to establish conception, diligence, and reduction to practice. Second, this evidence must be corroborated by a person other than the inventor(s). Neglecting these practices can result in a loss of the earliest possible priority date if this date is contested by another company.

Intellectual property policies and procedures are necessary to ensure that your company consistently maintains and preserves sufficient corroborated evidence to establish conception, reduction to practice, and diligence for each of your company's inventions.

The first inventorship rules are almost exclusively unique to the United States patent system. Other countries do not determine priority based on who was first to invent. Instead, most other countries in the world award priority to the first patent applicant to file for a patent. Such a system is called a *first-to-file* patent system. Under the first-to-file system, no attention is paid to conception, reduction to practice, or diligence. The United States has been under some international pressure to change from a *first-to-invent* to a *first-to-file* system, but has yet to take any major steps toward changing its laws. At the time of this writing, however, a United States Patent and Trademark Office Committee had recommended adopting the first-to-file system.

§ 12.16 Checklist

Intellectual property policies and procedures are a vital component of today's corporations. The following outlines why:

Intellectual property policies and procedures are necessary to:
  Establish and protect trade secrets by

1. Encouraging employees to keep your company's trade secrets confidential to prevent accidental disclosure
2. Defining for the employees what affirmative steps must be taken to keep trade secrets confidential
3. Documenting the affirmative steps taken to keep the trade secrets confidential for evidence in case of trial

4. Diminishing a competitor's chance of discovering the trade secret through proper means
5. Ensuring that employers of your company's former employees know that these employees have confidential trade secrets and are expected to maintain the trade secrets in confidence
6. Ensuring that business dealings with other companies are conducted under confidentiality for trade secret purposes.

Prevent loss of patent rights by

1. Preventing publication of an invention before patent protection is considered
2. Preventing the public use of an invention before patent protection is considered
3. Preventing the sale of, or offer to sell, an invention before patent protection is considered
4. Defining experimentation protocol to distinguish it from sales activity
5. Ensuring that business dealings with other companies include patent considerations
6. Ensuring the ability to establish your invention's date of conception and your company's diligence to reach an actual or constructive reduction of the invention to practice.

CHAPTER 13

COMPANY POLICIES AND PROCEDURES THAT MAXIMIZE PRESERVATION OF INTELLECTUAL PROPERTY RIGHTS

§ 13.1   Need for Policies and Procedures
§ 13.2   Employer/Employee Relationships
§ 13.3   —Preemployment Disclosure
§ 13.4   —Hiring New Employees from Competitor
§ 13.5   —Orientation for New Employees
§ 13.6   —Employee Agreement
§ 13.7   —Employment Manuals
§ 13.8   —Periodic Reminders of Intellectual Property Obligations
§ 13.9   —Seminars to Educate Employees
§ 13.10 —Procedures for Departing Employees
§ 13.11 Laboratory Procedures
§ 13.12 —Record Daily Activities of Engineers
§ 13.13 —Corroboration by Disinterested Employee
§ 13.14 —Maintain Progress Records
§ 13.15 —Catalog Engineering and Progress Notebooks
§ 13.16 —Maintain Records Pertaining to Daily Time Sheets of Personnel
§ 13.17 Security Procedures
§ 13.18 —Facility Restrictions
§ 13.19 —Handling Confidential Material
§ 13.20 Release Review Procedures
§ 13.21 —Distribution of Advertisements and Brochures

§ 13.22 —Publications in Trade and Professional Journals
§ 13.23 —Demonstrations of New Technology
§ 13.24 —Test Marketing New Products
§ 13.25 Patent Marking
§ 13.26 Copyright Marking
§ 13.27 Trademark Marking
§ 13.28 Technological Relationships with Other Companies
§ 13.29 —Initially Disclose Only General Information
§ 13.30 —Confidentiality Agreements
§ 13.31 —Stamp *CONFIDENTIAL* on All Documents Transferred to Business Partner
§ 13.32 —Record Transfer of Proprietary Information
§ 13.33 —Research and Development Relationships with Other Companies
§ 13.34 Channel New Ideas to Intellectual Property Counsel
§ 13.35 —Keep Decisions at Grass-roots Level
§ 13.36 —Educate Employees
§ 13.37 —Provide Incentive to Innovate
§ 13.38 Handling Unsolicited Ideas
§ 13.39 —Designate One Employee to Field All Unsolicited Ideas
§ 13.40 —Nonconfidential Disclosure Agreement
§ 13.41 —Reviewing Unsolicited Idea
§ 13.42 —Procedures for Designated Employee
§ 13.43 Intellectual Property Audit

§ 13.1 Need for Policies and Procedures

Company policies and procedures help preserve intellectual property rights by educating the company work force to appreciate the value of the company's intellectual property and to anticipate and prevent actions that may jeopardize these rights. Well-drafted and well-communicated policies and procedures can ensure, for example, that employees take affirmative steps to preserve company trade secrets, and that employees prevent unnecessary loss of patent rights due to premature use, sale, or publication of patentable technology. Most important, policies and procedures promote an employee awareness of intellectual property issues, keeping the employees conscious of how their daily actions may affect the company's proprietary intellectual property rights.

The policies and procedures discussed in this chapter are presented in nine categories:

1. Employee-related procedures
2. Laboratory procedures
3. Security procedures
4. Release review procedures
5. Marking procedures
6. Technological relationships with other companies
7. Channeling new ideas to intellectual property law counsel
8. Unsolicited proposal policies
9. Intellectual property audit procedures.

These policies and procedures are suggestions for enhancing your company's existing intellectual property program and serve as models for the types of intellectual policies and procedures you may wish to implement for your own company. The following sections may also function as a checklist to determine if your company's programs are adequately comprehensive.

The information in this chapter is presented in summary fashion to provide some guidance as to what types of policies and procedures are important. This discussion is not intended to be a legal primer on each area. Consult your patent counsel to determine which policies are appropriate for your particular business environment.

§ 13.2 Employer/Employee Relationships

The procedures in §§ 13.3 through 13.10 are designed for use in your company's employer/employee relationships. They include recruiting practices, programs for current employees, and programs for departing employees.

§ 13.3 —Preemployment Disclosure

Beginning at the first contact with a prospective employee during the recruiting process, your company's recruiters should inform prospective employees about intellectual property policies and procedures. The recruiters should explain to prospective employees how your company will expect all of the company's proprietary information to be kept secret. The prospective employees should also be made aware that the company will expect them to sign employee agreements as a condition for employment and that such agreements contain confidentiality and patent assignment clauses. The requirements of these clauses and their effect on the employees should be outlined during the initial meetings.

Prospective engineers and researchers should be made aware from the beginning that they will be exposed to vital trade secrets during their employment and that your company expects them to sign a confidentiality agreement to maintain these trade secrets in confidence as a condition for employment. They should further understand that all technological developments are proprietary to the company. It should be emphasized that under the employee agreement, they will be required to assign all patents produced as a result of their efforts to the company.

Of course, when employment negotiations dictate, your company may offer assignment clauses that are more favorable to the employee. Regardless of the terms, however, your company should demonstrate to the prospective employee at an early stage in the employee's relationship with your company that your company is sincere in its concern for the protection of its intellectual property rights. Begin this demonstration at the recruitment level.

Once your company offers a prospective employee a job and the prospective employee accepts the job, your company should send a document to the prospective employee that details its intellectual property policies and procedures. Your company should also send a copy of an employment agreement that the new employee will be expected to sign. This agreement should clearly state that the employee agrees to abide by the intellectual property policies and procedures required by the company. After reviewing these obligations to your company, a prospective employee may decide that the terms are unacceptable or that the prospective employee is unable to comply with the terms because of obligations to past employers. Ideally, your company and the prospective employee will identify any potential conflicts before employment is finalized.

Your company may also wish to send a form requesting that prospective employees acknowledge, by signing and returning the form, that they have read the employee agreement and that they understand that your company conditions its offer of employment upon compliance with the terms of the employee agreement.

§ 13.4 —Hiring New Employees from Competitor

Hiring a new employee from a competitor demands special attention because that employee may possess privileged proprietary information belonging to the competitor. Your company must be cautious not to open itself up to allegations of stealing a competitor's trade secrets through the hiring of the competitor's employees. One way to prevent such allegations is to isolate the employee from subjects that may present a conflict and to educate the new employee not to disclose the competitor's proprietary

§ 13.4 HIRING FROM COMPETITOR

information. If isolating the employee seems impractical, then reevaluate your motives for hiring the employee. If your motive is to benefit from the employee's knowledge of technological secrets gained from the previous employer, you are better off passing up the hiring opportunity.[1]

If you are able to isolate the new employee from situations that may raise a conflict, then recognize that your company should also have established special hiring procedures for former employees of competitors that require the new employee to remain silent regarding the competitor's proprietary information. The special hiring procedures might include the following special features:

1. Warn prospective employees not to disclose a competitor's proprietary information. Warn prospective employees who currently work, or have worked, for a competitor that they are obligated to keep secret their former employer's proprietary information. At the hiring stage, the prospective employee should sign an acknowledgement that (1) she will not disclose a competitor's trade secrets, (2) she understands that your company does not expect or desire the employee to reveal a competitor's trade secrets, and (3) she agrees to immediately report to your company's legal department or counsel any instance in which she is pressured by any company employee to disclose trade secrets.

2. Contact the competitor. Before your company hires a competitor's former employee, you may wish to inform the competitor of the proposed employment between its former employee and your company, if the circumstances permit. Try to assure the competitor that your company does not intend to allow the former employee to disclose or use any proprietary information acquired during employment with the competitor. If the competitor responds negatively, make a record of your attempt and the competitor's response.

   When your relationship with another company is sufficiently amicable, seek consent from the competitor to permit its former employee to work in a new field of technology at your company. Indeed, simply asking for the competitor's consent, whether or not the competitor responds, confirms that your company is acting in good faith in the hiring process, is mindful of its obligation not to improperly exploit the employee's knowledge, and is candid with the competitor

---

[1] *See, e.g.,* Central Soya, Inc. v. Geo. A. Hormel & Co., 581 F. Supp. 54, 219 U.S.P.Q. (BNA) 878 (W.D. Okla. 1983) (hiring a competitor's employee may be evidence of willfulness), *aff'd,* 723 F.2d 1573, 220 U.S.P.Q. (BNA) 490 (Fed. Cir. 1983).

about the field of technology assigned to the employee. These actions should be looked upon favorably if your company is later accused of misappropriation of trade secrets.
3. Conduct a security evaluation of the prospective employee. Conduct a security evaluation of your competitor's former employee before offering a position of employment. The security evaluation may range from an intensive evaluation to a mere follow up on a resume, depending upon the level of security required by the position. If, for example, your company contemplates hiring a person as a project engineer for a highly proprietary project, as a matter of policy, thoroughly investigate the employee's background and company loyalties. This action not only might reveal a potential conflict with a competitor, but also supports your company's affirmative steps toward maintaining the secrecy of its own confidential intellectual property.

§ 13.5 —Orientation for New Employees

After new employees are hired, your company should offer an orientation that thoroughly explains the company's intellectual property policies and procedures. Remind new employees hired from a competitor not to disclose their former employer's proprietary information to anyone in your company, with an explanation of the legal and practical consequences of such a disclosure.

§ 13.6 —Employee Agreement

When hiring new employees and introducing them to your company's intellectual property policies, your company should require the new employees to sign an employee agreement. These agreements must expressly set forth the employee's obligations to your company regarding intellectual property. The new employee should already be familiar with the document because your company sent a copy to the employee during the recruitment process.

The reasons for placing intellectual property clauses in employee agreements are compelling. First, courts are more likely to enforce an agreement containing express obligations toward intellectual property. Although a court might determine that an employee had an implied duty to keep confidential her former company's proprietary information in the absence of an agreement, the fact that the employee signed an agreement with express provisions designed to protect your company's proprietary information will prove beneficial.

§ 13.6 EMPLOYEE AGREEMENT

In *Eaton Corp. v. Giere*,[2] an appellate court concluded that an employee, Giere, had breached a duty of confidentiality owed to his former employer, Eaton Corporation, based upon a contractual duty and a common law duty. The court found that Giere showed drawings that contained proprietary information to prospective customers in direct violation of a provision in his employment agreement. Additionally, the court determined that even in the absence of this contractual duty, Giere had a duty under common law not to use trade secrets or confidential information obtained from his employer.

Second, an employee agreement can establish broader protection than that afforded a company without an express agreement. In other words, a court may enforce an obligation under a signed agreement even though the court would not have otherwise imposed the same obligation in the absence of the signed agreement. For example, a company cannot normally prevent a former employee from competing against it immediately following the employee's departure. The company might, however, prevent competition from a former employee if the employee had expressly agreed during her employment to a provision barring specified areas of competition against the company for a reasonable period of time. In this case, the written provision would increase the company's protection against loss of trade secrets by preventing the former employee from using the trade secrets in competition with the company for a period of time following the employee's departure. These written provisions, known as *restrictive covenants not to compete*, are discussed in more detail below. See also Kurt H. Decker, *Covenants Not to Compete* (John Wiley & Sons, 2d ed. 1993).

Third, a written agreement once again notifies the employee that the company has intellectual property rights it intends to protect. This reinforces the notion that the company values its trade secrets and expects its employees to take personal steps to guarantee the secrecy of the company's trade secrets, even after terminating their employment.

If employment negotiations permit, your company's employee agreements should include the following three provisions: a nondisclosure of trade secret provision, a restrictive covenant provision, and an assignment provision.

1. **Nondisclosure of trade secret provision.** A trade secret provision restricts an employee from disclosing or using any of your company's trade secrets, except in the course of employment. Nondisclosure provisions are important for enforcing your company's trade secret rights against a former employee who has misappropriated your company's trade secrets. A classic trade secret case, *Kewanee Oil Co. v.*

---

[2] 23 U.S.P.Q.2d (BNA) 1705 (Fed. Cir. 1992).

Bicron Corp.,[3] illustrates the usefulness of a nondisclosure provision in employee contracts. In this case, Harshaw, a division of Kewanee Oil spent 17 years and over $1 million to research and develop a technique to grow 17-inch crystals for use in the detection of ionizing radiation. The technique involved many processes, procedures, and manufacturing methods relating to purification of raw materials and the growth and encapsulation of the crystals. Some of these processes were maintained by Harshaw as trade secrets. No other company could duplicate this achievement.

An employee of the Kewanee Oil division then left to join Bicron. Fortunately for Kewanee Oil, the employee had already signed a nondisclosure agreement not to disclose the trade secrets. Amazingly, just eight months after the employee left, Bicron was able to grow a 17-inch crystal. Based on this evidence, the court found that Kewanee Oil owned trade secret rights to the crystal growth processes and that Bicron misappropriated these trade secrets when it used the information obtained by the former employee. The court was persuaded by the fact that the former employee disclosed the trade secrets to Bicron in breach of the nondisclosure agreement.

When drafting the nondisclosure provision, you must specifically define what your company considers to be its proprietary information. Failure to define the proprietary information covered by the nondisclosure provision may indicate that your company did not take sufficient affirmative steps to protect its trade secrets.[4] In addition, courts may not enforce a provision that does not specifically define the proprietary information. The courts may simply view the provision as overly broad and placing an undue burden on the employee to keep everything secret.[5]

2. **Restrictive covenant provision.** A restrictive covenant prohibits an employee from competing in a specified field for a stated period of time after termination of employment. Such agreements are viewed with suspicion because they can tend to restrict the ability of a former employee to successfully find new employment. Some state courts are reluctant to enforce such a provision, unless drafted narrowly, in view of a public policy not to unreasonably infringe an individual's

---

[3] 416 U.S. 470 (1974).

[4] Motorola, Inc. v. Fairchild Camera & Instrument Corp., 366 F. Supp. 1173, 177 U.S.P.Q. (BNA) 614 (D. Ariz. 1973).

[5] Motorola, Inc. v. Fairchild Camera & Instrument Corp., 366 F. Supp. 1173, 177 U.S.P.Q. (BNA) 614 (D. Ariz. 1973).

personal rights to seek employment.[6] In some states, notably California, such agreements are unenforceable.[7]

Most courts are willing to enforce a restrictive covenant provision if it reasonably defines the scope of technology and provides reasonable time and territory restrictions.[8] A scope of technology restriction is reasonable if it restricts activities pertaining only to the kind of technology the former employee had access to during employment.[9] For the time and territory restrictions, a restrictive covenant provision is reasonable if it restricts a former employee from competing in a specific geographical region and only for a specific period of time after employment necessary to protect your company's legitimate business interests.[10] The permissible size of a geographical region varies depending upon the market conditions, such as market size, the number of competitors, and the company's market position. With respect to time, a restrictive covenant for a maximum of about one to two years is generally permissible.[11]

3. **Assignment provision**. An assignment provision requires employees to assign all rights to any invention, trade secret, or copyrightable work they develop as a result of their employment with your company. The assignment provision should encompass rights to all information known by the employees as a result of their employment.

An assignment provision is the most widely accepted way for your company to protect its investment in its employees' inventions. In the absence of an assignment provision, your company may still obtain *shop rights* to certain inventions if the employee used company time and resources to conceive and develop the invention. A *shop right* is a royalty-free, nontransferable, and nonexclusive license to the invention. Of course, because a shop right license is nontransferable and nonexclusive, the employee may legally license the invention to a competitor. Further, obtaining shop rights often breeds

---

[6] California, Louisiana, Wisconsin, and Michigan have statutes that discourage restrictive covenants. J. Dratler, Jr., Intellectual Property Law: Commercial, Creative and Industrial Property §§ 4.02[1], [2] (1991).

[7] Cal. Bus. & Prof. Code § 16600.

[8] Hen & Alexander, Law of Corporations (3d ed. 1983); *see* Sires v. Luke, 544 F. Supp. 1155 (S.D. Ga. 1982).

[9] Computer Assocs. Int'l, Inc. v. Bryan, 784 F. Supp. 982 (E.D.N.Y. 1992); Business Intelligence Serv., Inc. v. Hudson, 580 F. Supp. 1068 (S.D.N.Y.1984).

[10] *Compare In re* Uniservices, Inc., 517 F.2d 492 (7th Cir. 1975) (one-year restrictive covenant for 75-mile radius upheld as reasonable) *with* Gary Van Zeeland Talent, Inc. v. Sandas, 84 Wis. 2d 202, 262 N.W.2d 242 (1978) (five-year restrictive covenant for 300-mile radius found to be unreasonable).

[11] *See In re* Uniservices, Inc., 517 F.2d 492 (7th Cir. 1975) (one-year restrictive covenant upheld as reasonable).

litigation between the former employee and the former employer. Therefore, rather than relying on shop rights, an express assignment provision in an employee agreement is a less expensive and more conclusive way to confirm your company's rights to the information or inventions developed by its employees.

In several states, however, a company may not be allowed to assume all rights to all inventions created by an employee during employment, even if such an assignment provision exists. Several states have enacted employee patent acts that limit the subjects of inventions which an employer can insist that its employees assign to it.[12] In general, these acts prohibit assignments of information or inventions for which no equipment, supplies, or facilities of the company are used.

Turning specifically to copyright protection, in the absence of an express copyright assignment clause, a company may be able to rely on the *work made for hire* provision in the copyright statute. This provides ownership rights in works made by an employee in the scope of employment. However, an express agreement governing title of copyrights is better.

§ 13.7 —Employment Manuals

Your company should include its intellectual property policies and procedures in any employment manual issued to employees. The manual should reiterate, in writing, your company's policies and procedures that were explained to new employees during orientation. The employment manual might also explain the functions of your intellectual property department (if you have one) and outline procedures for dealing with inventions, such as how inventions are channeled for review. The manual may also discuss how to establish an invention disclosure record describing the new invention. A brief explanation of the patent process in the manual would also be helpful to educate employees.

As a side issue, each manual can be a company trade secret because it contains certain valuable information that is not generally known outside of the company. Therefore, treat the manual with appropriate caution. Identify each manual with an identification number and record the identification number together with the name of the recipient employee. This record emphasizes to the employee that the manual may contain trade secrets and must therefore be handled with care. The record also identifies

---

[12] W. Jones, Protecting Intellectual Property from Within: In-House Programs, Employee Agreements, Non-Disclosure Agreements and Technical Assistance Agreements, presented June 8, 1988.

the employee responsible for a missing manual. Perhaps most important, the record shows a court that your company is taking affirmative steps to protect its trade secrets.

§ 13.8 —Periodic Reminders of Intellectual Property Obligations

Your company should periodically remind employees of their intellectual property obligations to your company. Your company should continually remind and update employees on what it considers to be its trade secrets and that confidentiality is mandatory. The proper approach to protecting these rights should also be reviewed to ensure that the rights are enforceable against others. Such reminders will help demonstrate to a court that your company has taken affirmative steps to protect its trade secret rights. Prime places for reminders include newsletters, company bulletin boards, intercompany memos, electronic-mail systems, and employee check stubs.

§ 13.9 —Seminars to Educate Employees

Your intellectual property department, or outside counsel that represents your company, should conduct yearly or biyearly seminars for each department in your company to educate and reeducate each employee with respect to current intellectual property policies and procedures. These seminars can be used to review your company's current activities in the intellectual property area, such as identifying company trade secrets and reviewing the Protection Analysis Model. During these seminars, the importance of adhering to company policies and procedures to prevent unnecessary loss of intellectual property rights must be reemphasized. This includes a refresher course on trade secret law and the bars to patentability. The seminars could also be used to demonstrate the value of a strong intellectual property portfolio and to motivate employees to work together with other employees toward obtaining and supporting a strong portfolio.

With your new understanding of the expanse of protectable intellectual property in even the smallest companies, you can now recognize that every employee of your company, from your maintenance crews to the Nobel-winning engineers, is entrusted with company trade secrets. Thus, employees at all levels in each department should attend the intellectual property policy seminars, including the obvious candidates such as project managers, marketers, and engineers, as well as less obvious candidates such as engineering technicians and machinery repairpersons. To minimize employee downtime and to boost attentiveness at the seminars, begin a program in which employees, as representatives from each department and support area, attend the seminars on a revolving basis and report on the seminar, by memorandum, to the other members of the department or support area.

The seminars are especially important for protection of trade secrets. The intellectual property department or counsel must preach the importance of trade secrets, both in terms of profit and market position and how easily trade secrets may be lost. Each company department must be taught that protecting trade secrets is a team effort of the entire company and that one accidental disclosure of a trade secret by any one member of the team may result in a competitively crippling blow to the company.

§ 13.10 —Procedures for Departing Employees

When an employee decides to leave your company, your company should remind the departing employee of the intellectual property obligations owed to the company. The following procedures are useful in preparing an employee for departure and will provide further evidence that your company is taking affirmative steps to maintain confidentiality:

1. **Examine departing employee's activities during the last weeks of employment.** Before holding a departure meeting, carefully examine the departing employee's activities during the last weeks of employment. If the employee is leaving to work for a competitor, the departing employee might have an incentive to take your company's proprietary information. You may wish to inquire whether the employee has ordered copies of special drawings or technical reports or whether that employee has been in restricted areas in which she is not customarily seen. Although you hope your employees are honest and have good explanations for any odd behavior in their waning weeks of employment, your company is best advised to take precautions rather than lose trade secrets to a competitor.

2. **Departure meeting.** Your company should conduct a departure meeting with the departing employee to review that employee's duties to your company. During the departure meeting, present the employment agreement that was signed by the departing employee when first hired, to reinforce those obligations expressly agreed to by the employee. Your company may even wish to have the departing employee sign an acknowledgement form stating that she understands the continuing obligations to your company to retain proprietary information in confidence. Specifically, the meeting must enforce that the departing employee has an obligation to keep specifically identifiable trade secrets confidential and to not disclose any subject matter that is in the process of being patented.

3. **Inquire into employee's new employment.** Your company may wish to inquire whether the employee's new employment is in a related technological field. This inquiry helps to assess the risk of proprietary information's leaking out to a competitor.

4. **Contact the departing employee's new employer.** If a departing employee is going to work for a competitor in a related technological field, your company may wish to inform the competitor of the employee's confidentiality obligations to your company. Also, you should discourage the competitor from placing the employee in a compromising position that would lead to the disclosure or use of your company's proprietary information. Failure to notify the competitor may allow the competitor to claim that it was an innocent and unknowing recipient of your company's proprietary information.[13] Recall the case from **Chapter 12** in which a court found Universal Slide Fasteners not liable to Conmar for alleged theft of Conmar's zipper trade secrets on the basis that Universal Slide Fasteners had no knowledge that its new employees (who had previously worked for Conmar) were using Conmar's zipper trade secrets.

5. **Demand the return of all proprietary information.** The departing employee should return all materials containing proprietary information. Classified materials might include laboratory notebooks, progress notebooks, sketches, drawings, personal notes, and employment manuals. Be sure to inquire about materials maintained by the employee at home. This is a practice quite prevalent among technical personnel.

6. **Follow-up letter to former employee restating obligations.** After the employee has left your company, send a follow-up letter to the departed employee restating her obligations of maintaining the proprietary information in confidence. For convenience, and to insure that the former employee gives the letter some careful consideration, the follow-up letter may be sent with the former employee's last paycheck.

§ 13.11 Laboratory Procedures

Recall from **Chapter 12** the requirements for first inventorship—conception, reduction to practice, diligence between conception and reduction to practice, and corroboration of these events by a disinterested person.

---

[13] Conmar Prod. Corp. v. Universal Slide Fasteners Co., 172 F.2d 150, 80 U.S.P.Q. (BNA) 108 (2d Cir. 1949).

These requirements are best evidenced through properly maintained engineering notebooks or other records. Accurate and corroborated engineering records during the conception and development stages of technology are often used to establish dates of conception and reduction to practice in a first inventorship dispute. In addition, maintaining progress records during the building and testing phases of a product helps to identify when an invention is sufficiently completed for purposes of the public use and on-sale bars to patentability. The procedures in §§ 13.12 through 13.16 are designed for the laboratory or research and development area in your company to ensure that it receives appropriate and accurate recordation and corroboration efforts from its employees.

§ 13.12 —Record Daily Activities of Engineers

The importance of documenting the daily activities of your company's technical personnel cannot be overstated. Your company should require that all engineers and scientists involved in research and development maintain daily notes of their efforts. The notes should be made regardless of their immediate conclusions as to the worth of their endeavors. Emphasizing to your employees that trade secret information involves both "know-how" and "know-not-how" reinforces to your engineers and scientists the importance of chronicling their failures as well as their successes.

Technical personnel should keep these daily notes in a bound paginated notebook, which is labeled conspicuously as *SECRET AND CONFIDENTIAL*. Date all notebook entries to provide a chronological concordance of the developmental stages of the invention. This procedure helps identify when the inventors first conceived the invention and accurately records when each developmental event occurred.

All entries should be written in clear, readable text with sufficient explanation to permit someone skilled in the technology to comprehend the inventive steps. Remember, the benefit from a legal standpoint of maintaining this notebook is to provide evidence of research and development before the filing date of the patent application for establishing an earlier invention date than the filing date of a corresponding patent application, and thus, earlier first inventorship. If a patent examiner, the Board of Patent Appeals and Interferences, or the federal courts ever require proof of an invention date earlier than the filing date of a company patent, these notebooks offer long-lasting evidence of the corresponding inventive steps. Therefore, a notebook presented in a clear, progressive, and explanatory commentary will greatly assist all concerned parties, and mostly your company.

The daily records should reveal all events, including mistakes. Correct errors in daily notebooks by drawing a single line through the incorrect text, rather than erasing. Then, if any inconsistencies exist after the correction, the writer can explain these inconsistencies in the notebook. The goal is to have a complete record of events leading to the invention.

§ 13.13 —Corroboration by Disinterested Employee

Some issues involving first inventorship demand corroborated proof, rather than unsupported statements of an inventor.[14] For this reason, each technical employee must have a disinterested employee or other person review, understand, and corroborate (by signing and dating) all entries in the author's notebook. The corroborating employee must possess sufficient skill to understand both the applicable technology and the specific notebook entries even though the corroborating employee is, preferably, not involved in the same company project as the author of the notebook. Routine corroboration of notebooks should be conducted weekly or bimonthly. However, breakthrough ideas or experimental advances should be documented and corroborated immediately on the same day that the breakthrough occurs.

After reviewing the entries, the corroborating employee should write in the inventor's notebook:

READ AND UNDERSTOOD BY

(signature of employee)
Date: _____

Preferably, your company can use blank technical notebooks with such a signature line preprinted at the bottom of each page. The preprinted signature line is then a reminder to technical personnel that they must corroborate information written on each page of the notebook.

§ 13.14 —Maintain Progress Records

In addition to engineering notebooks, employees who actually construct and test new products should also maintain daily progress records. These

---

[14] For example, the Patent and Trademark Office (PTO) and courts generally refuse to consider uncorroborated records and evidence submitted by the inventor to establish conception, diligence, and reduction to practice. Coleman v. Dines, 754 F.2d 353, 224 U.S.P.Q. (BNA) 857 (Fed. Cir. 1985).

progress records should note which components of the product are tested,[15] how well the components or the whole product performed in the test,[16] and whether improvements are necessary.[17] The progress records are useful to determine (1) whether the invention has been actually reduced to practice, and (2) whether the invention is sufficiently developed to invoke the on-sale bar to patentability under § 102. It is advisable to record progress events in a bound, paginated notebook, with all entries dated and signed by another person.

§ 13.15 —Catalog Engineering and Progress Notebooks

Your company should catalog and shelve the engineering and progress notebooks in a central storage facility. These notebooks identify valuable trade secrets of your company and thus require proper maintenance in a safe and organized facility.

The notebooks should be numbered and classified in terms of subject matter. Keep a catalog to facilitate easy retrieval and include in the catalog information concerning the type of subject matter, author (the engineer), dates covered in the notebook, and the assigned library code. Remember that the cataloging system must be sufficient so that an employer, when called upon to do so, can retrieve the notebooks for use as evidence in the Patent and Trademark Office (PTO) or the courts. If practicality permits, you may wish to cross reference other notebooks having the same subject matter or written by the same author. Maintaining an appropriate index that helps identify your company's proprietary information may help indicate that your company is taking affirmative steps to protect its trade secrets. In the *Motorola v. Fairchild* case discussed in **Chapter 12**,

---

[15] Listing the components tested helps indicate when the invention was first tested. If the invention is simply a component of a system, then testing other components of the system does not trigger the on-sale bar. *See, e.g.*, A.B. Chance v. RTE Corp., 854 F.2d 1307, 7 U.S.P.Q.2d (BNA) 1881 (Fed. Cir. 1988) (summary judgment invalidating a patent under § 102(b) is not appropriate when evidence showed that the critical components of the claimed invention had not been developed).

[16] T.P. Lab., Inc. v. Professional Positioners, 724 F.2d 965, 220 U.S.P.Q. (BNA) 577 (Fed. Cir. 1984) (looking to the dentist's notebook, which expressed the results of testing a new mouth positioner as "fair," "better," and "good," as evidence of the progress of the invention and when the dentist became satisfied that the invention worked for its intended purpose).

[17] Great N. Corp. v. Davis Core & Pad Co., 782 F.2d 159, 228 U.S.P.Q. (BNA) 356 (Fed. Cir. 1986) (the tests of a new foam support webbing for use in shipping performed before the one-year critical date did not invoke a bar to patentability because the tests resulted in cracked supports and were failures).

the court suggested that Motorola's failure to keep proprietary information in an orderly and safe fashion was one factor evidencing its failure to take affirmative steps to keep its trade secrets confidential.[18]

§ 13.16 —Maintain Records Pertaining to Daily Time Sheets of Personnel

In addition to technical notebooks, your company should require its technical employees to maintain narrative daily time sheets. These time sheets may establish an employee's exposure and access to particular proprietary information. If this practice proves too burdensome, your company should at least keep a record of the employees' absences.

The following hypothetical fact situation illustrates the importance of this procedure. An employee leaves your company for a competitor. Almost immediately, the competitor begins making a product very similar to your company's own product, a product to which the former employee had access when employed at your company. If your company believes that this former employee misappropriated its trade secrets with respect to this product, time sheets indicating that the employee contributed a significant number of hours on the development of this product may help indicate during litigation that the employee had sufficient access to misappropriate certain trade secrets of your company.

§ 13.17 Security Procedures

Security procedures begin with your company's fundamental security system, such as locking doors during nonwork hours, and plant security/alarm systems. These basic precautions should not be your only security procedures as far as intellectual property is concerned. Your company may wish to implement the security procedures discussed in §§ **13.18** and **13.19**, which are tailored to protect know-how and trade secrets.

§ 13.18 —Facility Restrictions

Prohibit access of all nonclassified personnel to key plant facilities. Failure to restrict access is a strong factor showing lack of affirmative conduct in maintaining trade secrets. In the *Motorola* case, a company permitted

---

[18] Motorola, Inc. v. Fairchild Camera & Instrument Corp., 366 F. Supp. 1173, 177 U.S.P.Q. (BNA) 614 (D. Ariz. 1973).

regular plant tours of a production line that the company claimed to be a trade secret.[19] The company placed no signs in the area warning of the presence of trade secrets, nor did the company offer any verbal warnings to the tour groups. In fact, the company allowed the people on the plant tour to take pictures. Based in part on this lack of security procedures, the court determined that the company failed to take reasonable steps to protect its trade secrets. Some facility restrictions include:

1. **Restrict access to sensitive areas.** Access to sensitive areas, such as research and development, testing, and production areas, should be restricted. These sensitive areas should be locked and perhaps guarded. Post signs identifying the area as restricted and keep a record of when and which classified employees enter and exit the sensitive area.
2. **Restrict access to sensitive material.** A logical extension of restricting access to sensitive areas is to restrict access to the work product from the sensitive areas. Your company should restrict access to sensitive material such as drawings, prints, or engineering and progress notebooks. Keep the sensitive material in a reasonably secure storage facility and permit only limited classes of personnel to examine these notebooks. Additionally, a log book should be provided to record who has accessed the materials.
3. **Impose security procedures for file facilities.** Assign a custodian to each storage facility containing sensitive materials and require each custodian to keep a notebook of who checked out materials. The technology storage facilities containing the notebooks should be locked every evening and any time during the day when the custodian is not present. Lock all file cabinets containing sensitive documents and computer storage discs. In this manner, your company can track and restrict the flow of trade secret information.
4. **Restrict access to computers.** Your company should avoid linking computers used in sensitive areas to computers used in nonsensitive areas. This procedure will prevent people from accidentally or purposefully accessing sensitive material via computer link. Also, passwords can be assigned to each classified employee working with computers in sensitive areas, whereby the password is designed solely for those particular computers.
5. **Restrict access to photocopiers.** Because employees may use photocopiers to make unauthorized copies of confidential material, such as engineering drawings, distribution schedules, customer lists, or

---

[19] Motorola, Inc. v. Fairchild Camera & Instrument Corp., 366 F. Supp. 1173, 177 U.S.P.Q. (BNA) 614 (D. Ariz. 1973).

marketing plans, your company should restrict access to photocopiers located where employees (even classified employees) may view sensitive documents. Your company may wish to centralize the photocopiers and assign certain employees to do all photocopying. These employees could ensure that the people requesting copies have proper authorization to copy the confidential documents. By keeping a log of properly made copies, your company will be able to later account for the properly requested copies and prove that it took steps to monitor the copying activities.

6. **Take visitor precautions.** Your company should provide only one entrance for visitors, with a receptionist or guard stationed at this entrance. All visitors should be required to sign a visitor's log and wear a badge identifying them as visitors. Visitors should be escorted by an employee while on the company premises. Do not conduct plant tours into restricted areas. If you must expose confidential information to visitors, do so only after the visitor signs a nondisclosure agreement. If you inadvertently expose any confidential information to a visitor, press the visitor to sign a nondisclosure agreement before leaving the facility.

§ 13.19 —Handling Confidential Material

Employees of your company must be reminded and encouraged to cautiously handle all material and documents that contain confidential proprietary information. This includes limiting and controlling reproductions of confidential material so that copies are not accidentally released to the public or competitors. Special care must be exercised to prevent such material from being sent to customers. Documents containing any proprietary information that are no longer needed should be shredded or otherwise destroyed. Do not feel secure against corporate espionage; competitors have been known to resort to rummaging through the trash to acquire their competitors' confidential information.

§ 13.20 Release Review Procedures

Your company may wish to adopt certain policies to limit the risk of accidental or premature disclosure of proprietary information. Such policies reduce the risk of losing patent rights in an invention through public use, sale, or publication and limit the risk of permanently losing a trade secret through inadvertent public disclosure.

Your company should designate appropriate personnel, including the members of the legal department, to review all speeches, trade show displays, news releases, and publications before release. This may prevent premature disclosure of an invention or accidental disclosure of a trade secret. The material should be reviewed for the following considerations: (1) disclosure of patentable subject matter that might affect domestic and foreign patent rights; (2) disclosure of the company's trade secrets; (3) disclosure of confidential information of another company with which the company is in a confidential relationship; and (4) disclosure of information that may be involved in a pending or future legal controversy.[20]

A trade secret is irreversibly lost when disclosed at a trade show or through speeches and publications.[21] The problem of accidental disclosure is particularly high during trade shows, where salespeople eagerly seek to attract potential customers. A salesperson's boasting about a product's attributes may reveal patentable or confidential information. With respect to patent rights, such speeches, trade shows, and publications may invoke the publication, public use, and on-sale bars of § 102(b). Therefore, a policy to review information before release assists in avoiding loss of trade secrets and patentability.

Release review procedures that your company should consider for inclusion in its intellectual property guidelines are discussed in §§ **13.21** through **13.24**.

§ 13.21 —Distribution of Advertisements and Brochures

Your company should forbid the release of advertisements and brochures that disclose new technology until the appropriate personnel, including your legal department or counsel, have approved the distribution. This approval is given only after thorough analysis of the effect that the distribution will have on potential or current intellectual property rights. It is also advisable not to circulate advertisements and brochures until the new technology has been evaluated under the Protection Analysis Model. See **Chapter 5**. If the technology is to be kept as a trade secret, such a policy will prevent accidental public disclosure of substantive information. If the technology is to be patented, the policy will prevent an employee from accidentally placing the invention on sale or publishing the invention and therefore prevents unnecessary loss of patent rights.[22]

---

[20] T. O'Brien, *Establishing a Company Policy and Program for Intellectual Property Rights*, 50 Alb. L. Rev. 551 (1986).

[21] *See, e.g.*, CVD, Inc. v. Raytheon, Co., 769 F.2d 842, 227 U.S.P.Q. (BNA) 7 (1st Cir. 1985) (a competent engineer could construct plaintiff's trade secret process based upon information disclosed to public, including papers published by employees; film shown at engineering conference; published photographs; and public speeches accompanied by slides of process), *cert. denied*, 475 U.S. 1016 (1986).

[22] *In re* Brigance, 792 F.2d 1103, 1107, 229 U.S.P.Q. (BNA) 988, 990 (Fed. Cir. 1986) (sales brochures advertising the invention are sufficient to invoke the on-sale bar).

§ 13.22 —Publications in Trade and Professional Journals

Engineers and researchers should not publish their discoveries and inventions in trade or professional journals until after the appropriate personnel, including the legal department, have analyzed the effect of the publication on potential or current intellectual property rights. Again, it is important to analyze all new technology under the Protection Analysis Model before any publications describe the new technology. If the technology is to be patented, this policy will prevent premature publication from barring patentability in the United States or abroad. If the technology is to be maintained as a trade secret, the policy will ensure that the employee does not accidentally disclose to the public material the company wishes to maintain in secrecy.

§ 13.23 —Demonstrations of New Technology

Employees should be prohibited from demonstrating their company's inventions to investors or customers until the appropriate personnel, including the legal department, approve the demonstration after analyzing the effect of the demonstration on potential or current intellectual properties. Again, this policy will help to prevent inadvertent disclosure of trade secret information. If patent protection is desired, this policy prevents possible triggering of the on-sale bar[23] or the public use bar[24] to patentability.

§ 13.24 —Test Marketing New Products

Refrain from test marketing a new product until after determining how, or if, your company will protect the new product under the intellectual property laws. Many companies test market their new products to a small sample population to assess how well the product may sell. The sample population may consist of a few random customers or of an entire geographic region. Test marketing, however, can invoke the on-sale or public use bars to patentability.[25] Furthermore, test marketing does not fall under

---

[23] *In re* Mann, 861 F.2d 1581, 8 U.S.P.Q.2d (BNA) 2030 (Fed. Cir. 1988).

[24] Harrington Mfg. Co. v. Powell Mfg. Co., 815 F.2d 1478, 2 U.S.P.Q.2d (BNA) 1364 (Fed. Cir. 1986).

[25] *In re* Smith, 714 F.2d 1127, 218 U.S.P.Q. (BNA) 976 (Fed. Cir. 1983). Construction Specialties, Inc. v. Arden Architectural Specialties, Inc., 20 U.S.P.Q.2d (BNA) 1874 (D. Minn. 1991).

the experimental use exception.[26] The experimental use exception is reserved for testing the operability and features of the product to determine whether the product has utility, not whether consumers are willing to buy the product. This policy helps your company avoid the public use and on-sale bars to patentability.

§ 13.25 Patent Marking

For the reasons discussed in **Chapter 8**, namely, notifying a competitor that any unauthorized making, using, or selling of your company's product is an infringement of its rights, it is necessary that your company clearly mark all products incorporating patented technology with the number of the patent covering the product. If a patent has not yet issued, mark the product with a notice of *patent pending* or *patent applied for*.

§ 13.26 Copyright Marking

All sales brochures, television commercials, instruction booklets, warranties, and other visually perceptible works should be marked with a copyright notice. The following notice is appropriate:

© 1992 COMPANY, INC.

Recall that the notice helps the copyright owner in litigation by preventing a defendant from mitigating damages by claiming that she "innocently infringed" the work because she was unaware that the work was copyrighted.[27] Your company's television commercials should also carry a notice for the same reasons.[28]

§ 13.27 Trademark Marking

Your company should place a notice symbol ® beside all federally registered trademarks. If the mark is not federally registered, a TM (or SM if services are involved) should be placed beside it. Such notice is important to alert competitors that your company intends to claim rights in the mark and that unauthorized use of the mark is prohibited.

---

[26] *In re* Smith, 714 F.2d 1127, 1134, 218 U.S.P.Q. (BNA) 976, 983 (Fed. Cir. 1983) (experimental use exception "does not include market testing where the inventor is attempting to gauge consumer demand for his claimed invention").

[27] 17 U.S.C. § 401(d) (1978).

[28] 17 U.S.C. § 402 (1978).

§ 13.28 Technological Relationships with Other Companies

Your company should devise and document special policies governing intellectual property issues in business relationships with other companies. For instance, your company may wish to disclose know-how and trade secrets to potential customers, licensees, and joint venture partners. Before disclosure, however, your company must ensure that the other company will respect and protect your company's trade secrets. The policies in §§ 13.29 through 13.33 are directed toward governing the flow of proprietary information to another company.

§ 13.29 —Initially Disclose Only General Information

At the initial meeting with a prospective business partner, it is advisable to discuss only general, nonproprietary information regarding the technology. In this manner, your company may educate the prospective partner about your company's operations and technology without first burdening them with signing a confidentiality agreement. This might psychologically enhance the relationship from the outset by alleviating any aura of distrust that may enshroud the presentation of a confidentiality agreement.

§ 13.30 —Confidentiality Agreements

Once the prospective partner expresses a sincere interest in further negotiations, request that the prospective partner sign a written confidentiality agreement before your company discloses any of its know-how, trade secrets, or soon-to-be patented products. The confidential disclosure agreement (also known as a *secrecy agreement*) requires in general that both companies maintain in confidence proprietary information presented to them.

§ 13.31 —Stamp CONFIDENTIAL on All Documents Transferred to Business Partner

Before the release of any company documents to the prospective partner, stamp all documents *CONFIDENTIAL*. The *CONFIDENTIAL* stamp warns the business partner that the technology presented is confidential and is to be maintained in secrecy during the business relationship and after the relationship has ended. Further, the *CONFIDENTIAL* stamp gives notice to the business partner that your company intends to take measures to protect and enforce the confidentiality of its technological information.

§ 13.32 —Record Transfer of Proprietary Information

During the business relationship, keep careful records of all proprietary information transferred to the other company. Such records should include a list of what information was exchanged, the date of the disclosure, the representative from the other company to which disclosure was made, the company employee who made the disclosure, and the reasons for the transfer.

§ 13.33 —Research and Development Relationships with Other Companies

Due to financial or manufacturing limitations, many companies often join together to research, develop, build, and test new products. A problem arises, however, when the relationship appears to be more commercial than developmental. Recall from the discussion in **Chapter 12** that inventions that have been offered for sale or used publicly may not qualify for patent protection for failure to satisfy the on-sale or public use bars to patentability. Yet, in some situations, the experimental use exception may step in to preclude the effect of these bars.

When scrutinizing a partnership relationship, the federal courts look to whether the codevelopment agreement between two companies was primarily for commercial gain. If one company's soon-to-be patented technology is jointly developed by both companies and the relationship appears to be commercial, the business relationship will most likely invoke the public use or on-sale bars to patentability. On the other hand, if the relationship resembles legitimate, technical codevelopment, the experimental use exception will most likely apply so that the public use and on-sale bars do not prevent patentability.

To illustrate the problem, suppose TransWay, a manufacturer of automobile transmissions, has an arrangement with one of its customers, U.S. Car Company, an automobile manufacturer. The arrangement allows U.S. Car to assist in the final stages of development and to test TransWay's transmissions to make them suitable for use in U.S. Car automobiles. Once a new transmission is ready for market, TransWay sells the new

§ 13.33 RESEARCH AND DEVELOPMENT   229

transmission to U.S. Car. Because U.S. Car is both a codeveloper and a customer, the joint development and testing activities may be characterized as a part of a larger commercial relationship. In other words, TransWay may have entered into the relationship primarily to ensure sales to U.S. Car, and then cloaked the relationship in terms of research and development. If the relationship is found to be primarily for commercial gain, the joint venture activity will invoke the public use or on-sale bar to patentability and the experimental use exception will not apply. If, however, the relationship is found to be primarily for determining to the satisfaction of the inventors that the transmissions properly function in their intended use, patentability may be saved by the experimental use exception to the on-sale bar. The following procedures are designed to prevent joint research and development relationships from being improperly characterized as commercial relationships.

1. **Retain control over any experiments and tests performed by the joint partner.** To qualify as an experimental use, the inventor must retain control over the experiments being performed by another company.[29] Activities suggesting that the inventor within your company is retaining control over the experimentation include the inventor's imposing conditions with respect to testing and reporting, requiring test reports, placing restrictions on any use of the product, and placing restrictions regarding any sale or resale of the product.[30]

    Before allowing another company to test your company's new products, have the other company sign an agreement including the following conditions: (1) forbid the other company from reselling, publicly using, or otherwise publicly disclosing the invention (restricting resale is important because a sale by a third party is sufficient to invoke the on-sale bar for the company[31]); (2) request that the other company deliver regular progress reports of the experiments to the inventor; (3) ensure that your inventor assists in conducting the experiments, or in the alternative, that your inventor be permitted to periodically inspect the experiments and offer recommendations for the future direction of the experimentation.

2. **Avoid using salespeople in codevelopment relationships.** Avoid involving salespeople when interacting with a partner company that

---

[29] *In re* Hamilton, 882 F.2d 1576, 11 U.S.P.Q.2d (BNA) 1890 (Fed. Cir. 1989).

[30] *See, e.g.*, Western Marine Elec. v. Furuno Elec. Co., 764 F.2d 840, 226 U.S.P.Q. (BNA) 334 (Fed. Cir. 1985) (a letter offering the invention for sale, which imposed no conditions of reporting, testing, or control, nor any restrictions over resale or use, triggered the on-sale bar).

[31] J.A. LaPorte, Inc. v. Norfolk Dredging Co., 787 F.2d 1577, 229 U.S.P.Q. (BNA) 435 (Fed. Cir. 1986).

will be testing your company's products. All dealings with the other company should be conducted only by personnel from engineering or research and development. The involvement of salespeople may indicate that the primary purpose of the business relationship was commercialization of the product (an activity traditionally controlled by salespeople) rather than experimentation (an activity traditionally controlled by technical employees). In one case, a court found that the display of a prototype floor mat at a trade show constituted public use because such display was aimed at commercial exploitation, not experimentation to improve a product. One factor was that a salesman conducted the demonstration, and not an engineer.[32]

3. **Provide the products to be tested free of cost.** If possible, supply all products to be tested by the other company free of cost. Although payment for the product does not necessarily negate experimental use,[33] payment (especially at a profit) is evidence tending to support that the primary purpose of the sale is commercial exploitation.[34]

§ 13.34 Channel New Ideas to Intellectual Property Counsel

Critical to an effective intellectual property program are procedures for forwarding technological ideas to your intellectual property department or counsel for protection consideration. The Protection Analysis Model in **Chapter 5** is designed to assist you in determining if know-how should be protected and what type of protection should be used. When the know-how has been identified as warranting protection, follow the procedures that you have implemented for bringing the know-how to the attention of the intellectual property department so that the formalities of securing protection may begin.

These procedures are generally company specific, and thus vary widely from company to company. No set of procedures is perfect for every company. The guidelines in §§ **13.35** through **13.37**, however, may prove useful in drafting your company's set of procedures for informing the intellectual property department about new ideas.

---

[32] Construction Specialties, Inc. v. Arden Architectural Specialties, Inc., 20 U.S.P.Q.2d (BNA) 1874 (D. Minn. 1991).

[33] Baker Oil Tools, Inc. v. Geo Vann, Inc., 828 F.2d 1558, 1564, 4 U.S.P.Q.2d (BNA) 1210, 1214 (Fed. Cir. 1987) (payment does not per se make a § 102(b) bar); *In re* Dybel, 524 F.2d 1393, 1399, 187 U.S.P.Q. (BNA) 593, 597 (C.C.P.A. 1975) (a bona fide experimental use may involve incidental income).

[34] T.P. Lab., Inc. v. Professional Positioners, Inc., 724 F.2d 965, 220 U.S.P.Q. (BNA) 577 (Fed. Cir. 1984).

§ 13.35 —Keep Decisions at Grass-roots Level

Decision-making authority to protect know-how should be delegated to employees at the grass roots level, where the innovation is taking place. Generally, engineers and research scientists can best appreciate the utility and limitations of innovative know-how. For example, IBM makes it the responsibility of its individual engineer and the line manager to submit ideas to the intellectual property department.[35] The line manager prioritizes the know-how and recommends which know-how warrants protection. Allocating this power to engineers and line managers encourages awareness of intellectual property among these grass-roots employees. It thereby increases the number of proposals forwarded to the intellectual property department.

§ 13.36 —Educate Employees

Engineers and scientists should be educated about the legal requirements of patents and trade secrets. Engineers often make the erroneous assumption that their innovations are not inventive enough to be patentable, or that patents are awarded only to pioneering discoveries and not merely to improvements in existing technology. As a result, uninformed engineers fail to recognize and submit ideas that could be valuable to your company. Teach your engineers and scientists that they need not reinvent the wheel to obtain a patent. Teach them that know-how need only be useful, novel, and nonobvious to be patentable; that minor improvements over existing technology are worthy of protection consideration; and that improvement patents may prove to be the most valuable in the marketplace. Teach them that trade secret protection is in itself valuable in the event that patent protection is not available, and that trade secret protection is fairly easy to obtain. Finally, educate the employees to use the Protection Analysis Model so they gain a global perspective about analyzing intellectual property.

§ 13.37 —Provide Incentive to Innovate

Your company may wish to provide some incentive for the engineers and scientists to develop valuable intellectual property. Incentives are particularly useful in companies that require their engineers to submit invention

---

[35] R. Smith, Management of a Corporate Intellectual Property Law Department, *reprinted in* AIPLA Bull., Spring Meeting Plenary Session, May 4, 1989.

Table 13-1
Top Motives or Incentives for Encouraging Inventions

1. Love of inventing
2. Desire to improve
3. Financial gain
4. Necessity or need
5. Desire to achieve
6. Part of work
7. Prestige
8. Altruistic reasons.

disclosures to the intellectual property department or counsel for protection review. Because the invention disclosure system depends upon motivated engineers, incentives often encourage these engineers to submit all of their new ideas. Such incentives can range from company recognition to financial compensation.

Thomas Savitsky, senior patent attorney for Eastman Chemical Company, conducted a survey of 118 United States companies with respect to their invention compensation systems.[36] Mr. Savitsky found that about half of the companies had some form of special compensation system for employee inventions, and that such systems could lead to increased invention disclosure and inventor cooperation. Cash incentives were found to range from $100 to $500 per patent application to a sharing of the profits resulting from the invention (for example, $1,000 to $175,000 awards at Texas Instruments).

Other forms of incentives are also important. For example, the inventors could be given plaques in formal or informal ceremonies that recognize their important contributions. In a survey of 710 inventors, Mr. Savitsky found that financial gain was only the third most motivating factor among inventors, behind love of inventing and desire to improve. His list of the top motives or incentives mentioned by the inventors surveyed is provided in **Table 13-1**.

§ 13.38 Handling Unsolicited Ideas

Companies often receive new ideas from various outside sources. The ideas may range from patentable subject matter (such as a suggestion on how to improve a product) to a simple campaign slogan (such as a trademark for a new product or an advertising concept). The ideas are received

---

[36] Savitsky, *Compensation for Employee Inventions*, 73 J. Pat. Off. Soc'y 645 (1991).

through many different channels: mail, telephone, advertisement in a trade journal, an unannounced plant visit, or disclosure to a company employee. Establishing procedures to deal with unsolicited ideas is important because use of such ideas, whether accidental or purposeful, without the consent of the outsider might result in a lawsuit for misappropriation of an idea.

On the other hand, most companies do not want to discourage unsolicited ideas because they feel that public relations demand a cordial demeanor toward outsiders. Furthermore, direct feedback from customers can be of considerable value to your company. To protect against claims of an outsider that your company unfairly stole unsolicited ideas, your company should implement procedures for handling unsolicited ideas from outside sources, including the procedures in §§ 13.39 through 13.42.

§ 13.39 —Designate One Employee to Field All Unsolicited Ideas

Your company should designate one employee (not necessarily a member of the intellectual property department) to field all incoming ideas from outsiders. If the idea is submitted in writing, those in the mailroom should immediately forward the documents to this employee. If the outsider calls the company, forward the phone call to this designated employee. For situations in which the outsider approaches a company employee during off-hours, the employee should be taught to decline discussing the idea and to request that the outsider contact the designated employee directly.

§ 13.40 —Nonconfidential Disclosure Agreement

As a matter of policy, require all outsiders who submit an idea to sign a nonconfidential disclosure agreement before anyone in the company other than the designated person gives consideration to the proposed idea. This agreement generally requires that the outsider waive all rights to confidentiality and all rights to the idea that are not protectable under the patent laws. An express nonconfidential disclosure agreement helps defeat a claim by the outsider that your company breached a confidential relationship with the outsider by using the unsolicited idea.[37] You may delegate the responsibility of ensuring that the outsider sign the nonconfidential disclosure agreement to the employee designated to field all unsolicited ideas.

Regardless of whether the outsider agrees to sign the agreement, always keep a copy of what was sent to your company by the outsider. If the

---

[37] Haglund v. Dow Chem., Co., 218 U.S.P.Q. (BNA) 55 (E.D. Cal. 1982).

outsider refuses to sign, keep the copy in a secure place, *away* from your employees in the relevant field.

§ 13.41 —Reviewing Unsolicited Idea

As a general matter, do *not* let any employees, particularly those to whom the idea would be most relevant, review the idea until the outsider signs the nonconfidential disclosure agreement. This prevents any accusations that your company learned of the idea from the outsider, rather than independently developing the idea, and then used it without compensating the outsider. Further, if an employee of your company independently comes up with the same idea, your company will want to prove that the employee's discovery was an independent invention and not a result of the outsider's disclosure. A strict policy of refusing to review unsolicited ideas absent a nonconfidential disclosure agreement is an important part of such proof. On the other hand, your company may have tremendous difficulty defending a lawsuit if the outsider can prove that: (1) no nonconfidential disclosure agreement was signed, and (2) your company used the idea in some manner or disclosed the idea to others.

In the few instances when your company wishes to review an invention and the inventor refuses to sign a nonconfidential disclosure agreement, your company and the inventor can negotiate and sign a special *confidential* disclosure agreement. This agreement will typically protect the inventor's disclosure unless the company can document its own prior invention of the disclosed subject matter.

§ 13.42 —Procedures for Designated Employee

The designated employee should follow procedures designed to prevent other employees from accidentally seeing the unsolicited idea before the outsider signs the nonconfidential disclosure agreement. Consider implementing one of the following two sets of procedures:

PROCEDURE 1
> Immediately return the unsolicited disclosure to the inventor with a form letter stating that the correspondence received only clerical review because it appeared to be an unsolicited disclosure absent a suitable nonconfidential disclosure agreement. Ask the inventor to sign a nonconfidential disclosure agreement and then resubmit the unsolicited disclosure along with the signed agreement.

- OR -

PROCEDURE 2

1. File the unsolicited idea in a safety file and request that the outsider sign the nonconfidential disclosure agreement.
2. If the outsider refuses to sign the nonconfidential disclosure agreement, retain the unsolicited idea in the safety file.
3. If the outsider signs the nonconfidential disclosure agreement, pass the unsolicited idea to the intellectual property department or the relevant engineering department for evaluation.

§ 13.43 Intellectual Property Audit

Your company's intellectual property department should conduct an annual intellectual property audit to examine the policies and procedures discussed in this chapter.[38] During the audit, a member from the intellectual property department or outside intellectual property counsel can visit company departments, unannounced, to evaluate each department's handling of intellectual property issues.

The purpose for this audit is threefold. First, the audit determines whether your company is taking affirmative steps to keep secret its trade secrets. Are employees careful not to disclose trade secrets? Are the security procedures and facility restrictions being enforced? Is the company careful in its dealings with other companies? Interestingly, the intellectual property audit is itself evidence of a company's taking affirmative steps to maintain trade secrets.

Second, the audit evaluates employee awareness of the harms of public disclosure, including publication, public use, or sale of proprietary technology. Are employees adequately educated regarding intellectual property? Are the procedures for new employees and departing employees being followed? Are laboratory and progress notebooks being used to the greatest practical extent? Are notebook entries being corroborated? Are sales personnel and marketers being careful not to prematurely disclose technology before a patent application on the technology is filed? Are dealings with joint venture partners being handled with intellectual property concerns in mind?

Third, the audit reviews the compatibility of existing policies with proposed company enhancements to ascertain whether current procedures and policies require adjustment. For instance, if your company plans to install a new computer system, then additional safety procedures may be necessary to ensure protection of trade secrets accessible by the computer system. If your company reorganizes its sales and engineering staffs, then

---

[38] *See* Epstein & Levi, *Protecting Trade Secret Information: A Plan for Proactive Strategy*, 43 Bus. Law. 887–914 (1988).

you may need to correspondingly reorganize the roles that individuals will assume during experimentation of new ideas to prevent the appearance of commercialization of the new idea. Your natural changes in the company will thus dictate changes in the established intellectual property policies that you have adopted. An annual audit will help identify these changes.

CHAPTER 14

MANAGING THE INTELLECTUAL PROPERTY PORTFOLIO

§ 14.1   Monitoring the Industry
§ 14.2   —Monitoring Activities of Other Companies
§ 14.3   —Product Clearance
§ 14.4   —Policing for Infringers of Company's Rights
§ 14.5   —Checklist
§ 14.6   Intellectual Property Program Review
§ 14.7   —Roundtable Meetings to Plan Protection Strategies
§ 14.8   —Product Team Meetings on Intellectual Property Issues

§ 14.1   Monitoring the Industry

Your company should implement a few necessary procedures aimed at scouting the progress of competitors and policing for potential infringing activities. These procedures are grouped into three types of activities: (1) monitoring the activities of other companies, (2) monitoring to prevent infringement of competitors' intellectual property, and (3) policing for infringers of your company's intellectual property.

§ 14.2   —Monitoring Activities of Other Companies

General information with respect to your competitors' activities can be easily obtained by:

1. Regularly reviewing the United States Patent and Trademark Office (PTO) *Official Gazette*
2. Routinely running patent assignment searches

3. Subscribing to a trademark watch service
4. Reviewing professional and trade literature
5. Compiling files of competitive literature
6. Attending and monitoring trade shows.

1. *Official Gazette.* The PTO publishes each week an *Official Gazette* (OG), which lists all newly issued patents and their abstracts and all newly registered trademarks. Periodic review of the OG will keep you informed as to competitors' design efforts and their intellectual property holdings in your technical field. This review is typically conducted by the intellectual property counsel.

    In addition, relevant portions of the OG should be copied and circulated to particular product groups who are specialists in the technological area. The design-level engineers have a better appreciation for the newly patented technology and whether such patents will jeopardize any of the company's present products.

    The OG also lists trademarks that have been published before registration. If any trademark is identical to one employed by your company, or is confusingly similar, then your company may wish to oppose registration of the mark.

    The OG is therefore a tremendous resource for analyzing competitors' activities and should be regularly and routinely eviewed by legal, managerial, engineering, and marketing personnel.

2. *Patent assignment searches.* Several on-line computer search services are now available. In part, these services maintain large computer databases that include the text of United States and foreign patents that issued after a certain date, together with field codes identifying the respective assignees of the patents. The services can be accessed by modem to a local computer, which can be located on the premises of your company.

    With these services, you can routinely determine what patents have issued to your competitors by searching for your competitor's name as an assignee on any issued patent. In this way, you will learn which technologies your competitors are working on and what types of protections they have obtained. Some databases also allow you to search patents for specific types of claim language or specific language in the patent abstract. Each of these can be a useful tool in uncovering the pursuits and positions of your competitors.

3. *Trademark watch services.* If your company has valuable trademarks it wants to protect and prevent from being eroded by other companies' use of similar marks, your company may wish to subscribe to a trademark watch service. For a reasonable fee, trademark watch firms can keep your company apprised of any new trademarks that

appear to be similar to your company's marks. The services are typically very useful and provide an extra layer of insurance along with or in place of scanning the weekly *Official Gazette* for similar trademarks.

4. *Professional literature.* Your company should also subscribe to professional and trade journals applicable to its business. Many articles published in such journals are written by people who are developing new technology. It is not uncommon for an inventor to first file for a patent on a new technology and then publish the discoveries in a journal. Because the patent application may take one or two years to issue (if it issues at all), the journals may provide information on new technology before the technology is publicly described in its corresponding patent.

5. *Competitive literature.* Many companies have recognized the value of watching competitors from a financial and marketing interest and have accordingly compiled files of competitive literature, Dunn and Bradstreet reports, and other information. These same files can provide valuable information into the potential intellectual property pursuits of your competitors. Additionally, valuable information concerning competitors' potential intellectual property pursuits may be learned from their promotional materials, specification sheets, user manuals, and service manuals.

6. *Trade shows.* Trade shows are one of the best sources of information on new technologies and thus on your competitors' potentially protectable intellectual property. First, the new technologies will be on display for all to see. Second, the boasts of competitors' sales representatives can suggest which products (or portions of products) are considered unique and therefore potentially protectable by the competitors.

§ 14.3 —Product Clearance

Before your company places a new product on the market, it should determine whether the product will infringe another company's patent. The process of checking for possible infringement is known as *product clearance*. Associated with this product clearance should be procedures to ensure that the trademark selected for your new product does not infringe another's trademark.

A patent gives your company the right to *exclude* others from making, using, or selling the invention, *not* the right to make, use, or sell the invention. Therefore, even though a new product is covered in part, or in whole, by a patent owned by your company, the product may still infringe another company's patent. (Recall from **Chapter 2** the ladder example, in which Treetop's improved, self-supporting ladder was protected by a patent, yet still infringed Acme's basic ladder patent.)

A product clearance, normally performed by the intellectual property department or counsel, essentially consists of conducting a patent search at the PTO. This search is very similar to the patentability search step in the Protection Analysis Model (**Chapter 8**). If the new product is not covered by any valid and enforceable claims of any extant patents, the product can be cleared for production and sale. On the other hand, if the new product is likely to infringe a valid and enforceable claim of another company's patent, your company should evaluate the risks of the product being held an infringement, the opportunities available for licensing, and the possibilities of designing a new, noninfringing product.

As part of a product clearance, conducting a trademark search before release of a new mark associated with the new product is advisable. More important, failure to make such a timely trademark search before release of a new trademark may be construed as a careless disregard for another's trademark rights if your new mark turns out to infringe.[1] This step is essentially the trademark search step in the Protection Analysis Model discussed in **Chapter 11**. The trademark search should indicate whether the new mark is confusingly similar to, and thus might infringe, another's trademark.

The purposes of conducting a product clearance are twofold. First, product clearance minimizes the risk of infringing another company's patent. This then avoids being forced into potentially lengthy and expensive infringement litigation. Second, product clearance reduces the risk of a finding of willful infringement by your company. Remember, a finding of willful infringement can result in tripling the actual damages.[2] Some courts impose on a company an affirmative duty to exercise care in determining whether that company's product infringes another company's patent, before manufacturing, using, or selling the product.[3] Product clearance may prove that the duty was met.

Additionally, if you are concerned about whether your product may infringe another's patent, be sure to promptly obtain an opinion from an outside patent attorney, if possible, before your questionable product goes to market. Typically, good-faith reliance on a reasoned opinion before and after engaging in any acts that may later be charged as infringing is an

---

[1] Sands, Taylor & Wood v. Quaker Oats Co., 18 U.S.P.Q.2d (BNA) 1457 (N.D. Ill. 1990), *rev'd on other grounds*, 24 U.S.P.Q.2d 1001 (7th Cir. 1992).

[2] 35 U.S.C. § 284 (1954).

[3] *See, e.g.*, S.C. Johnson & Son, Inc. v. Carter-Wallace, Inc., 614 F. Supp. 1278, 225 U.S.P.Q. (BNA) 1022 (S.D.N.Y. 1985), *aff'd in part, vacated in part*, 781 F.2d 198, 228 U.S.P.Q. (BNA) 367 (Fed. Cir. 1986).

important factor in determining whether your company acted in good faith.[4] Conversely, failure to obtain the opinion may be evidence that your company acted with willful disregard of another's patent rights.[5]

§ 14.4 —Policing for Infringers of Company's Rights

As courts are increasingly recognizing the contributions that intellectual properties provide and their associated monetary values, systems that maximize exploitation of a company's intellectual property opportunities are becoming increasingly important. A company that continually seeks new intellectual properties and exploits the intellectual properties that it obtains can remain financially healthy. The company maintains a competitive edge by protecting its improved and desirable products. Further, the company strengthens this edge by forcing compensation from those competitors that emulate its patented products.

The task of policing for potential infringers is virtually complete when a company combines competitive monitoring with a corporate awareness of its own intellectual property. By instituting well-prescribed policies for protecting and exploiting your company's intellectual properties, employees become attentive to the company's intellectual property portfolio and to the activities of competitors. Accordingly, employees should be quick to identify an infringing product, mark, or process.

The monitoring activities provide the impetus for your company to investigate potential infringements. Take, for example, a marketer who sees a competitive product displayed at a trade show and describes the products to his manager. An informed manager might recall a patent that was similar to the product described by the marketer. At this point, the manager can contact the legal department with his findings and an infringement review can begin. The key, then, is training employees to be well versed in their own intellectual property portfolio and encouraging them to keep their eyes and ears open.

Once a potential infringer has been identified, your intellectual property department or counsel will begin an infringement review. This review may include purchasing a potentially infringing product, purchasing a product bearing a potentially infringing mark, investigating a potentially infringing process, or a variety of other fact-finding activities.

---

[4] Central Soya Co. v. Geo. A. Hormel & Co., 723 F.2d 1573, 220 U.S.P.Q. (BNA) 490 (Fed. Cir. 1983).

[5] Great N. Corp. v. Davis Core & Pad Co., 782 F.2d 159, 228 U.S.P.Q. (BNA) 356 (Fed. Cir. 1986).

When the fact-finding is complete, the intellectual property department or counsel will compare the potentially infringing product, process, or mark with the intellectual property owned by the company. From this, the company can ascertain the probability that an infringement has occurred, whether any damage was caused by the infringement and how much, and an approximate cost of obtaining a judgment to that effect. A business decision can then be made about whether to attempt to license an intellectual property, whether to litigate over the infringement, or whether to do nothing, based on a benefit/cost/risk analysis.

If the intellectual property department or counsel concludes that a competitor is in fact infringing your company's products, your company must not delay in enforcing its intellectual property rights. An unreasonable delay may result in a loss of these rights with respect to that competitor. Delays of over six years are regularly found to be unreasonable[6] and shorter delays are possibly unreasonable.[7]

The enforcement clock begins running when your company has knowledge, or reasonably should have knowledge, of the infringing product. If, for example, as a result of your company's monitoring efforts, a project manager learns that a competitor's product may infringe one of your company's patents, the period for determining unreasonable delay might begin as of the date the manager learned of the product. Accordingly, once an potential infringement is identified, your company must take precautions to ensure that it does not unreasonably delay after the identification.

If your company delays too long, the infringing competitor may have a legally valid defense against infringement known as *laches* or *estoppel*. The laches defense precludes your company from collecting otherwise available damages that were incurred before the filing of an infringement suit.[8] In a worse case, the estoppel defense precludes your company from collecting any past or future damages.[9]

Company employees must understand that their knowledge of potential infringements not only provides opportunities to exploit a company's intellectual property, but can also begin a time period against which the same opportunities can be lost. Your company must therefore have policies that instruct employees to quickly disclose to their manager or the legal

---

[6] A.C. Aukerman Co. v. R.L. Chaides Constr. Co., 960 F.2d 1020, 22 U.S.P.Q.2d (BNA) 1321 (Fed. Cir. 1992) (en banc); Hottel Corp. v. Seaman Corp., 833 F.2d 1570, 4 U.S.P.Q.2d (BNA) 1939 (Fed. Cir. 1987).

[7] Advance Hydraulics, Inc. v. Otis Elevator Co., 525 F.2d 477, 186 U.S.P.Q. (BNA) 1 (7th Cir. 1975), *cert denied*, 423 U.S. 869 (1975).

[8] Olympia Werke Aktiengesellschaft v. General Elec. Co., 712 F.2d 74, 219 U.S.P.Q. (BNA) 107 (4th Cir. 1983).

[9] Olympia Werke Aktiengesellschaft v. General Elec. Co., 712 F.2d 74, 219 U.S.P.Q. (BNA) 107 (4th Cir. 1983).

department any facts that they learn that support a finding of infringement against a competitor.

Because opportunities to exploit intellectual property rights can be lost as a result of unreasonable delay, standards for disclosing information that is learned in the monitoring process must be part of your company's standards for monitoring competitive activities. If your company loses opportunities to exploit intellectual properties, the losses should be a matter of choice and never a matter of forgetting about the existence of an intellectual property owned by the company or forgetting about the existence of a potentially infringing competitive product. When the company learns of the facts supporting infringement, the issue should be reported to the legal department and investigated without undue delay.

§ 14.5 —Checklist

Monitoring the activities of competitors within your company's industry is an important aspect of effective management of an intellectual property portfolio. Broadly characterized, your company should implement the following monitoring procedures:

1. **Monitor the activities of other companies.** This procedure includes regular review of the *Official Gazette*, assignment searching, reading professional and trade literature, subscription to a trademark watch service, review of competitors' literature, and attendance at trade shows.
2. **Product clearance procedures.** Such procedures help prevent your company from prematurely releasing a product or mark that clearly infringes a competitor's patent or trademark rights.
3. **Police for infringers of your company's products and marks.**

§ 14.6 Intellectual Property Program Review

An important key to managing an intellectual property portfolio is to provide a formal protocol for reviewing the portfolio. As market conditions change and the company sets new goals and strategies, the intellectual property portfolio must adapt responsively to provide maximum protection for any future business endeavor.

A formal intellectual property program review is one way to ensure that the intellectual property portfolio is current with the company's goals and strategies. This formal program is a regular review of the intellectual property portfolio to determine whether the company's products and internal secrets are being adequately protected.

The purpose of the intellectual property program review is threefold. First, the review forces you to evaluate the intellectual property portfolio on a regular basis. Second, it provides a formal setting in which employees from different departments can discuss and plan for better coordination between the portfolio and the company products. Third, the program review allows you to reexamine previous protection decisions.

For larger companies, the intellectual property program review is preferably conducted through two different sets of meetings: (1) a roundtable meeting for higher level management and (2) routine product meetings for the product management level. For smaller companies, the same objectives can be satisfied by a single review committee that meets routinely to reexamine the company intellectual property program and evaluate the portfolio. For the smaller company, then, the single review committee can perform both the roundtable and the team meeting functions described in §§ 14.7 and 14.8.

§ 14.7 —Roundtable Meetings to Plan Protection Strategies

A roundtable meeting should be conducted quarterly to evaluate your company's global intellectual property strategy. An intellectual property committee should be created to attend this meeting, with the committee including, at the very least, the chief intellectual property counsel and the vice presidents from all company departments.

During the roundtable meetings, the intellectual property committee should address issues including:

1. Company policies and procedures directed toward intellectual property
2. Current domestic and foreign market positions and the adequacy of intellectual property protection in these markets
3. Future market opportunities
4. Licensing activities
5. Joint venture prospects.

These issues should not be addressed casually, but should be critically analyzed. Specific conclusions should be developed and verbalized at the meeting so each participant leaves the meeting with a common understanding about the company's immediate and long-term intellectual property goals.

Too many opportunities to protect or exploit intellectual properties are lost by companies as a result of miscommunication (or lack of communication) between upper management and the engineers and marketers working on a particular project. This is in part due to misunderstandings among engineers and marketers as to the company's product and marketing goals, in part due to upper management's lack of clear and uniform understanding of the company's intellectual property goals, and in part due to upper management's inability to remain abreast of all lucrative intellectual properties that are developed and marketed by project-level employees.

The participation of upper management in the roundtable meeting to agree on a unified set of intellectual property goals is one way that miscommunication between upper management and project employees can be prevented. Another recommended method is to give project-level employees periodic opportunities to participate in the roundtable meetings. This reinforces to the project employees that the company considers its intellectual property pursuits and protections important priorities. Also, project employee participation offers each of the upper management personnel an opportunity to review the development and marketing activities that are occurring throughout the company from the employees that are actually performing these functions.

To minimize downtime among project-level employees, the project-level employees can attend the roundtable meetings on a rotational basis. For example, one engineer and one marketer from select project groups would participate in one roundtable meeting. In the next quarter, another group of engineers and marketers would participate, and so on until all engineers and marketers have participated. In this way, a particular project group may be represented at the roundtables by at least one engineer or marketer perhaps twice per year. Each engineer and marketer might then attend a roundtable every several years, depending on the size of the project-level work force.

The rotation is important both to upper management and to project-level employees. At each roundtable meeting, upper management receives input from a diversified group of engineers and marketers regarding the successes, setbacks, goals, and predictions of the various product groups that are represented. From this, upper management can better understand what is occurring in the engineering and commercial arenas as well as the directions of technological change and how the company as a whole can change its goals and objectives accordingly. For the project-level employee, the roundtable meeting offers indirect training in the company's long-range goals for developing new products and for exploiting existing products and intellectual properties.

To further the value of the roundtable discussions to all employees, those project-level employees that participate in a particular roundtable meeting may orally report to their fellow project group employees by describing what they learned at the meeting.

In summary, in the roundtable environment, upper management gains a clear understanding of the activities of the company as a whole from the reports of project-level employees. Upper management can then resolve immediate and short-term intellectual property goals and verbalize the goals to facilitate a uniform understanding among the management team. Finally, the management team is able to personally analyze how the actions of its respective project-level employees are promoting (or impeding) the company's progress toward its intellectual property goals.

§ 14.8 —Product Team Meetings on Intellectual Property Issues

Companies typically conduct routine product team meetings that involve representatives from various company departments who have ties to a particular product. These meetings vary from brainstorming sessions for determining new product directions to trouble-shooting sessions for correcting problem areas in existing products.

It is important to consider protection related issues at these routine meetings. Protecting a company's new technology or product trademark is as important as setting a price or target marketing a consumer group. Without protection, even well-designed and marketed products may not survive the intense competitive pressure from a copycat producer (with virtually no research and development costs). If practical, a member from the intellectual property department or counsel should attend each product meeting to ensure a proper handling of proprietary-related issues. Using the Protection Analysis Model from **Chapter 5** to develop protection strategies concurrently with the development and marketing of particular products provides a flexible approach to analyzing these issues and selecting between alternative forms of protection.

APPENDIXES

A. Example of a Patent
B. Example of a Design Patent
C. Sample Trademark Registration
D. Form for Registration of a Copyrighted Work

APPENDIX A

EXAMPLE OF A PATENT

United States Patent [19]
Lee et al.

[11] Patent Number: 5,125,010
[45] Date of Patent: Jun. 23, 1992

[54] LAP COUNTING SYSTEM

[76] Inventors: Lewis C. Lee, W. 3114 Sheridan Ct., Spokane, Wash. 99205; T. Lester Wallace, 600 Sharon Park Dr. A103, Menlo Park, Calif. 94025

[21] Appl. No.: 597,159

[22] Filed: Oct. 15, 1990

[51] Int. Cl.^{5} G01C 22/00; G06M 1/22; G06M 3/02
[52] U.S. Cl. 377/24.2; 377/5; 377/112; 482/55
[58] Field of Search 377/5, 24.2, 112; 272/71

[56] References Cited

U.S. PATENT DOCUMENTS

4,518,266	5/1985	Dawley	377/24.2
4,530,105	7/1985	Rabinowitz	377/24.2
4,700,369	10/1987	Siegal et al.	377/24.2
4,780,085	10/1988	Malone	272/71
4,823,367	4/1989	Kreutzfeld	377/24.2
4,932,045	5/1990	Kasoff et al.	377/24.2

FOREIGN PATENT DOCUMENTS

| 0234482 | 10/1986 | Japan | 377/24.2 |
| 2176036 | 12/1986 | United Kingdom | 377/24.2 |

Primary Examiner—John S. Heyman
Attorney, Agent, or Firm—Wells, St. John & Roberts

[57] ABSTRACT

The present invention relates to a lap counting system having a radio communication range between a radio transmitter and a radio receiver. The lap counting system increments a lap count each time the distance between the receiver and the transmitter becomes smaller than the communication range.

18 Claims, 5 Drawing Sheets

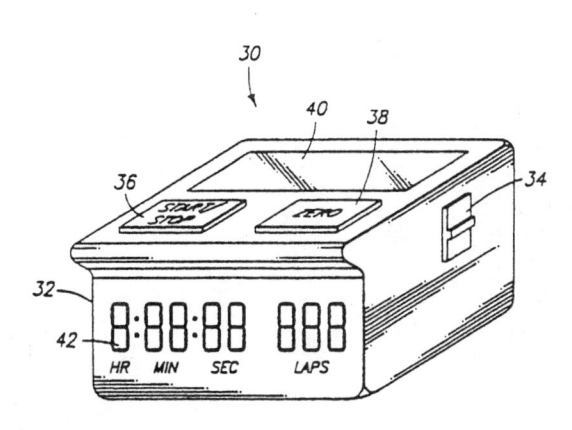

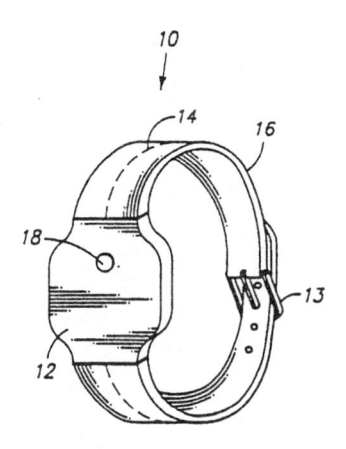

249

250   EXAMPLE OF A PATENT

U.S. Patent   June 23, 1992   Sheet 1 of 5   **5,125,010**

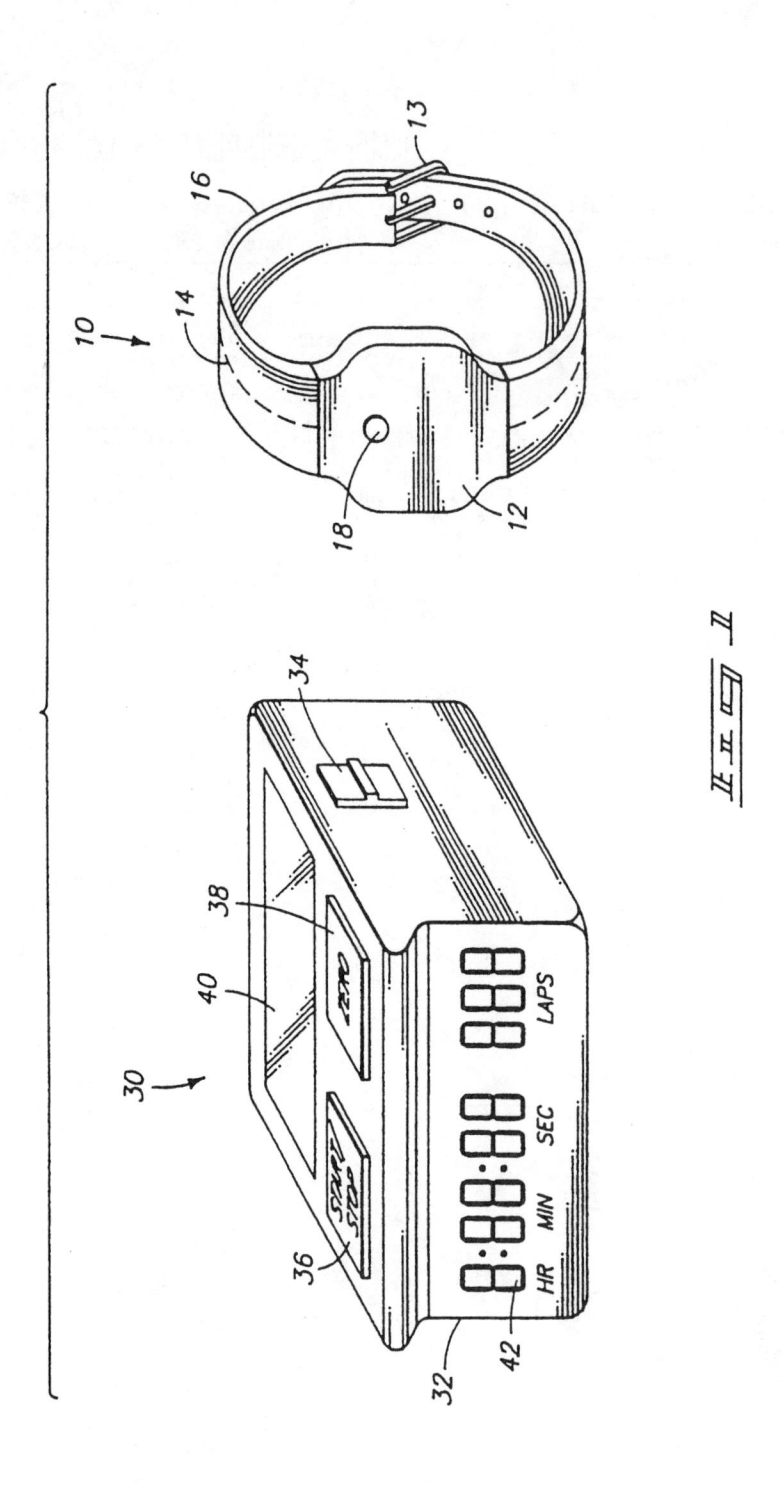

EXAMPLE OF A PATENT

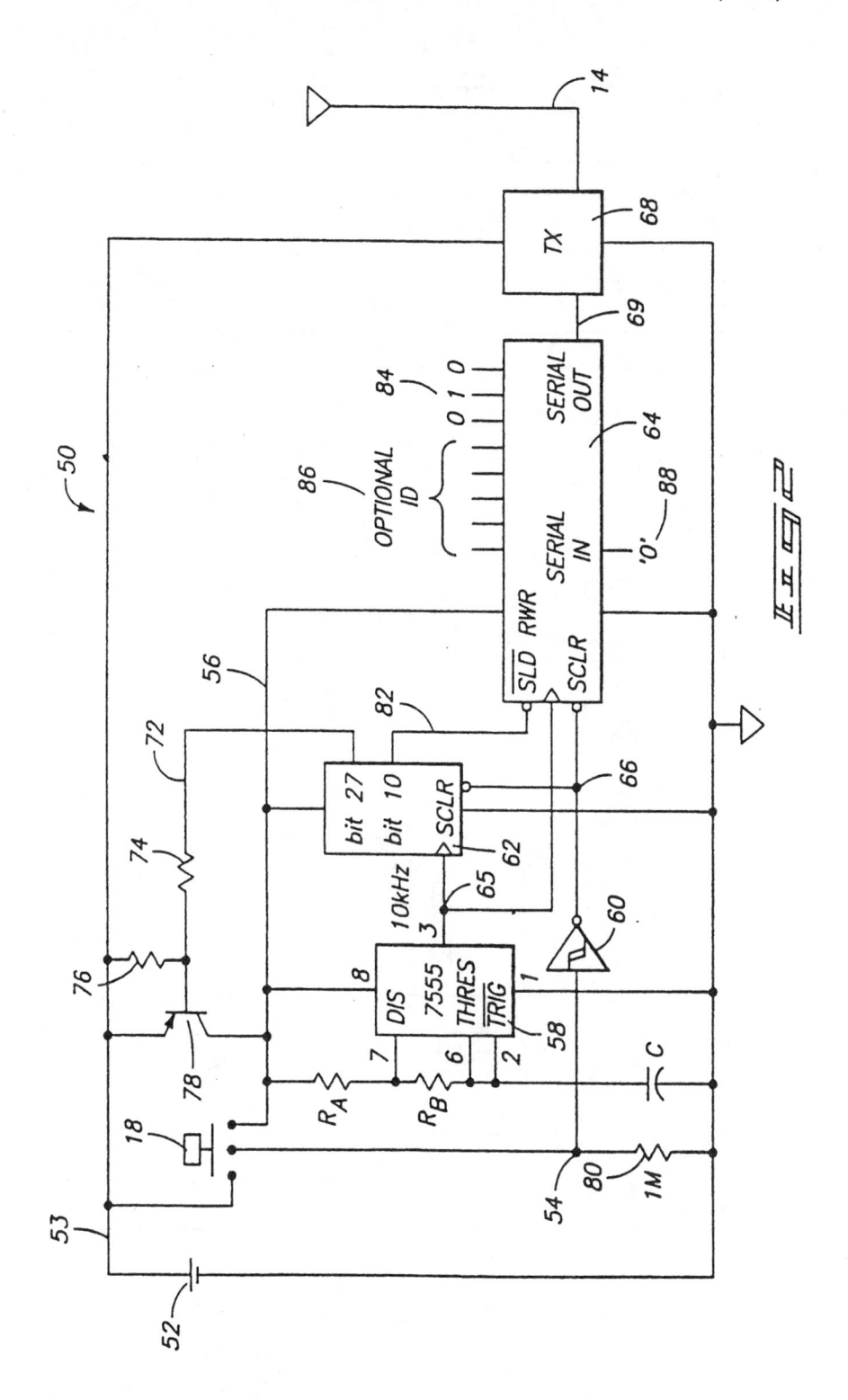

EXAMPLE OF A PATENT

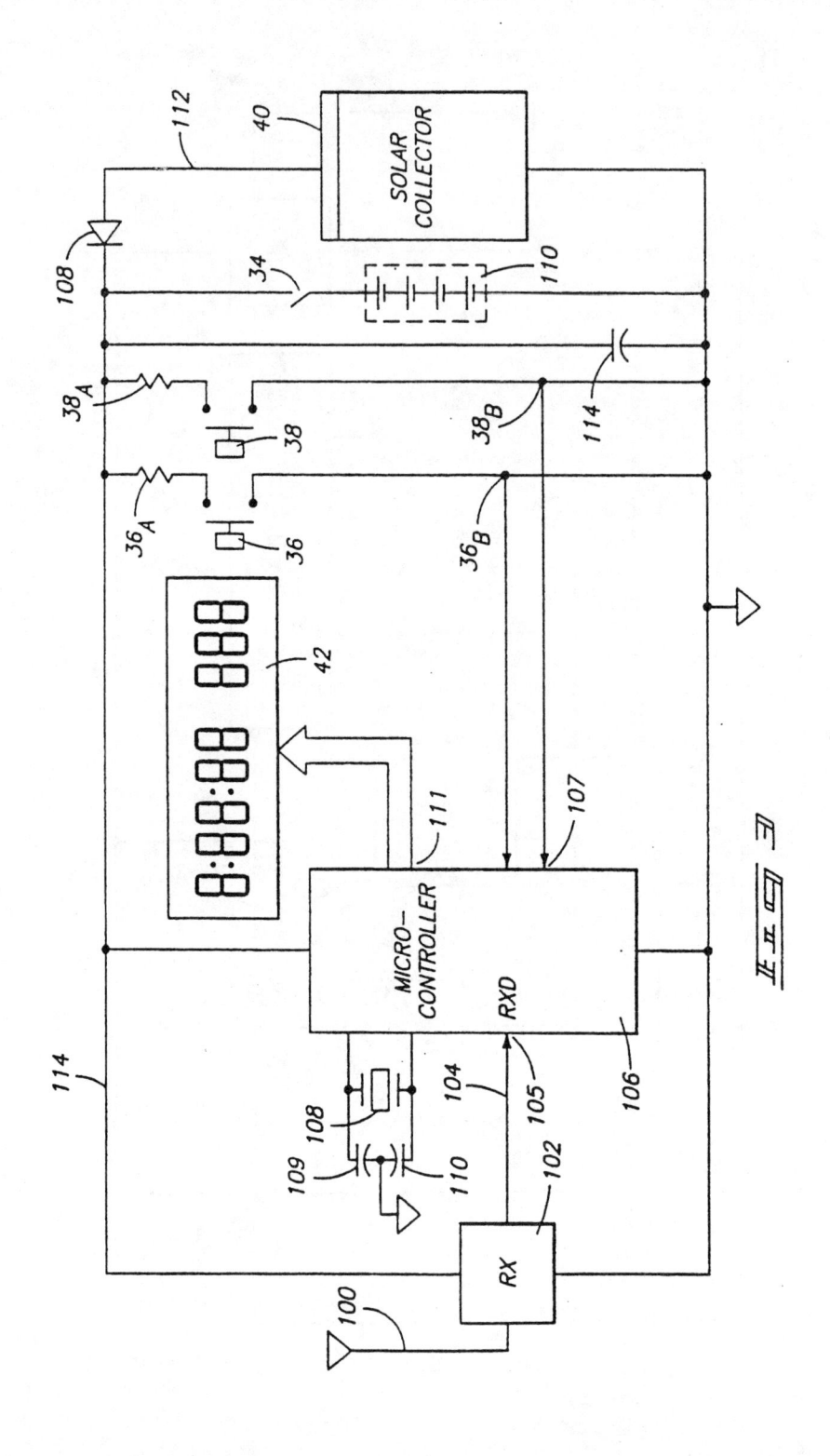

EXAMPLE OF A PATENT

U.S. Patent   June 23, 1992   Sheet 4 of 5   5,125,010

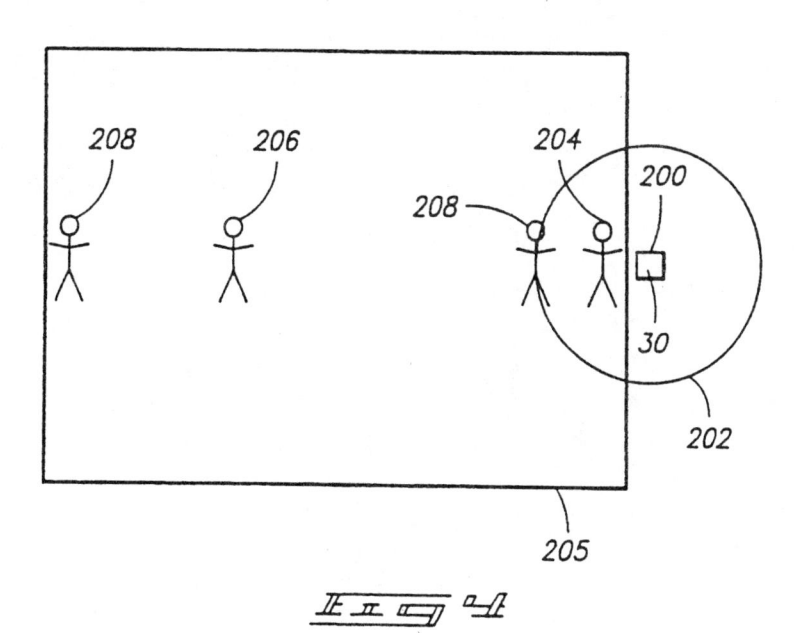

Fig 4

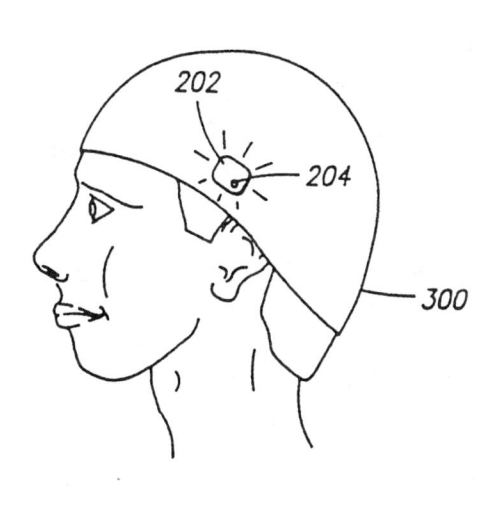

Fig 6

254   EXAMPLE OF A PATENT

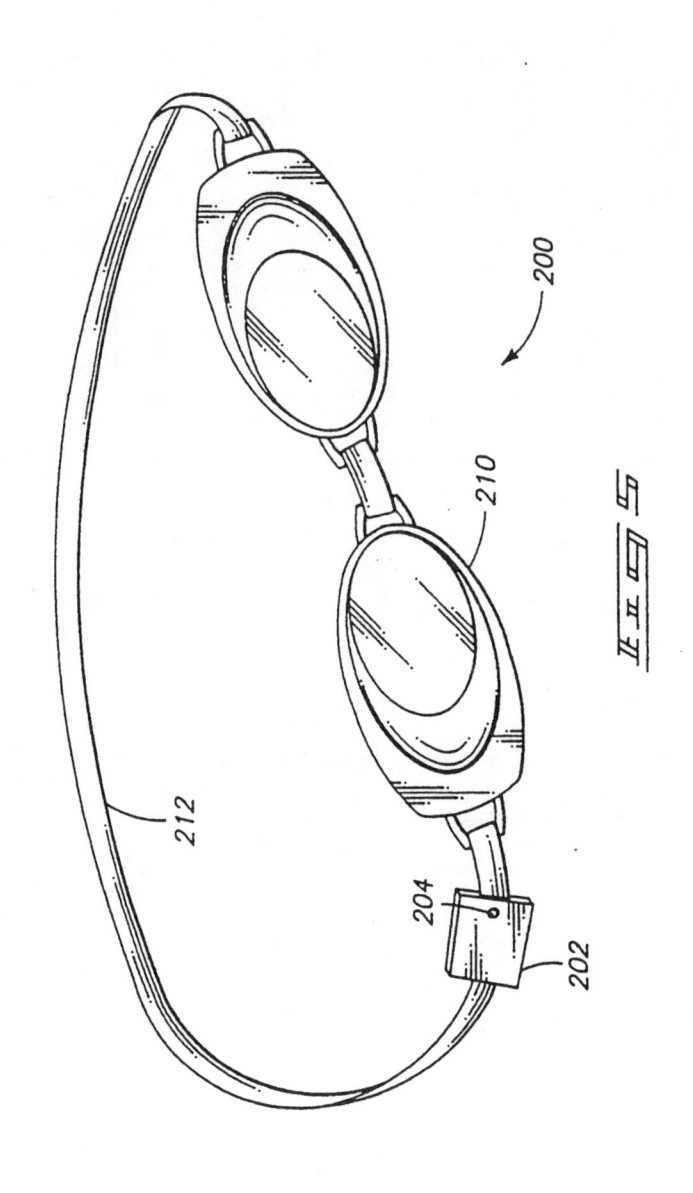

U.S. Patent   June 23, 1992   Sheet 5 of 5   5,125,010

FIG. 5

EXAMPLE OF A PATENT

5,125,010

LAP COUNTING SYSTEM

BACKGROUND OF THE INVENTION

1. Field of the Invention

The present invention relates to a lap counter, and more particularly, to a lap counting system having a radio communication range between a radio transmitter and a radio receiver which increments a lap count each time the distance between the receiver and the transmitter becomes smaller than the communication range.

2. Background and Related Art

In certain sporting events, such as swimming and track, athletes traverse the same course multiple times during a single workout. As a result, these athletes must maintain a count of the number of laps completed. Mentally maintaining this lap count is burdensome in that the athlete may lose track of the number of laps or may, for psychological reasons, not want to count each grueling lap. These athletes have thus expressed an interest in a lap counting device which would maintain an accurate lap count during their workouts.

The lap counting device should be foremost reliable, inexpensive, and easy to use. It should also be portable and lightweight so that the athletes can easily carry it to the pool or track, and it should be compact for easy storage.

Various lap counting systems have been developed. However, none of these systems satisfy all of the above mentioned attributes. For example, some lap counting systems employ ultrasonic transducers to detect the athlete on each lap. These systems have serious drawbacks in that they cannot discriminate between different athletes, for example, between different swimmers swimming in the same lane, or between different runners on the same track. Furthermore, because ultrasonic systems are directional and line-of-sight, ultrasonic systems must be mounted in a special manner along the pool or track.

Other lap counting systems employ infrared transducers. These systems have serious drawbacks similar to those of the ultrasonic systems. In addition, because the athlete must wear either an infrared transmitter or a receiver, the athlete must consciously directionally orient the unit he/she wears toward the stationary unit to trigger a counting of each lap.

Some lap counting systems, designed specially for swimmers, require the swimmer to touch a pad to effectuate a count. These lap counting systems have several serious drawbacks: the pads are difficult to mount to the side of the pool, the pads are easily dislodged, the pads are expensive, the pads may be touched by other swimmers which disrupts an accurate count for the desired swimmer, physical switches within the pad are unreliable, and swimmers must locate and touch the pads each lap.

SUMMARY OF THE INVENTION

The present invention has been designed to solve the above mentioned drawbacks inherent in prior art lap counters. The present invention is a lap counting system having a radio communication range between a radio transmitter and a radio receiver. The lap counting system increments a lap count each time the distance between the receiver and the transmitter becomes smaller than the communication range.

By employing radio frequency communication, the unit placed by the pool or track does not need to be specially mounted. Nor, does the athlete need to orient his/her unit toward the poolside or trackside unit.

The present invention also eliminates the expense and problems associated with pads employed in the prior art swimming systems.

BRIEF DESCRIPTION OF THE DRAWING

These and other advantages will become more apparent from the detailed description of the preferred embodiment along with the following drawings:

FIG. 1 shows a lap counting system according to a first embodiment of the present invention;

FIG. 2 is a schematic of the swimmer's unit;

FIG. 3 is a schematic of the poolside unit;

FIG. 4 illustrates the operation of the present invention in a swimming pool;

FIG. 5 shows an embodiment of the present invention involving goggles for swimmers; and

FIG. 6 shows another embodiment of the present invention involving a swim cap for swimmers.

DESCRIPTION OF THE PREFERRED EMBODIMENT

The preferred embodiment of the present invention described hereinbelow is adapted for use by swimmers. However, it is to be understood that other sporting events having a redundant course, such as track, fall within the contemplation of the present invention.

FIG. 1 shows one embodiment of a lap counting system according to the present invention. The lap counting system has a swimmer's unit 10 which includes a radio transmitter, and a poolside unit 30 which includes a radio receiver. The swimmer's unit 10 is shown in the form of a water-resistant wrist watch having a housing 12, a wrist band 16 and a clasp 13 which may be worn by the swimmer. The radio transmitter is contained in a housing 12 and a radio antenna 14 is located in the wrist band 16. An activate push-button 18 is located on the housing 12 to activate the transmitter circuitry.

The poolside unit 30 has a water-resistant housing 32, a power ON/OFF switch 34, a START/STOP push-button 36, a ZERO push-button 38, a solar collector 40, and an LCD display 42. The START/STOP push-button 36 and the ZERO push-button 38 are relatively large to facilitate easy depression by the swimmer when initiating a lap counting session. The LCD display 42 has two sections, a time section and a lap section. The time section has a single display digit for an hours value, two display digits for a minutes value and two display digits for a seconds value. These display digits are correspondingly labelled as "HR" for hours, "MIN" for minutes, and "SEC" for seconds. The lap section has three display digits for a lap count and is labelled "LAPS" for number of laps counted. The entire poolside unit 30 is sealed to prevent water from entering the housing 32 through push-buttons 36 and 38, ON/OFF switch 34, solar collector 40, or LCD display 42.

The poolside unit 30 also has a base portion comprising an insulative rubber mat or plural rubber pegs which permit the unit to be insulated from a wet surface alongside the pool. Because the present invention employs RF communication, the poolside unit 30 need not be specially mounted in a specific orientation as required by conventional infrared and ultrasonic systems. Further, the poolside unit 30 does not require any special pads or the like.

EXAMPLE OF A PATENT

The following disclosure describes the circuitry of the swimmer's unit 10 and the poolside unit 30.

SWIMMER'S UNIT

FIG. 2 shows the circuitry of the radio transmitter 50 employed in the swimmer's unit 10 shown in FIG. 1. The transmitter 50 transmits for a period of approximately 1.8 hours upon momentary depression of activate push-button 18. After this time, the swimmer's unit 10 is disabled to conserve battery power, and to extend the life of battery 52.

When activate push-button 18 is depressed, node 54 and internal power line 56 are coupled to battery 52 via battery power line 53. As a result, square wave generator 58, Schmidt trigger inverter 60, counter 62, and shift register 64 begin to operate. Square wave generator 58 outputs a square wave clock signal of approximately 10 kHz on node 65 to clock counter 62 and shift register 64. This 10 kHz frequency is determined by the values of resistors R_A, R_B and capacitor C. The positive voltage at node 54 causes Schmidt trigger inverter 60 to force node 66 low and to clear counter 62 and shift register 64. Because transmitter 68 is deactivated whenever output 69 from shift register 64 is low, the cleared shift register results in a deactivated transmitter and no transmission occurs from antenna 14.

Because counter 62 is also cleared, the bit-27 output 72 of counter 62 is low. A voltage divider is therefore formed between resistors 76 and 74, transistor 78 is turned on, and internal power line 56 is connected to battery power line 53 through transistor 78. Internal power line 56 is therefore "latched" high when activate push-button 18 is depressed, thereby remaining high for a predetermined time after activate push-button 18 is released.

When activate push-button 18 is released by the swimmer, resistor 80 pulls down node 54 causing node 66 to go high. Counter 62 is thus no longer cleared and begins incrementing. While the bit-10 output 82 of counter 62 is low, shift register 64 is held in a parallel load condition. Because the first bit of start bits 84 is a "0", transmitter 68 remains deactivated. When counter 62 increments to the point that the bit-10 output 82 goes high, shift register 64 is released and the start bits "010", followed by identification code 86, are sequentially shifted out and transmitted via transmitter 68.

The identification code 86 may be set during construction of the swimmer's unit 10 by cutting traces to power and ground on the swimmer's unit circuit board. Alternatively, identification code 86 may be set by flipping a dedicated dip switch provided for this purpose or by blowing fuses or the like in a custom or semi-custom designed integrated circuit.

After start bits 84 and identification code 86 are shifted out of shift register 64, the output of the shift register 64 returns to a low level because the serial input 88 to shift register 64 is tied low. This remains so until bit-10 line 82 again goes low. A radio frequency transmission is therefore made from transmitter 68 each 2^{10} times as long as the period of the square wave. With the square wave frequency being set at 10 kHz, a transmission will occur approximately ten times each second. The duration of each transmitted bit is the period of the square wave.

The parallel loading and shifting out of the start bits 84 and the identification code 86 continues repeatedly until the bit-27 output 72 of counter 62 finally goes high. This occurs 2^{27} periods of the square wave (approximately 1.8 hours) after the swimmer releases activate push-button 18. Transistor 78 is then switched off, battery power line 53 is disconnected from internal power line 56, and battery power is conserved when the transmitting unit is no longer being used. Pullup resistor 76 ensures that transistor 78 remains off during the period that counter 62 is not powered.

The approximate 1.8 hour period of operation for the swimmer's unit 10 is chosen to be somewhat longer than a long workout of a serious lap swimmer. If a swimmer wishes to swim longer, activate push-button 18 may be depressed again for another 1.8 hours of use. On the other hand, the present invention may be easily adopted to operate for a duration shorter than the 1.8 hour period. For example, the bit-26 output of counter 62 may be used to establish an approximate 0.9 hour period of operation.

Numerous low power radio frequency oscillators known in the art, such as single stage Hartley, Colpitts, and Pierce type oscillators can function as transmitter 68. The strength of the radio signal arriving at the poolside unit 30 from transmitter 68 should be of such a signal strength so that the distance at which poolside unit 30 begins to receive transmissions is significantly less than the length of an average lap swimming pool. This short distance allows the radio frequency oscillator to be powered with a low voltage on the order of 3 volts. The distance at which receiver 102 (discussed below with reference to FIG. 3) begins to receive transmissions from transmitter 68 should be approximately five feet. In this embodiment where antenna 14 is relatively short due to the antenna's being placed in wrist band 16, the frequency of the carrier signal should be kept as low as possible to reduce the attenuating effect of the transmitter's being frequently surrounded by water.

The low voltage supply requirement of the transmitter 68, along with the power saving deactivating feature of swimmer's unit 10, allow a single inexpensive lithium battery 52 to power swimmer's unit 10 for a period of 10 years. The fact that the swimmer's unit 10 only transmits for a very small portion of the time allows the power consumption of the transmitter 68 during transmissions to be as high as required to achieve the required signal strength at the poolside unit 30. Because the swimmer's unit 10 is capable of operating for 10 years with a single battery, the transmitter 50 may be permanently sealed in water resistant housing 12 during manufacturing. Therefore, the cost of providing a way to replace battery 52 is avoided.

Poolside Unit

FIG. 3 shows the circuitry of poolside unit 30 shown in FIG. 1. Poolside unit 30 receives transmissions on antenna 100 which is located inside housing 32. Amplitude modulation (AM) receiver circuit 102 removes the radio frequency carrier and outputs a bit stream of the modulating signal over line 104 to the receive data RXD input pin 105 of micro-controller 106 RXD input pin 105 is the pin customarily provided on microcontrollers for receiving serial asynchronous bit streams.

Microcontroller 106 has on-board RAM for program execution and data manipulation, on-board EEPROM for program and data storage, on-board timer circuits capable of keeping time of day, output port 111 for outputting data to LCD display 42, and parallel input port 107 for receiving input information from START/STOP and ZERO push-buttons 36 and 38.

Crystal 108 and capacitors 109 and 110 are connected in standard fashion to the oscillator of microcontroller 106.

Microcontroller 106 controls LCD display 42 by writing data from output port 111. LCD display 42 may incorporate a driver chip with internal registers and/or circuitry for driving the actual LCD display. Alternatively, microcontroller 106 contains the circuitry for directly driving the actual LCD display.

When depressed, START/STOP and ZERO push-buttons 36 and 38 cause nodes 36B and 38B to be pulled high to power line 114 through resistors 36A and 38A, respectively. Microcontroller 106 reads the logic level of nodes 36B and 38B and debounces these values digitally via input port 107.

Solar collector 40 and batteries 110 are provided to power the circuitry of poolside unit 30. When adequate solar radiation is incident on solar collector 40 (positioned on the upper surface of poolside unit 30 as shown in FIG. 1), solar collector 40 outputs a powering voltage onto line 112, through diode 108, and onto power line 114. Diode 108 prevents power from power line 114 from bleeding back through solar collector 40 when solar collector 40 is not supplying an adequate voltage to power the poolside unit 30. By employing solar collector 40 as a power source, a swimmer merely needs to place poolside unit 30 in the sun or under building lights to effectuate a power supply. Because solar collector 40 is always connected to power line 114, the swimmer will know that poolside unit 30 is powered because zeros will appear on LCD display 42 if poolside unit 30 has adequate power.

In the event there is not adequate solar radiation, poolside unit 30 is optionally powered by removable batteries 110 shown in a dashed box. ON/OFF switch 34 is provided to prevent battery drain when poolside unit 30 is not in use. Batteries 110 can therefore be switched onto or off of power line 114 via switch 34. A removable hatch in the back of the receiver housing 32 allows spent batteries to be removed and replaced. Capacitor 114 is provided between power line 114 and ground.

System Operation

The operation of the lap counting system according to the present invention is discussed below with reference to FIG. 4. The swimmer places poolside unit 30 at location 200 along side of pool 205. Incident solar radiation on solar collector 40, or power from batteries 110, powers poolside unit 30. After being reset on power up, microcontroller 106 causes "0:00:00 000" to be displayed on LCD display 42.

The swimmer then depresses the activate push-button 18 on the swimmer's unit 10 he/she is wearing. Because the swimmer is within the communication range 202 of the lap counting system, the swimmer is able to see that the transmissions are being received because microcontroller 106 causes one of the colons in the time section of LCD display 42 to flash. Once the swimmer has checked that the lap counting system is functioning and that transmissions are being received, the swimmer enters the pool at location 204. The swimmer depresses START/STOP push-button 36 once and notes that the swim time being displayed is incrementing. The swimmer then begins swimming to the other side of the swimming pool away from the poolside unit 30 at location 200.

The poolside unit 30 detects when no transmissions have been received within a predetermined period of time (for example, five seconds). When this occurs, the poolside unit 30 assumes that the swimmer has swum out of communication range 202 of the system. The swimmer then continues to swim across pool 205 as depicted in FIG. 4 as successive locations 206 and 208. The next time the poolside unit 30 receives a predetermined number of transmissions in a second predetermined period of time (for example, ten transmissions in 5 seconds), the poolside unit 30 assumes that the swimmer has returned from the opposite side of the pool and into communication range 202. The poolside unit 30 therefore increments the lap count by two when the swimmer is about at location 208 indicating that the swimmer has swum two laps.

This sequence is repeated as the swimmer swims laps. If the swimmer wants to take a break, the swimmer depresses the START/STOP push-button 36 again. Both the lap counter and the timer are stopped. When the swimmer wishes to start swimming again after the break, he/she pushes START/STOP push-button 36 and poolside unit 30 continues counting laps and timing from where it left off. In the alternative, if the swimmer wishes to start timing and lap counting anew, the swimmer depresses ZERO push-button 38 which restarts the counting sequence from time zero and lap zero.

When the swimmer completes his/her workout, he/she stops poolside unit 30 by depressing START/STOP push-button 36. The total swim time and the number of laps are then easily read from LCD display 42. The swimmer's unit 10 will automatically turn itself off 1.8 hours after activate push-button 18 was depressed at the beginning of the workout. The poolside unit 30 will remain powered as long as solar collector 40 receives adequate incident solar radiation or as long as batteries 110 are switched on via ON/OFF switch 34.

The probability that two swimmers using the lap counting system will swim in the same pool at the same time within communication range of the other swimmer's system is very low. Even if this does occur, the probability that the swimmer's unit of one swimmer will be picked up by the other swimmer's poolside unit is reduced to practically zero because the swimmer's units are programmed with different identification codes 86. To guard against the poolside unit's deciphering transmissions from other sources as transmissions from its associated swimmer's unit, the identification code 86 of each swimmer's unit may contain an error detection code such as a cyclic redundancy check (CRC) code. The poolside unit will therefore be able to calculate what CRC code should have been transmitted with each received identification code. After comparing this calculated CRC code with the CRC code received, false transmissions can be identified and ignored.

The poolside unit 30 has stored in EEPROM nonvolatile memory the identification code 86 corresponding to the swimmer's unit 10. The poolside unit 30 is programmed with the identification code 86 by having one and only one swimmer's unit 10 within the communication range of poolside unit 30. START/STOP push-button 36 and ZERO push-button 38 are then simultaneously pushed to instruct poolside unit 30 to store in EEPROM the received identification code. The microcontroller 106 uses this stored identification code to decipher transmissions received in the future. A poolside unit 30 only acknowledges transmissions which have the identification code 86 with which that poolside unit 30 has been programmed. The poolside unit 30 may also be reprogrammed to receive a different identification code from another swimmer's unit 10 in the event, for example, that the battery of the original swimmer's unit expires or is lost.

Accordingly, the present invention permits the poolside unit 30 to discriminate between swimmers without any special mounting orientation as required by conventional lap counting systems. Many prior art devices, such as ultrasonic detecting systems, are incapable of discriminating between swimmers. Other prior art devices, which are capable of discrimination, such as infrared detecting systems, require specific, and often awkward, orientation.

OTHER EMBODIMENTS OF THE PRESENT INVENTION

FIG. 5 shows another embodiment of the swimmer's unit according to the present invention. Swimmer's unit 200 comprises water-resistant housing 202 which is secured to a swimmer's goggles 210. The swimmer's unit 200 also has an activate push-button 204 which operates identically to the activate push-button 18 discussed above. The antenna for the swimmer's unit 200 is housed in housing 202. In an alternative variation of this embodiment, the swimmer's goggles 210 may be specially designed to contain the circuitry of FIG. 2. In other embodiments, the antenna is housed in head band 212.

FIG. 6 depicts an embodiment in which the transmitter circuitry is contained in housing 202 which is in turn incorporated into swim cap 300. Activate pushbutton 204 operates as does pushbutton 18 discussed above. Placement of the transmitter in a wrist watch, a pair of goggles, or a swim cap ensures that the radio transmitter is frequently above the surface of the water during swimming. Because the transmitter makes about ten transmissions per second, radio wave attenuation and reflection due to the transmitter's being under water will not seriously impede system performance.

In another embodiment of the present invention, the circuitry of swimmer's unit 10 of FIG. 2 may be simplified by eliminating shift register 64. Although the resultant system no longer discriminates between swimmers, there is an advantage of reduced unit cost. No cutting of traces or setting of dip switches is required. Further, because the probability of two swimmers, both having non-discriminating systems, swimming near enough in a pool to trigger erroneously the other swimmer's poolside unit is small, this embodiment is both functional and economical.

In yet another embodiment, the present invention is adapted to display the total distance traveled during the swimmer's workout. The microcontroller 106 of the poolside unit 30 is programmed to calculate this total distance by multiplying the number of laps times the distance of each lap. There are numerous ways in which the distance of each lap can be programmed into the microcontroller 106. For example, the swimmer could depress and hold START/STOP push-button 36 for a preset time period (five seconds) which would trigger a LAP mode. Once LAP mode is entered, START/STOP push-button 36 and ZERO push-button 38 become incrementing and decrementing buttons to set a desired distance as displayed on the lap section of the LCD display 42. If the pool was a 10 meter pool, the swimmer would increment up (using for example, START/STOP push-button 36) to a value 10 shown on the LCD display 42. To leave the LAP mode, the START/STOP pushbutton is again depressed and held for the five second preset time period.

After the workout, the swimmer may reenter the LAP mode to reveal the total distance which is then displayed on the lap section of the LCD display 42. The units of measure correspond to the units of the initially entered distance. To ensure that the distance is fully displayed, the lap section of the LCD display 42 may be adapted to have four digits, rather than the three digits shown in FIG. 1.

Other calculations, such as average lap time, may also be obtained by the present invention. Of course, the LCD display 42 may include dedicated distance and average lap time sections in addition to the those time and lap sections depicted in the preferred embodiment described above.

In another embodiment, the system involves an additional poolside unit called the relay unit. The circuitry of the relay unit is very similar to that of the poolside unit except that receiver 102 comprises both a receiver and a transmitter. The transmitter is modulated on and off by microcontroller 106 so that serial bit sequences are transmitted from antenna 100. This relay unit is located at the opposite end of the pool from the poolside unit to check that the swimmer penetrates a second communication range of the relay unit at the opposite end of the pool. The relay unit detects that this second communication range has been penetrated in the same way that the poolside unit detects that the swimmer has penetrated its communication range.

When the second communication range has been penetrated, the relay unit transmits a serial bit sequence different from that sent from the swimmer's unit back to the poolside unit. The relay unit may transmit the same identification code, however, if the sum of the first communication range and second communication range is less than the length of the pool. The poolside unit still requires only one receiver 102 because the same radio frequency is transmitted by the relay unit as is transmitted by the transmitting unit.

It is to be understood that the invention is not limited to the disclosed embodiment, but is intended to cover various modifications and equivalent arrangements included within the spirit and scope of the appended claims.

We claim:

1. A lap counting system comprising:
remote means comprising:
  attaching means for attaching the remote means to a user;
  transmitting means for transmitting a radio signal; and
  a timing means which causes said transmitting means to transmit a plurality of bursts of said radio signal during a first period, each of said plurality of bursts being followed by a second period in which said radio signal is not transmitted;
  an activate electrical contact means for causing the transmitting means to transmit alternately said plurality of bursts and said second periods during a third period of time after said activate electrical contact means is activated, said timing means deactivating the transmitting means from transmitting said bursts after expiration of said third period of time from the last activation of said activate electrical contact means; and

central means comprising:
  receiving means for receiving said radio signal, said receiving means having a communication range with said transmitting means, the receiving means outputting a reception signal indicative of when said transmitting means enters said communication range;
  processing means for incrementing a lap count when said reception signal indicates that said transmitting means enters said communication range; and
  display means for displaying said lap count.

2. The lap counting system of claim 1, wherein said attaching means comprises a water resistant housing with one of (1) a wristband, (2) swim goggles, and (3) a swim cap.

3. The lap counting system of claim 1, wherein said remote means transmits a remote identification code modulated on said radio signal, wherein said reception signal output from the receiver means is indicative of the remote identification code, and wherein said central means only increments said lap count when the remote identification code indicated by the reception signal matches a preset central identification code.

4. The lap counting system of claim 2, wherein said central means comprises a memory which stores the central identification code.

5. The lap counting system of claim 1 wherein said central means further comprises a solar collector means for powering said central means.

6. The lap counting system of claim 1, wherein said central means further comprises a timer circuit.

7. The lap counting system of claim 6, wherein said central means further comprises a first electrical contact means and a second electrical contact means, successive activations of said first electrical contact means starting and stopping said timer circuit respectively, and activation of said second electrical contact means resetting said timer circuit.

8. The lap counting system of claim 1, wherein said central means further comprises an electrical contact means, activation of said electrical contact means causing said lap count to be reset to zero.

9. The lap counting system of claim 6, wherein said display means is also for displaying an indication of time, said indication of time being output from said timer circuit.

10. The lap counting system of claim 1, wherein said central means further comprises batteries for powering said central means.

11. The lap counting system of claim 1, wherein said display means comprises a liquid crystal display.

12. A lap counting system comprising:
remote means comprising:
  attaching means for attaching the remote means to a user; and transmitting means for transmitting a radio signal;
central means comprising:
  receiving means for receiving said radio signal, said receiving means having a communication range with said transmitting means, the receiving means outputting a reception signal indicative of when said transmitting means enters said communication range;
  processing means for incrementing a lap count when said reception signal indicates that said transmitting means enters said communication range; and

display means for displaying said lap count; and
relay means for receiving said radio signal from said transmitting means and for transmitting a second radio signal to said central means, the relay means being disposed outside of said communication range of said transmitting means and said receiving means, the relay means and the central means having a second communication range which is greater than said communication range of said transmitting means and said receiving means;
wherein said processing means only increments said lap count from a first lap count to a second lap count when said central means receives the second radio signal from said relay means after said lap count was set to said first lap count.

13. A lap counting system comprising;
remote means comprising:
  generating means for producing a continuous series of pulses;
  counting means coupled to said generating means for incrementally counting to a desired predetermined value, each incremental count being made upon receipt of a pulse from said generating means; and
  transmitting means operatively coupled to said counting means for transmitting a radio signal when said counting means reaches the predetermined value;
central means comprising:
  receiving means for receiving said radio signal; and
  processing means operatively coupled to said receiving means for incrementing a lap count when said receiving means receives the radio signal.

14. A lap counting system according to claim 13 wherein said receiving means and said transmitting means define a communication range, said receiving means only receiving said radio signal when said transmitting means is within the communication range.

15. A lap counting system according to claim 13 further comprising a shift register coupled between said counting means and said transmitting means, said shift register outputting an identification code to said transmitting means when said counting means reaches the predetermined value.

16. A lap counting system according to claim 13 wherein said counting means counts to a second predetermined value, said remote means being deactivated when said counting means reaches the second predetermined value.

17. A lap counting system comprising:
remote means comprising:
  generating means for producing a continuous series of pulses;
  counting means coupled to said generating means for incrementally counting a first predetermined number of counts and a second predetermined number of counts greater than the first predetermined number of counts, each incremental count being made upon receipt of a pulse from the generating means; and
  transmitting means operatively coupled to said counting means for transmitting a radio signal each time said counting means reaches the first predetermined number of counts, said transmitting means transmitting the radio signal for a time less than a time required for said counting means to reach the first predetermined number of counts, said transmitting means ceasing to

transmit the radio signal when said counting means reaching said second predetermined number of counts; and

central means comprising:

receiving means for receiving the radio signal; and processing means operatively coupled to said receiving means for incrementing a lap count when said receiving means receives the radio signal.

18. A lap counting system according to claim 17 further comprising a shift register coupled between said counting means and said transmitting means, said shift register outputting an identification code to be transmitted by said transmitting means each time said counting means reaches the first predetermined number of counts.

* * * * *

APPENDIX B

EXAMPLE OF A DESIGN PATENT

United States Patent [19]
Chu

[11] Patent Number: Des. 301,142
[45] Date of Patent: ** May 16, 1989

[54] COMPUTER MOUSE

[75] Inventor: Robin Chu, San Francisco, Calif.

[73] Assignee: Keytronic Corporation, Spokane, Wash.

[**] Term: 14 Years

[21] Appl. No.: 232,918

[22] Filed: Aug. 16, 1988
[52] U.S. Cl. D14/114
[58] Field of Search .... D14/100–117; D13/32, 38; D21/48; 74/471 XY; 178/18, 19; 340/706, 709, 710

[56] References Cited
U.S. PATENT DOCUMENTS

D. 283,818 5/1986 Skaggs D14/114
D. 284,284 6/1986 Manock et al. D14/114
D. 288,569 3/1987 Ida D14/114
D. 288,930 3/1987 Barbera et al. ... D14/114
D. 291,318 8/1987 Kim D14/114
D. 292,927 11/1987 Burnstem et al. .. D14/114
4,550,316 10/1985 Whetstone et al. . 340/710
4,613,853   9/1986 Hosogoe et al. ... 340/710

FOREIGN PATENT DOCUMENTS

107130– 6/1985 Japan 340/710
160429_ 8/1985 Japan .

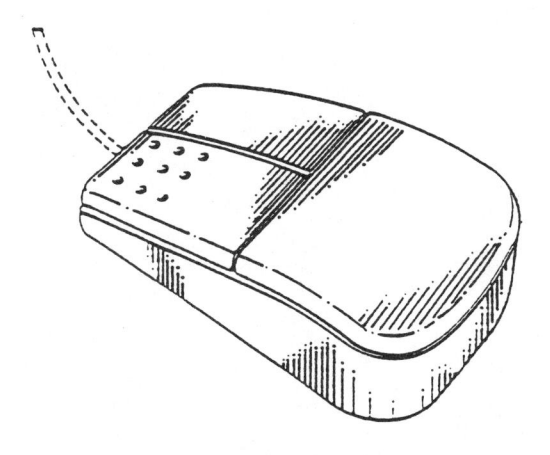

OTHER PUBLICATIONS

IBM Technical Disclosure Bulletin–Oct. 1984, p. 3042.
The Hirez Mouse Brochure.
GVC Brochure, "250 DPI Optical Mouse".
Winner Brochure, "We Cover the Whole Market".
Advertisement from *Computer Reseller News*, Monday, Mar. 28, 1988.
Microsoft Brochure, "Guide to Microsoft Products for the MS-DOS and XENIX Operating Systems".
MSC Technologies, Inc. Brochures (3).
Microsoft Brochure, "The Microsoft Mouse".

Primary Examiner—Susan J. Lucas
Assistant Examiner—Freda S. Nunn
Attorney, Agent, or Firm—Wells, St. John & Roberts

[57] CLAIM

The ornamental design for computer mouse, as shown and described.

DESCRIPTION

FIG. 1 is a top, front perspective view of a computer mouse showing my new design;
FIG. 2 is a top plan view thereof;
FIG. 3 is a front elevational view thereof;
FIG. 4 is a rear elevational view thereof;
FIG. 5 is a left side elevational view thereof;
FIG. 6 is right side elevational view thereof.
The electric cord is shown in broken lines for illustrative purposes only.

262   **EXAMPLE OF A DESIGN PATENT**

U.S. Patent   May 16, 1989   Sheet 1 of 2   **D301,142**

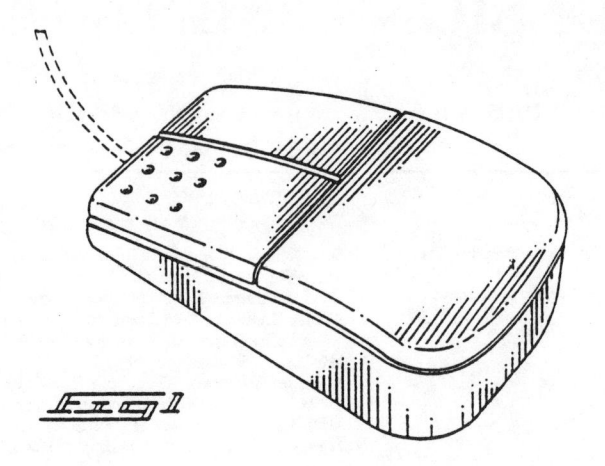

FIG 1

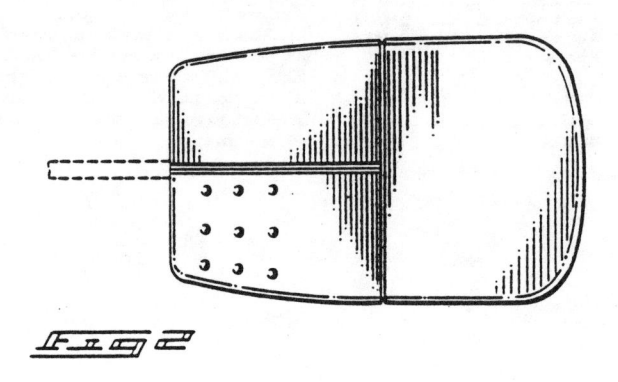

FIG 2

EXAMPLE OF A DESIGN PATENT 263

U.S. Patent May 16, 1989 Sheet 2 of 2 D301,142

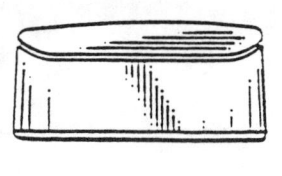

Fig 3

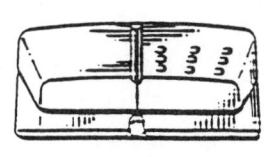

Fig 4

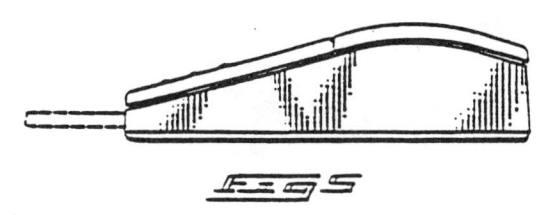

Fig 5

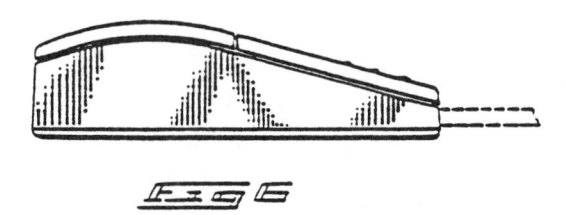

Fig 6

APPENDIX C

SAMPLE TRADEMARK REGISTRATION

Int. Cl.: 30

Prior U.S. Cl.: 46

United States Patent and Trademark Office   Reg. No. 1,439,355
Registered May 12, 1987

TRADEMARK
PRINCIPAL REGISTER

OLYMPIC FOODS, INC. (WASHINGTON CORPORATION)
P.O. BOX 3183
605 N. FANCHER RD.
SPOKANE, WA 99202, ASSIGNEE OF BUCKAROO BAGELS, INC. (WASHINGTON CORPORATION) SPOKANE, WA 99204

FOR: BAGELS, BAGEL CRUMBS, BAGEL STUFFING MIX, MIX TO MAKE BAGELS AND FRANKFURTERS WRAPPED IN BAGEL DOUGH, IN CLASS 30 (U.S. CL. 46).

FIRST USE 5-0-1982; IN COMMERCE 5-0-1982.

NO CLAIM IS MADE TO THE EXCLUSIVE RIGHT TO USE "BAGELS", APART FROM THE MARK AS SHOWN.

SER. NO. 534,994, FILED 4-29-1985.

JERRY L. PRICE, EXAMINING ATTORNEY

APPENDIX D

FORM FOR REGISTRATION OF A COPYRIGHTED WORK

FORM TX
UNITED STATES COPYRIGHT OFFICE

REGISTRATION NUMBER

TX / TXU
EFFECTIVE DATE OF REGISTRATION

Month Day Year

DO NOT WRITE ABOVE THIS LINE. IF YOU NEED MORE SPACE, USE A SEPARATE CONTINUATION SHEET.

1 TITLE OF THIS WORK ▼

PREVIOUS OR ALTERNATIVE TITLES ▼

PUBLICATION AS A CONTRIBUTION If this work was published as a contribution to a periodical, serial, or collection, give information about the collective work in which the contribution appeared. Title of Collective Work ▼

If published in a periodical or serial give: Volume ▼   Number ▼   Issue Date ▼   On Pages ▼

2 NAME OF AUTHOR ▼   DATES OF BIRTH AND DEATH
a   Year Born ▼   Year Died ▼

Was this contribution to the work a   AUTHOR'S NATIONALITY OR DOMICILE   WAS THIS AUTHOR'S CONTRIBUTION TO
"work made for hire"?   Name of Country   THE WORK   If the answer to either
☐ Yes   OR ⎰ Citizen of ▶   Anonymous?   ☐ Yes ☐ No   of these questions is
☐ No   ⎱ Domiciled in ▶   Pseudonymous? ☐ Yes ☐ No   "Yes," see detailed instructions

NOTE
Under the law, the "author" of a "work made for hire" is generally the employer, not the employee (see instructions). For any part of this work that was "made for hire" check "Yes" in the space provided, give the employer (or other person for whom the work was prepared) as "Author" of that part, and leave the space for dates of birth and death blank.

NATURE OF AUTHORSHIP Briefly describe nature of the material created by this author in which copyright is claimed. ▼

b NAME OF AUTHOR ▼   DATES OF BIRTH AND DEATH
                                                   Year Born ▼   Year Died ▼

Was this contribution to the work a   AUTHOR'S NATIONALITY OR DOMICILE   WAS THIS AUTHOR'S CONTRIBUTION TO
"work made for hire"?   Name of country   THE WORK   If the answer to either
☐ Yes   OR ⎰ Citizen of ▶   Anonymous?   ☐ Yes ☐ No   of these questions is
☐ No   ⎱ Domiciled in ▶   Pseudonymous? ☐ Yes ☐ No   "Yes," see detailed instructions

NATURE OF AUTHORSHIP Briefly describe nature of the material created by this author in which copyright is claimed. ▼

c NAME OF AUTHOR ▼   DATES OF BIRTH AND DEATH
                                                   Year Born ▼   Year Died ▼

Was this contribution to the work a   AUTHOR'S NATIONALITY OR DOMICILE   WAS THIS AUTHOR'S CONTRIBUTION TO
"work made for hire"?   Name of Country   THE WORK   If the answer to either
☐ Yes   OR ⎰ Citizen of ▶   Anonymous?   ☐ Yes ☐ No   of these questions is
☐ No   ⎱ Domiciled in ▶   Pseudonymous? ☐ Yes ☐ No   "Yes," see detailed instructions

NATURE OF AUTHORSHIP Briefly describe nature of the material created by this author in which copyright is claimed. ▼

3 YEAR IN WHICH CREATION OF THIS   DATE AND NATION OF FIRST PUBLICATION OF THIS PARTICULAR WORK
WORK WAS COMPLETED This information   Complete this information Month ▶ _____ Day ▶ _____ Year ▶ _____
                    must be given   ONLY if this work
          ◀ Year   in all cases.   has been published.   ◀ Nation

4 COPYRIGHT CLAIMANT(S) Name and address must be given even if the claimant is the   APPLICATION RECEIVED
same as the author given in space 2. ▼
                                                                                           ONE DEPOSIT RECEIVED

See instructions   TWO DEPOSITS RECEIVED
before completing
this space
          TRANSFER If the claimant(s) named here in space 4 are different from the author(s) named   REMITTANCE NUMBER AND DATE
          in space 2, give a brief statement of how the claimant(s) obtained ownership of the copyright. ▼

MORE ON BACK ▶ • Complete all applicable spaces (numbers 5-11) on the reverse side of this page.   DO NOT WRITE HERE
                • See detailed instructions.   • Sign the form at line 10.   Page 1 of _____ pages

267

FORM FOR REGISTRATION

EXAMINED BY	FORM TX
CHECKED BY	
☐ CORRESPONDENCE Yes	FOR COPYRIGHT OFFICE USE ONLY
☐ DEPOSIT ACCOUNT FUNDS USED	

DO NOT WRITE ABOVE THIS LINE. IF YOU NEED MORE SPACE, USE A SEPARATE CONTINUATION SHEET.

PREVIOUS REGISTRATION Has registration for this work, or for an earlier version of this work, already been made in the Copyright Office?
☐ Yes ☐ No If your answer is "Yes," why is another registration being sought? (Check appropriate box) ▼
☐ This is the first published edition of a work previously registered in unpublished form.
☐ This is the first application submitted by this author as copyright claimant.
☐ This is a changed version of the work, as shown by space 6 on this application.
If your answer is "Yes," give: **Previous Registration Number** ▼   **Year of Registration** ▼

5

DERIVATIVE WORK OR COMPILATION Complete both space 6a & 6b for a derivative work; complete only 6b for a compilation.
a. Preexisting Material Identify any preexisting work or works that this work is based on or incorporates. ▼

b. Material Added to This Work Give a brief, general statement of the material that has been added to this work and in which copyright is claimed. ▼

See instructions before completing this space

6

—space deleted—

7

REPRODUCTION FOR USE OF BLIND OR PHYSICALLY HANDICAPPED INDIVIDUALS   A signature on this form at space 10, and a check in one of the boxes here in space 8, constitutes a non-exclusive grant of permission to the Library of Congress to reproduce and distribute solely for the blind and physically handicapped and under the conditions and limitations prescribed by the regulations of the Copyright Office: (1) copies of the work identified in space 1 of this application in Braille (or similar tactile symbols); or (2) phonorecords embodying a fixation of a reading of that work; or (3) both.

a ☐ Copies and Phonorecords   b ☐ Copies Only   c ☐ Phonorecords Only   See instructions

8

DEPOSIT ACCOUNT If the registration fee is to be charged to a Deposit Account established in the Copyright Office, give name and number of Account.
Name ▼   **Account Number** ▼

CORRESPONDENCE Give name and address to which correspondence about this application should be sent.   Name/Address/Apt/City/State/Zip ▼

Area Code & Telephone Number ▶

Be sure to give your daytime phone ◀ number

9

CERTIFICATION* I, the undersigned, hereby certify that I am the
Check one ▶
☐ author
☐ other copyright claimant
☐ owner of exclusive right(s)
☐ authorized agent of

of the work identified in this application and that the statements made by me in this application are correct to the best of my knowledge.

Name of author or other copyright claimant, or owner of exclusive right(s) ▲

Typed or printed name and date ▼ If this is a published work, this date must be the same as or later than the date of publication given in space 3.
_____ date ▶ _____

☞   Handwritten signature (X) ▼

10

MAIL CERTIFICATE TO	Name ▼	YOU MUST: • Complete all necessary spaces • Sign your application in space 10
Certificate will be mailed in window envelope	Number Street Apartment Number ▼	SEND ALL 3 ELEMENTS IN THE SAME PACKAGE: 1. Application form 2. Non-refundable $10 filing fee in check or money order payable to Register of Copyrights 3. Deposit material
	City State ZIP ▼	MAIL TO: Register of Copyrights Library of Congress Washington, DC 20559

11

* 17 U.S.C. § 506(e): Any person who knowingly makes a false representation of a material fact in the application for copyright registration provided for by section 409, or in any written statement filed in connection with the application, shall be fined not more than $2,500.

April 1989—200,000   ☆ U.S. GOVERNMENT PRINTING OFFICE: 1989—241-428/80,018

TABLE OF CASES

Case name	Book §
A.B. Chance Co. v. RTE Corp., 854 F.2d 1307, 7 U.S.P.Q.2d (BNA) 1881 (Fed. Cir. 1988)	§§ 12.12, 13.14
Abele, *In re*, 684 F.2d 902, 214 U.S.P.Q. (BNA) 682 (C.C.P.A. 1982)	§ 2.5
A.C. Aukerman Co. v. R.L. Chaides Constr. Co., 960 F.2d 1020, 22 U.S.P.Q.2d (BNA) 1321 (Fed. Cir. 1992)	§ 14.4
Advance Hydraulics, Inc. v. Otis Elevator Co., 525 F.2d 477, 186 U.S.P.Q. (BNA) 1 (7th Cir.), *cert. denied*, 423 U.S. 869 (1975)	§ 14.4
A.H. Emery Co. v. Marcan Prod. Corp., 389 F.2d 11, 156 U.S.P.Q. (BNA) 529 (2d Cir.), *cert. denied*, 159 U.S.P.Q. (BNA) 799 (1968)	§§ 2.48, 2.49, 12.3
Allen, *Ex parte*, 2 U.S.P.Q.2d (BNA) 1425 (Bd. Pat. App. & Interferences 1987)	§ 2.5
Arco Indus. Corp. v. Chemcast Corp., 633 F.2d 435, 208 U.S.P.Q. (BNA) 190 (6th Cir. 1980)	§§ 2.58, 12.3
Baker Oil Tools, Inc. v. Geo Vann, Inc., 828 F.2d 1558, 4 U.S.P.Q.2d (BNA) 1210 (Fed. Cir. 1987)	§ 13.33
Barmag Barmer Maschinenfabrik AG v. Murata Mach., Ltd., 731 F.2d 831, 221 U.S.P.Q. (BNA) 561 (Fed. Cir. 1984)	§ 12.12
Becton Dickinson & Co. v. C.R. Bard, 922 F.2d 792, 17 U.S.P.Q.2d (BNA) 1097 (Fed. Cir. 1990)	§ 2.2
B.F. Sturtevant v. Massachusetts Hair & Felt Co., 124 F.2d 95, 51 U.S.P.Q. 420 (1st Cir. 1941)	§ 12.12
Black, Sivalls & Bryson, Inc. v. Keystone Steel Fabrication, 584 F.2d 946, 199 U.S.P.Q. (BNA) 385 (10th Cir. 1978)	§ 2.48
Brigance, *In re*, 792 F.2d 1103, 229 U.S.P.Q. (BNA) 988 (Fed. Cir. 1986)	§§ 12.12, 13.21
Brulotte v. Thys Co., 379 U.S. 29, 143 U.S.P.Q. (BNA) 264 (1964)	§ 9.20
Burger King of Fla., Inc. v. Hoots, 403 F.2d 904, 159 U.S.P.Q. (BNA) 706 (7th Cir. 1968)	§ 2.35
Burke Elec. Co. v. Independent Pneumatic Tool Co., 234 F. 93 (2d Cir.), *cert. denied*, 241 U.S. 682 (1916)	§ 12.12
Business Intelligence Servs., Inc. v. Hudson, 580 F. Supp. 1068 (S.D.N.Y. 1984)	§ 13.6
Cadillac Gage Co. v. Verne Eng'g Corp., 203 U.S.P.Q. (BNA) 473 (Mich. Cir. Ct. 1978)	§ 2.55
Caveney, *In re*, 761 F.2d 671, 226 U.S.P.Q. (BNA) 1 (Fed. Cir. 1985)	§ 12.12

TABLE OF CASES

Central Soya, Inc. v. Geo. A. Hormel & Co., 581 F. Supp. 54, 219 U.S.P.Q. (BNA) 878 (W.D. Okla.), *aff'd*, 723 F.2d 1573, 220 U.S.P.Q. (BNA) 490 (Fed. Cir. 1983)	§§ 13.4, 14.3
Clark v. Bunker, 453 F.2d 1006, 172 U.S.P.Q. (BNA) 420 (9th Cir. 1972)	§§ 2.49, 12.3
Coleman v. Dines, 754 F.2d 353, 224 U.S.P.Q. (BNA) 857 (Fed. Cir. 1985)	§§ 12.15, 13.13
Computer Assocs. Int'l Inc. v. Bryan, 784 F. Supp. 982 (E.D.N.Y. 1992)	§ 13.6
Conmar Prod. Corp. v. Universal Slide Fasteners Co., 172 F.2d 150, 80 U.S.P.Q. (BNA) 108 (2d Cir. 1949)	§§ 12.6, 13.10
Constant v. Advanced Micro-Devices, Inc., 848 F.2d 1560, 7 U.S.P.Q.2d (BNA) 1057 (Fed. Cir.), *cert. denied*, 488 U.S. 892 (1988)	§ 12.10
Construction Specialties, Inc. v. Arden Architectural Specialties, Inc., 20 U.S.P.Q.2d (BNA) 1874 (D. Minn. 1991)	§§ 13.24, 13.33
Cronyn, *In re*, 890 F.2d 1158, 13 U.S.P.Q.2d (BNA) 1070 (Fed. Cir. 1989)	§ 12.10
CTS Corp. v. Piher Int'l Corp., 527 F.2d 95, 188 U.S.P.Q. (BNA) 419 (7th Cir. 1975), *cert. denied*, 424 U.S. 978 (1976)	§ 12.12
CVD, Inc. v. Raytheon, Co., 769 F.2d 842, 227 U.S.P.Q. (BNA) 7 (1st Cir. 1985), *cert. denied*, 475 U.S. 1016 (1986)	§ 13.20
Defiance Button Mach. Co. v. C&C Metal Prod. Corp., 759 F.2d 1053, 225 U.S.P.Q. (BNA) 797 (2d Cir. 1985)	§ 3.5
Diamond v. Chakrabarty, 447 U.S. 303, 206 U.S.P.Q. (BNA) 193 (1980)	§ 2.5
Digital Dev. Corp. v. International Memory Sys., 185 U.S.P.Q. (BNA) 136 (S.D. Cal. 1973)	§ 6.16
D.L. Auld Co. v. Chroma Graphics Corp., 714 F.2d 1144, 219 U.S.P.Q. (BNA) 13 (Fed. Cir. 1983)	§ 12.12
Dybel, *In re*, 524 F.2d 1393, 187 U.S.P.Q. (BNA) 593 (C.C.P.A. 1975)	§§ 12.13, 13.33
Eaton Corp. v. Giere, 23 U.S.P.Q.2d (BNA) 1705 (Fed. Cir. 1992)	§ 13.6
E.I. Du Pont de Nemours & Co., *In re*, 476 F.2d 1357, 177 U.S.P.Q. (BNA) 563 (C.C.P.A. 1973)	§ 2.40
E.I. Du Pont de Nemours & Co. v. Christopher, 431 F.2d 1012, 166 U.S.P.Q. (BNA) 421 (5th Cir.), *cert. denied*, 400 U.S. 1024, 168 U.S.P.Q. (BNA) 385 (1970)	§ 2.54
Elizabeth v. Nicholson Pavement Co., 97 U.S. 126 (1878)	§ 12.13
Ferrari S.p.A. Esercizio Fabriche Automobile E Corse v. Roberts, 944 F.2d 1235, 20 U.S.P.Q.2d (BNA) 1001 (6th Cir. 1991), *appeal pending*, 60 U.S.L.W. 878 (U.S. 1992)	§ 8.11
Gary Van Zeeland Talent, Inc. v. Sandas, 84 Wis. 2d 202, 262 N.W.2d 242 (1978)	§ 13.6

TABLE OF CASES

Georgia-Pacific Corp. v. U.S. Plywood-Champion Papers, Inc., 318 F. Supp. 1116, 166 U.S.P.Q. (BNA) 235 (S.D.N.Y. 1970)	§ 4.4
Graver Tank Co. v. Linde Air Prod. Co., 339 U.S. 605, 85 U.S.P.Q. (BNA) 328 (1950)	§§ 2.2, 2.11
Great N. Corp. v. Davis Core & Pad Co., 782 F.2d 159, 228 U.S.P.Q. (BNA) 356 (Fed. Cir. 1986)	§§ 3.10, 12.12, 13.14, 14.3
Haglund v. Dow Chem. Co., 218 U.S.P.Q. (BNA) 55 (E.D. Cal. 1982)	§ 13.40
Hall, *In re*, 781 F.2d 897, 228 U.S.P.Q. (BNA) 453 (Fed. Cir. 1986)	§ 12.10
Hamilton, *In re*, 882 F.2d 1576, 11 U.S.P.Q.2d (BNA) 1890 (Fed. Cir. 1989)	§§ 3.3, 13.33
Harrington Mfg. Co. v. Powell Mfg. Co., 815 F.2d 1478, 2 U.S.P.Q.2d (BNA) 1364 (Fed. Cir. 1986), *cert. denied*, 479 U.S. 1030 (1987)	§§ 12.10, 12.11, 13.23
Hazeltine Corp. v. United States, 820 F.2d 1190, 2 U.S.P.Q.2d (BNA) 1744 (Fed. Cir. 1987)	§ 12.15
Hottel Corp. v. Seaman Corp., 833 F.2d 1570, 4 U.S.P.Q.2d (BNA) 1939 (Fed. Cir. 1987)	§ 14.4
Iwahashi, *In re*, 888 F.2d 1370, 12 U.S.P.Q.2d (BNA) 1908 (Fed. Cir. 1989)	§ 2.5
J.A. LaPorte, Inc. v. Norfolk Dredging Co., 229 U.S.P.Q. (BNA) 435 (Fed. Cir. 1986)	§ 13.33
Jones, *In re*, 373 F.2d 1007, 153 U.S.P.Q. (BNA) 77 (C.C.P.A. 1967)	§ 2.5
Jostens, Inc. v. National Computer Sys., Inc., 318 N.W.2d 691, 214 U.S.P.Q. (BNA) 918 (Minn. 1982)	§ 3.6
Jungersen v. Ostby & Barton Co., 335 U.S. 560, 80 U.S.P.Q. (BNA) 32 (1949)	§ 4.25
K-2 Ski Co. v. Head Ski Co., 506 F.2d 471, 182 U.S.P.Q. (BNA) 724 (9th Cir. 1974)	§ 4.7
Kewanee Oil Co. v. Bicron Corp., 416 U.S. 470, 181 U.S.P.Q. (BNA) 673 (1974)	§§ 2.48, 13.6
King Instrument Corp. v. Otari Corp., 767 F.2d 853, 226 U.S.P.Q. (BNA) 402 (Fed. Cir. 1985)	§ 4.4
Koerhring Co. v. National Automatic Tool Co., 362 F.2d 100, 149 U.S.P.Q. (BNA) 887 (7th Cir. 1966)	§ 12.11
Mann, *In re*, 861 F.2d 1581, 8 U.S.P.Q.2d (BNA) 2030 (Fed. Cir. 1988)	§§ 12.11, 12.12, 13.23
Marconi Wireless Tel. Co. v. United States, 320 U.S. 1 (1943)	§ 12.15
Massachusetts Inst. of Technology v. AB Fortia, 774 F.2d 1104, 227 U.S.P.Q. (BNA) 428 (Fed. Cir. 1984)	§ 12.10
Mazer v. Stein, 347 U.S. 201, 100 U.S.P.Q. (BNA) 325 (1954)	§ 5.8
McCreery Eng'g Co. v. Massachusetts Fan Co., 195 F. 498 (1st Cir. 1912)	§ 12.12

TABLE OF CASES

Metallizing Eng'g Co. v. Kenyon Bearing & Auto Parts Co., 153 F.2d 516, 68 U.S.P.Q. (BNA) 54 (2d Cir. 1946)	§ 12.12
Miller, *In re*, 418 F.2d 1392, 164 U.S.P.Q. (BNA) 46 (C.C.P.A. 1969)	§ 2.5
Milliken Research Corp. v. Dan River, Inc., 739 F.2d 587, 222 U.S.P.Q. (BNA) 571 (Fed. Cir. 1984)	§ 12.11
Minnesota Mining & Mfg. Co. v. General Elec. Co., 167 F. Supp. 37, 119 U.S.P.Q. (BNA) 65 (D.D.C. 1958)	§ 12.15
Mogen David Wine Corp., *In re*, 372 F.2d 539, 152 U.S.P.Q. (BNA) 593 (C.C.P.A. 1967)	§ 5.8
Molecular Research Corp. v. CBS, Inc., 793 F.2d 1261, 229 U.S.P.Q. (BNA) 805 (Fed. Cir. 1986), *cert. denied*, 479 U.S. 1030 (1987)	§ 12.11
Motorola, Inc. v. Fairchild Camera & Instrument Corp., 366 F. Supp. 1173, 177 U.S.P.Q. (BNA) 614 (D. Ariz. 1973)	§§ 3.7, 12.3, 13.6, 13.15, 13.18
Olympia Werke Aktiengesellschaft v. General Elec. Co., 712 F.2d 74, 219 U.S.P.Q. (BNA) 107 (4th Cir. 1983)	§ 14.4
Palin Mfg. Co. v. Water Technology, Inc., 221 U.S.P.Q. (BNA) 640 (Ill. App. Ct. 1982)	§ 12.7
Panduit Corp. v. Stahlin Bros. Fibre Works, Inc., 575 F.2d 1152, 197 U.S.P.Q. (BNA) 726 (6th Cir. 1978)	§ 4.4
Polaroid Corp. v. Eastman Kodak Co., 16 U.S.P.Q.2d (BNA) 1481 (D. Mass. 1990)	§§ 1.31, 3.9
Preemption Devices, Inc. v. Minnesota Mining & Mfg. Co., 732 F.2d 903, 221 U.S.P.Q. (BNA) 841 (Fed. Cir. 1984)	§ 12.10
RCA Corp. v. Data Gen. Corp., 887 F.2d 1056, 12 U.S.P.Q.2d (BNA) 1449 (Fed. Cir. 1989)	§§ 3.2, 12.12
Regents of the Univ. of Cal., Inc. v. Howmedica, 503 F. Supp. 846, 210 U.S.P.Q. (BNA) 727 (D.N.J. 1981), *aff'd*, 676 F.2d 687 (3d Cir. 1982)	§ 12.10
Reiner v. I. Leon Co., 285 F.2d 501, 128 U.S.P.Q. (BNA) 25 (2d Cir. 1960)	§ 4.25
Sands, Taylor & Woods v. Quaker Oats Co., 18 U.S.P.Q.2d (BNA) 1457 (N.D. Ill. 1990), *rev'd on other grounds*, 24 U.S.P.Q.2d 1001 (7th Cir. 1992)	§§ 3.11, 14.3
S.C. Johnson & Son, Inc. v. Carter-Wallace, Inc., 614 F. Supp. 1278, 225 U.S.P.Q. (BNA) 1022 (S.D.N.Y. 1985), *aff'd in part, vacated in part*, 781 F.2d 198, 228 U.S.P.Q. (BNA) 367 (Fed. Cir. 1986)	§ 14.3
Schalk v. Texas, 823 S.W.2d 633, 21 U.S.P.Q.2d (BNA) 1838 (Tex. Crim. App. 1991)	§ 12.3
Schulenburg v. Signatrol, 33 Ill. 2d 379, 212 N.E.2d 865, U.S.P.Q. (BNA) 167 (1965)	§ 2.48
Shatterproof Glass Corp. v. Libbey-Owens Ford Co., 758 F.2d 613, 225 U.S.P.Q. (BNA) 634 (Fed. Cir.), *cert. denied*, 474 U.S. 976 (1985)	§§ 12.12, 12.15
Sikes v. McGraw-Edison, 671 F.2d 150, 217 U.S.P.Q. (BNA) 1086 (5th Cir.), *cert. denied*, 458 U.S. 1108 (1982)	§ 12.4

TABLE OF CASES

Case	Section
Sikes v. McGraw-Edison, 665 F.2d 731, 213 U.S.P.Q. (BNA) 983 (5th Cir.), *cert. denied*, 458 U.S. 1108 (1982)	§ 12.4
Sires v. Luke, 544 F. Supp. 1155 (S.D. Ga. 1982)	§ 13.6
Smith, *In re*, 714 F.2d 1127, 218 U.S.P.Q. (BNA) 976 (Fed. Cir. 1983)	§§ 3.4, 12.11, 13.24
Smith v. Dravo Corp., 203 F.2d 369, 97 U.S.P.Q. (BNA) 98 (7th Cir. 1953)	§ 12.3
Spada, *In re*, 911 F.2d 705, 15 U.S.P.Q.2d (BNA) 1655 (Fed. Cir. 1990)	§§ 6.20, 12.10
Stratoflex, Inc. v. Aeroquip Corp., 713 F.2d 1530, 218 U.S.P.Q. (BNA) 871 (Fed. Cir. 1983)	§ 2.7
Syntex Ophthalmics, Inc. v. Novicky, 745 F.2d 1423, 223 U.S.P.Q. (BNA) 695 (Fed. Cir. 1984)	§ 2.48
Tansel, *In re*, 253 F.2d 241, 117 U.S.P.Q. (BNA) 188 (C.C.P.A. 1958)	§ 12.15
Telex Corp. v. International Business Mach. Corp., 510 F.2d 894, 184 U.S.P.Q. (BNA) 521 (10th Cir. 1974), *cert. denied*, 423 U.S. 802 (1975)	§ 2.48
Theis, *In re*, 610 F.2d 786, 204 U.S.P.Q. (BNA) 188 (C.C.P.A. 1979)	§ 12.13
Timely Prod. Corp. v. Arron, 523 F.2d 288, 187 U.S.P.Q. (BNA) 257 (2d Cir. 1975)	§ 12.12
T.P. Lab., Inc. v. Professional Positioners, Inc., 724 F.2d 965, 220 U.S.P.Q. (BNA) 577 (Fed. Cir.), *cert. denied*, 469 U.S. 826 (1984)	§§ 12.9, 12.13, 13.14, 13.33
UMC Elec. Co. v. United States, 816 F.2d 647, 2 U.S.P.Q.2d (BNA) 1465 (Fed. Cir. 1987), *cert. denied*, 484 U.S. 1025 (1988)	§§ 12.12, 12.13, 12.15
Union Carbide Corp. v. American Can Co., 724 F.2d 1567, 220 U.S.P.Q. (BNA) 584 (Fed. Cir. 1984)	§ 2.7
Uniservices, Inc., *In re*, 517 F.2d 492 (7th Cir. 1975)	§ 13.6
Universal Athletic Sales Co. v. American Gym Recreational & Athletic Equip. Corp., 546 F.2d 530, 192 U.S.P.Q. (BNA) 193 (3d Cir. 1976), *cert. denied*, 430 U.S. 984 (1977)	§ 12.10
Warner-Lambert Pharmaceutical Co. v. John J. Reynolds, Inc., 178 F. Supp. 655, 123 U.S.P.Q. (BNA) 431 (S.D.N.Y. 1959)	§ 9.20
Water Serv., Inc. v. Tesco Chem., 410 F.2d 163, 162 U.S.P.Q. (BNA) 321 (5th Cir. 1969)	§ 2.48
Waterman v. McKenzie, 138 U.S. 252 (1891)	§ 4.8
Weiner King, Inc. v. Weiner King Corp., 615 F.2d 512, 204 U.S.P.Q. (BNA) 820 (C.C.P.A. 1980)	§ 2.42
Western Electro-plating Co. v. Henness, 180 Cal. App. 2d 442, 4 Cal. Rptr. 434 (1960)	§ 2.48
Western Marine Elec. v. Furuno Elec. Co., 764 F.2d 840, 226 U.S.P.Q. (BNA) 334 (Fed. Cir. 1985)	§ 13.33

Willis v. Suppa, 209 U.S.P.Q. (BNA) 406 (Bd. Pat. Int. 1980) § 12.15

Yamamoto, *In re*, 740 F.2d 1569, 222 U.S.P.Q. (BNA) 934
 (Fed. Cir. 1984) § 9.14

INDEX

ADVERTISEMENT DISTRIBUTIONS
  Intellectual property rights, company policies maximizing preservation § 13.21

ADVERTISING
  Copyright protection, appropriateness of §§ 10.3, 10.4
  Intellectual property protection, most appropriate selection of § 5.7
  Trademark protection, appropriateness of § 11.11

ADVERTISING AND QUANTITY OF SALES, MANNER OF
  Trademark protection, appropriateness of § 11.11
  Trademarks § 2.39

AFFIRMATIVE STEPS
  Company intellectual property policies and procedures, necessity of § 12.3
  Trade secret and patent protection, choosing between § 9.10
  Trade secrets § 2.52

AFFIXATION
  Trademarks § 2.37

APPLICATION, INTENT TO USE
  Trademark protection, appropriateness of § 11.7

ASSET VALUE
  Protection § 6.17
  Value and benefits of intellectual property § 4.24

ASSIGNMENT OR LICENSE FOR REVENUE
  Patent protection, appropriateness of § 8.5

ASSIGNMENT PROVISION
  Intellectual property rights, company policies maximizing preservation § 13.6

ATTORNEYS AND ATTORNEYS' FEES
  See also INTELLECTUAL PROPERTY RIGHTS, COMPANY POLICIES MAXIMIZING PRESERVATION
  Intellectual property issues, dangers of failing to consider §§ 3.10, 3.11
  Intellectual property protection, most appropriate selection of § 5.5
  Patent protection, appropriateness of §§ 8.3, 8.7, 8.14
  Patents §§ 2.9, 2.13
  Trade secret and patent protection, choosing between § 9.10
  Trade secret protection, threshold level protection § 7.2
  Trade secrets § 2.56
  Value and benefits of intellectual property §§ 4.4–4.6

AUDIT, INTELLECTUAL PROPERTY
  Intellectual property rights, company policies maximizing preservation § 13.43

AUTHORSHIP, ORIGINAL
  Copyrights § 2.26
  Protection § 6.3

AWARDS
  See PUNITIVE AWARDS

BACKUP PROTECTION
  Patent protection, appropriateness of § 8.11

BARGAINING POSTURE, CORPORATE
  Patent protection, appropriateness of § 8.5
  Protection § 6.15

BARS TO PATENTABILITY
  See also SECTION 102 BARS TO PATENTABILITY

BARS TO PATENTABILITY
(Continued)
Company intellectual property policies and procedures, necessity of § 12.9

BENEFITS OF INTELLECTUAL PROPERTY
See VALUE AND BENEFITS OF INTELLECTUAL PROPERTY

BEST MODE
See ENABLEMENT AND BEST MODE

BOOK, HOW TO USE
Intellectual property, importance of § 1.6

BREACH OF CONTRACT
Company intellectual property policies and procedures, necessity of § 12.4

BROCHURES
Intellectual property rights, company policies maximizing preservation § 13.21

BUFFERING TECHNIQUE
Patent protection, appropriateness of § 8.5
Value and benefits of intellectual property § 4.19

BUSINESS RELATIONSHIPS
Company intellectual property policies and procedures, necessity of § 12.7

CASES, LESSONS FROM ACTUAL
See INTELLECTUAL PROPERTY ISSUES, DANGERS OF FAILING TO CONSIDER

CLAIMS
Patents §§ 2.2, 2.3

CLOSED MARKETS, EXPLOITING IN
Value and benefits of intellectual property § 4.14

COLLATERAL FOR SECURED FINANCING
Patent protection, appropriateness of § 8.5

COMMERCIALIZE RIGHTS AFFORDED BY COPYRIGHT
Copyright protection, appropriateness of § 10.6

COMMERCIALLY-ACCEPTABLE ALTERNATIVES
Patent protection, appropriateness of § 8.6

COMMON LAW TRADEMARKS
Trademark protection, appropriateness of § 11.4
Trademarks § 2.35

COMPANY GOALS
Protection § 6.10

COMPANY INTELLECTUAL PROPERTY POLICIES AND PROCEDURES, NECESSITY OF
Generally § 12.1
Checklist § 12.16
First inventorship § 12.15
Novelty requirement, failing to satisfy
–Generally § 12.9
–Foreign patent rights, loss of § 12.14
–On-sale bar § 12.12
–Printed publication bar § 12.10
–Public use bar § 12.11
–Public use or sale activity, experimentation incident to § 12.13
Patent laws § 12.8
Secrecy and affirmative steps requirements, satisfying § 12.3
Trade secret laws § 12.2
Trade secrets, preventing unnecessary loss of
–Generally § 12.4
–Former employee and innocent new employer § 12.6
–Inadvertent disclosure § 12.5
–Trade secret matters in business relationships § 12.7

COMPANY PROFILE
Protection § 6.13

COMPETITION
Protection §§ 6.5, 6.6, 6.9

COMPETITIVE DESIGNS, EFFECT ON
Patent protection, appropriateness of § 8.5

COMPETITOR, HIRING NEW EMPLOYEES FROM
Intellectual property rights, company policies maximizing preservation § 13.4

INDEX

COMPOSITIONS OF MATTER
  Patents § 2.5
COMPUTERS, RESTRICTED ACCESS TO
  Intellectual property rights, company policies maximizing preservation § 13.18
CONFIDENTIAL INFORMATION, FAILURE TO IDENTIFY
  Intellectual property issues, dangers of failing to consider § 3.6
CONFIDENTIAL MATERIAL, HANDLING
  Intellectual property rights, company policies maximizing preservation § 13.19
CONFIDENTIALITY
  See also DISCLOSURE AGREEMENT, NONCONFIDENTIAL
  Trade secret protection, threshold level protection § 7.3
CONFIDENTIALITY AGREEMENTS
  Intellectual property rights, company policies maximizing preservation § 13.30
CONSTRUCTIVE NOTICE
  Patent protection, appropriateness of § 8.18
CONSUMER SURVEYS
  Trademark protection, appropriateness of § 11.11
  Trademarks § 2.39
CONSUMERS' TESTIMONY
  Trademarks § 2.39
COPYRIGHT MARKING
  Intellectual property rights, company policies maximizing preservation § 13.26
COPYRIGHT OFFICE
  See UNITED STATES COPYRIGHT OFFICE
COPYRIGHT PHASE
  Intellectual property protection, most appropriate selection of § 5.6
COPYRIGHT PROTECTION, APPROPRIATENESS OF
  Commercialize rights afforded by copyright § 10.6
  Copyright notice placed on the work § 10.3

COPYRIGHT PROTECTION, APPROPRIATENESS OF
(Continued)
  Copyright phase of Protection Analysis Model § 10.1
  Published work § 10.4
  Registration, advantages of § 10.5
  Subject matter, satisfying the legal requirements for copyright protection § 10.2
COPYRIGHT REMEDIES
  Value and benefits of intellectual property § 4.5
COPYRIGHTS
  Actions not necessary but recommended § 2.28
  Copyright protection, how company secures § 2.33
  Definition § 2.23
  Duration of copyright protection § 2.30
  Exclusive right to copy and distribute work § 2.29
  Infringers, enforcement against § 2.32
  Intellectual property, importance of §§ 1.1, 1.3–1.6
  Know-how § 2.60
  Legal framework and requirements of copyrights
  –Generally § 2.24
  –Fixation § 2.27
  –Original authorship § 2.26
  –Subject matter § 2.25
  Narrowness of protection § 2.31
  Protection §§ 6.1, 6.3, 6.4
  Trade secret protection, threshold level protection § 7.2
COSTS
  See also PRICING CONSIDERATIONS; PROTECTION
  Patent protection, appropriateness of §§ 8.6, 8.7, 8.11
  Protection §§ 6.6–6.8, 6.16
  Trade secret and patent protection, choosing between §§ 9.10, 9.16
  Trade secret protection, threshold level protection § 7.2
  Trademark protection, appropriateness of § 11.11

INDEX

COURT, ENFORCEMENT AND BURDEN IN
Trade secret and patent protection, choosing between § 9.15

COVENANTS, RESTRICTIVE
Intellectual property rights, company policies maximizing preservation § 13.6

CROSS-LICENSING
Patent protection, appropriateness of § 8.5
Value and benefits of intellectual property § 4.11

CUSTOMER BASE, POTENTIAL
Patent protection, appropriateness of § 8.6

CUSTOMER DEMAND
Patent protection, appropriateness of § 8.6

CUSTOMER PREFERENCE
Protection § 6.9

CUSTOMER RECEPTIVENESS
Patent protection, appropriateness of § 8.6

CUSTOMER WORTH, RANGE OF
Patent protection, appropriateness of § 8.6

DAMAGES
Company intellectual property policies and procedures, necessity of § 12.4
Copyright protection, appropriateness of § 10.5
Intellectual property, importance of §§ 1.2, 1.3
Protection § 6.4
Trade secret protection, threshold level protection § 7.2
Value and benefits of intellectual property §§ 4.5–4.7

DEFINITIONS
Copyrights § 2.23
Design patents § 2.15
Know-how § 2.59
Patents § 2.1
Trade secrets § 2.46
Trademarks § 2.34

DEPARTING EMPLOYEES, PROCEDURES FOR
Intellectual property rights, company policies maximizing preservation § 13.10

DESIGN PATENT PROTECTION, APPROPRIATENESS OF
See PATENT PROTECTION, APPROPRIATENESS OF

DESIGN PATENTS
Definition § 2.15
Design patent protection, how company secures § 2.22
Know-how § 2.60
Legal framework and requirements of design patents
–Generally § 2.16
–Novelty and non-obviousness § 2.20
–Originality § 2.19
–Ornamental § 2.18
–Subject matter § 2.17
Patent protection, appropriateness of § 8.11
Protection § 6.1
Scope of design patent protection § 2.21

DISCLOSURE AGREEMENT, NONCONFIDENTIAL
Intellectual property rights, company policies maximizing preservation § 13.40

DISCLOSURE, INADVERTENT
Company intellectual property policies and procedures, necessity of § 12.5
Intellectual property issues, dangers of failing to consider § 3.5
Trade secret and patent protection, choosing between § 9.14

DISCLOSURE, PREEMPLOYMENT
Intellectual property rights, company policies maximizing preservation § 13.3

DISCOVERY
Trade secret and patent protection, choosing between §§ 9.8, 9.16

DISINTERESTED EMPLOYEES, CORROBORATION BY
Intellectual property rights, company policies maximizing preservation § 13.13

DISTINCTIVENESS
Patent protection, appropriateness of § 8.11
Trademark protection, appropriateness of § 11.11

INDEX

DISTINCTIVENESS *(Continued)*
  Trademarks § 2.39
DOCTRINE OF EQUIVALENTS
  Patents § 2.11

ECONOMIC DESIRABILITY
  See PATENT PROTECTION, APPROPRIATENESS OF
EDUCATION
  Intellectual property rights, company policies maximizing preservation §§ 13.9, 13.36
EMPLOYEE AGREEMENT
  See INTELLECTUAL PROPERTY RIGHTS, COMPANY POLICIES MAXIMIZING PRESERVATION
EMPLOYEE-RELATED PROCEDURES
  Company intellectual property policies and procedures, necessity of § 12.6
  Trade secret protection, threshold level protection § 7.3
EMPLOYER/EMPLOYEE RELATIONSHIPS
  See INTELLECTUAL PROPERTY RIGHTS, COMPANY POLICIES MAXIMIZING PRESERVATION
ENABLEMENT AND BEST MODE
  Patents § 2.9
ENGINEERING AND PROGRESS NOTEBOOKS
  Intellectual property rights, company policies maximizing preservation § 13.15
ENGINEERS, RECORDING DAILY ACTIVITIES OF
  Intellectual property rights, company policies maximizing preservation § 13.12
EQUIVALENT PRODUCTS
  See also DOCTRINE OF EQUIVALENTS
  Patents § 2.11
ESTOPPEL
  Intellectual property portfolio, managing § 14.4
EUROPEAN PATENT OFFICE (EPO)
  Patent protection, appropriateness of § 8.17
EXCLUSIVE RIGHTS
  Patent protection, appropriateness of § 8.5

EXCLUSIVE RIGHTS *(Continued)*
  Trademark protection, appropriateness of §§ 11.4, 11.11
  Value and benefits of intellectual property § 4.2
EXPERIMENTAL USE EXCEPTION
  Company intellectual property policies and procedures, necessity of § 12.13
EXPERIMENTATION INCIDENT TO PUBLIC USE OR SALE ACTIVITY
  Company intellectual property policies and procedures, necessity of § 12.13

FACILITY RESTRICTIONS
  Intellectual property rights, company policies maximizing preservation § 13.18
FAIR USE
  Copyrights § 2.29
FEDERAL CIRCUIT, CREATION OF
  Value and benefits of intellectual property § 4.26
FIRST INVENTORSHIP
  Company intellectual property policies and procedures, necessity of § 12.15
FIXATION
  Copyrights § 2.27
FOOD AND DRUG ADMINISTRATION (FDA)
  Value and benefits of intellectual property § 4.16
FOREIGN COMPETITION
  Intellectual property, importance of § 1.4
FOREIGN MARKETS, INTEREST SECURED IN
  Protection § 6.11
  Value and benefits of intellectual property § 4.21
FOREIGN PATENT APPLICATIONS
  Patent protection, appropriateness of § 8.17
FOREIGN PATENT RIGHTS, LOSS OF
  Company intellectual property policies and procedures, necessity of § 12.14

INDEX

FRAUD
Company intellectual property policies and procedures, necessity of § 12.4

FREEDOM OF INFORMATION ACT
Value and benefits of intellectual property § 4.23

GRANTBACKS
Patent protection, appropriateness of § 8.5
Value and benefits of intellectual property § 4.12

GRANTING OF PATENTS
Patent protection, appropriateness of § 8.18

GUT FEELINGS
Patent protection, appropriateness of § 8.6

HEAD-START PERIOD
Value and benefits of intellectual property § 4.7

IMPROVEMENT PATENTS
Patent protection, appropriateness of § 8.6

INCENTIVES TO INNOVATE
Intellectual property rights, company policies maximizing preservation § 13.37

INDUSTRY, MONITORING
See INTELLECTUAL PROPERTY PORTFOLIO, MANAGING

INDUSTRY STANDARD, ESTABLISHING
Value and benefits of intellectual property § 4.17

INFRINGEMENT
Copyright protection, appropriateness of §§ 10.3, 10.5
Copyrights § 2.32
Intellectual property, importance of § 1.4
Intellectual property issues, dangers of failing to consider §§ 3.8–3.11
Intellectual property portfolio, managing § 14.4
Intellectual property rights, company policies maximizing preservation § 13.26

INFRINGEMENT *(Continued)*
Patent protection, appropriateness of § 8.5
Patents § 2.13
Protection §§ 6.4, 6.17, 6.20
Trade secret and patent protection, choosing between § 9.17
Trademarks § 2.44

INFRINGEMENT OF INTELLECTUAL PROPERTY, REMEDIES FOR
See VALUE AND BENEFITS OF INTELLECTUAL PROPERTY

INJUNCTIONS
Trade secret and patent protection, choosing between § 9.17
Trade secret protection, threshold level protection § 7.2
Value and benefits of intellectual property § 4.6

INTANGIBLES
See VALUABLE INTANGIBLES

INTELLECTUAL PROPERTY, IMPORTANCE OF
See also VALUE AND BENEFITS OF INTELLECTUAL PROPERTY
Definition § 1.1
How to use book § 1.6
Why intellectual property is important
–Generally § 1.2
–Foreign competition § 1.4
–Litigation § 1.3
–Valuable asset § 1.5

INTELLECTUAL PROPERTY ISSUES, DANGERS OF FAILING TO CONSIDER
Cases, lessons from actual
–Generally § 3.1
–Case 1: loss of patent rights as result of patent holder's marketing activity § 3.2
–Case 2: loss of patent rights caused by business partner's sales activities § 3.3
–Case 3: loss of patent rights as result of prior public use § 3.4
–Case 4: loss of trade secret rights as result of inadvertent disclosure § 3.5

INTELLECTUAL PROPERTY
ISSUES, DANGERS OF FAILING
TO CONSIDER *(Continued)*
–Case 5: loss of trade secret rights as result of failing to adequately identify confidential information § 3.6
–Case 6: loss of trade secret rights as result of failing to take affirmative steps to maintain secrecy § 3.7
–Case 7: monetary loss for patent infringement § 3.8
–Case 8: monetary loss for patent infringement § 3.9
–Case 9: monetary loss for willful patent infringement § 3.10
–Case 10: monetary loss for trademark infringement § 3.11

INTELLECTUAL PROPERTY POLICIES, COMPANY
See COMPANY INTELLECTUAL PROPERTY POLICIES AND PROCEDURES, NECESSITY OF

INTELLECTUAL PROPERTY PORTFOLIO, MANAGING
Industry, monitoring
–Generally § 14.1
–Activities of other companies, monitoring § 14.2
–Checklist § 14.5
–Policing for infringers of company's rights § 14.4
–Product clearance § 14.3
Program review
–Generally § 14..6
–Product team meetings on intellectual property issues § 14.8
–Roundtable meetings to plan protection strategies § 14.7

INTELLECTUAL PROPERTY PROTECTION, MOST APPROPRIATE SELECTION OF
Best protection alternative § 5.1
Common scenario § 5.2
Protection analysis model
–Generally § 5.3
–Copyright phase § 5.6
–Know-how and trade secret phases § 5.4
–More than one type of protection available § 5.8
–Patent phase § 5.5

INTELLECTUAL PROPERTY PROTECTION, MOST APPROPRIATE SELECTION OF *(Continued)*
–Trademark phase § 5.7

INTELLECTUAL PROPERTY RIGHTS
Trade secret and patent protection, choosing between §§ 9.7, 9.11, 9.12, 9.14

INTELLECTUAL PROPERTY RIGHTS CHECKLIST
Know-how § 2.60

INTELLECTUAL PROPERTY RIGHTS, COMPANY POLICIES MAXIMIZING PRESERVATION
Audits § 13.43
Copyright marking § 13.26
Employee agreement
–Generally § 13.6
–Employment manuals § 13.7
–Periodic reminders of obligations § 13.8
–Procedures for departing employees § 13.10
–Seminars to educate employees § 13.9
Employer/employee relationships
–Generally § 13.2
–Hiring new employees from competitor § 13.4
–Preemployment disclosure § 13.3
Intellectual property counsel, channeling new ideas
–Generally § 13.34
–Educating employees § 13.36
–Keeping decisions at grass-roots level § 13.35
–Providing incentive to innovate § 13.37
Laboratory procedures
–Generally § 13.11
–Corroboration by disinterested employee § 13.13
–Daily time sheets of personnel, maintaining records § 13.16
–Engineering and progress notebooks § 13.15
–Progress records, maintaining § 13.14
–Recording daily activities of engineers § 13.12

INDEX

INTELLECTUAL PROPERTY
RIGHTS, COMPANY POLICIES
MAXIMIZING PRESERVATION
(Continued)
  Need for policies and procedures
    § 13.1
  Orientation for new employees
    § 13.5
  Patent marking § 13.25
  Release review procedures
    –Generally § 13.20
    –Demonstrations of new technology
      § 13.23
    –Distribution of advertisements and
      brochures § 13.21
    –Publications in trade and
      professional journals § 13.22
    –Test marketing new products
      § 13.24
  Research and development
    relationships with other companies
    § 13.33
  Security procedures
    –Generally § 13.17
    –Facility restrictions § 13.18
    –Handling confidential material
      § 13.19
  Technological relationships with
    other companies
    –Generally § 13.28
    –Confidentiality agreements § 13.30
    –Initially disclose only general
      information § 13.29
    –Record transfer of proprietary
      information § 13.32
    –Stamping "CONFIDENTIAL" on
      all documents transferred to
      business partner § 13.31
  Trademark marking § 13.27
  Unsolicited ideas
    –Generally § 13.38
    –Designated employee procedures
      § 13.42
    –Designating one employee to field
      all unsolicited ideas § 13.39
    –Nonconfidential disclosure
      agreement § 13.40
    –Reviewing unsolicited idea § 13.41
INTENDED REGION OF USE
  Trademark protection,
    appropriateness of § 11.4

INTENT TO USE
  See also USE OR INTENT TO USE
  Intellectual property protection, most
    appropriate selection of § 5.7
  Trademark protection,
    appropriateness of § 11.13
INTERFERENCE
  Company intellectual property
    policies and procedures, necessity
    of § 12.15
INTERNATIONAL TRADE
  COMMISSION (ITC)
  Value and benefits of intellectual
    property § 4.27
INTERSTATE COMMERCE
  Trademarks §§ 2.35, 2.38
INVENTORSHIP
  See FIRST INVENTORSHIP

KNOW-HOW
  Definition § 2.59
  Intellectual property, importance of
    § 1.1
  Intellectual property protection, most
    appropriate selection of § 5.4
  Intellectual property rights checklist
    § 2.60
  Protection §§ 6.1, 6.17

LABORATORY PROCEDURES
  See INTELLECTUAL PROPERTY
    RIGHTS, COMPANY POLICIES
    MAXIMIZING PRESERVATION
LACHES
  Intellectual property portfolio,
    managing § 14.4
LANHAM ACT
  Trademarks §§ 2.35, 2.37, 2.38
LAWSUIT PREVENTION OR
  SETTLEMENT
  Value and benefits of intellectual
    property § 4.15
LEGAL FRAMEWORK AND
  REQUIREMENTS
  See also COPYRIGHTS; DESIGN
    PATENTS; KNOW-HOW;
    PATENTS; TRADE SECRETS;
    TRADEMARKS
  Copyright protection,
    appropriateness of § 10.2
  Patent protection, appropriateness of
    § 8.2

LEGAL FRAMEWORK AND
REQUIREMENTS *(Continued)*
  Trade secret and patent protection,
    choosing between § 9.6
  Trade secret protection, threshold
    level protection § 7.1
  Trademark protection,
    appropriateness of § 11.2
LICENSE FOR REVENUE
  See ASSIGNMENT OR LICENSE
    FOR REVENUE
LICENSES, IDENTIFIABLE
  Patent protection, appropriateness of
    § 8.6
LICENSING POTENTIAL
  See also CROSS-LICENSING;
    GRANTBACKS
  Protection § 6.14
  Trade secret and patent protection,
    choosing between § 9.20
LIKELIHOOD OF CONFUSION
  Trademarks § 2.40
LIMITED RESOURCES
  Protection § 6.16
LITERATURE, COMPETITIVE
  Intellectual property portfolio,
    managing § 14.2
LITERATURE, PROFESSIONAL
  Intellectual property portfolio,
    managing § 14.2
LITIGATION
  Intellectual property, importance of
    § 1.3

MACHINES
  Patents § 2.5
MANUALS, EMPLOYMENT
  Intellectual property rights, company
    policies maximizing preservation
    § 13.7
MARK, EXCLUSIVE USE OF
  See also COPYRIGHT MARKING;
    PATENT MARKING;
    TRADEMARK MARKING
  Trademarks § 2.42
MARK IN USE
  Trademark protection,
    appropriateness of § 11.14
MARK IN USE, REGULAR
  APPLICATION FOR
  Trademark protection,
    appropriateness of § 11.8

MARK, SELECTION OF NEW
  Trademark protection,
    appropriateness of § 11.10
MARKET CONTROL, ENHANCED
  Patent protection, appropriateness of
    § 8.5
MARKET SHARE, CONTROL
  Value and benefits of intellectual
    property § 4.19
MARKETING ACTIVITY
  Intellectual property issues, dangers
    of failing to consider § 3.2
  Protection §§ 6.11, 6.12
  Trade secret and patent protection,
    choosing between § 9.19
MARKETS, ENTERING NEW
  See also FOREIGN MARKETS,
    INTEREST SECURED IN
  Value and benefits of intellectual
    property § 4.20
MARKS, ABSENCE OF CONFUSION
  WITH SIMILAR
  Trademarks § 2.40
"MATERIAL TO PATENTABILITY,"
  DUTY TO DISCLOSE
  INFORMATION KNOWN TO BE
  Patent protection, appropriateness of
    § 8.15
MISAPPROPRIATION
  Company intellectual property
    policies and procedures, necessity
    of § 12.4
MONETARY LOSSES
  Intellectual property issues, dangers
    of failing to consider §§ 3.8–3.11

NONFUNCTIONALITY
  Trademarks § 2.41
NONOBVIOUSNESS
  Design patents § 2.20
  Patent protection, appropriateness of
    §§ 8.2, 8.14
  Patents § 2.7
  Trade secret and patent protection,
    choosing between § 9.3
NOVELTY
  Company intellectual property
    policies and procedures, necessity
    of § 12.14
  Design patents § 2.20
  Patent protection, appropriateness of
    §§ 8.2, 8.14

NOVELTY *(Continued)*
  Patents § 2.6
  Trade secret and patent protection, choosing between §§ 9.3, 9.6
  Trade secrets § 2.51
NOVELTY REQUIREMENT, FAILING TO SATISFY
  See COMPANY INTELLECTUAL PROPERTY POLICIES AND PROCEDURES, NECESSITY OF

OFFICIAL GAZETTE
  Intellectual property portfolio, managing § 14.2
ON-HAND DOCTRINE
  Company intellectual property policies and procedures, necessity of §§ 12.9, 12.12
ON-SALE BAR
  Company intellectual property policies and procedures, necessity of § 12.12
  Patents § 2.6
ORIENTATIONS
  Intellectual property rights, company policies maximizing preservation § 13.5
ORIGINALITY
  Design patents § 2.19
ORNAMENTAL
  Design patents § 2.18
OWNERSHIP EVIDENCE
  Trademark protection, appropriateness of § 11.4

PARIS CONVENTION
  Patent protection, appropriateness of § 8.17
PATENT AND TRADEMARK OFFICE (PTO)
  See UNITED STATES PATENT AND TRADEMARK OFFICE (PTO)
PATENT APPLIED FOR
  Intellectual property rights, company policies maximizing preservation § 13.25
PATENT ASSIGNMENT SEARCHES
  Intellectual property portfolio, managing § 14.2

PATENT COOPERATION TREATY (PCT)
  Patent protection, appropriateness of § 8.17
PATENT MARKING
  Intellectual property rights, company policies maximizing preservation § 13.25
PATENT PENDING
  Intellectual property protection, most appropriate selection of § 5.5
  Intellectual property rights, company policies maximizing preservation § 13.25
  Patent protection, appropriateness of §§ 8.5, 8.11, 8.16
  Value and benefits of intellectual property § 4.23
PATENT PHASE
  Intellectual property protection, most appropriate selection of § 5.5
  Patent protection, appropriateness of § 8.1
PATENT PROTECTION, APPROPRIATENESS OF
  See also TRADE SECRET AND PATENT PROTECTION, CHOOSING BETWEEN
  Design patent protection, appropriateness of
  –Generally § 8.9
  –Design patent protection, desirability from business perspective § 8.11
  –Subject matter, satisfying design patent requirements § 8.10
  Duty to disclose information known to be "material to patentability" § 8.15
  Economic desirability
  –Generally § 8.3
  –Cost variable C, factors affecting § 8.7
  –Patent value formula § 8.4
  –Patent value formula, checklist of factors for § 8.8
  –Value probability variable Pv, factors affecting § 8.6
  –Value variable V, factors affecting § 8.5
  Foreign patent applications § 8.17
  Patent, granting of § 8.18

INDEX

PATENT PROTECTION,
APPROPRIATENESS OF
(Continued)
   "Patent pending," label products with § 8.16
   Patent phase of Protection Analysis Model § 8.1
   Patent protection, file for § 8.14
   Patent rights, maintaining and commercializing § 8.19
   Patent search and reevaluating patentability § 8.13
   Subject matter, satisfying legal requirements for patent protection § 8.2
   Trade secret or patent protection? § 8.12

PATENT REMEDIES
   Value and benefits of intellectual property § 4.4

PATENT RIGHTS, LOSS OF
   Intellectual property issues, dangers of failing to consider §§ 3.2–3.4

PATENT RIGHTS, MAINTAINING AND COMMERCIALIZING
   Patent protection, appropriateness of § 8.19

PATENT VALUE FORMULA
   Patent protection, appropriateness of §§ 8.3–8.8

PATENTS
   See also DESIGN PATENTS; IMPROVEMENT PATENTS; PIONEERING PATENTS
   Company intellectual property policies and procedures, necessity of § 12.8
   Definition
   –Generally § 2.1
   –Patent claims, defining patented subject matter § 2.3
   –Patent claims, how to read § 2.2
   Duration of copyright protection § 2.12
   Infringers, enforcement against § 2.13
   Intellectual property, importance of §§ 1.1, 1.4–1.6
   Intellectual property issues, dangers of failing to consider §§ 3.8–3.10
   Know-how § 2.60

PATENTS *(Continued)*
   Legal framework and requirements of patents
   –Generally § 2.4
   –Enablement and best mode § 2.9
   –Nonobviousness § 2.7
   –Novelty § 2.6
   –Subject matter § 2.5
   –Utility § 2.8
   Patent protection, how company secures § 2.14
   Protection §§ 6.1, 6.4, 6.9, 6.12, 6.15
   Protection extends to equivalent products § 2.11
   Right to exclude § 2.10
   Trade secret protection, threshold level protection § 7.2
   Trade secrets, patenting of by others § 2.57

PATENTS, INCREASING STRENGTH OF
   See VALUE AND BENEFITS OF INTELLECTUAL PROPERTY

PERSONAL PROPERTY
   Intellectual property, importance of § 1.1

PHOTOCOPIERS, RESTRICTED ACCESS TO
   Intellectual property rights, company policies maximizing preservation § 13.18

PIONEERING PATENTS
   Patent protection, appropriateness of § 8.6
   Trade secret and patent protection, choosing between § 9.18

PLANT PATENT
   Patents § 2.1

POLICING
   Intellectual property portfolio, managing § 14.4
   Trade secret and patent protection, choosing between § 9.13

PRICE EROSION
   Value and benefits of intellectual property § 4.4

PRICING CONSIDERATIONS
   Patent protection, appropriateness of § 8.6

PRINTED PUBLICATION BAR
   Company intellectual property policies and procedures, necessity of § 12.10

INDEX

PRINTED PUBLICATION BAR *(Continued)*
  Patents § 2.6
PRIOR ART
  Patent protection, appropriateness of § 8.13
PRIOR PUBLIC USE
  Intellectual property issues, dangers of failing to consider § 3.4
PROCESSES
  Patents § 2.5
PRODUCT CLEARANCE
  Intellectual property portfolio, managing § 14.3
PRODUCT LIFE CYCLE, EXTENDING
  Patent protection, appropriateness of § 8.5
  Value and benefits of intellectual property § 4.22
PRODUCT TEAM MEETINGS ON INTELLECTUAL PROPERTY ISSUES
  Intellectual property portfolio, managing § 14.8
PROFIT MARGIN
  Patent protection, appropriateness of § 8.6
PROGRAM REVIEW
  See INTELLECTUAL PROPERTY PORTFOLIO, MANAGING
PROGRESS RECORDS, MAINTAINING
  Intellectual property rights, company policies maximizing preservation § 13.14
PROPERTY
  See INTELLECTUAL PROPERTY, IMPORTANCE OF; PERSONAL PROPERTY; REAL PROPERTY
PROPRIETARY INFORMATION, RECORDING TRANSFER OF
  Intellectual property rights, company policies maximizing preservation § 13.32
PROTECTION
  See also BACKUP PROTECTION; PATENT PROTECTION, APPROPRIATENESS OF; TRADE SECRET PROTECTION, THRESHOLD LEVEL PROTECTION

PROTECTION *(Continued)*
  Copyright protection, appropriateness of § 10.2
  Copyrights §§ 2.30–2.33
  Design patents §§ 2.21, 2.22
  Factors
  –Generally § 6.2
  –Asset value importance § 6.17
  –Company goals § 6.10
  –Company market position and strategy § 6.11
  –Company profile § 6.13
  –Market mature enough to accept technology § 6.12
  –Subject matter, company's products made more competitive through § 6.6
  –Subject matter, economic practicality of § 6.7
  –Subject matter, exclusive ownership of § 6.4
  –Subject matter, helping to reduce company's cost with § 6.8
  –Subject matter, helping to satisfy customer preference with § 6.9
  –Subject matter, improved corporate bargaining posture with § 6.15
  –Subject matter, knowing § 6.3
  –Subject matter, licensing potential of § 6.14
  –Subject matter, preventing competitors from owning § 6.5
  –Subject matter, valuable to warrant expenditure of limited resources § 6.16
  Intellectual property protection, most appropriate selection of § 5.8
  Know-how, everything begins as § 6.1
  Patent protection, appropriateness of §§ 8.6, 8.9, 8.11, 8.12, 8.14
  Patents §§ 2.11–2.14
  Protection alternatives § 6.20
  Protection factors checklist § 6.18
  Protection favored, all things being equaled § 6.19
  Trade secret and patent protection, choosing between §§ 9.3, 9.6, 9.9, 9.10, 9.21
  Trade secrets §§ 2.54–2.58
  Trademark protection, appropriateness of § 11.2

INDEX

PROTECTION *(Continued)*
  Trademarks §§ 2.43–2.45
PROTECTION ANALYSIS MODEL
  See also INTELLECTUAL
    PROPERTY PROTECTION,
    MOST APPROPRIATE
    SELECTION OF
  Copyright protection,
    appropriateness of § 10.1
  Patent protection, appropriateness of
    § 8.1
  Protection, generally this heading
  Trade secret protection, threshold
    level protection §§ 7.1, 7.2
  Trademark protection,
    appropriateness of § 11.1
PROTECTION FACTORS
  CHECKLIST
  Protection § 6.18
PUBLIC DOMAIN
  Protection § 6.20
PUBLIC USE BAR
  Company intellectual property
    policies and procedures, necessity
    of § 12.11
  Patents § 2.6
PUBLISHED WORKS
  See also TRADE AND
    PROFESSIONAL JOURNALS,
    PUBLICATIONS IN
  Copyright protection,
    appropriateness of §§ 10.4, 10.5
  Intellectual property protection, most
    appropriate selection of § 5.6
  Protection § 6.20
  Trade secret and patent protection,
    choosing between § 9.3
PUNITIVE AWARDS
  Trade secret protection, threshold
    level protection § 7.2

QUANTITY OF SALES
  See ADVERTISING AND
    QUANTITY OF SALES,
    MANNER OF

REAL PROPERTY
  Intellectual property, importance of
    § 1.1
REGISTRABLE SUBJECT MATTER
  Intellectual property protection, most
    appropriate selection of § 5.7

REGISTRABLE SUBJECT MATTER
  (Continued)
  Protection § 6.1
REGISTRATION
  See TRADEMARK PROTECTION,
    APPROPRIATENESS OF
REGISTRATION, ADVANTAGES OF
  Copyright protection,
    appropriateness of § 10.5
RELEASE REVIEW PROCEDURES
  See also INTELLECTUAL
    PROPERTY RIGHTS,
    COMPANY POLICIES
    MAXIMIZING PRESERVATION
  Trade secret protection, threshold
    level protection § 7.3
REMEDIES
  Trade secret and patent protection,
    choosing between § 9.17
REQUIREMENTS
  See LEGAL FRAMEWORK AND
    REQUIREMENTS
RESEARCH AND DEVELOPMENT
  (R & D) EXPENDITURES,
  RECOUPMENT OF
  Patent protection, appropriateness of
    § 8.5
  Value and benefits of intellectual
    property § 4.18
RESEARCH AND DEVELOPMENT
  (R & D) RELATIONSHIPS WITH
  OTHER COMPANIES
  Intellectual property rights, company
    policies maximizing preservation
    § 13.33
RIGHT TO EXCLUDE
  Patents § 2.10
RIGHTS, ABILITY TO ASSIGN
  Value and benefits of intellectual
    property § 4.8
RIGHTS, ABILITY TO LICENSE
  See VALUE AND BENEFITS OF
    INTELLECTUAL PROPERTY
ROUNDTABLE MEETINGS TO
  PLAN PROTECTION
  STRATEGIES
  Intellectual property portfolio,
    managing § 14.7
ROYALTY REVENUE
  Protection § 6.14
  Trade secret and patent protection,
    choosing between § 9.17

ROYALTY REVENUE *(Continued)*
Value and benefits of intellectual property § 4.10

SALES ACTIVITIES
Intellectual property issues, dangers of failing to consider § 3.3
Trademark protection, appropriateness of § 11.11

SECOND SOURCES
Value and benefits of intellectual property § 4.13

SECONDARY CONSIDERATIONS
Patents § 2.7

SECONDARY MEANING
Intellectual property protection, most appropriate selection of § 5.7
Trademark protection, appropriateness of §§ 11.2, 11.11
Trademarks §§ 2.35, 2.37, 2.38

SECRECY
Company intellectual property policies and procedures, necessity of § 12.3
Trade secrets § 2.49

SECRECY AGREEMENT
Intellectual property rights, company policies maximizing preservation § 13.30

SECTION 102 BARS TO PATENTABILITY
Company intellectual property policies and procedures, necessity of §§ 12.9, 12.10
Patents § 2.6

SECURITY PROCEDURES
See also INTELLECTUAL PROPERTY RIGHTS, COMPANY POLICIES MAXIMIZING PRESERVATION
Trade secret protection, threshold level protection § 7.3

SELF-INFLICTED BARS
Company intellectual property policies and procedures, necessity of § 12.9

SEMINARS TO EDUCATE EMPLOYEES
Intellectual property rights, company policies maximizing preservation § 13.9

SERVICE MARKS
Trademarks § 2.34

SHOP RIGHTS
Intellectual property rights, company policies maximizing preservation § 13.6

STATEMENT OF USE
Intellectual property protection, most appropriate selection of § 5.7

SUBJECT MATTER
See also PROTECTION; REGISTRABLE SUBJECT MATTER
Copyright protection, appropriateness of § 10.2
Copyrights § 2.25
Design patents § 2.17
Intellectual property protection, most appropriate selection of § 5.4
Know-how § 2.60
Patents § 2.5
Trade secret and patent protection, choosing between § 9.4
Trade secrets § 2.48
Trademark protection, appropriateness of § 11.2
Trademarks § 2.36

SURVEYS
See CONSUMER SURVEYS

TARIFF ACT OF 1930
Value and benefits of intellectual property § 4.27

TECHNOLOGICAL APPEARANCE
Patent protection, appropriateness of § 8.5

TECHNOLOGICAL RELATIONSHIPS WITH OTHER COMPANIES
See also INTELLECTUAL PROPERTY RIGHTS, COMPANY POLICIES MAXIMIZING PRESERVATION
Trade secret protection, threshold level protection § 7.3

TECHNOLOGY
Copyright protection, appropriateness of § 10.2
Intellectual property rights, company policies maximizing preservation §§ 13.23, 13.28–13.33

INDEX

TECHNOLOGY *(Continued)*
  Patent protection, appropriateness of §§ 8.6, 8.11
  Protection §§ 6.2, 6.5, 6.10, 6.12, 6.13, 6.15, 6.20
  Trade secret and patent protection, choosing between §§ 9.5, 9.18

TECHNOLOGY EXCHANGES
  Value and benefits of intellectual property § 4.11

TECHNOLOGY, TESTING OF
  Value and benefits of intellectual property § 4.16

TEST MARKETING NEW PRODUCTS
  Intellectual property rights, company policies maximizing preservation § 13.24

TESTIMONY
  See CONSUMERS' TESTIMONY

THEFT, LEGAL RECOURSE FOR THEFT OF TRADE SECRET
  Protection § 6.17
  Trade secrets § 2.56

TIME SHEETS OF PERSONNEL, DAILY MAINTENANCE OF
  Intellectual property rights, company policies maximizing preservation § 13.16

TRADE AND PROFESSIONAL JOURNALS, PUBLICATIONS IN
  Intellectual property rights, company policies maximizing preservation § 13.22

TRADE SECRET AND PATENT PROTECTION, CHOOSING BETWEEN
  Generally, story § 9.1
  Checklist of trade secret versus patent protection factors § 9.21
  Factors
  –Generally § 9.2
  –Burden in court, enforcement and § 9.15
  –Cost of enforcing § 9.16
  –Duration of protection § 9.9
  –Intellectual property, breadth of § 9.12
  –Intellectual property rights, preservation of § 9.11
  –Intellectual property rights, risk of losing § 9.14

TRADE SECRET AND PATENT PROTECTION, CHOOSING BETWEEN *(Continued)*
  –Intellectual property rights, scope of § 9.7
  –Legal requirements, patent protection has stricter § 9.6
  –Licensing § 9.20
  –Market readiness § 9.19
  –Patent protection, availability of § 9.3
  –Policing § 9.13
  –Protection, cost of obtaining and maintaining § 9.10
  –Remedies § 9.17
  –Subject matter nature, likelihood of keeping secret § 9.4
  –Subsequent and independent discovery by another § 9.8
  –Technology, life expectancy of § 9.5
  –Technology, pioneering § 9.18

TRADE SECRET PROTECTION, THRESHOLD LEVEL PROTECTION
  Legal requirements for trade secret protection § 7.1
  Trade secret attributes § 7.2
  Trade secret rights, maintaining § 7.3

TRADE SECRET REMEDIES
  Value and benefits of intellectual property § 4.7

TRADE SECRET RIGHTS, LOSS OF
  Intellectual property issues, dangers of failing to consider §§ 3.5–3.7

TRADE SECRETS
  Copyright protection, appropriateness of § 10.4
  Definition § 2.46
  Duration of trade secret protection § 2.55
  Improper taking, protection against § 2.54
  Intellectual property, importance of § 1.6
  Intellectual property protection, most appropriate selection of § 5.4
  Know-how § 2.60
  Legal framework and requirements of trade secrets
  –Generally § 2.47
  –Affirmative steps § 2.52

TRADE SECRETS *(Continued)*
- Novelty § 2.51
- Secrecy § 2.49
- Subject matter § 2.48
- Value § 2.50

Patent protection, appropriateness of § 8.12

Protection §§ 6.1, 6.2, 6.4, 6.6, 6.9, 6.15, 6.16, 6.19

Rights may not be exclusive § 2.53

Technological trade secrets, others may patent § 2.57

Theft, legal recourse for § 2.56

Trade secret protection, how company secures § 2.58

Trade secret protection, threshold level protection §§ 7.2, 7.3

TRADE SECRETS, PREVENTING UNNECESSARY LOSS OF

See COMPANY INTELLECTUAL PROPERTY POLICIES AND PROCEDURES, NECESSITY OF

TRADE SHOWS

Intellectual property portfolio, managing § 14.2

TRADEMARK MARKING

Intellectual property rights, company policies maximizing preservation § 13.27

TRADEMARK PHASE

Intellectual property protection, most appropriate selection of § 5.7

TRADEMARK PROTECTION, APPROPRIATENESS OF

Checklist of registration factors § 11.5

Subject matter, satisfying the legal requirements for trademark protection § 11.2

Trademark maintained, properly used, and commercialized § 11.15

Trademark phase of Protection Analysis Model § 11.1

Trademark registration
- Generally § 11.6
- Intent to use application § 11.7
- Regular application for mark in use § 11.8

Trademark registration allowed
- Generally § 11.12
- Intent to use § 11.13
- Mark is in use § 11.14

TRADEMARK PROTECTION, APPROPRIATENESS OF *(Continued)*

Trademark registration when not allowed
- Generally § 11.9
- Keeping mark and generating secondary meaning § 11.11
- New mark, selection of § 11.10

Trademark registration, desirability of § 11.4

Trademark search § 11.3

TRADEMARK REMEDIES

Value and benefits of intellectual property § 4.6

TRADEMARK WATCH SERVICES

Intellectual property portfolio, managing § 14.2

TRADEMARKS

See also COMMON LAW TRADEMARKS

Definition § 2.34

Duration of trademark protection § 2.43

Exclusive use of mark § 2.42

Federal trademark protection, how company secures § 2.45

Intellectual property, importance of §§ 1.3, 1.6

Intellectual property issues, dangers of failing to consider § 3.11

Know-how § 2.60

Legal framework and requirements of trademarks
- Generally § 2.35
- Absence of confusion with similar marks § 2.40
- Affixation § 2.37
- Distinctiveness § 2.39
- Nonfunctionality § 2.41
- Subject matter § 2.36
- Use or intent to use § 2.38

Protection §§ 6.1, 6.3

Trade secret protection, threshold level protection § 7.2

Trademark infringers, enforcement against § 2.44

UNIFORM COMMERCIAL CODE (UCC)

Value and benefits of intellectual property § 4.23

INDEX

UNIFORM TRADE SECRET ACT (UTSA)
   Trade secrets §§ 2.46–2.49, 2.52, 2.58
UNITED STATES COMMISSIONER OF PATENTS AND TRADEMARKS
   Patents § 2.1
UNITED STATES COPYRIGHT OFFICE
   Copyright protection, appropriateness of §§ 10.1–10.5
   Copyrights § 2.32
UNITED STATES PATENT AND TRADEMARK OFFICE (PTO)
   Company intellectual property policies and procedures, necessity of § 12.15
   Design patents § 2.22
   Intellectual property portfolio, managing § 14.2
   Intellectual property protection, most appropriate selection of §§ 5.5, 5.7
   Patent protection, appropriateness of §§ 8.13–8.15, 8.17, 8.18
   Patents § 2.14
   Trade secret and patent protection, choosing between §§ 9.5, 9.10, 9.14
   Trademark protection, appropriateness of §§ 11.2, 11.4, 11.11
   Trademarks §§ 2.39, 2.45
   Value and benefits of intellectual property § 4.23
UNITED STATES SUPREME COURT
   Value and benefits of intellectual property § 4.25
UNSOLICITED IDEAS
   See INTELLECTUAL PROPERTY RIGHTS, COMPANY POLICIES MAXIMIZING PRESERVATION
USE OR INTENT TO USE
   Trademarks § 2.38
UTILITY
   Know-how § 2.60
   Patent protection, appropriateness of §§ 8.9, 8.11
   Patents § 2.8

VALIDITY EVIDENCE
   Trademark protection, appropriateness of § 11.4

VALUABLE ASSET
   Intellectual property, importance of § 1.6
VALUABLE INTANGIBLES
   Value and benefits of intellectual property § 4.23
VALUE
   Trade secrets § 2.50
VALUE AND BENEFITS OF INTELLECTUAL PROPERTY
   Generally § 4.1
   Asset value § 4.24
   Control market share § 4.19
   Exclusive rights § 4.2
   Foreign markets, interest secured in § 4.21
   Infringement of intellectual property, remedies for
   –Generally § 4.3
   –Copyright remedies § 4.5
   –Patent remedies § 4.4
   –Trade secret remedies § 4.7
   –Trademark remedies § 4.6
   New markets, entering § 4.20
   Patents, increasing strength of
   –Generally § 4.25
   –Federal circuit, creation of § 4.26
   –International Trade Commission (ITC) § 4.27
   Product life cycle, extending § 4.22
   Recoupment of research and development expenditures § 4.18
   Rights, ability to assign § 4.8
   Rights, ability to license
   –Generally § 4.9
   –Closed markets, exploiting in § 4.14
   –Grantbacks § 4.12
   –Industry standard, establishing § 4.17
   –Lawsuit prevention or settlement § 4.15
   –Royalty revenue § 4.10
   –Second sources § 4.13
   –Technology exchanges § 4.11
   –Technology testing § 4.16
   Valuable intangibles § 4.23
VISITOR PRECAUTIONS
   Intellectual property rights, company policies maximizing preservation § 13.18

WORK, COPYRIGHT NOTICES FOR
   See also PUBLISHED WORKS

WORK, COPYRIGHT NOTICES
FOR *(Continued)*
   Copyright protection,
    appropriateness of § 10.3
WORK, EXCLUSIVE RIGHT TO
COPY AND DISTRIBUTE
   Copyrights § 2.29

WORK MADE FOR HIRE
   Copyrights §§ 2.30, 2.33
   Intellectual property rights, company
    policies maximizing preservation
    § 13.6